Essays in British Accounting Research

Essays in British Accounting Research

Edited by **Michael Bromwich**
and **Anthony Hopwood**

Pitman

PITMAN PUBLISHING LIMITED
39 Parker Street, London WC2B 5PB

PITMAN PUBLISHING INC
1020 Plain Street, Marshfield, Massachusetts

Associated Companies
Pitman Publishing Pty Ltd, Melbourne
Pitman Publishing New Zealand Ltd, Wellington
Copp Clark Pitman, Toronto

First published in Great Britain 1981

Text set in 10/12 pt Linotron 202 Times, printed and bound in Great Britain at The Pitman Press, Bath

ISBN 0 273 01596 6

Contents

Preface

Stephen A Zeff,
Herbert S Autrey Professor of Accounting, Rice University

The publication of this volume of provocative and wide-ranging essays testifies to the progress made by British academic accountancy in the last decade. Prior to the 1970s, the number of full-time accounting academics in tertiary institutions was quite small, and the number who were actively engaged in research still smaller. Early attempts to raise the standard of British academic accounting had not been marked by conspicuous success. The Accounting Research Association, founded so optimistically in the 1930s by Cosmo Gordon and Ronald Edwards (as he was then known), failed to survive the war. The active programme of research developed by the Incorporated Accountants' Research Committee, the courageous journal known as *Accounting Research*, and the other enterprises set in motion by Bertram Nelson, Sewell Bray, and Leo T. Little did not survive the integration of the Society of Incorporated Accountants and the Institutes of Chartered Accountants in 1957. The Parker Report of 1961 discouraged efforts at bringing universities and the profession into collaboration (but see Bertram Nelson's refreshing dissent in an appendix to the Report).

But attitudes soon began to change. In the 1960s, tertiary institutions in Britain began to establish courses in business studies. Business schools were opened in London and Manchester. By the beginning of the 1970s, there was in Britain—as elsewhere in the world—a rising demand by students for courses in accountancy, and, one by one, British universities established Chairs in accounting and kindred subjects, frequently in departments of economics. (The views of some economists toward university study in accountancy have been slow to change, and not a few British accounting academics who were attached to economics departments apparently experienced a tension with economists not unlike that which prompted Hatfield to write his famous 'An Historical Defense of Bookkeeping' in 1923.) Although the teaching loads were, and continue to be, heavy, many of the mostly young academics embarked on ambitious programmes of research. Two journals were launched in 1969–70: the *Journal of Business Finance*, which was reconstituted in 1974 under the title, *Journal of Business Finance and Accounting*; and *Accounting and Business Research*, published by the same body that had scuttled *Account-*

ing Research in another era. In 1976, *Accounting, Organizations and Society* joined the march.

At this stage in the evolution of British accounting research, the essays gathered for this volume perform several useful functions. First, they survey much of the salient work and identify the principal themes which have been addressed thus far. Secondly, they raise questions about the directions taken and the quality of what has been done. Thirdly, they propose an agenda for future research. In making these assessments, the contributors to this collection compare and contrast the lines and modes of inquiry in Britain with those observable in North America. But the differences between recent British and North American research may be explained, not by geography, but by culture, institutions, and history.

The role of universities in the formation of accounting academics has been quite different in Britain than in North America. North American accounting academics have, for the most part, been educated in business schools, and, until the last ten or fifteen years, they tended not to have been extensively exposed to the disciplines of economics, psychology, and mathematics (including statistics). The contents of *The Accounting Review* prior to the late 1960s bear out this generalisation. By the early 1970s, however, most new assistant professors in North America were much better schooled in research methods borrowed from other disciplines than were their predecessors. The tradition in Britain has been quite different. While some of today's accounting academics have 'graduated' from the ranks of qualified accountants, others have done studies in economics or accounting departments. Some have done both. Moreover, the placement of accounting academics in economics departments has influenced the questions addressed and the methods employed in their research. Training in research methodology has not been as intensive or widespread in Britain as it has in the United States.

The longer economics tradition associated with British accounting academics does much to explain the active interest, over many years, of British researchers in opportunity cost theory and income theory. The long line of British enquiries into these questions is well brought out in the essays by Arnold and Scapens, and Whittington. In particular, the 'value to the owner' school has been championed, almost without exception, by Britons and Australians, although the germ of the idea is often traced to Bonbright, an American public utilities economist. The writings emanating from this school had an obvious impact on the Report of the Sandilands Committee, and, through that report, also upon certain utterances of the Financial Accounting Standards Board in the U.S.A.

Another distinctive feature of the British accounting literature has been the numerous articles devoted to 'cash flow accounting'. Lee and Lawson have been the two prime movers, and it is fitting that they both be represented in this volume. In his paper, Lee reviews the arguments in favour of 'cash flow accounting'. Like many essays in this volume, Lee's is a helpful annotation on the pertinent literature, citing British as well as American writings on the subject. Lawson, in an empirical study, suggests some of the consequences of the disparity between measured profit performance and measured 'cash flow' performance.

The essays by Tomkins and Perrin seem, to me, to suggest agendas for academic research rather than an impressive record of achievement. Some work, to be sure, has been done, but, as in North America, the non-business sectors have attracted considerably less interest among academics. A trend toward serious research in public sector accounting has, however, become noticeable in North America in the last half-dozen years (spurred, one suspects, by the financial predicament of New York City), but it is difficult to say whether the incentives for such research in North America and Britain will succeed in shifting resources further in that direction. Both papers in this volume propose a wide range of issues worthy of research.

Parker's essay represents a more thorough treatment (with particular attention to possible British work) of a theme which was developed in the report of the Committee on Accounting History of the American Accounting Association, in 1970. I was the chairman of that committee. It was created by AAA President, Sidney Davidson, following my suggestion that the Association do what it could to encourage more and better work in accounting history, which had been a neglected field in North America. He responded by asking me to chair a committee to recommend an AAA role, and the committee's report was the result. Unfortunately, the Association did not accept the challenge, but I hope that Parker will be more successful. Few incentives are present in North America to encourage younger academics, especially, to conduct research in accounting history. In Britain, one can perhaps be more optimistic.

In North America, as in Britain, it is difficult to assess the increment to knowledge produced thus far by the outpouring of modern empirical research in accounting. New insights into the uses which are made of accounting information have been provided, but one could question whether the substantial investment of research resources since the late 1960s has yielded corresponding benefits in the form of new knowledge. One can, therefore, understand Peasnell's pessimistic appraisal of British empirical research. In the social sciences, we perhaps expect too much of our empirical research, particularly when comparisons are drawn with results in the physical sciences. But we work with variables that are less susceptible to rigorous empirical study, and even carefully guarded generalisations may be difficult to draw. Nonetheless, in order to be able to make defensible accounting choices we will require much better knowledge about the interactions between accounting information and individuals, organisations, markets, and society. I, therefore, join Peasnell in hoping that the necessary resources will be devoted to raising British empirical research to an even higher plane of quality and usefulness.

Cooper, in his wide-ranging analysis, examines the contributions which contingency theory can make to the design of accounting systems and to the greater usefulness of management accounting. Bhaskar, in an extensive review of work which has applied quantitative methods to a variety of problems in management accounting (a difficult literature, indeed), helps interpret, both for the researcher and practitioner, many of the noteworthy developments—as well as prospects for future lines of enquiry. Lowe draws on his earlier work to argue for an 'extroversion' and a coming of age of the literature on MIS design.

In his paper, Bromwich outlines the contributions of economics and social choice theory to the increasingly complex process of setting accounting standards. In Britain and North America, standard-setting was virtually ignored as a topic of research until the late 1960s, and the research since then on both sides of the Atlantic has confronted accounting policy-makers—much to their discomfort, I should imagine—with arguments and evidence that their decisions carry economic, social, and political consequences. It is a fascinating and almost boundless subject, and one of the largest questions of the 1980s centres on the role which these alleged consequences will play in accounting policy-making—and what will become of the standard-setting process if they do play a role.

The perceived schism between the work of researchers and the interests of practitioners and policy-makers is raised by Flint and Shaw (and also by Peasnell). To some extent, this widening schism is one of the costs unavoidably incurred when, within a single generation, the states of accounting research and of preparation for the accounting profession both undergo radical change. Research has suddenly become more rigorous and scientific, which, during the period of transition, will make it less intelligible to non-researchers. No-one can deny that there has been a revolution in accounting research methods in the last ten to fifteen years. But, during the same period, there has also been a revolution in the manner of entry to the British accounting profession. What was, not so many years ago, a profession which included very few university graduates—indeed, university attendance was positively discouraged in many quarters—may soon be confining its intake to university graduates (but not necessarily those specialising in accounting). If, for those students who do university studies in accounting, British academics—unlike North Americans—instil in their students a respect for rigorous research and an appreciation for the results which sound research can produce, it is reasonable to expect a better understanding between professionals and academics. The publication of this collection of essays should further this understanding, as almost all of its contents can be read and comprehended by professionals as well as academics.

The keen interest of the Social Science Research Council in the cause of accounting research has, indeed, been welcome, and I am pleased and honoured to have been invited by the editors to collaborate, if only in a small way, in this useful undertaking. I hope that it will lead to more and better research and to closer and more fruitful links between researchers and the professional accounting bodies.

Introduction

The last decade has witnessed a growing interest in the United Kingdom in accounting research. With a rapid expansion in university teaching of accounting and finance, there has been a major inflow of new people into the academic community. Although, initially, a great deal of the available effort was devoted to teaching and to the administration of newly established departments, more serious attention now is being given to research and scholarly inquiry. Perhaps for the first time there is a fair sized, viable and active accounting research community in the U.K. Of equal importance, there are signs that accounting practitioners have started to recognize the contribution which new knowledge can make to the development of accounting practice. For, as in many other countries, questions of accounting policy have entered the arena of public debate. With pressures for greater organizational accountability and disclosure, further standardization of the accounting craft, a growing awareness of the roles which accounting and financial management can play in improving organizational efficiency and effectiveness and, not least in importance, a more informed and critical media, aspects of accounting have come to be examined, debated and challenged in new ways. Accounting has come to be recognized as a socially important, but not unproblematic, area of management activity, and one in which there is a need for new insights and developments.

The debates over inflation accounting forcefully illustrated these tendencies. Emerging out of both an inflationary economy and the establishment of institutions for the regulation and standardization of accounting, the discussions quickly illustrated both the problematic nature of accounting in practice, and the ways in which debate in the area is dependent upon the existence of bodies of thought which can provide a basis for understanding and evaluating practical options and alternatives. Possibly for the first time, accounting research was demonstrably shown to be relevant to the development of accounting practice. Practitioners, let alone academics, publicly argued over the merits of alternative theoretical perspectives and their practical consequences. Moreover, the inflation accounting debate also illustrated the reality of the broader economic, social and organizational significance of the accounting function. From an early stage inflation accounting alternatives were discussed in the context of policy questions related to the management of the national economy, industrial and corporate strategy, and the communication and use of corporate information in a more pluralistic society where the interests of the capital markets are considered alongside those of the state, professional institutions and managerial responses to the organized labour movement.

Although obviously a central debate of the last decade, the discussion of inflation accounting is only one of a number of issues which have contributed to a growing recognition of the wider significance of accounting and the need for new insights and understandings. Mention also might be made of issues such as the appropriate institutional locus and processes of accounting standard setting, the growing concern with the disclosure of information to employees and trade unions, and the roles which accounting might play in furthering the efficiency and accountability of public institutions.

A New Research Initiative

Aware of the importance of such issues and the need for further research, the Management and Industrial Relations Committee of the U.K. Social Science Research Council launched an Accounting Research Initiative in 1976. Building on the recommendations of the Tricker (1975) report entitled 'Research in Accountancy—A Strategy for Further Work', the initiative sought to provide both general and specific stimuli to accounting research with funds being made available for particular areas of research, the establishment of research networks and the discussion of research in progress.

The specific areas identified for immediate research funding were inflation accounting and information disclosure to employees and trade unions. In the area of inflation accounting, funds have been made available for two studies of the impact of inflation on management accounting and organizational decision-making, an aspect of the problem relatively neglected to date by researchers world wide. A two-year professorial fellowship also has been established with the aim of providing an overview of both the current state of knowledge in the area and the nature of the debates that have taken place in the U.K. Aware of the paucity of research on the currently contentious issue of disclosing information, both financial and otherwise, to employees and trade unions, the SSRC initially supported four research projects on this topic and has subsequently allocated funds to a fifth. The fact that these projects adopted very different perspectives and used an array of methodologies was seen as an advantage at this stage in the development of knowledge.

In the case of two further areas of accounting research the SSRC aimed to provide relatively modest funds which might help to establish a viable network of potential researchers and stimulate the identification of topics worthy of subsequent research funding. With such objectives in mind, seminar groups on Management Accounting and on the Social and Political Aspects of Accounting were established under the chairmanship of Michael Bromwich and Professor Bengt Stymne (of the Stockholm School of Economics), respectively. It is a sign of practitioner interest that the former group is co-funded by the Institute of Chartered Accountants in England and Wales and the Institute of Cost and Management Accountants. Both have so far succeeded in pulling together interested groups of researchers, and others, and show the potential to provide a necessary stimulus for encouraging future research in their respective areas of concern.

The SSRC also organized a series of national accounting research conferences as part of its initiative—a particularly important factor in a country which has not had a rich and sustained tradition of scholarly discussion in the accounting area. The first such conference, held at the Oxford Centre for Management Studies in January 1977, played a key role in launching the initiative, bringing it to the attention of the relatively newly appointed accounting professoriate and an active group of younger scholars. A subsequent gathering in 1978 provided a worthwhile opportunity for discussing the organizational as well as the intellectual constraints on research, and it resulted in a number of ideas which subsequently were incorporated into SSRC discussions and decisions. Finally, in December 1979, a major conference was organized at the London Graduate School of Business Studies to review the current state of accounting research in the U.K. Based, because of costs, on a series of invited papers from only a segment of the academic population, this latter conference, nevertheless, aimed to provide insights into both earlier research traditions and emerging issues and concerns. These papers form the basis of the present volume.

Past Traditions and Current Issues

A number of the essays which follow focus on the understandings that have begun to merge from important areas of past as well as current research. The discussions of income theory, costing theory and cash flow accounting are particularly important in this respect. Drawing on substantive traditions of inquiry in the U.K. they provide insights into the nature of the problems that have been investigated, the theoretical perspectives that have been drawn on and both the conclusions and the remaining uncertainties.

Other essays reflect more recent research interests. Professional concerns with accounting regulation, for instance, are resulting in a growth of interest in both the institutional processes of accounting standard-setting and its more fundamental conceptual characteristics. Similarly, the shifting structure of the economy and changing patterns of political belief are stimulating interest in accounting problems in the public sector, at both the national and local levels. It also is possible that the uncertainties of the accounting present have encouraged an increasing number of accounting researchers to investigate the processes through which accounting has come to be as it now is.

The initial inspiration for some current research no doubt came from across the Atlantic. Be that as it may, some of the subsequent essays illustrate how the very different institutional bases and traditions of inquiry already are influencing the type of research that is being undertaken in areas such as the empirical study of accounting, the application of quantitative methods and the investigation of the behavioural and organizational aspects of both accounting and information systems. The sophisticated methodologies that are so characteristic of American empirical inquiries can, we think, be contrasted with the more descriptive approaches in the U.K. and in the behavioural and organizational areas the contrasts are becoming even more evident. For whilst inquiries in the U.S.A. still emphasize a psychological perspective, British work increasingly is reflecting more organizational and societal levels of analysis.

Unfortunately, the conference was not able to provide a comprehensive overview of either current or emerging accounting research in the U.K. No papers focused on auditing research or more traditional management accounting research concerns, for instance, despite the fact that the latter has been the subject of a number of inquiries and the former is now starting to attract more interest. Of particular significance, however, is the absence of papers on the issues raised by the growing practical concern with the disclosure of information to employees and trade unions, and its use by these groups.

Increasingly, the accounting function in the U.K. is being viewed in a more pluralistic context, as was evidenced by the form and recommendations of The Corporate Report published by the then Accounting Standards Steering Committee in 1975. Managerial groups, for instance, are having to grapple with the difficulties of communicating financial information and any implied economic messages to an employee and trade union audience. Equally, however, trade unionists and some of their supporters in the academic community are starting to investigate the problems with using accounting information in the context of both collective bargaining and the formulation of wider industrial policies by the organized labour movement. Consideration is being given to the consequences of broader legislative disclosure requirements, the roles which accounting has played in industrial policy making and the possibilities for formulating accounting policies which can more adequately reflect the concerns and needs of a broader array of social interests. Perhaps not unsurprisingly, the emerging patterns of research are starting to relate more explicitly to the research traditions of continental Europe and Scandinavia rather than to those which have emerged in a very different social, institutional and political context in the U.S.A.

Despite a number of such gaps, we nevertheless hope that the essays collected in this volume provide a useful summary of some of the important areas of past and current accounting research in the U.K. It is certainly our hope that they might help to bring to the attention of a wider audience in the U.K. and elsewhere both the substantive progress that has been achieved and some of the problems that are currently being investigated by the growing number of members of the British accounting research community.

Some Future Directions

Now that a viable research community is in the process of being established in the U.K., what are the issues and problems that might concern it in the years ahead? Of course, making such predictions is a hazardous task at the best of times, and particularly so in an area which has newly emerged and which itself is concerned with the creation of new insights and possibilities. We nevertheless think that some of the concerns and approaches of today are pointing towards a number of possibilities for tomorrow. So, with due caution, to these we now turn.

Already mention has been made of the growing recognition of the pluralistic nature of the accounting context. Whilst much early research and theorizing was orientated towards the accounting needs of the capital market and of a management group who were presumed to be striving to meet its performance demands, current research already is adopting a wider perspective. For instance, attention is being given to the consequences for accounting standard-setting of conflicting information needs, to the roles which accounting and auditing might play in furthering corporate accountability and to the ways in which the wider disclosure of information might provide a broader basis for the consideration of industrial development policies. Moreover, the growing interest in accounting in the public sector also points to a similar expansion of research orientations. For there too, research is now starting to consider the roles which accounting might be able to play in furthering not only traditional conceptions of economic efficiency but also more widely conceived notions of both effectiveness and accountability.

It is likely that such a changing view of both the context in which accounting operates and the roles which it does and might serve will continue to influence what issues are seen as problematic, and thereby the loci of research. Already in the area of financial accounting standard-setting, for instance, problems are starting to be seen in terms of both their technical characteristics and the ways in which they have emerged at the interface between the bodies concerned with accounting regulation, the institutions of the accounting profession and agencies representing not only industrial and commercial interests but also those of the State. Whilst technical considerations will remain of considerable importance, there already are indications that such interests will be complemented by attempts to understand the institutional and political processes that are implicit in standard setting, the roles played by a whole array of economic and social interests and issues, and not least in importance, the complex ways in which knowledge of accounting comes to bear on its practice. For example, rather than focusing on the presumed needs and decision models of very particular groups of users of accounting information, which was a predominant concern of the past, current research is striving to ascertain just who are the users and how the information is used, the roles which it plays and is seen to play, and the consequences which it has.

It is our belief that such shifting research perspectives are of the utmost importance. By striving to provide understandings of the processes of accounting change and the ways in which accounting is implicated in economic and social action they have the potential to provide bases for debating the accountings that might be in ways that are not divorced from the complexities of the accounting present.

Interestingly, not dissimilar perspectives are emerging in the study of management accounting and information systems. Again, there are signs that past emphases on the creation of the technically new are beginning to be complemented by a concern with understanding how management accounting systems have come to be, the roles which they serve and the consequences which they have for organizational functioning and performance. Rather than continuing to articulate ever more normative possibilities, so many of which have differed radically from what appears to be done, a few researchers are starting to ascertain just what is the current state of practice, the factors underlying its development and the problems which it is facing. Foresaking the desk for the factory and the office, such researchers are starting to draw on a wider array of insights from disciplines such as organization theory and sociology in order to understand the ways in which accounting is implicated in organized endeavour.

Research which so strives to understand the complexities of accounting in action undoubtedly will present both opportunities and frustrations to the scholars of the future. It certainly will not be easy to develop perspectives which will help us to appreciate either the accounting context or the pressures for development and change. Nor should we minimize the problems of introducing and gaining acceptance for those methodologies which might more adequately illuminate the accounting condition. On the other hand, difficult as such problems may be, they at least offer some possibility for moving towards the integration of accounting research into the mainstream of social science enquiry. Of equal importance, the emerging research interests also have the potential to contribute more directly to the practice of accounting. For by trying to understand both accounting as it is and as it might become, there is a real chance that we will be able to create a greater interplay between the practice of, and research into, accounting—a factor which we consider to be of the greatest significance.

Acknowledgements

Finally, we would like to acknowledge the help and support provided by a number of individuals and organizations.

The role of the Social Science Research Council has been a particularly important one. Both by its funding of the conference on which the present volume is based and its more general concern for furthering accounting research in the U.K., the SSRC has provided such a vital stimulus in the last few years. In this respect we would particularly like to mention the efforts of Bob Tricker, whose report on the state of accounting research in the U.K. provided an essential basis for action, Professor Dorothy Wedderburn who was Chairman of the Management and Industrial Relations Committee of the SSRC for much of the time when the accounting research initiative was being considered and planned, and Professor Chris Higgins who has been a supportive and facilitative Chairman of the SSRC's Accounting Steering Committee. Our appreciation is also extended to the many members of the SSRC secretariat who have played such a vital role throughout the initiative, particularly to Michael Brennen, Chris Caswill, Gerda Loosemore-Reppen and Paul Long.

On such occasions it is unusual to mention one's publisher. However, we would like to acknowledge the help provided by Alfred Waller and Eric Dalton of Pitmans. They have proved to be enthusiastic supporters of the whole project and a source of a great deal of help and advice.

Last, but by no means least, we would like to thank our secretaries, Melinda Smallwood and Meg Wells for their help in not only organizing the conference but also dealing so efficiently with the seemingly endless correspondence generated by the subsequent editorial process.

Anthony Hopwood
Michael Bromwich

1 The British contribution to income theory

Geoffrey Whittington
Professor of Accounting and Finance, University of Bristol

1 Scope and Plan of the Paper

The theory and measurement of income has attracted a voluminous literature during the 20th century, and it is not proposed to attempt a comprehensive survey of the whole field. In order to make the subject manageable, the following constraints will be imposed:

(a) the main objective will be to survey the current state of the art, rather than to provide a comprehensive historical survey of the literature which led to the present state of knowledge;

(b) the concept and measurement of business income is the central concern of this paper and the financial accounting literature the main source of reference. The concepts of personal income and national income are not considered, although welfare economics provides many useful insights into the fundamental assumptions and objectives of accounting (and is likely to be of even greater relevance in the future: see, for example, the recent survey of the economic literature on real income measurement, Sen (1979)). It should be noted that the measurement of business income also has underpinnings in welfare economics, e.g. it is often assumed, implicitly or explicitly, that accounts should provide information which will enable shareholders or management to make profit (or net present wealth) maximizing investment decisions, and this objective presumably has its origins in the concept of Pareto efficiency which can (under certain important restrictive assumptions) be achieved by competitive, profit-maximizing behaviour. (See, for example, Edwards and Bell (1961), p. 271, footnote 2.) Useful introductory surveys of welfare economics are Winch (1971) and Mishan (1966). A good illustration of how the results of welfare economics can be applied to a problem of business income is Bromwich (1977);

(c) 'theory' is taken to apply to any idea or proposal supported by deductive rather than inductive reasoning, i.e. to *a priori* rather than empirical work;

(d) it is not proposed to attempt a comprehensive treatment of inflation accounting, which is an overlapping, but partially disjointed, field;

(e) although the British contribution to income theory will be emphasized, it is not proposed to confine the discussion to British contributions to the field. To do so would be hopelessly one-sided and insular, and would ignore the essentially international character of the debate.

The plan of the rest of the paper is as follows. In section 2, a brief historical perspective is provided. This is followed in section 3 by a summary of the present state of income theory. Specific problem areas of the subject are then examined. In section 4, two aspects of the relationship between the measurement of income and the purpose for which it is used are considered. In recent years, there has been some exploration of income as a measure of dividend-paying capacity ('distributable profit'), and of income as a basis for taxation, and these are selected as examples of the 'different incomes for different purposes' approach. Section 5 considers two techniques of income measurement which have received much attention recently. In the British literature, the idea of 'value to the owner' has been given particular emphasis as an asset valuation basis, and that of the 'gearing adjustment' has received similar emphasis in the area of capital maintenance. Finally, an attempt is made to draw some conclusions for the directions in which future research might develop.

2 Historical Development and Present State of the Art

Two important and distinct strands can be discerned in the evolution and current state of the theory of income measurement. The first is what might be called the 'pure theory', i.e. the development of an 'ideal' model of income, which relies heavily on the work of economists. The second is the concern with measuring income in practice, and is more closely associated with accountants. The best work of the latter type (such as Edwards and Bell (1961)) relies on the theory for its foundation, and the most immediately useful theory from the accountant's standpoint is that which makes assumptions which might apply in the real world. It is perhaps worth emphasizing that the economist's standpoint is sometimes different, being concerned with the properties of abstract models of the economy in which income measurement may not play a central role and a degree of abstraction may be permissible. It is often overlooked that Hicks's (1946) definition is merely an aside in a work on rather abstract economic theory. However, many fruitful insights have been obtained by a systematic comparison of the accountant's and the economist's approach (e.g. R. S. Edwards (1937), Alexander (1950), and Solomons (1961)).

There is no comprehensive survey of this literature, but the best and by far the most common starting point (especially for British work) is the collection of readings edited by Parker and Harcourt (1969). The Introduction to Parker and Harcourt has also become a classic in its own right, and synthesizes much of the earlier work. Certain other important early contributions are included in Baxter and Davidson (1977), and Zeff (1976), provides a valuable collection of early contributions from the U.S.A. for the period 1918–35. An extremely useful survey of the main competing theories of asset valuation will be found in Sterling (1971). Finally, there is a number of classic works such as Bonbright (1937) and Canning (1929) which are not easily anthologized and which can therefore be studied only in their original (somewhat forbidding) form. For developments during the past ten years it is necessary to rely almost entirely on the original sources, although Lee (1974) provides a partial survey, a useful bibliography and numerical examples of the main competing systems of income measurement.

All that will be attempted here will be to summarize the present state of the art, and even this involves a degree of simplification which may be unacceptable to some.

(1) The Pure Theory

The seminal contributor to the first strand in the literature, the pure theory of income, was Irving Fisher (1906). His influence pervades the subsequent development of the subject, as is demonstrated by the frequency with which his work is cited. His basic definition of income was a measure of personal income, grounded in welfare economics, and he, therefore, measured income in terms of consumption. However, it is important not to overlook the fact that Fisher also had a concept of what he called 'earnings', i.e. consumption plus the increase (or less the decrease) in wealth. This is much closer to the conventional definition of income for a business enterprise and Fisher (1930) approved of Canning's (1929) proposal that Fisher's 'earnings' concept should be the model for measuring the profit and loss of a business. Fisher measured wealth in terms of the discounted present value of future receipts (or, in the case of an individual, consumption), so that his earnings measure was a form of the neoclassical economic income model which is still used as one possible standard by which to judge a system of accounting measurement, e.g. Barton (1974) and Scapens (1978), although it should be noted that neither of these authors is optimistic about economic income as a practical method of measurement, Barton dismissing the 'surrogate' hypothesis and Scapens preferring short-run profit as a practical alternative.

The definition of economic income which is most often quoted is that of Hicks (1946). Hicks, like Fisher, assumes that consumption is the ultimate motive of all economic activity. It should be noted that Hicks offers three different definitions of income:

(a) 'income No. 1 is . . . the maximum amount which can be spent during a period if there is to be an expectation of maintaining intact the capital value of prospective receipts (in money terms)';

(b) 'income No. 2 . . . (is) . . . the maximum amount the individual can spend this week, and still expect to be able to spend the same amount in each ensuing week';

(c) 'income No. 3 must be defined as the maximum amount of money which the individual can spend this week, and still expect to be able to spend the same amount *in real terms* in each ensuing week'.

In each case 'spending' is assumed to be identical with consumption: when the two differ, because of the existence of durable consumption goods, an attempt should be made to measure consumption (e.g. by resort to prices in second-hand consumption goods markets).

Each of the measures defined above is an *ex ante* concept, but there is a parallel set of three *ex post* income concepts. Clearly, *ex post* income is of more relevance to the financial accountant, who is typically concerned to report past events rather than projecting the future (although the latter seems likely to play an increasingly important role in financial statements; see, for example, *The Corporate Report*, Accounting Standards Steering Committee 1975, pp. 55–6). However, even the measurement of *ex post* Hicksian income involves taking a view as to the future, in the case of a continuing business enterprise, since it is necessary to value closing assets by discounting expected future receipts, unless an acceptable market value is available. Furthermore, there is the problem of defining the capital to be maintained intact. Each of Hicks's definitions contains a different capital maintenance concept, but each of these is unambiguous only under conditions of certainty. If we introduce uncertainty, then the valuations of both opening and closing capital will vary depending upon whether they are viewed from the beginning or the end of the period: if we choose to measure income *ex post* this might imply that we should revalue opening capital, not as it was actually valued at the beginning of the period, but as it would have been valued in the light of the information available at the end of the period. The problems of unanticipated, or 'windfall', gains are discussed fully by Kaldor (1955) and Solomons (1961), both of whom reach pessimistic conclusions about the practical usefulness of income (in Kaldor's case as a tax base and in Solomons' case as a measure of economic performance). Solomons (1961) reached the conclusion that 'so far as accounting is concerned, the next twenty-five years may subsequently be seen to have been the twilight of income measurement'.

This theme will be taken up later, but, first, it is necessary briefly to trace the second strand of the literature, that which concentrates upon the technique of measuring income in practice.

(2) Income Measurement

The most basic work of this type is largely empirical in content, describing accounting practice and attempting to deduce the concepts of income and capital which underly practice, but the best works of this type have evaluated practice in the light of theory. An outstanding work in this mould is part of Canning (1929), and R. S. Edwards's series of papers (1937) are an excellent British contribution. Gilman (1939) and the report by the Study Group on Business Income (1952) are examples of the more empirically based approach.

An alternative approach to practical methods of income measurement has been to ignore (or largely ignore) present practices, and devise hypothetical accounting systems which are, nevertheless, compatible with the practical constraints necessary for feasibility in the real world, a type of constraint often ignored by those concerned with pure theory. Of this type of approach the replacement cost school is perhaps the most widely represented in the literature, owing its origins to the response to hyper-inflation in Germany in the 1920s when Schmidt (1921), (1930), (1931) was its most prominent advocate. Contemporary with Schmidt was the creation of the Dutch replacement cost school of Limperg and Goudeket (1960), which, in turn, has had a clear influence on Gynther (1966) (1975), one of the most trenchant current advocates of replacement cost accounting, and, in the more practical field, on the Sandilands Committee (1975). This approach to replacement cost accounting might be termed the 'pure' (or pejoratively, the 'extreme') form, since it uses replacement cost to define the capital maintenance concept, thus requiring the maintenance of the capital specific to the accounting entity before a profit is recognized (as in Sandilands 'operating profit'). In its most extreme form it requires physical capital maintenance.

There is, however, a more pragmatic school of replacement cost accounting, and here the British contribution is particularly strong. The main characteristics of this approach are that capital maintenance is defined in terms of general purchasing power (a 'proprietary' approach as opposed to the 'entity' approach described in the preceding paragraph), and that the use of replacement cost for asset valuation is usually justified on the grounds that it will typically represent the 'value to the owner' (otherwise known as 'deprival value' or 'opportunity value') of the assets. Examples of this approach are Sweeney (1935 and 1936), Baxter (1967 and 1975), Wright (1970) and Gee and Peasnell (1976). Value to the owner has attracted considerable attention recently, and has been adopted in the current cost accounting systems proposed by the Sandilands Committee and various other committees or professional bodies in the English-speaking world. These systems have had some difficulty with the capital maintenance concept, general purchasing power not having found universal favour. Another British contribution in this field, which will be discussed later, is the idea of a gearing adjustment (as expounded, for example, in Kennedy (1978)), which provides an alternative capital maintenance concept.

Standing apart from both of these replacement cost schools of thought is the classic work of Edwards and Bell (1961). Although Edwards and Bell's preferred income measure 'business profit' is based upon replacement cost, they also have a measure of 'realizable profit' which is based upon selling prices. Their justification for preferring replacement cost is one of the less well-developed parts of their work. Their main contribution was to propose a segmentation of aspects of the firm's activities, separating realized holding gains from unrealized holding gains, and separating real gains from nominal gains. It will be argued in the next section of this paper that their scheme is a manifestation of the current trend away from the idea of a single income number, and possibly away from income measurement itself. Tippett (1979) provides a similar interpretation of Edwards and Bell's work.

A final alternative is provided by the 'net realizable value', 'exit value' or 'current cash equivalent' valuation basis, whose most articulate contemporary advocate is Chambers, whose writings on this subject are voluminous. A recent listing will be found in Chambers (1977). Another distinguished advocate is Sterling (1970). Canning (1929) was an early exponent of this approach, although he was prepared to temper his advocacy with an element of expediency in valuing assets which are held for use and do not have a ready second-hand market. Chambers argues that the 'current cash equivalent' is the one valuation basis which is always relevant in decisions concerning the disposition of a firm's assets. Thomas (1974) argues that this is one of the few valuation bases which avoids the allocation problem (i.e. the problem of allocating the total value of an entity to the individual assets which jointly generate that value, or the problem of allocating the cost of a durable asset between the various periods over which it is used), although he claims that it does not avoid the aggregation problem (i.e. groups of assets may sell for more, or less, than the sum which individual assets will realize when sold separately). Net realizable value also has considerable intuitive appeal, being close to the everyday concept of value (Tweedie (1977) provides evidence of this). However, critics such as Baxter (1967), Edwards and Bell (1961), and Edwards (1975) tend to stress the greater relevance of replacement cost in valuing assets which are held for use in a continuing entity.

What is notable about all the above systems of accounting measurement is that none claims to yield a perfect representation of the economist's income measure, except in very special circumstances. For example, it is well known (see, for example, Robichek and Myers (1965), chapter 2, which gives a useful numerical illustration) that, over the full lifetime of an accounting entity (i.e. from the initial injection of cash to final liquidation) total income will be the same, irrespective of the valuation base adopted, and will equal economic income, although there may be differences due to whether real or money capital is maintained. However, the typical accounting problem is to measure the periodic income of a continuing entity, and the valuation basis used in the allocation of income to a particular period then becomes important, except in those special cases in which all values are identical, as in Edwards and Bell's 'stationary state' ((1961), pp. 6–11). Thus, the practical methods of income measurement which are available have no necessary identity with the economist's (highly subjective and therefore impractical) model of income. There are two possible responses to this: either practical techniques must be refined and their theoretical properties explored so that they can be related to the economist's model, which is seen as an ideal, or practical techniques should be devised in such a manner that they generate information which satisfies the perceived needs of the users of accounting information, irrespective of whether or not it conforms with an abstract definition of income. The latter alternative would be a fulfilment of Solomons' prediction quoted earlier.

3 The Current State of the Art: Income Measurement or 'Fuzzy Communication'?

It has long been recognized that a single income measure will not serve all purposes. Daines (1929) made an early attempt to list some of the diverse purposes which income measurement might be required to serve, and was particularly scathing in his condemnation of the inhibiting effect on accounting practice of the dividend distribution laws. An early British contribution which relates income measurement to the specific purposes for which it is used is Edwards (1938), and nearly all subsequent writers on the subject specify the uses which they have in mind. Nevertheless, it is by no means clear that the use-oriented approach is universally accepted by practitioners or the users of financial statements.

A further development of the use-oriented approach which has become apparent in recent years is the view that the measurement of income in any form may be inappropriate to users' needs. The British contribution to this development has been considerable. Solomons' scepticism about the future of income measurement has already been quoted. One alternative suggested by Solomons was cash flow or funds flow reporting, which has its roots in the ideas of Irving Fisher and was extant in the 1920s (e.g. it is mentioned by Daines (1929)), and developed by Vatter (1947). In recent years two of its most consistent advocates have been Lawson (1971 and 1976) and Lee (1972 and 1974). Cash flow reporting is perhaps the most revolutionary alternative to income measurement. The more common response to the difficulties of measuring income is to produce a figure or set of figures representing something called 'income', but to pay more attention to the components of the final net figure than to the figure itself. The object of this is to give the user of accounts the opportunity to assess the reliability of the final income number and its appropriateness to his needs, and, if necessary, to construct his own alternative. The Edwards and Bell system can be viewed as an example of such a system (Tippett,

1979). The distinctions between operating and holding gains, realized and unrealized gains, and real and monetary gains can all be viewed as giving the user of accounts information about different aspects of the entity's activities which might have different degrees of relevance to his needs, different predictive value or different risk attributes, although the validity of some of their dichotomies has been questioned (Drake and Dopuch, 1965). In stating their theoretical framework, Edwards and Bell (Chapters 2 and 3) are clear that they do not attempt to measure economic income, which involves the estimation of subjective goodwill, but are instead concerned to measure the economic progress of the firm in terms of current market prices. They emphasize the importance of the comparison of the *ex post* outcome with the *ex ante* expectation rather than the size of the final income number, as a means of assessing managerial performance. Equally, the current cost accounting system proposed by the Sandilands Committee (1975) provides some information of this type and has even been described as being concerned with measuring cash flow rather than income (Kay, 1977). This concern is even more apparent in some of the writings of Gibbs (1976 and 1979).

There has been a substantial body of theoretical work which has provided an analytical basis for this rejection of economic income as the ideal model for financial reporting, and it has contained a strong British contribution. Barton (1974 and 1976) contended that *ex ante* economic income is an inappropriate model for the *ex post* accounting measurement of the economic performance of a business enterprise. Bromwich (1975) demonstrated that market imperfections could render both replacement cost and net realizable value inappropriate surrogates for present value. Peasnell (1977) and Bromwich (1977) simultaneously and independently argued that 'there is no reason to suppose that accountants have a comparative advantage in measuring income' and they should therefore concentrate on reporting those items of information about the entity of which they have special knowledge and which enter the process of income measurement, rather than carrying out the final evaluation. In fact, the final evaluation to which each author refers is the calculation of the present value of the business, by estimating future cash flows, which can by-pass income measurement altogether. Peasnell stresses the difficulty of assessing the discount rate relevant to the individual firm, and Bromwich emphasizes the differences which may occur between individual shareholders, when they enjoy consumer's surplus from the ownership of shares.

Beaver and Demski (1979) have recently neatly encapsulated this literature, suggesting that the role of income reporting is as information, a means of 'noisy communication', which strikes the right balance between excessive detail and over-simplification. They identify the situation where this could be the role of income, rather than the representation of 'true' economic income, as occurring whenever markets are imperfect or incomplete. Complete markets occur when there are markets for all goods in all possible states of the world. If markets are complete, uncertainty can be traded away by dealing in the appropriate market (e.g. commodity futures). In practice, it is not possible to trade in every commodity or insure against every contingency. Since perfect and complete markets impose stringent requirements which do not appear to be met in the real world in which accountants operate and under which accounting reports might not be required anyway, accountants should concentrate on the properties of their reports as a means of effective communication of relevant data, rather than as an estimate of a 'true' ideal income number.

This is not to say that theoretical work has concentrated solely on the task of discrediting the economist's model of income as an ideal by which to judge accounting measures. There is, indeed, a tradition which has lasted at least half a century (Canning, 1929), of using the economist's model as an ideal. Alexander (1950) is a good example of this. More recently, the idea of accounting values as surrogates for economic values has been explored analytically, particularly by Revsine (1970, 1973 and 1976), who demonstrates that, under certain highly restrictive assumptions, replacement cost operating profit can be regarded as a measure of *ex ante* economic income and holding gains as a measure of unexpected (windfall) gains. The restrictive assumptions necessary for this result to hold have been criticized by Barton (1974 and 1976). This, in turn, evoked an elegant response from Cook and Holzmann (1976) who demonstrate that, in long-run perfectly competitive equilibrium, the replacement cost of assets should equal their discounted present value ('economic value') but they concede that the 'surrogate' relationship fails when their assumptions are violated. On their assumptions 'exit' (sale) values would equal replacement cost and be equally good surrogates for economic values. A British contribution by Scapens (1978) investigates the possibility of measuring short-run economic profit in accounts. In a more practical context, Scott (1976) makes suggestions for reforming accounting practice so as to approximate the measurement of 'standard stream' economic income. Merrett's (1975) proposal for a 'capitalizable distribution' measure of profit is in a similar vein. There is also considerable literature concerned with the circumstances in which accounting rates of return will equal the economist's internal rate of return (Harcourt (1965), Vatter (1966), Kay (1976), Whittington (1979)), but this yields results which are more relevant to average rates of return over several periods than to the problems of reporting for single periods.

However, although it is useful to impose a pattern on the literature by classifying it in this manner, it would be misleading to suggest that there is a fundamental disagreement as to the relationship between economic models and accounting measurements of income. There is widespread agreement that economic models can be represented in accounts only in restrictive circumstances. One current task of theoretical research in this field is to define the precise conditions in which economic models are relevant and feasible. There is also considerable scope for empirical work in this field, for example, in assessing the practical importance of divergences between different valuation bases.

To summarize the present state of the art, the following developments are observable in the current literature and seem likely to be important in the future.

(1) Different Incomes for Different Purposes

As was described earlier, this idea has been extant for at least fifty years. However, a search of the literature suggests that relatively little work has been done which starts with the purpose and works back to the required measure of income. The more common approach has been to define a system of income measurement and explore whether its properties are consistent with an often ill-specified purpose or set of purposes.

(2) Dis-aggregation of Accounting Income Measures

The provision of relevant information to enable a 'do-it-yourself' income measurement by the user of information requires further investigation. The Edwards and Bell system has been described as fitting into this pattern, and an example of one controversial area of their system which has attracted critical attention is the validity of the distinction between holding gains and operating gains (Drake and Dopuch (1965), Prakesh and Sunder (1979): Kay (1977) criticizes this distinction in the context of the Sandilands Report).

(3) Alternative Valuation Bases

Once it is accepted that different income measures will best serve different uses, and that different users may evaluate various items of information differently, the possibility arises that more than one valuation base might be used in financial reports. Edwards and Bell (1961, Chapters 3 and 8) consider this view favourably, and Kennedy (1978) has recently devised an appropriation statement which would show a number of alternative capital maintenance concepts. However, the proposal that multiple valuations should be reported has been rejected, for example, by Chambers (1972), on the ground that it would lead to inefficiency of communication. On the other hand, the practice of showing inflation-adjusted data in a supplementary statement is already recommended by various professional bodies (e.g. ED18, Accounting Standards Committee (1976)), and this might be regarded as the beginning of an important trend.

(4) Complementary and Alternative Information

For many potential uses, an income measure is not sufficient in itself and is only useful when supplemented by other information (Barton, 1975, p. 4). For example, in the next section of this paper we shall review the concept of distributable profit, which may be of some use in the dividend decision but requires to be supplemented by information concerning present and future liquidity (Egginton, 1979). Furthermore, in some uses, an income measure will itself be an input in calculating another number (e.g. Scott (1976) suggests that 'standard stream' income can be discounted to yield an estimate of present value). As has been argued elsewhere (Whittington, 1974), rational economic decisions about the disposal of assets usually require an evaluation of alternative uses, so that the reporting of a single value, or the means of obtaining it, is unlikely to satisfy the information requirements of such a decision. More work needs to be done to ascertain the full range of accounting data which are required to supplement income measures in specific uses.

In some cases, these data may be alternatives to income. Cash flow accounting is a potential competitor to income measurement, but it can also be viewed (e.g. in the case of the dividend decision) as complementary to it. A revival of interest in the balance sheet is another possibility, a balance sheet containing current net realizable values having obvious relevance to a number of potential uses of accounts (Chambers, 1966). A suggestion made recently (Macdonald, 1974) is that the balance sheet should not necessarily be articulated with the income statement, since net realizable value may be the best single valuation basis for the balance sheet, whereas replacement cost may be the appropriate valuation basis in charging assets consumed in earning operating profit. In this context, it is notable that Edwards and Bell's argument (1961, pp. 90–94) for charging physical replacement cost against operating profit seems quite plausible for the purpose which they have in mind but leads to a holding gain of dubious validity, since the asset showing the gain would not justify replacement at its present cost. Finally, forecast data may play an increasing role in financial reporting. Edwards and Bell, for example, stress the importance of evaluating their *ex post* income measures by comparing them with *ex ante* projections.

Having surveyed the history, current state, and likely developments of income measurement, we turn to specific areas where a distinct British contribution is discernible. First, following on from the 'different incomes for different purposes', theme which figures so prominently in the earlier discussion, two topics, distributable profit and income as a tax base, are further considered. Secondly, two areas are examined in which it appears that theorists have first devised a system and then tried to relate its properties to different uses. The two systems are value to the owner as a method of asset valuation and the measurement of real capital using a gearing adjustment. Both are incorporated in the present proposals for implementing current cost accounting in the U.K. (Accounting Standards Committee, 1979).

4 Different Incomes for Different Purposes—Two British Contributions

(1) Distributable Profit

Company law governing dividend payments has had an important influence on the measurement of profit by accountants (French, 1977, Daines, 1929), and the determination of the profit available for distribution to shareholders can be relied upon to make an appearance in most lists of the uses which a profit statement is supposed to serve. Recently, the idea of 'distributable' profit has been given new impetus by the prominence accorded to it in the Sandilands Report, and in the various subsequent British professional proposals for the implementation of current cost accounting. It has received further attention as a justification for the introduction of the monetary working capital adjustment, advocated by Gibbs (1976) and incorporated into the recent ED24 (ASC, 1979).

The exploration by theorists of the idea of distributable profit has not been as extensive as might have been expected, but some useful contributions have been made. Forker (1977) has proposed a system of reserve accounting which would make appropriations from profit for the change in the real burden of replacement, arising from price changes, as estimated by the management of the business. Sale and Scapens (1978) set out 'to explore the validity of the current cost profit measure proposed by the Sandilands Committee (and endorsed in ED18 and the Hyde Guidelines) as an indicator of dividend paying ability'. They conclude that the Sandilands proposals substantially meet this aim, but propose that a monetary working capital adjustment should be added. More recently, Egginton (1979) has provided a thorough analysis of the idea of distributable profit and concludes that 'financial accounting theory would be healthier without the distractions of the distributable profit concept; its demise would allow other purposes of profit measurement to receive more attention, and the object of prudence associated with the distributable profit concept could be more effectively pursued in other ways'. He argues that prudence may, in fact, require either expansion or contraction of the company's capital base, depending upon its economic circumstances. Profit measurement, on the other hand, assesses the hypothetical (and not necessarily prudent) distributions which would maintain capital intact, where 'capital maintenance can serve as a neutral benchmark against which to measure a company's success in increasing its command over resources in an accounting period'. He then explores various concepts of capital maintenance and finds them all potentially inconsistent with the idea of prudence in the distribution decision. He concludes that what he calls 'financial capacity' is that which should be maintained in order to satisfy the dictates of prudence, and suggests various pragmatic financing constraints as being more appropriate legal devices for imposing prudence on dividend distribution decisions.

Superficially, it might seem that Egginton's critique implies a wholesale dismissal of the arguments of the advocates of distributable profit. Closer examination shows, however, that this is not the case, although it does result in a more precise and limited role for the idea of distributable profit. It is clear that profit measures based upon capital maintenance ideas are not sufficient, or even particularly relevant, information for the dividend decision; this is the central theme of Egginton's critique. However, there is an alternative justification for distributable profit which treats distribution as a hypothetical benchmark, just as capital maintenance can be regarded as a benchmark. For example, Sale and Scapens write that: 'Distributable Operating Flow does not purport to measure the amount that should or will be distributed . . . DOF indicates the level of dividend which could be maintained into the indefinite future if the business continues with its current level of profits and if the environmental factors remained unchanged'. This approach treats 'distributable operating flow' as indicating maximum sustainable income, and recalls Hicks' consumption maintenance definition of income and can be related to Edwards and Bell's view of *ex post* operating profit as having predictive content as to future potential operating profit. It is, however, a limitation of the Sale and Scapens analysis that the authors do not explore the conditions under which the 'environmental factors' do give rise to a situation where maintaining real operating capacity is identical with maintaining the value of operating profit.

This deficiency is partly made good by a paper by Scott (1976) who advocates the use of the 'standard stream' (Hicks no. 2 and 3) approach in accounting and provides some guidelines as to how it might be implemented in practical accounting. Scott does not confine himself to artificial situations, and his discussion of the treatment of various types of gain (e.g. those due to changes in expectations) is analytically illuminating, although his claims for the verifiability by auditors of this system would be unlikely to find favour in professional circles. Merrett (1975) develops a 'capitalizable distribution' basis for profit measurement which is essentially similar to Scott's proposal but is not so clearly grounded in the Hicksian definition of income. Another economist, Kay (1977), also criticizes the Sandilands report for its alleged failure to recognize explicitly that 'Current Cost Profit is not a measure of profit at all, but a measure of cash flow'. It is 'the cash flow which the business would have generated in the course of the year had it neither expanded not (*sic*) contracted the scale of its operations'. Kay goes on to advocate the development of a system of cash flow accounting, in preference to the standard stream income approach suggested by Scott, which raises 'what are really very intractable issues'.

(2) Taxation

Taxation has long been one of the major purposes for which income has been measured, in practice, and models of income have been constructed by theorists. For example, Irving Fisher (1906 and 1942) was concerned to show that his 'income as consumption' avoided the double taxation which results if income is measured as 'earnings' (the income out of which the savings are made is taxed, and the return on the savings is taxed, so that the post-tax rate of return on savings is lower than the pre-tax rate of return on investment).

Writers on accounting income have typically listed taxation as one of the objectives for which accounting income will be used (e.g. Edwards and Bell, 1961), but, as Morley (1974, Chapter 4) points out 'too many . . . (writers on accounting theory) . . . have concentrated exclusively on accounting for decision-making and have thereby failed to contribute to the development of an equitable system for taxing profit'. For example, the Sandilands Report, although it recognizes the importance of defining the corporation tax base, is surprisingly vague as to how tax should be based upon its proposed system of reporting: in particular, there is no discussion about the taxation of holding gains. Morley attempts to remedy this by considering the economic implications of basing company taxation in Britain on the 'indexed historic cost' accounting profit proposed in ED8 (Accounting Standards Steering Committee, 1973). His conclusion, which is based largely on his view that widespread indexation of the tax system is impracticable, is that such a reform of the corporation tax base alone is undesirable.

Morley's approach is to evaluate a specific piecemeal reform in the context of the present British tax system. The Report of the Meade Committee (Meade, 1978) attempts the much more ambitious task of devising complete model tax systems (at least for direct taxation), within which the selection of the corporation tax base is based upon its compatibility with the rest of the system. Compatibility, in this case, implies consistency with the aims of the system, in terms of the economic objectives of equity and efficiency which it is designed to achieve, in addition to administrative compatibility. Thus, the Meade Report deduces the appropriate tax base from the economic objectives of the tax system, rather than starting from the tax base and considering its compatibility with the objects of taxation. It is therefore a true use-oriented approach (the author should temper this fulsome praise by declaring an interest as a signatory of the Meade Report).

The Meade Report proposes two basic alternative tax systems, one which is income-based and one which is expenditure-based. It also considers two types of corporation tax base (Chapter 12), flow of funds and a real profit measure. The flow of funds basis assesses corporation tax on the net outflow from the company to its shareholders. It, therefore, avoids all the valuation and capital maintenance problems associated with measuring profit. It is, incidentally, much closer to the present corporation tax base than might appear superficially, since accelerated depreciation and stock appreciation relief are substantial modifications of the profit base. The economic properties of the flow of funds tax are similar to those of an expenditure tax; in particular, it involves no tax barrier between the pre-tax rate of return on investment and the post-tax rate of return on saving. This type of corporation tax would be consistent with either of the two alternative direct tax systems proposed (income or expenditure based).

Many other aspects of both personal and corporate taxation are also discussed in the Meade Report. The only further reference to it which can be made here is that, in the discussion of ideal income measures (chapter 3), a capital maintenance approach (income as net withdrawals plus net increase in wealth) is preferred to the consumption maintenance, or 'standard stream' approach (the level of consumption maintainable in future periods, which involves excluding windfall gains due to changes in expectations or interest rates), because the latter is too subjective as a tax base. Furthermore, expenditure is preferred to either measure of income because of its greater ease of objective measurement. However, it should be noted that this argument does not necessarily follow through to other purposes for which financial reports are prepared: the need for objectivity is particularly acute in the case of designing an administratively feasible tax system.

A common conclusion to be drawn from our two samples of how user needs might be translated into income measures is that income has only a limited role to play. This does not mean that income measurement has no role at all: indeed, it might be much more effectively applied if too much burden were not placed upon a single number, and if income measures were not asked to perform tasks for which they are inappropriate.

5 Two Techniques of Income Measurement

The next topics for discussion are practical techniques of income measurement. Although it is perhaps more satisfying intellectually to start from the decision and deduce the information requirements from this, the information which can be supplied will be constrained by practical circumstances, such as uncertainty or the cost of supplying too great a variety of information. It is, therefore, a legitimate and useful activity to consider what practical measurement techniques are available and assess their relevance to various decision needs. Both the techniques discussed below can be placed in this category. They have been selected for discussion for two reasons. Firstly, British writers have been prominent in the evolution and advocacy of both techniques. Secondly, both techniques have been incorporated in recent professional proposals for current cost accounting (e.g. the current U.K. ED24 (ASC, 1979)).

(1) Value to the Owner

Value to the owner or 'deprival value' is an eclectic valuation technique: it can value an asset at either net realizable value (NRV), replacement cost (RC) or discounted value in present use (PV). Its basic purpose is to establish the loss which a firm would suffer if deprived of an asset. Replacement cost therefore sets a ceiling on deprival value in those cases in which it would be worthwhile replacing the asset, so that the deprival value argument is often used to justify replacement cost as a general asset valuation basis (e.g. Parker and Harcourt, 1969).

The origins of 'the value to the owner idea' appear to be in the U.S. in the 1920s, although a single source has not been established. It is customary to attribute the idea to Bonbright (1937). Sweeney (1933) cites Bonbright (without reference to any particular publication) as the source of the argument that replacement cost (of the service rather than the specific asset) is normally the appropriate valuation of an item of capital 'under conditions of intelligent free competition': presumably this argument was based upon 'value to the owner' reasoning. However, Canning (1929) had also devised rules of the value to the owner type for the valuation of fixed assets, basing his reasoning upon 'opportunity differences'. His work influenced that of Wright (1964, 1965, 1968 and 1970), who developed the application of 'value to the owner' rules in the context of depreciation (1964 and 1968), stock valuation (1965), and financial accounting generally (1970). The writers who acknowledge direct allegiance to Bonbright are the LSE triumvirate, Baxter (1967, 1971 and 1975), Edey (1974) and Solomons (1966), and also Parker and Harcourt (1969) and Stamp (1971). Of these, Solomons was the first to set out the value to the owner rules in the familiar inequality form, later popularized by Parker and Harcourt (1969) and adopted by numerous other writers.

Baxter's (1967) advocacy of value to the owner in an influential review of Chambers (1966) led to considerable controversy, especially in the pages of Abacus. Chambers (1970) attacked value to the owner as referring specifically to a situation in which the firm was deprived of the asset, a situation which he felt was appropriate to an insurance valuation (which was one of the purposes which Bonbright had in mind) but not to the general problem of financial reporting. He also objected to the subjectivity involved in calculating PV. He was taken to task by Wright (1971) for seeming to identify PV with value to the owner, whereas PV would be the relevant 'value to the owner' only in relatively rare circumstances. Stamp (1971) proposed that PV could be dispensed with even in this case by measuring 'netback' (the higher of PV or NRV) as NRV. The 'value to the owner rule' can be defined as: 'choose the lower of "netback" or RC'. Stamp's rule was subsequently criticized by Yoshida (1973) on the ground that PV is relevant in determining the final value even when it does not emerge as the final value, and by Wanless (1974) who maintained that the situation in which PV is the value to the owner might be quite common.

Chambers (1971), replied to Wright, maintaining that the use of PV introduced an unacceptable degree of subjectivity and also objecting to the hybrid nature of value to the owner, which was alleged to violate the criteria for homogenous measurement. Chambers also demonstrated certain ambiguities in Bonbright's definitions. Ma (1976) also entered this debate, emphasizing the ambiguity of PV when the asset is part of a joint productive process, so that the problem of allocation (Thomas, 1969) arises. This criticism seems to be inappropriate: as Edey (1974) points out, if the asset concerned is essential to a joint operation, the PV of the whole operation *will* be relevant to the asset holding decision, and RC will become the deprival value. It might be argued that deprival value is specifically designed to prevent the attribution of an excessive value in such a case.

In 1975, value to the owner was adopted by the Sandilands Committee and since then it has been the asset valuation base of all British proposals for current cost accounting. It was also proposed by the Richardson Committee Report in New Zealand (1976) and by the 1975 Australian Preliminary Exposure Draft (Institute of Chartered Accountants in Australia and Australian Society of Accountants), both of which adopted Stamp's proposal for avoiding the calculation of PV as value to the owner. This gave further impetus to theoretical work exploring the rationale of value to the owner.

Two statements from the LSE school on the use of value to the owner in financial reporting, by Baxter and by Edey, were published in the year preceding the Sandilands Report. Baxter's case is essentially pragmatic ('such a standard is grounded in common sense', Baxter (1975), p. 125), stressing that 'deprival value' (Baxter's term for value to the owner) avoids certain apparently anomalous valuations which would result from applying a single valuation method (RC, NRV or PV) in all circumstances (hence the apparent irrelevance of Ma's criticism). Edey (1974) deals particularly with the problem of aggregation and concedes that, for collections of interdependent assets, the only satisfactory method of applying deprival value is in aggregate, i.e. to calculate PV, NRV and RC for the group of assets, which may imply valuing the firm as a whole, a formidable task, in practice.

Following the publication of the Sandilands Report, Gee and Peasnell (1976) provided 'A Pragmatic Defence of Replacement Cost' in the context of the Sandilands system. They explore each of the six possible relationships between PV, NRV and RC and appraise them in terms of their likely frequency, the circumstances under which they might arise, and the valuation problems arising from those circumstances. They conclude (with some reservations) that RC is likely to be a satisfactory valuation basis in most cases, and that the simplicity resulting from having a single valuation basis is likely to compensate for any consequential loss of accuracy. As this is an extension of Stamp's 'netback' method of simplifying value to the owner, it might be dubbed the Lancaster method.

A second theme in the Gee and Peasnell paper is the problem of aggregation, a problem stated earlier by Edey (1974). They concede the difficulty of interpreting the sum of the RC of individual assets, but they point out that this problem of 'over-imputation' of individual values can arise equally under the conventional 'value to the owner' rules, and so does not invalidate the case for their simplified approach. The theme of aggregation is explored further in Peasnell (1978). This uses Thomas' (1969 and 1974) arguments concerning the 'incorrigibility' of allocation rules to demonstrate that the total value of a firm's assets under the conventional 'value to the firm' rule (as used in current cost accounting) is rendered arbitrary by interaction effects between assets, which make the allocation of PV dependent upon the precise definition, and level of disaggregation of deprival. This paper also considers interactions due to risk. The author concludes that the valuation of intangible assets and their separation from the valuation of other assets require urgent consideration in current cost accounting. However, he does not discuss the fundamental issue of what the total value of assets in a 'value to the owner' system *ought* to mean; he appears to believe that it should sum to the PV of the whole firm, but the author's own work elsewhere (Peasnell, 1977) suggests that accountants 'do not have a comparative advantage in calculating PV' and should not attempt it.

A paper by Bromwich (1977b) has recently explored another aspect of value to the owner—its claim to be rooted in the economist's concept of opportunity cost. Bromwich demonstrates that this claim is valid only in closely defined circumstances, when the best alternative is that defined by the deprival situation, or when value to the owner is numerically equal to (and therefore a surrogate for) opportunity cost. Thus, the connection between 'value to the owner' and the opportunity cost concept is not as strong as is sometimes suggested.

In conclusion, the 'value to the owner' concept has been advocated and explored by a number of British writers. It has had the distinction of being adopted as a basis for reforms of accounting practice, and there is no denying its intuitive appeal as a pragmatic compromise between competing valuation methods. However, it is, to some extent, still a technique in search of a justification, and it requires further analysis and development. The aggregation problem is serious, and the connection with opportunity cost is both tenuous and of dubious relevance. The more fundamental problem is, however, that value to the owner has never been demonstrated to arise out of a particular information requirement of a potential user of financial reports (other than that of an insurer). We need to know whether it is intended, in aggregate, as a surrogate for PV or merely as a set of piecemeal valuations of individual assets, and, if the latter, how it is to be used. We also need to know more about the properties of the income measures to which it gives rise, and why these are to be preferred to income measures based upon replacement cost, net realizable value, or even historic cost.

(2) The Gearing Adjustment

The gearing adjustment shares with value to the owner the distinction of having recently been espoused by the ASC (1977 and 1979) as the basis of proposed reforms of accounting practice. It also shares the less desirable attribute of being somewhat imperfectly related to specific information needs of users of financial reports. It is another example of a 'general purpose' technique which has been developed to deal with a specific problem, in this case, the problem of dealing with gains on borrowing and losses on monetary assets within the current cost accounting system.

The gearing adjustment was originally a German creation, the basic idea being the creation of Schmidt; his 1930 (pp. 237–8) and 1931 papers are an accessible account of his ideas for English readers. His work was the main source of inspiration for the 1975 recommendation by the German Institute of Chartered Accountants, which was the first professional pronouncement to advocate a form of gearing adjustment. The German recommendations, and their relationship to the work of Schmidt, are described in Coenenberg and Macharzina (1976).

However, the gearing adjustment was re-invented, apparently independently, by a group of British writers, Godley and Cripps, Kennedy, and Gibbs in a series of articles published in *The Times* between 1974 and 1976. This literature has been surveyed by Kennedy (1978). It was clearly influential in the thinking behind the *Submission on ED18* by the London Society of Chartered Accountants (May 1977), which was, in turn, influential in the move towards the adoption of the Hyde Guidelines (ASC, 1977).

The origins of the gearing adjustment in the U.K. lay in the corporate liquidity crisis of 1974 and in Merrett and Sykes' article about this (1974). Their article was influential in the introduction of stock appreciation relief, which removed stock appreciation from the tax base, in the autumn of 1974, lightening the tax burden, and therefore easing the liquidity problem. The general principle of eliminating holding gains in the calculation of operating profit was followed by the Sandilands Report (1975). This implied an 'entity' view of capital, i.e. the value of capital to be maintained intact was to be determined by reference to changes in the specific value of the company's assets, not by the application of a general purchasing power index. Godley and Wood (1974) had objected to this approach in the case of a loan-financed business, showing by means of numerical examples that the shareholders of such a business did make a distributable profit from stock appreciation and should, therefore, be taxed on this gain. Day (1974) pointed out that this applied only to a loan-financed business.

The gearing adjustment, proposed by Godley and Cripps (1975) reconciled these two views. Holding gains on assets should be treated as profit to the extent that they were loan-financed. Therefore, a proportion of holding gains should be credited to profits, the proportion being the gearing ratio of the firm. As Kennedy (1978) points out, this implies that, insofar as assets are loan-financed, the holding gain recognized is the same as that under 'real terms' accounting (as, for example, proposed by the CCAB, 1975), the total gain being current replacement cost less historic cost, although the 'real terms' approach would divide the gain, in a period of general inflation, into a gain on borrowing and a real holding gain. Insofar as assets are equity-financed, however, the gearing adjustment leaves holding gains 'below the line': they are not recognized as part of profit, because equity capital is effectively up-dated by the index appropriate to the specific assets of the entity. Thus, insofar as there are real holding gains in an all equity-financed firm, they will not be included in profit under the gearing-adjustment system, and this profit will therefore be less than 'real terms' profit, which would include holding gains, i.e. those gains due to the specific price of the asset rising faster than a general purchasing power index (see Forker, 1979).

Kennedy (1978) has proposed a 'simplified income statement' which would record 'real terms' proprietary profit as well as various income measures suggested by proponents of the gearing adjustment. It is difficult to quarrel with this eclectic approach to the appropriation statement, which seems to be one way to achieve the reporting of 'different incomes for different purposes'. However, it is possible to question the specific usefulness of profit calculations based upon the gearing adjustment, and their superiority to 'real terms' accounting. The 'entity' valuation of equity capital, which excludes real holding gains from profit, seems to imply that the firm must remain intact in its present form, and that no profit results even when the current value of that form rises in real terms. In fact, it might be hoped that maintenance of current operating capacity in the face of higher real assets would lead to a higher real level of operating profit, resulting from the maintenance of the real rate of return. If this were not the case, we might question the assumption of operating capacity maintenance: this might not be in the best interest of shareholders. Kennedy describes operating profit, less interest and after the gearing adjustment, as 'proprietary profit'. This is a proprietary concept, insofar as these two adjustments have been made to reflect profit attributable to equity, but the method of *measuring* equity for capital maintenance purposes is *entity*-based, reflecting the values of the specific assets of the firm which are assumed to be maintained, rather than proprietary, reflecting the general purchasing power of shareholders. It is, therefore, possible to contest Kennedy's view that his 'proprietary profit' is 'the most suitable figure for use as a *base* for dividend distribution policy' (Kennedy, 1978, p. 63).

A second deficiency of the gearing adjustment system is the failure to separate the gain on borrowing from holding gains on assets. To anyone who accepts constant purchasing power as the ideal measurement standard for capital maintenance (such as Sweeney (1936) and Baxter (1975)), this involves a serious loss of information, pooling gains on financing (the borrowing gain) with gains on investment (asset gains). Kennedy proposes a system which should combine this information with the gearing adjustment.

Finally, the relationship of the gearing adjustment to particular uses is ill-specified. Merrett and Sykes (1974) were clearly concerned with a liquidity crisis rather than a profits crisis (holding gains do not give rise to a cash flow even when they can be regarded as an economic gain which is of the nature of a profit). A concern with liquidity has remained throughout the debate, particularly in the writings of Gibbs (1975, 1976 and 1979), and it is not entirely clear that the central concern is always with profit rather than cash flow (a point made by Edey, 1979). Taxation appears to be a central concern of Godley and Wood (1974), and Godley and Cripps (1975), although Kennedy (1978) shrewdly avoids any commitment on this issue.

The liquidity theme in the debate seems to be responsible for a recent variant of the gearing adjustment, the 'split-level' adjustment, proposed by Gibbs (1976), described with approval by Kennedy (1978), adopted in ICI's published accounts, and recommended for professional implementation by ED24 (ASC, 1979). This involves, as a first stage, adjusting operating profit by a charge for the additional monetary working capital necessary to maintain the operating capacity of the business. This charge is analogous to the cost of sales adjustment and, like that adjustment, is based upon *specific* indices relating to items of expenditure by the firm, not the general indices which 'real terms' (or CPP) accounting would attribute to monetary assets and liabilities. Since it cannot be argued that the *value* of specific items of monetary working capital has changed according to a specific index (since, unlike stocks, they are of fixed value in money terms), this adjustment implies a concern with distributable cash flow (the rise in monetary working capital pre-empts a portion of cash flow) rather than with profit measurement (which is concerned with changes in the *value* of assets and of capital). It will be recalled that Sale and Scapens (1978) advocate such an adjustment to reflect 'distributable operating flow'. The second stage of the 'split-level' adjustment is merely the gearing adjustment defined so as to avoid double adjustment of those monetary items included in the first stage.

It should be noted that neither the Hyde Guidelines nor the ED24 proposals does full justice to the Godley/Cripps/Kennedy/Gibbs approach, because they do not propose the writing back to profits of unrealized holding gains. Both Kennedy (1978) and Gibbs (1979) make this point forcefully. The professional proposals are therefore tempered by prudence and will tend to understate profits (by the ideal standard described by these authors) in a period when unrealized holding gains are positive.

In summary, the gearing adjustment is likely to have an important effect on the practice of accounting. For advocates of 'real terms' accounting it can be looked upon as a simple approximation which is an improvement upon the Sandilands system of current cost accounting. From the point of view of income theory, it shares two attributes with other current developments. First, it is none too firmly grounded in user information needs, although it is related to the idea of 'distributable profit', discussed earlier. (This may not do full justice to Kennedy, who makes a rudimentary attempt to relate information to uses in his 1978 paper, and who discussed the problem of share valuation rigorously and elegantly in his 1976 paper, concluding that no form of inflation adjustment is required for this purpose.) Secondly, it is not entirely clear whether it is concerned with the measurement of income or the measurement of cash flow. If it is concerned with the measurement of income, the capital maintenance concept which it embodies requires a clearer justification. Alternatively, it might be possible to justify the gearing adjustment as a means of implementing an income maintenance concept: the maintenance of operating capacity and gearing suggests that equity income also might be maintained, but it remains to be demonstrated that the assumptions necessary for this to be the case are plausible, particularly in a period of changing prices.

Conclusion

The theory of income measurement is a vast field, and this paper has only skimmed the surface: the trade-off between breadth of coverage and depth of treatment has been particularly difficult to establish. However, the following conclusions are suggested (rather than asserted) in a spirit of due humility. Some of these have already been stated in more detail at the end of section 2, at pp. 10–11 *ante*.

(a) Economic income is precisely measurable only under very restrictive circumstances, and these tend to be ones in which an income measure would not be required anyway, such as perfectly competitive static equilibrium. However, the search for 'surrogates' for economic income continues, and is likely to perform the useful function of delineating the boundaries of economic income as a practical measurement concept.

(b) The most important lesson to be drawn from the study of economic income is that the future, rather than the past, is relevant for decisions. Thus, a useful attribute of an *ex post* income measure (or its components) would be some ability to predict the future. This 'prediction' might be a conditional projection, e.g. it might depend upon prices changing at specified rates, or reinvestment being undertaken at a certain level and these conditions might not, in fact, be fulfilled *ex post.* Nevertheless, it seems possible that such *ex ante* projections could be useful for both decision and control purposes, and ideas of this type seem to lie behind a number of current developments in income theory (e.g. Edwards and Bell (1961), Merrett (1975), Scott (1976), Sale and Scapens (1978)). This suggests that the implementation of the 'Hicks Number 3' or 'standard stream' definition of income requires further investigation. Past work on the 'surrogate' (or 'indirect measurement') hypothesis has concentrated on *values* (e.g. whether RC or NRV approximate PV) rather than *flows* (e.g. whether a particular *ex post* profit measure approximates an *ex ante* 'standard stream' which could be capitalized in order to estimate PV). The 'standard stream' approach is not new: it was seen as the crucial role of income or 'earnings' measurement by Canning (1929), but much of the subsequent literature has concentrated on the 'Hicks Number 1' approach (distributions by the entity *plus* change in net worth). Where 'standard stream income' measurement becomes 'cash flow reporting' may also be a matter for debate. It is easy to separate the two concepts in their abstract forms, but practical systems of reporting may involve elements of both, cf. Kay's (1977) critique of Sandilands and the discussion of distributable profit in section 3, pp. 12–14 *ante*.

(c) Different measures of income may be needed for different purposes, but surprisingly little work has been done to derive relevant income measures (or related information) from the needs of different purposes, and this should be an important field for future research. However, the demands of the accounting profession and unsophisticated users are likely to be a continuing stimulus to the development of 'general purpose' measures and techniques, such as the gearing adjustment or the 'value to the owner' valuation basis.

(d) As a result of (a) and (c), above, there has been an increasing concentration on useful methods of dis-aggregating and segmenting income measures into their components, with the object of enabling the user to make his own assessment of income. Much more needs to be done in empirical, as well as theoretical research, to establish the usefulness of such methods. The feasibility of reporting multiple valuation bases also deserves further exploration.

(e) There is a range of supplementary information which might complement income measures, once the idea that income measures will provide us with definitive numbers is abandoned. *Ex ante* forecasts of income were suggested by Edwards and Bell (1961) as the obvious standard by which to evaluate their proposed *ex post* income measures. Flow of funds and cash flow data (including forecasts) might complement income measures in important uses such as dividend decisions or lending decisions by creditors. The independent role of the balance sheet (i.e. not merely as an accrual sheet for the income statement) also deserves more attention.

(f) As a result of these developments, income measurement may be bypassed altogether in some cases. For example, for many potential users present value might be more useful than income. The calculation of present value may, of course, involve the calculation of an income measure as an interim step, but there may be alternative routes, such as balance sheet valuations or cash flow forecasts, which bypass income measurement entirely.

(g) It is not clear that it is useful to apportion this essentially international debate on national lines, but Britain has produced the most widely-quoted definition of income (Hicks), and the Cassandra of income measurement (Solomons), whose bold prediction (1961) anticipated a number of important current trends. For the rest, if it is necessary to characterize the British approach, it has been pragmatic and eclectic (both of these characteristics can be seen very clearly in Baxter, 1975), paying commendable attention to practical constraints, and it may be for this reason that (for better or for worse) professional proposals for current cost accounting bear the mark of a number of ideas advanced by academics. British writers usually owe allegiance to a decision-oriented approach to establishing users' needs, although progress in deriving forms of accounting information to meet specific decision requirements has been limited. This emphasis may be due partly to the relatively primitive state of empirical research in Britain, which has meant that the 'efficient markets' approach to assessing the utility of accounting information has not achieved the same prominence in Britain as in the U.S.A.

(h) In summary, the trends described earlier amount to a considerable shift in the emphasis of income measurement with economic income as a receding ideal. However, it seems likely that a flow measure, or measures, analogous to income will play an important role in the theory and practice of financial accounting for a considerable time to come. Whether or not we should describe such a measure as income is a matter of unprofitable semantics.

References

Accounting Standards Steering Committee, *ED8: Accounting for Changes in the Purchasing Power of Money*. A.S.S.C. (January 1973).

Accounting Standards Steering Committee, *The Corporate Report*. A.S.S.C. (July 1975).

Accounting Standards Steering Committee, *ED18, Current Cost Accounting*. A.S.S.C. (November 1976).

Accounting Standards Committee, *Inflation Accounting—an Interim Recommendation by the Accounting Standards Committee* ('The Hyde Guidelines'). A.S.C. (November 1977).

Accounting Standards Committee, *ED24, Current Cost Accounting*. A.S.C. (April 1979).

Alexander, S. S., 'Income Measurement in a Dynamic Economy'. Originally pp. 1–97 of Study Group on Business Income (1950). Revised by David Solomons and reprinted in Baxter and Davidson (1977).

Barton, A. D., 'Expectations and Achievements in Income Theory', *The Accounting Review* (October 1974).

Barton, A. D., *An Analysis of Business Income Concepts*, ICRA Occasional Paper No. 7. International Centre for Research in Accounting, University of Lancaster (1975).

Barton, A. D., 'Surrogates in Income Theory: A Reply', *The Accounting Review* (January 1976).

Baxter, W. T., 'Accounting Values: Sale Price versus Replacement Cost', *Journal of Accounting Research* (Autumn 1967).

Baxter, W. T., *Depreciation*. Sweet and Maxwell (1971).

Baxter, W. T., *Accounting Values and Inflation*. McGraw-Hill (1975).

Baxter, W. T. and Davidson, S. (eds.), *Studies in Accounting*, 3rd edition. Institute of Chartered Accountants in England and Wales (1977).

Beaver, W. and Demski, J., 'The Nature of Income Measurement', *The Accounting Review* (January 1979).

Bonbright, J. C., *Valuation of Property* (2 vols.). McGraw-Hill (1937).

Bromwich, M., 'Asset Valuation with Imperfect Markets', *Accounting and Business Research* (Autumn 1975).

Bromwich, M., 'The Use of Present Value Valuation Models in Published Accounting Reports', *The Accounting Review* (July 1977).

Bromwich, M., 'The General Validity of Certain "Current" Value Asset Valuation Bases', *Accounting and Business Research* (Autumn 1977b).

Canning, J. B., *The Economics of Accountancy: A Critical Analysis of Accounting Theory*. Ronald Press (1929).

CCAB, *Initial Reaction to the Report of the Inflation Accounting Committee*. Accounting Standards Committee, London (October 1975).

Chambers, R. J., *Accounting, Evaluation and Economic Behavior*. Prentice-Hall (1966).

Chambers, R. J., 'Second Thoughts on Continuously Contemporaneous Accounting', *Abacus* (September 1970).

Chambers, R. J., 'Value to the Owner', *Abacus* (June 1971).

Chambers, R. J., 'Multiple Column Accounting—Cui Bono?', *Chartered Accountant in Australia* (March 1972).

Chambers, R. J., *An Autobibliography*, ICRA Occasional Paper No. 15 (International Centre for Research in Accounting, University of Lancaster, 1977).

Coenenberg, A. and Macharzina, K., 'Accounting for Price Changes: an Analysis of Current Developments in Germany', *Journal of Buiness Finance and Accounting* (Spring 1976).

Cook, J. S. and Holzmann, O. J., 'Current Cost and Present Value in Income Theory', *The Accounting Review* (October 1976).

Daines, H. C., 'The Changing Objectives of Accounting', *The Accounting Review* (June 1929). Reprinted in Zeff (1976).

Day, A. C. L., Article in *The Observer* (3 November 1974).

Drake, D. F. and Dopuch, N., 'On the Case for Dichotomizing Income', *Journal of Accounting Research* (Autumn 1965).

Edey, H. C., 'Deprival Value and Financial Accounting', pp. 75–83 of H. C. Edey and B. S. Yamey (eds.), *Debits, Credits, Finance and Profits*. Sweet and Maxwell (1974).

Edey, H. C., 'Sandilands and the Logic of Current Cost', *Accounting and Business Research* (Summer 1979).

Edwards, E. O. and Bell, P. W., *The Theory and Measurement of Business Income*. University of California Press (1961).

Edwards, E. O., 'The State of Current Value Accounting', *The Accounting Review* (April 1975).

Edwards, R. S., 'The Nature and Measurement of Income', *The Accountant*, July–October 1938. Revised and reprinted in Baxter and Davidson (1977).

Egginton, D. A., 'Distributable Profit and the Pursuit of Prudence', University of Bristol mimeo (1979), forthcoming in *Accounting and Business Research*.

Fisher, I., *The Nature of Capital and Income*. Macmillan (1906).

Fisher, I., 'The Economics of Accountancy', *American Economic Review* (December 1930).

Fisher, I. and Fisher, H. W., *Constructive Income Taxation*. Harper (1942).

Forker, J. J., 'CCA and CPP: a Suggested Basis for Reconciliation', *Accounting and Business Research* (Autumn 1977).

Forker, J. J., 'Inflation Accounting, Capital Maintenance Concepts and the Measurement of Income', University of Bristol mimeo (1979), forthcoming in *Accounting and Business Research*.

French, E. A., 'The Evolution of the Dividend Law of England', pp. 306–331 of Baxter and Davidson (1977).

Gee, K. and Peasnell, K. V., 'A Pragmatic Defence of Replacement Cost', *Accounting and Business Research* (Autumn 1976).

Gibbs, M., 'Why Sandilands is not the full answer', *The Times* (18 September 1975).

Gibbs, M., 'A better answer to the problem of inflation accounting', *The Times* (23 February 1976).

Gibbs, M. and Seward, W., *ED24—Morpeth's New Proposals*. Phillips and Drew (30 April 1979).

Gilman, S., *Accounting Concepts of Profit*. Ronald Press (1939).

Godley, W. and Wood, A., 'Stock Appreciation and the Crisis of British Industry', Department of Applied Economics, Cambridge, mimeo (October 1974), and articles in *The Times* (7 October and 12 October 1974).

Godley, W. and Cripps, F., 'Profits, stock appreciation and the Sandilands Report', *The Times* (1 October 1975).

Goudeket, A., 'An Application of Replacement Value Theory', *Journal of*

Accountancy (July 1960). Revised and reprinted, with a Postscript by E. B. MacDonald, in Baxter and Davidson (1977).

Gynther, R. S., *Accounting for Price-Level Changes: Theory and Procedures.* Pergamon (1966).

Gynther, R. S., 'Why Use General Purchasing Power', *Accounting and Business Research* (Spring 1975).

Harcourt, G. C., 'The Accountant in a Golden Age', *Oxford Economic Papers* (March 1965). Reprinted in Parker and Harcourt (1969).

Hicks, J. R., *Value and Capital.* Clarendon Press (1946). Pp. 171–181 of the second edition (1946) are reprinted in Parker and Harcourt (1969).

Institute of Chartered Accountants in Australia and Australian Society of Accountants, *A Method of 'Current Value Accounting'.* Preliminary Exposure Draft (June 1975).

Kaldor, N., 'The Concept of Income in Economic Theory', *An Expenditure Tax.* Allen and Unwin (1955) pp. 54–78. Reprinted in Parker and Harcourt (1969).

Kay, J. A., 'Accountants, too, could be happy in a Golden Age: The Accountant's Rate of Profit and the Internal Rate of Return', *Oxford Economic Papers* (November 1976).

Kay, J. A., 'Inflation Accounting—A Review Article', *The Economic Journal* (June 1977).

Kennedy, C., 'Inflation Accounting, Profits, Profitability and Share Valuation', *Journal of Business Finance and Accounting* (Spring 1976).

Kennedy, C., 'Inflation Accounting: Retrospect and Prospect', *Cambridge Economic Policy Review* (No. 4, 1978).

Lawson, G. H., 'Cash Flow Accounting', *The Accountant* (28 October and 4 November 1971).

Lawson, G. H., 'The Rationale of Cash Flow Accounting', *The Investment Analyst* (December 1976).

Lee, T. A., 'A Case for Cash Flow Reporting', *Journal of Business Finance* (Summer 1972).

Lee, T. A., *Income and Value Measurement: Theory and Practice.* Nelson (1974).

Lee, T. A., 'Enterprise Income: Survival or Decline and Fall?', *Accounting and Business Research* (Summer 1974).

London Society of Chartered Accountants, *Submission on ED18* (May 1977).

Ma, R., 'Value to the Owner Revisited', *Abacus* (December 1976).

MacDonald, G., 'Deprival Value: Its Use and Abuse', *Accounting and Business Research* (Autumn 1974).

Meade, J. E., *The Structure and Reform of Direct Taxation*, Report of a Committee chaired by Professor J. E. Meade. Institute for Fiscal Studies, George Allen and Unwin (1978).

Merrett, A. J. and Sykes, A., Article in *The Financial Times* (30 September 1974).

Merrett, A. J., 'Indexing Company Accounts', pp. 61–76 of T. Liesner and M. King (eds.), *Indexing for Inflation.* Heinemann (1975).

Mishan, E. J., *Welfare Economics: Ten Introductory Essays* (2nd edition). Random House (1966).

Morley, M. F., *The Fiscal Implications of Inflation Accounting.* Institute for Fiscal Studies and Chartered Accountants Trust for Education and Research (1974).

Parker, R. H. and Harcourt, G. C. (eds.), *Readings in the Concept and Measurement of Income.* Cambridge University Press (1969).

Peasnell, K. V., 'A Note on the Discounted Present Value Concept', *The Accounting Review* (January 1977).

Peasnell, K. V., 'Interaction Effects in CCA Accounting', *Accounting and Business Research* (Spring 1978).

Prakesh, P. and Sunder, S., 'The Case Against Separation of Current Operating Profit and Holding Gain', *The Accounting Review* (January 1979).

Revsine, L., 'On the Correspondence Between Replacement Cost Income and Economic Income', *The Accounting Review* (July 1970).

Revsine, L., *Replacement Cost Accounting*. Prentice-Hall (1973).

Revsine, L., 'Surrogates in Accounting Theory: A Comment', *The Accounting Review* (January 1976).

Richardson Committee Report, *The Report of the Committee on Inquiry into Inflation Accounting* (New Zealand Government Printer, 1976).

Robichek, A. A. and Myers, S. C., *Optimal Financing Decisions*. Prentice-Hall (1965).

Sale, T. and Scapens, R., 'Current Cost Accounting as a Surrogate for Dividend Paying Ability', *Accounting and Business Research* (Summer 1978).

Sandilands Committee, *Inflation Accounting. Report of the Inflation Accounting Committee under the Chairmanship of F.E.P. Sandilands* (Cmnd. 6225, H.M.S.O., September 1975).

Scapens, R., 'A Neoclassical Measure of Profit', *The Accounting Review* (April 1978).

Schmidt, F., *Die organische Bilanz im Rahmen der Wirtschaft*. Gloeckner (1921)

Schmidt, F., 'The Importance of Replacement Value', *The Accounting Review* (September 1930). Reprinted in Zeff (1976).

Schmidt, F., 'Is Appreciation Profit?', *The Accounting Review* (December 1931). Reprinted in Zeff (1976).

Scott, M. FG., *Some Economic Principles of Accounting: A Constructive Critique of the Sandilands Report*, IFS Lecture Series No. 7. Institute for Fiscal Studies (1976).

Sen, A. K., 'The Welfare Basis of Real Income Comparisons: A Survey', *Journal of Economic Literature* (March 1979).

Simons, H. C., *Personal Income Taxation*. University of Chicago Press (1938). An extract on 'The definition of income' is reprinted in Parker and Harcourt (1969).

Solomons, D., 'Economic and Accounting Concepts of Income', *The Accounting Review* (July 1961). Reprinted in Parker and Harcourt (1969).

Solomons, D., 'Economic and Accounting Concepts of Cost and Value', Chapter 6 of M. Backer (ed.), *Modern Accounting Theory*. Prentice-Hall (1966).

Stamp, E., 'Income and Value Determination and Changing Price Levels: An Essay Towards a Theory', *The Accountant's Magazine* (June 1971).

Sterling, R. R., *Theory of the Measurement of Enterprise Income*. University Press of Kansas (1970).

Sterling, R. R. (ed.), *Asset Valuation and Income Determination, A Consideration of the Alternatives*. Scholars Book Co. (1971).

Study Group on Business Income, *Five Monographs on Business Income*. American Institute of Accountants (1950).

Study Group on Business Income, *Changing Concepts of Business Income*. American Institute of Accountants (1952).

Sweeney, H. W., 'Stabilised Depreciation', *The Accounting Review* (September 1931). Reprinted in Zeff (1976).

Sweeney, H. W., 'Capital', *The Accounting Review* (September 1933). Reprinted in Zeff (1976).

Sweeney, H. W., 'The Technique of Stabilized Accounting', *The Accounting Review* (June 1935). Reprinted in Zeff (1976).

Sweeney, H. W., *Stabilized Accounting*. Harper (1936).

Thomas, A. L., *The Allocation Problem in Financial Accounting Theory*, Studies in Accounting Research, 3. American Accounting Association (1969).

Thomas, A. L., *The Allocation Problem: Part Two*, Studies in Accounting Research, 9. American Accounting Association (1974).

Tippett, M., 'An Inefficient Means of Information Retrieval?', *The Accountant's Magazine* (November 1979).

Tweedie, D. P., 'Cash Flows and Realisable Values: the Intuitive Accounting Concepts? An Empirical Test', *Accounting and Business Research* (Winter 1977).

Vatter, W. J., *The Fund Theory of Accounting*. University of Chicago Press (1947).

Vatter, W. J., 'Income Models, Book Yield and Rate of Return', *The Accounting Review* (October 1966).

Wanless, P. T., 'Reflections on Asset Valuation and Value to the Firm', *Abacus* (December 1974).

Whittington, G., 'Asset Valuation, Income Measurement and Accounting Income', *Accounting and Business Research* (Spring 1974).

Whittington, G., 'On the Use of the Accounting Rate of Return in Empirical Research', *Accounting and Business Research* (Summer 1979).

Winch, D. M., *Analytical Welfare Economics*. Penguin Books (1971).

Wright, F. K., 'Towards a General Theory of Depreciation', *Journal of Accounting Research* (Spring 1964). Reprinted in Parker and Harcourt (1969).

Wright, F. K., 'A Theory of Inventory Measurement', *Abacus* (December 1965).

Wright, F. K., 'Measuring Asset Services: A Linear Programming Approach', *Journal of Accounting Research* (Autumn 1968).

Wright, F. K., 'A Theory of Financial Accounting', *Journal of Business Finance* (Autumn 1970).

Wright, F. K., 'Value to the Owner: a Clarification', *Abacus* (June 1971).

Yoshida, H., 'Value to the Firm and the Asset Measurement Problem', *Abacus* (June 1973).

Zeff, S. A., *Asset Appreciation, Business Income and Price-Level Accounting, 1918–1935*. Arno Press (1976).

Commentary on
'The British contribution to income theory'

Edward Stamp
ICRA, University of Lancaster
Research Professor of Accounting

Professor Whittington's paper illustrates very clearly the confused state of thinking on income theory. Whittington himself is not confused; indeed, his paper is admirably lucid. Yet its clarity of exposition serves to remind us of how much theoretical analysis remains to be done before accountants can pretend to know what it is they mean when they speak of 'income'. A recently published ICRA Occasional Paper by Tweedie (1979), provides further evidence of the wide divergence of thought among accountants on this topic. As the work of Whittington and of Tweedie demonstrates, there has been far too much of what one might describe as the re-invention of the wheel, and the various proposals for dealing with capital maintenance and gearing adjustments (to take just two examples) provide ample evidence of this.

There are other reasons for our confusion. What is thought to be the most important will be dealt with at the end of this commentary. But we might also observe that in addition to generating a proliferation of different concepts of income, accountants are also prone to confuse the issue by re-labelling concepts that have been in existence for many years.

An illustration of this is provided by the concept of value to the owner. Bonbright (1937) developed the concept, and his ideas were brought to the attention of accountants by Baxter (as I explained in an article a few years ago [1977]). Unfortunately, in the early 1970s when the ideas began to catch on, Baxter and some of his colleagues at LSE decided to re-label the concept 'deprival value' (Baxter, 1971). This move seems to me to have been particularly unfortunate, since not only does it result in two different names being applied to the same thing, but also because the term 'deprival value' makes the whole concept appear to depend upon a rather unlikely event taking place. Indeed, as I have demonstrated elsewhere (1979), Bonbright's conclusions are equally valid if we address our attention to the benefits attaching to ownership, and think of 'opportunity values' rather than 'deprival values'. Clearly, owners of assets are generally far more interested in the former than in the latter. However, although I have written several articles arguing that such a positive approach should be adopted, I would not suggest that Bonbright's term should be replaced by 'opportunity value' because I believe that to do so would only serve to confuse readers and practitioners.

Whittington takes value to the owner and the gearing adjustment as two areas in income theorizing where major British contributions have been made. I believe it is also worth pointing out an important corollary of this, namely that the American contribution in these areas has been negligible (Bonbright is, of course, an American but he was not writing for accountants). This is odd, in view of the generally dominant position of the U.S. in the development of accounting theory. The situation is exacerbated by the fact that most American writers seldom seem to read British or other foreign journals, and there has consequently been little attempt by American scholars to develop thinking that has been initiated in Britain, the Netherlands and Australia. I suspect there is a real danger that when the Americans eventually catch up with these ideas we shall be presented with yet further examples of the phenomenon of the re-invention of the wheel.

Incidentally, it is interesting to note Whittington's reference to the role of the efficient market hypothesis in American thinking. It is noteworthy that none of this has led to any significant developments in income theorizing, and the main impact on income measurement seems to have been the argument that efficient market research demonstrates that disclosure rather than measurement standards are all that is really required in many areas (such as depreciation, tax allocation, inventory valuation, etc.).

Whittington's paper has some surprising omissions. Thus he has very little to say on the important question of the use of specific and general price indexes in the development of income concepts. A good deal of this has been done in Britain, and once again there is very little recent American writing on this subject (Peasnell and Skerratt, 1976).

Whittington also neglects significant work done in the Netherlands. Although he makes a passing reference to Limpberg and Goudeket, more attention deserves to be given to the fruitful and well co-ordinated efforts of Dutch academics and practitioners in the field of income theory. It has influenced British thought, and much of it has already been translated into practice in the Netherlands. (He has not neglected other foreign work, and he has even managed to claim an Australian for England—a feat which our cricket selectors might wish they could emulate.)

I am also surprised that he omits any reference to the work of Hatfield and of Paton. In particular, Paton's book (written with Littleton), *An Introduction to Corporate Accounting Standards* (AAA, 1940) was very influential in the 1940s and 1950s on both sides of the Atlantic. Nor is there any reference to the work of the Association of Certified Accountants and (as it then was) the Institute of Cost and Works Accountants in producing, in 1952, the books *Accounting for Inflation*, and *The Accountancy of Changing Price Levels*. (It is interesting to note that the former of these two works is shortly to be republished by the Scholars Book Company.) There is also the booklet written by Sir Edmund Parker when he was

President of the English Institute in 1968, *Accounting for Stewardship in a Period of Inflation.* This is similar to the earlier AAA booklet *Price Level Changes in Financial Statements: Basic Concepts and Methods*, written by Perry Mason and published in 1956. Although neither of these two booklets could be described as a theoretical treatise they represent very important links between the theory of general price level adjustments and the world of practice, and we ought not to overlook such connections. Without them income theorizing would be sterile.

Finally, we have to consider the overriding question of what we mean when we speak of income. Unless we can define this with precision it is unrealistic to expect businessmen to be able to measure it. Whittington's paper demonstrates that we are more confused on this subject now than people thought they were 30 years ago.

I believe the real problem lies in the attempts of people like Chambers who argue that financial statements ought to be 'isomorphic', and that accounting is essentially similar to map-making. The difficulties are compounded by writers such as Sterling who argue that accounting is, or ought to be, a 'science'.

It really does not take much reflection to realize that income is *not* represented by something which exists in the real world, and it is therefore not something which is open to discovery in the way that a physicist can discover an electron and measure its properties. Income is a mental construct, a concept whose value depends upon its utility to those who use it. This utility will depend upon environmental conditions, and these can obviously vary from time to time, from place to place, and from person to person. Research into all of these matters may well determine which measures of 'income' are most useful. But neither empirical research nor theoretical work will ever, in my view, be able to determine which measurement, or which concept, is right in the sense that it embodies some final truth. That kind of scientific truth does not exist in accounting, and we are wasting our time if we look for it.

References

Baxter, W. T., *Depreciation.* Sweet and Maxwell (1971).

Bonbright, J. C., *The Valuation of Property.* McGraw-Hill (1937).

Peasnell, K. V. and Skerratt, L. C. L., *Current Cost Accounting: The Index Number Problem* (Lancaster: ICRA Occasional Paper No. 8, 1976).

Stamp, E., 'ED18 and Current Cost Accounting: A Review Article', *Accounting and Business Research* (Spring 1977).

Stamp, E., 'Financial Reports on an Entity: *ex uno plures*', Chapter 8 of R. R. Sterling and A. L. Thomas (eds.), *Accounting for a Simplified Firm having Depreciable Assets.* Scholars Book Co. (1979).

Tweedie, D. P., *Financial Reporting, Inflation and the Capital Maintenance Concept* (University of Lancaster: ICRA Occasional Paper No. 19, 1979).

2 The setting of accounting standards: the contribution of research

Michael Bromwich
Professor of Finance and Accounting, University of Reading

Accounting standards are defined here as uniform rules for external financial reporting applicable either to all or to a certain class of entity. These rules seek to prescribe the preferred accounting treatment from the available set of methods for treating a given accounting problem. This paper examines some of the controversies that surround the setting of accounting standards by reviewing the contribution of research to the solution of these debates, and by considering its promise for this task in the future. The first section provides an historical perspective, examining the extant British (mainly English) literature. Comparative references will be made to the American literature. The objective is to give some feel for the way the concerns with standard-setting of the practising and academic arms of the profession have changed.

The second part considers one of the most exciting developments in accounting research today, the explicit use of rigorous models from economics and social choice theory to improve the understanding of the standard-setting problem. As this literature is mainly American, it is reviewed here to bring it more clearly to the attention of British writers. It is believed that the strong economic theme which runs through much of the British academic accounting literature might lend some additional insights if focused on this area.

Research of an economic character is stressed, although it needs to be integrated with the results of studies having a more explicit concern with sociological and political themes. These latter studies are still very much in their infancy (Gerboth, 1973, and May and Sundem, 1976) and space constraints mean that reference to them cannot give adequate regard to their importance.

To give a perspective to the review of the British evolution of accounting standards, it should be appreciated that the British experience has followed a different pattern from that of the U.S.A. An important theme for the American accounting profession since the mid-1930s has been the setting of accounting standards for published accounting reports in a variety of guises and with varying degrees of compulsion attached to the use of such standards (Zeff, 1972). The exciting, but often frustrating, task of evolving such standards has been pursued continually, with varying intensity, in America, the activity increasing greatly in recent times.

The first British attempt to lay down non-mandatory guidelines was in the early 1940s. The arrangements then adopted were employed without major change until the late 1960s. Moreover, the subject of accounting standards did not stimulate the same interest in British accounting writers as it did in American authors. Only a few voices were addressed to the subject in Britain until the 1970s. Even the recent British literature lacks the analytical approach which is becoming dominant in the U.S.A. It only weakly reflects the increasing recognition in the U.S.A. that the setting of accounting standards may be a political and social process. The promise offered by approaches to standard setting which pay attention to these latter factors is considered in the last part of this paper.

However, there are some common themes running through the evolution of accounting standards in both countries. Alterations in standard setting processes and institutions seem to have served as ways of resolving accounting crises. The British and American approaches both seem directed to damping down brush fires, that is, attempting to solve the specific accounting problems of interest at any given time, rather than seeking, what has been called, 'an agreed conceptual framework' (ASC, 1978, para. 7.7). Important phenomena which seem to exist in America, but which have hardly appeared in Britain, are the recurring cycles of disillusionment with the various standard setting processes and institutions. (Evidence supporting the existence of these cycles is easily obtained, see Zeff (1972), section III, Garner (1960), Hawkins (1963) and Hendriksen (1977), Chapters 2 and 3.) The reasons for the similarities and differences in the patterns of evolution of accounting standards in the two countries are unclear, but the following historical review of the British developments may contribute to their understanding.

The Development of Accounting Standards in the United Kingdom[1]

The Early Years

The lack of concern with accounting standards in the U.K. until the late 1930s was exemplified by the Royal Mail case in 1931 with its clear, if implicit, suggestion that 'good' financial accounting practice was that which the 'best' firms of auditors vouchsafed (Hastings, 1949). The lessons of this case, and a number of attacks launched in the late 1930s on conventional financial accounting, could have formed an auspicious environment for the first formal attempt to set guidelines for financial accounting in 1942. Indeed, the attacks, originating with an LSE group (Edwards, 1937 and 1938, and Coase, 1938), could have given British endeavours a better foundation than the support rendered to similar American efforts (which

1 This section draws heavily on Zeff's (1972) masterly review, 'The Forging of Accounting Principles in Five Countries', see also ICAEW (1966).

had started 12 years earlier with the Special Committee on Co-operation with Stock Exchanges) by their academics. The British group was concerned with the theoretical foundations of accounting and the integration of accounting and economics (Edwards, 1938), rather than with the codification of best practice which often seemed to be the objective of American academics. However, it was never really reconstituted after the Second World War. British accounting policy-makers seemed unswayed by both these academic efforts and the few voices which sought to get professional recognition of the difficulties surrounding the task of setting accounting guidelines. The most extraordinary of these, especially given his usually more conventional views, was that of P. D. Leake when he asserted to the Leeds Chartered Accountants' Student Society in 1931 that '. . . accounting science must directly concern itself not only between individual and individual, but between bodies of employers and bodies of employed and also between individual and the State, individuals and municipality and between nation and nation'.

Zeff's (1972, p. 7) evidence suggests that the institutional arrangements which led to the Institute of Chartered Accountants in England and Wales taking an interest in standard-setting in the 1940s arose for quite other purposes. A solution was needed to the discontent expressed by non-practising members of the Institute who felt that it did little for them, and that they were excluded from decision-making concerning the profession. They could neither be members of the Institute's Council nor, therefore, sit on the Institute's committees. The foundation of the Taxation and Financial Relations Committee, the broad charge of which was 'to consider matters affecting taxation and the financial relationship of the business community with the Inland Revenue and other Government Departments' was part of a compromise that allowed the Council to continue to be composed mainly of practising members. It has been claimed that allowing non-practising and non-Council members to form part of the membership of this committee injected a new spirit into the Institute (Zeff, 1972, p. 9). This, and contemporary criticism of financial accounting may have eased the committee's way when it asked for power to draft pronouncements on accounting principles in 1942. This request was promptly acceded to by the Council of the Institute, and 29 guidance statements on accounting were issued between 1942 and 1969.

That such recommendations were regarded as of great importance is clear from the procedure adopted for their promulgation. They had to be approved by an overwhelming majority of Council and had to be deemed necessary by that body and had to survive a complicated exposure process amongst the Institute's members. The deliberations concerning recommendations were kept entirely confidential to the Institute's members, and decisions concerning them seemed to be controlled by the 'establishment' of the Institute.

By 1949 the committee had produced a number of solid, thorough, pronouncements which were seemingly well-received. These covered a wide range of topics, many of which were of great importance. The subjects tackled ranged from the tax to be reported in accounting statements, through the disclosure of reserves and provisions, consolidated accounts and depreciation, to the valuation of stock-in-trade. These recommendations tended to be conservative, prudent, and based on conventional practice, but their reception by the profession speaks well of the committee's ability to assess the acceptability of their recommendations.

This early standard-setting procedure may hold lessons for the Accounting Standards Committee (the current British standard-setting organization). In particular, the tortuous exposure procedure may have ensured the acceptability of the recommendations to the Institute's members, but only at the cost of great delay in the issue of recommendations.

Reliance on conservatism led to problems when a recommendation on 'Rising Price Levels in Relation to Accounts' sought to maintain historical cost accounting, in the face of arguments concerning the effects of inflation on conventional determined profits and the resultant high taxation on such profits (see, for example, *Some Accounting Terms and Concepts*, Cambridge University Press, 1951, the report of a committee jointly appointed by the English Institute and the National Institute for Economic and Social Research). Moreover, most of the other professional accounting bodies had reservations about this recommendation and tended to favour replacement cost-based systems.

The influence, prestige and power of the English Institute and, one suspects, the desire to avoid conflict, are evidenced by the acceptance of the Institute's view when it reiterated its position in 1952. This confirmation again attracted criticism from a number of influential people and organizations, including some of the other accounting bodies. Joint meetings between some of these bodies were held, but no further important developments in the inflation accounting debate occurred on the initiative of the professional bodies for approximately 20 years.

An important theme for the understanding of future developments and problems in standard-setting is highlighted by the above brief review. The procedure used for approving recommendations indicates that these were seen as something for accountants to decide upon. With a few exceptions, only those recommendations which commanded acceptance within the profession were eventually promulgated. It can be argued that this view of the proprietary interest of accountants in accounting standards has not yet been entirely abandoned.

After the controversy over inflation accounting, the Taxation and Financial Relations Committee continued its endeavours to codify best practice without any major opposition until the mid-1960s. Indeed, many observers can be found to attest to the committee's effectiveness during this period.

The fairly untroubled reception generally accorded to its recommendations is illustrated by the lack of concern among British accounting academics with this area of activity. Until the late 1960s, only two notable academic contributions concerning standard-setting seem to have emerged. The first of these was by Baxter (1953) and the essence of his concern was the lack of theoretical foundation for recommendations on accounting practice. He wondered whether 'it is wise for any group of men to say what is true or right in matters of theory'—a cause of equal anxiety today. Baxter's view was that, although there are pitfalls to be avoided in laying down practical rules, such recommendations in accounting are probably useful. In contrast, the temptation to lay down 'principles' of accounting should be avoided because such activities lead to rigidity. They may inhibit progress, both in research and in educational areas, and may discourage desirable innovations in practice. In a remarkably prescient footnote he recommends the task that many researchers have recently taken up: 'to examine the question of what safeguards (if any) are needed if a private group is to make rules, almost with the force of law, that affect non-members'.

Kitchen (1954) also made comments pertinent to accounting standards when he critically reviewed the *Terminology of Cost Accountancy* (Institute of Cost and Works (now Management) Accountants, 1953). In this neglected work, he did a considerable service to future researchers, for he considered analytically the difficulties in seeking to define accounting terms. He shows that this is not a simple matter. It is, perhaps, therefore, not surprising that those who attempt the more ambitious task of setting accounting standards run into difficulties. The first point he makes is that although the advantage of a common language is clear, often definitions are unnecessary in that they provide tools for which there are few users. Indeed, they may be positively dangerous where they have strong authority behind them. This weight of authority may freeze the natural process of evolution in the meanings of words. It may also cause great confusion where the approved definitions sit uneasily with their natural usage. Of more importance is that the choice of a definition will almost certainly require an implicit selection between rival theories. If this is true for individual words, how much more likely is it to apply to even simple accounting standards?

Given this lack of concern in the literature with accounting guidelines, the committee continued on its untroubled way until the mid-1960s. During this time, ten new recommendations were issued including the treatment of taxation, investment grants and the accounts of investment trust companies.

This fairly serene scene can be contrasted with the American experience between the 1940s and 1960s which appears, at least in retrospect, to have been a harbinger of the problems which appeared in Britain in the late 1960s. From 1936 until 1959 the body charged with standard-setting in the

U.S.A. was the Institute of Certified Public Accountants' Committee on Accounting Procedure. Academic accountants in America were far more active than their British counterparts (May, 1958 and Chambers, 1955). However, the committee found itself diverted throughout the period from following their advice in seeking a general intellectual approach to accounting problems by the imperative of solving problems of current urgency (Blough, 1967). It was this latter concentration which probably led to the committee's replacement by the Accounting Principles Board in 1959 (Spacek, 1969 and Seawell, 1959). That the committee tended, like its British counterpart, to be conservative, careful, slow and dominated by the accounting profession did not save it.

The need for research was so well taken that the new Board did not issue any accounting guidelines until some basic studies had been completed (Moonitz, 1960 and Sprouse and Moonitz, 1962). These, however, proved too radical for the accounting establishment. There is, perhaps, a lesson here for those who believe that thorough-going research will ultimately provide the solution to accounting problems. Research is not sufficient for this purpose—acceptance of the findings is also necessary. The Board thereafter reverted to the usual practice of solving immediate problems and, after a time, began to run into all the problems that plagued its predecessor, and which began to cause difficulties for its British counterpart in the late 1960s, to which the focus now returns.

The Turbulent Years

In the late 1960s a storm of criticism arose in the U.K. against the accounting profession's efforts to set guidelines. Accounting methods had been found wanting in a number of financial debacles that are still notorious today. These included the collapse of Rolls Razor Ltd, in 1964, just after publishing 'clean' accounts, the vast difference between AEI's profit forecast for 1967 and the large loss reported after its takeover by GEC, partly resulting from the use of different accounting principles. Finally, there was the failure of the Leasco-Pergamon takeover, central to which was the use of different valuation bases for the same items by the two companies. The strong concern felt by many was sharpened and given greater authority by Stamp (1969a, 1969b and Stamp and Marley, 1970). At the time, most U.K. academic accountants agreed with Stamp's plea to base accounting recommendations on the underlying theoretical concepts and with his urging of a full-scale research programme to aid in discovering these concepts. Experience in the U.S. of this route to 'better' standards may now lead some to be more sceptical.

These accounting crises also led many in the profession to feel that there was a threat of government intervention if the profession was not seen to be able to put its own house in order. This threat corresponds with the

American experience that the ultimate authorities in the community will not remain passive forever in the face of accounting controversies.

The sources of British criticism of the profession do not entirely reflect American experience. Most objections to American standard-setting organizations seem to come from the industrial and academic sectors whereas the sources of British complaints are wider spread, and seem to put the interests of the investor in a more prominent position. It was this type of pressure which led the English Institute to issue a 'Statement of Intent on Accounting Standards in the 1970s' (*Accountancy*, January 1970).

The Introduction of Accounting Standards

This statement of intent had four major objectives: the narrowing of difference and variety in accounting principles, the disclosure of accounting bases, the disclosure of departures from established definitive standards and the wider exposure of major new proposals. The desirability of these objectives may be self-evident, but it has not yet been demonstrated that their achievement will ensure that the accounting crises which preceded the statement do not recur. The immediacy of extinguishing current bush fires still seems to dominate the search for a standard-setting mechanism for the longer run.

The establishment of the Accounting Standards Steering Committee by the English Institute followed quickly after the statement. The Institute was almost immediately joined by the Scottish and Irish bodies. Two other bodies joined in 1971 and the Institute of Public Finance and Accountancy became a member from 1976. The committee was then re-established as a joint committee of these six accounting bodies the deletion of the word 'steering' from its title, perhaps, signalling that its period of apprenticeship was over.

Fifteen accounting standards (Statements of Standard Accounting Practice, SSAPs) have so far been issued and there are seven exposure drafts (EDs) outstanding. The list of standards and exposure drafts covers a large number of topics which lack any obvious theoretical connection. The earliest exposure drafts and standards were, in part, a response to the financial crises the existence of which helped to create the committee. Thus SSAP1 was concerned with accounting for the results of associate companies, SSAP2, addressed the disclosure of accounting policies, and SSAP3 tackled the computation of earnings per share.

Other topics for which SSAPs have been issued cover a wide range, including accounting for government grants, the treatment of extraordinary items and prior year adjustments, stocks and work in progress, accounting for depreciation, for research and development and the compilation of group accounts. Probably the most important exposure drafts on issue are those concerned with current cost accounting and with accounting for foreign currency transactions.

Some of the issued standards have caused a few difficulties in application; for example, those dealing with earnings per share, value added tax and the treatment of corporate taxation. The acceptance of others has been problematic. The history of the various inflation accounting proposals (see SSAP7, ED18 and ED24) requires a paper of its own. Criticism of the standard which stipulated the recognition of all deferred tax liabilities required the original standard to be withdrawn and replaced by another which said that provision need be made only for foreseeable liabilities. A similar scenario arose over research and development. Even the standard concerned with depreciation—a subject which one would expect accountants to feel at home with—has had to be delayed in implementation.

A plethora of reasons have been suggested to account for the adverse reception of some of the committee's proposals. Its membership is still confined to qualified accountants and many believe its opinions reflect mainly the views of practising members. The Accounting Standards Committee does, however, devote a considerable amount of its resources to consultation. It is estimated that over 100,000 copies of an exposure draft of a proposed standard are circulated. There is also a consultative group with a wide membership.

These consultative activities cannot be said to be aimed at persuasion—comments on exposure drafts are invited but do not receive a response in any formal or published way. The committee does not, generally, attempt to defend itself from attacks by lobbies which are often able to obtain a great deal of publicity. Public debate concerning a proposed standard may, therefore, often seem one-sided and may encourage the already strong tendency for the committee to minimize controversy by giving priority to immediate problems.

The committee appeals infrequently to theoretical concepts either to support or defend its exposure drafts. This is not surprising for most of the preliminary research studies are conducted by practising accountants who may tend to advocate what they see as 'best practice' and approach their task from an auditing point of view.

These and other research studies are not obviously integrated into proposed standards. The only standard that is primarily theoretical in content is SSAP2, which provides a list of fundamental accounting concepts, without reference to any theoretical models used in their derivation (see also the *Corporate Report*, ASSC, 1975). The only other major public use of theoretical notions by the committee has been to support its views in the inflation accounting debate.

The Recent Literature

Only recently could the Accounting Standards Committee hope to turn to the British academic accounting literature. Little, or none, of this literature in the 1960s addressed the problem of standard-setting. One of the earliest contributions of the 1970s was by a practitioner (Morison, 1970). In a wide-ranging and thoughtful article, he made a number of very sensible statements concerning accounting standards. He asserted that the critics of financial accounting are concerned to obtain uniformity of treatment and suggested two differing views of uniformity. The first is that accounting theory should be such that only one accounting treatment can be deduced for any one set of facts. He made the familiar point that there is, as yet, no way of selecting the ideal accounting model from the large number of available alternatives. Morison attacked the second view which he labelled the 'let's settle for one view anyhow' school using the arguments first published by Baxter (1953). He advocated allowing 'all flowers to bloom', providing that the treatment chosen is clearly explained, and the reasons are given for the belief that a 'true and fair' view is thereby achieved.

How such choices can be justified without recourse to some generally accepted theoretical model, is not clear. In particular, some may doubt the implicit assumption that accountants are 'seekers after truth' who are able entirely to suppress their personal interests and those of their employers.

In the mid-1970s, articles concerning accounting standards began to appear more frequently in the British literature. Most were critical of existing standard-setting practice and argued polemically for a more explicitly normative approach and for research into 'fundamentals'. Examples are Jones (1975), Tempelaar (1975), Edey (1977), Gibbs (1977) and McMonnies (1977). Weetman (1977) attempted to appraise how well the objectives set out in the 1970 statement of intent had been achieved. Even this exercise, which should lend itself to a rigorous treatment, was approached in an impressionistic way.

Reasoning of the type used by Edey (1977) had a major influence on the Accounting Standards Committee (1978) when they coined a distinction between those users' objectives which are 'legally orientated, in which certainty . . . is the main aim' and 'those needs which are orientated more towards economic factors, in which judgement may be more important than certainty'.

Edey supports accounting standards because they speed up the process of communication if they are accepted and used. The utility of standards as communication devices does not depend upon whether they are agreed by all to be optimal. It is sufficient that they are acceptable. He differs with Baxter (1953), who felt that standards might inhibit the development of accounting, for his impression is that 'the issue of standards has brought about a great increase in the amount of open argument and controversy'.

Edey classifies standards into four types. Type 1 simply says 'you must tell people what you are doing', and argues that 'the case for this disclosure seems overwhelmingly strong'. Type 2 standards seek uniformity of presentation. Standards of this type have rarely been issued in Britain. Type 3 recommendations concern the disclosure of specific items. Edey is in favour of standards concerned with disclosure and presentation, mainly as devices to improve communication but also out of respect for the well-established cannons of statistical presentation. Type 4 requirements are those concerned with income measurement and valuation; Edey supports the views of most researchers when he argues that these standards should not be made mandatory whilst agreement is lacking on a conceptual framework of accounting.

Edey's analogy with statistics may be thought weak, for the required depth of detail to be disclosed concerning the accounting policies adopted is less than is required by statistical methodology. The detail presently given in accounting reports generally allows neither the determination of the steps used in deriving the accounting figures, nor the verification of the published figures. Thus, a listing of accounting policies in the detail presently required may mislead and the meaning of such policies may be difficult to determine.

Moreover, requirements to disclose accounting policies are akin to exercises in definition and, therefore, may be subject to the criticisms that Kitchen (1954) levelled against those seeking authoritative definitions of accounting terms. The selection of those accounting policies which must be disclosed requires the implicit use of a theory or theories.

The argument that Type 3 requirements (the disclosure of specific items) are unobjectionable is also doubtful. The only obvious difference between items covered by Type 3 and by Type 4 standards is that the argument concerning the former is not presently being waged. Such arguments may be only in abeyance and may break out again at any time. Reporting specific accounting items, in whatever way may be regarded as acceptable, at any given time, is no more theoretically legitimate than reporting favoured solutions to Type 4 controversies. Moreover, the classification of accounting items, as subject to Type 3 requirements, may be thought to inhibit accounting development when a view less sanguine than Edey's is taken of the Accounting Standards Committee's willingness to allow both deviations from extant standards and alteration of standards. A sceptic reading the foreword to the British series of standards might feel that the only ground allowed for using an alternative treatment is the impracticability of the relevant standard, for other deviations are regarded as exceptional. Similarly, the committee's willingness to revise standards might seem a little less than wholehearted, for they say only that revisions will take place from time to time.

In 1978, the Accounting Standards Committee initiated a review of the standard-setting process in the light of the experience gained over its first ten years (ASC, 1978). The invitation to comment was met by a large response (see ASC (1979), which gives a good coverage of professional and other views). That these comments are published is a very useful by-product of the committee's activities which could be extended to the comments on all standards. A dominant theme in these responses was that without a generally accepted conceptual framework for accounting, the committee cannot properly discharge its functions. The envisaged characteristics of such a framework differ substantially from one commentator to another. Most of the responses were assertive and polemical, and appeals to theory were of a general nature. It is, therefore, not surprising that authorities tended to be at variance in their conclusions (Lafferty (1970), Mumford (1978) and Stamp (1979)). Stamp gives a clear and forceful summary of the criticisms that many researchers have made of the committee's endeavours.

The British Experience: Conclusions

This brief review of the British experience with accounting standards and of the research aimed at improving such standards might suggest a number of themes common to the American experience and others which are unique to Britain. The British experience suggests that most of the symptoms that have accompanied the failure of the various American standard-setting institutions can be identified, in some degree, at the present time in the U.K. Whether the diseases producing these symptoms will prove less virulent and more susceptible to cure in the different environment remains to be seen.

The above review of the British developments in standard-setting indicates that political and socio-economic aspects of standard-setting are of increasing importance. The controversy over what has come to be called 'inflation accounting' illustrates, again, that at the limit, the government is not a passive observer of self regulation by the accounting profession. In Britain, opposition to standards seems often to have been overcome not by a choice between rival theories. Rather it has been tackled in a number of pragmatic ways—by a compromise standard being issued, by the acceptance of the opposition's view, and by exempting the most powerful opposition from controversial requirements.

As these crucial problems have hardly been taken up in the British literature, the next section reviews mainly the American efforts. The earlier U.S. literature, concerned with the political and economic aspects of accounting standards, has spawned a large number of academic enquiries. These are of a much more analytical and rigorous character than is often usual in the accounting literature and offer considerable promise for solving some of the problems associated with the setting of accounting standards.

Possible Directions of Future Research[2]

The Politics of Standard-Setting

A number of recent American studies have attempted to explain the existence of the cycles of disillusionment experienced in America with accounting standards and standard-setting institutions. Moonitz (1968 and 1974) was struck by the seemingly easy acceptance in the U.S. of audit standards, compared with the controversies that have surrounded general accounting standards. He argues that the community sees the former as technical matters, the effects of which are perceived as confined to the accounting profession. It is difficult to understand how the community can so deceive itself. His tentative solutions to the controversy surrounding accounting standards include separating the standards issuing organization from the entity charged with enforcing standards and the diminution of the influence of practical auditors on accounting standards.

Horngren has written a number of articles attempting to get accounting standard-setting recognized as a political process (1972, 1973 and 1976). Starting with the view that impeccable logic and heavy support within the standard-setting organization are not sufficient for the successful implementation of an accounting standard, he argues that acceptance by the relevant sectors of the community is a necessary condition to assure the success of a standard. He, therefore, sees it as necessary to recognize that the ultimate authorities in the accounting area, Congress and the Securities and Exchange Committee in America, will not remain passive in the face of the standard-setting activities. He sees the existing framework as a co-operative effort between the public and private sectors which requires the skilful marketing of standards to ensure their acceptability. A similar view has been expressed by Gerboth (1973) who argues that 'the politicization of accounting rule-making is not only inevitable but just . . . when a decision-making process depends on public confidence, the critical issues are not technical, they are political'.

The potential problems with placing the emphasis on acceptability are well-known. A consensus may result in compromise standards lacking in intellectual rigour. Alternatively, a compromise may require that a number of treatments for a given problem be allowed, not all of which are thought desirable. Under these circumstances a standard may be shaped to appeal to those who have the greatest bargaining power, thereby making the standard-setting authority liable to the charge that they have accepted, for example, the views of enterprise managers (Moonitz, 1968, and Chatov, 1977). Another problem is that the search for compromise may either cause the standard-setting process to become stagnant or result in a log

2 Parts of this section rely on my article in *Accountancy Age* (1979). Permission to reproduce is gratefully acknowledged.

jam. It is not clear that any standard-setting framework, so far instituted, has sufficient authority to overcome these problems.

In contrast to these concerns with acceptability, which may take extreme forms (see Hawkins (1975)), Solomons has suggested (1978) that the standard-setting authority should employ the criterion of neutrality, some might think indifference a better word, relative to the different modes of individual behaviour which promulgated standards may induce when selecting between the accounting measurements. For Solomons, neutrality in accounting does not relate to the behavioural consequences of accounting but rather is concerned with attaining representational accuracy of physical phenomena. He sees accounting as financial map-making. With this view, the objective for the accountant should be to measure and report on those phenomena that have an existence in their own right, such as cash flows, contractual rights and market values. Neutral accounting standards will, of course, variously affect different members of the community. These effects are, presumably, seen either as falling where they may or being a matter of indifference to the accountant *qua* accountant.

The problems of obtaining acceptance for neutral accounting standards would seem at least as strong as those attaching to the more conventional utterances of the standard-setting organizations. Further, even if it were possible to free accounting figures from value judgements, the consequent redistribution of wealth on the implementation of Solomons' suggestions would cause additional difficulties of this type. Some would doubt whether there are many accounting items which can easily be reduced to their physical essentials in a way that everyone would agree upon as Solomons argues is the case with maps. Any such agreements concerning maps often disappear when, for example, a given mountain is shaded, say, pink to portray the territorial claims of one nation or another.

The recognition that standard-setting may be a social and political process came late to the British literature. Muiss (1977) described the recent Dutch experience of standard-setting and suggested that in Holland there is an '*a priori*' commitment to seek standards which are feasible in terms of their acceptability to the community. Proposed standards are considered by the two principal social partners, the employers and the trade unions, with the accounting profession acting as the 'great helmsman'. Some of the problems with this approach are well-presented by Morison (1970). In addition, there could be great scope for horse-trading and log-rolling between the parties. Those with less bargaining power could be neglected in these deliberations.

The few other British articles that have considered these problems have done so in an impressionistic way (Bromwich, 1979). Hope (1979) argues that the standard-setting process is a political one, and that the Accounting Standards Committee may be able to gain political acceptability by seeking to make only those incremental changes to existing practice, and to existing standards, which are acceptable to the community. He also asserts the importance of evaluating the social benefits and costs of individual standards, and doubts whether the Accounting Standards Committee is a suitable vehicle for this task (for an American view, see Buckley, 1976).

The next sections of this paper briefly review the contribution of some recent academic endeavours, which build on the above concern with the political aspects of accounting standards. They also outline the impetus for future research offered by these recent developments. The basic characteristic which allows these approaches to be conveniently delineated from other research efforts (apart from the use of more technical and well-established models borrowed from economics and social choice theory) is a wish to question the fundamentals of the standard-setting process, and of accounting theory generally. There are, of course, a large number of disciplines which could be used to analyse accounting standards considered in a wider social context. However, attention is confined here to the results of applying economics and social choice theory. This not only reflects my specific interests and understandings, but also is founded on a view that other disciplines have not yet been used as successfully as those to be reviewed.

Some Suggested Causes of Present Difficulties in Standard-Setting

Taking an economist's perspective, some of the problems associated with determining a conceptual framework for accounting occur because of the lack of the usual type of market on which accounting information can be traded (Gonedes and Dopuch, 1974, and Sterling and Harrison, 1974). Demands for accounting information cannot be expressed by making bids for the desired information in a free market. Rather, enterprises are supposed to provide the same package of information, at a minimal cost, to all users. This information may satisfy merely the conventional minimum standards and legal requirements for accounting information. The absence of the usual price system for accounting information means that, in general, there is no clear mechanism whereby those with needs, unsatisfied by the conventional published statements can easily make this known and thereby attract resources into their provision. A number of people such as investment analysts, brokers and financial journalists do, however, at least claim to have access to non-public information. Such a provision must reflect their superior bargaining power relative to the general user of accounting information. The explicit or implicit price which emerges from these activities will, therefore, neither reflect society's preferences for accounting data nor the opportunity cost of its provision.

Accounting, Public Goods and Free Riders

Benston (1976) and others argue that the absence of an explicit price mechanism is of little importance. Those enterprises that believe that issuing such information above the minimum legally and conventionally required would improve the value of their securities on the market, would provide such information. There are a number of problems with this view. The most important of these stems from society's dislike of 'inside trading' with its insistence that no one should be excluded from information published by enterprises. Gonedes and Dopuch (1974) show, using perfectly competitive markets, that if such exclusion were allowed, the market mechanism for accounting information could work in the normal way (Demsetz, 1970). But without this exclusion of 'free riders' (those who do not pay for information), a rational person will neither buy information nor, in the case considered here, bid up the prices of those securities issued by enterprises that provide additional information. For any extra information will flow to all, irrespective of whether or not they have paid for it. Indeed, there is some suggestion that something of this effect will remain even where exclusion of non-purchasers of information is possible. The actions taken by informed traders in attempting to capitalize on their knowledge will, in perfectly functioning markets, affect prices. Those who have not paid for the information can, by observing price behaviour, learn some or all of the information possessed by informed traders. This will make inside information less valuable (Grossman, 1977).

It is normally argued that the existence of 'free riders' constitutes evidence that published accounting information shares some of the characteristics of what are called public goods. The essence of such goods is that their supply is not, as with a normal good, reduced by the consumption of any individual (Samuelson, 1954). An individual's consumption of a typical good, say an apple, reduces the supply by one unit whereas his or her consumption of public goods like, say, defence or deterrence, does not alter the amount of these goods available to others. Few, if any, goods have only public characteristics, but the existence of such characteristics may mean that the usual market mechanism cannot easily function (Samuelson, 1954 and 1969). It is, therefore, argued (Gonedes and Dopuch, 1974) that the prohibition on inside trading gives accounting information some public goods characteristics (Gonedes, 1976, but see Watts, 1976).

One useful piece of research would, therefore, seem to be to compare the damage done to the functioning of the market mechanism by the outlawing of inside trading relative with the gains that accrue to the less wealthy users of accounting information under conventional accounting systems.

The problem of free riders in accounting could, if it were thought socially desirable, be removed by allowing inside trading. The consequent redistribution of wealth following such a relaxation might be regarded as too large to be politically acceptable. Detailed analysis of this assertion requires the use of social and political as well as economic criteria.

The general view in the economics literature is that the problems for the usual market mechanism caused by 'non-exclusion' are so great that some type of non-market system is required to ensure the supply of the good under consideration (McMillan, 1979, and Musgrave, 1969). The mechanism presently adopted in Britain and the U.S., to ensure the supply of accounting information in the presence of free riders, is a combination of legally enforced disclosure rules and the use of rule-making bodies such as the Financial Accounting Standards Board and the Accounting Standards Committee with somewhat weak powers of enforcement.

The problem of non-exclusion does partly disappear under this system for these rule-making bodies have some power to enforce their solutions on the suppliers of accounting information. The cost of meeting these requirements implies some wealth redistribution away from those who bear the cost (consumers of enterprise products, enterprise equity-holders and the government). These are left to fall where they may with the existing standard-setting arrangements. Much of the economics literature concerning these questions investigates arrangements whereby the costs of supplying public goods fall directly, via taxes, on consumers of the good, in proportion to the benefits they perceive from the good (Head, 1972). Such a system, if attainable, would solve the non-exclusion problem, for all would be taxed on the basis of the benefits they receive. However, the utilization of such schemes in accounting requires much greater government intervention than many people would support. It also requires that the government can accurately discover individual preferences and define and measure individual consumption using a tax base which is generally acceptable in the community.

Public Goods and the Supply of Accounting Information

With the current institutional arrangements for the supply of accounting information, the costs of providing published accounting statements are borne by one or more of the following: the consumer of the products of the enterprises issuing accounting statements; the holders of enterprise equity; and the taxpayer, via the tax deductability of such costs. The system works imperfectly because those who bear the costs of providing accounting information have little incentive to supply the amount desired by the community. This is especially the case, if as many suspect, the incremental cost of supplying accounting information falls as the number of users supplied increases. The problem of the declining cost of accounting information is a special case of the problem of joint supply (Samuelson, 1954), which arises when having decided to supply one individual with a good, demands from others can be met without extra cost. There is, generally, little incentive for a free market supplier to produce output (accounting information) in the face of decreasing costs below average costs, unless the supplier has some monopoly power. Thus the supply of accounting information is unlikely to be socially optimal, since users of accounting information who would be willing to pay the social cost of meeting their demands for information may be denied their requirements.

Declining costs or joint supply provides another reason for the existence of public goods. This aspect of accounting information has not been analysed in the accounting literature. The problems exist independently of whether there are free riders in the market for accounting information (Head, 1962 and 1972), for this latter problem can presumably always be removed by political action. Joint supply is regarded as the more basic characteristic of public goods in at least some of the economics literature (Samuelson, 1954 and 1969). One important research endeavour is to extend the analysis of Gonedes and Dopuch (1974) to cover this aspect of accounting information.

Any solution to under-provision requires a knowledge of user-preferences, but there are no incentives for those asked about their preferences concerning public goods to reveal the truth (Head, 1962) unlike in the usual market system. Individuals, when questioned, know that any supply of the public good will be available to all and will be financed by all. The supply of the public good thus depends on what the whole community can be expected to pay. Each individual, therefore, has an incentive to reduce his own contribution by understating preferences. This reasoning leads to the view that it is likely that public goods in joint supply, which may include accounting information, will be under-provided even when supplied by non-market institutions. A good deal of thought in economics has been applied to investigating systems of taxation which would give individuals incentives to reveal their true preferences (Clarke, 1971 and 1972). Such systems or mechanisms cannot be used within the usual standard-setting framework, for standard-setters have no taxing ability, and, by their actions, can affect only some of the costs faced by the users and suppliers of accounting information. Knowledge of even these costs by standard-setting bodies must be limited, given their restrictive membership and consultative arrangements. Thus, government intervention can be expected if the revelation of 'true preferences' for accounting information is found to be a major problem.

There are many ways such intervention could be structured (some of these are discussed by Gonedes and Dopuch, 1974). The large cost and severe disruption associated with imposing taxes on the users of accounting information make it more likely that intervention will be restricted to prescription of the information to be conveyed by published accounting statements.

One role of existing standard-setting organizations could be that of forestalling such intervention, by demonstrating that existing or alternative standard-setting mechanisms can more efficiently obtain the government's desired ends than government intervention. Certainly, a comparative analysis of the benefits and costs of the existing standard-setting systems and those involving greater government intervention, along the lines used in the Benston Study (1976) of corporate disclosure in the U.K. and the U.S., is likely to be a useful piece of research. If such a study did indicate that the public good aspects of accounting were empirically significant, this might dispel some of the prejudices presently surrounding the idea of government intervention in accounting.

Perhaps a more attractive solution to the preference revelation problem is to 'tie in' the sale of a public good to that of a private good. The consumer of a private good could, for example, be forced to pay something towards the cost of producing accounting reports if all enterprises practised average cost pricing. This seems to describe how the provision of accounting information is presently financed. The amount of information supplied with such a system will be sub-optimal since that part of the price which represents a fee for accounting reports will not reflect individual preferences. Moreover, there may be little incentive for an enterprise to increase the quantity of information it offers. The product of the enterprise which sells a joint product consisting of a private good and accounting information will not be preferred to that of enterprises offering only the private good unless free riders can be excluded (Stigler, 1974). Thus, the analysis of public goods and accounting comes full circle.

Recognition of all these problems of the demand for, and supply of, public goods has led some economists to suggest that informal mechanisms may grow up which allow individual desires to be expressed and bargained over (Arrow, 1970). It is difficult to argue that the existing standard-setting bodies serve this role, for few individuals and enterprises are involved in the bargaining process concerning accounting standards. It, also, has been argued that the consequences of difficulties with public goods may be reduced by the creation of 'norms of social behaviour'. Such norms may serve to restore some of the incentives for beneficial co-operation (Arrow, 1970). Standard-setting organizations may have a role here.

Much of the professional literature in America (e.g. AICPA, 1973 and FASB, 1976) and more especially in Britain (ASC, 1978) implicitly takes the view that many of the problems examined in both this section and the previous one could be resolved within the context of a self-regulating accounting profession, provided that a generally agreed conceptual framework for accounting could be found. What such a framework entails differs substantially from one writer to another. For example, the Accounting Standards Committee seem to have in mind a model which can be used to resolve most accounting controversies, whereas the Trueblood Report (AICPA, 1973) seemed to imply an agreement to a set of fairly generally defined objectives for financial statements. The next section reviews the promise offered by this approach, again concentrating on those discussions which draw heavily on economic theory.

A Universally agreed Conceptual Framework

Much of the theoretical accounting literature seeks to aid decision-making by providing valuations, which also permit the computation of income measures, that can be used by everybody (for representative sample of this literature, see Parker and Harcourt, 1969). The determination of such valuations and income measures implies the existence of an accepted accounting framework. It will be argued here that reformers of accounting practice who follow this path have set themselves an impossible task.

The difficulty associated with seeking a single model which aids everyone in their valuation problems is that no generally acceptable method of arriving at such a model exists, given that tastes differ between individuals and that people seek to use published accounting information to solve a variety of problems (Demski, 1974). The selection of such an accounting model therefore requires a trade-off between the welfare of members of the community. The present consensus in the literature is that such choices can be made unequivocally only with perfect markets in complete equilibrium. In these situations accounting reports would replicate information conveyed by market prices (Ohlson, 1975, and Bromwich, 1977). In other contexts, many accounting statements would aid some members of the community and harm others. For example, a revision to accounting statements which leads to the release of 'bad' news concerning an enterprise's fortunes will harm existing equity holders, but may improve the lot of other investors. Moreover, both groups may be able to exploit non-users of the information. One area of accounting research where efforts are likely to be rewarded is that of ascertaining whether individuals do have common preferences concerning given items of accounting information (Cushing, 1977).

Decisions concerning the use of accounting systems require some type of comparison of the welfare of those who gain and those who are harmed. There exists no method of selecting between rival accounting systems if the reasonable assumption is made that the tastes of all individuals are to be reckoned in the choice of the accounting system to be used. It has been demonstrated by Arrow (1963) that the methods which might be considered for making such choices, such as majority voting, infringe some supposedly innocuous requirements which might be placed on the choice system (Sen, 1970). Among these requirements are that the system chosen should not be dictatorial but should permit all those choices which harm no-one and improve the lot of at least one person (that is, which are pareto optimal). For example, allowing the majority to decide an issue may infringe Arrow's condition that the community's preferences should be transitive (Sen, 1970).

These findings suggest that standard-setting bodies should not be seduced by the blandishments of those who argue that they should seek some universally agreed model. Such a model may exist, but, with the current state of knowledge, no method is available for discovering it and for obtaining the community's agreement to its utilization.

Cushing (1977) attempts to blunt the edge of this attack by calling on the literature which questions some of Arrow's assumptions. He argues that these assumptions may be reasonable at the level of the individual but not when society as a whole is considered. He also advocates a partial approach to accounting standards. The best rule or standard for a given accounting problem is to be sought using benefit/cost analysis, holding constant the accounting principles used in all other areas of controversy.

Other research efforts in the area of social choice may offer some positive aid to the Accounting Standards Committee and the Financial Accounting Standards Board (Mueller, 1976). For example, majority voting can be relied on in situations where the issue is the degree of detail to be provided concerning a given item of accounting information, provided that the welfare of all individuals first increases as more detail is supplied, and then declines as diminishing returns to extra detail set in, that is, where preferences are single peaked (Sen, 1970). *A priori*, it might be thought that several accounting issues are of this character. These findings do not carry over to multi-dimensional issues where the problem involves simultaneous choices between the information to be provided concerning two or more accounting issues.

Given the problems associated with social choice mechanisms, some writers have explored other avenues to see whether they have any promise for those who seek to promulgate acceptable accounting standards. Finance theory, and economics generally, has progressed by making a set of fairly arbitrary assumptions about the market in which securities are traded and about the individuals trading in it. Some powerful theoretical results have been obtained by assuming that markets are perfect and that the individual is concerned only with the return and risk offered by a security. For a survey of these results see, for example, Fama (1977), but, see also, Roll (1977).

Applications of findings obtained in this way in accounting are still new but do show considerable promise. Much of the current empirical work by accounting academics utilizes this theory, as does much of analytical accounting theory (Foster, 1978). The theory, for example, gives limited support to the use of present value accounting (Bromwich, 1977). Further developments, aimed at relaxing the fairly restrictive assumptions of finance theory, will increase its value in solving problems in standard-setting.

One especially interesting development is the finding that even with incomplete markets (where all desired trades cannot be consummated), investors with differing preferences may still be unanimous as to whether a given project is worthwhile to a specific enterprise. This occurs where the projects being considered offer risk and return characteristics already available to investors (Ekern and Wilson, 1974), and where competitive markets prevail. In both cases, investors may still disagree about items other than project acceptability (Hart, 1979). Given this unanimity concerning project acceptability, it should be possible to derive accounting variables of use to all investors, irrespective of their preferences. Other promising results yield hope that some of the difficulties of selecting a social choice mechanism can be overcome, by accepting a 'second best' approach and instituting enquiries as to the possibility of delineating optimal accounting models for restricted circumstances.

An Immediate Partial Solution

Setting general all-purpose accounting standards might be regarded as attempting to choose between information systems without recourse to individual preferences and decision problems (Demski, 1973). Judgements of this type between information systems can be made only if the systems being considered are comparable in terms of fineness (McGuire, 1972). Such systems are those where an information process provides at least all the information available from competing systems and may also yield additional amounts. A balance sheet showing replacement cost figures and historic cost figures in separate columns would be comparable, in this sense, with conventional balance sheets.

Many of the suggested reforms for accounting statements imply information systems which are not comparable in this way. For example, there seems no way of converting accounting statements prepared according to the Accounting Standards Committee's ED18 into those compiled according to the principles of ED8, without access to additional information. A choice between such non-comparable information systems can be made only by consulting the preferences of the individuals in mind, and considering the decision problems for which they hope to use accounting information. Thus, progress can be made only by making extensive value judgements about which set of people should be aided by accounting standards.

Further relief from the difficulty of achieving comparability between information systems is obtained if the effects on an individual's welfare of the solution to one accounting problem are separate from the effects of all other standards (Cushing, 1977). Choice here may be easier than when selection from more comprehensive accounting models is required, because the simpler alternatives are more readily rendered comparable in terms of the information they convey. The conditions which allow the choice of an accounting standard for a given problem to be made without considering the effects of its interaction with other standards on the welfare of those in the community are known (Bromwich, 1980). These conditions are fairly restrictive but, when applicable, they substantially reduce the problems facing accounting standard-setting organizations.

Conclusions

This article reflects a personal selection of some important contributions to accounting thought. Most of the lines of investigation considered are of sufficient maturity to give some confidence that they are likely to have an effect on the evolution of accounting standards. Even more recent developments may turn out to be yet more promising. The most obvious example is the use in accounting of the theory of agency. This recognizes that those who are meant to work in the interests of others (for example, enterprise management relative to investors and workers) may attempt to maximize their own welfare. It is argued that much of accounting can be understood in terms of attempts to overcome this difficulty, by allowing the principal to monitor the agent's activities and to assure himself that his best interests are being pursued. This theory has been used to tackle a variety of accounting problems (Jensen and Meckling, 1976, Ng, 1978, and Watts and Zimmerman, 1979).

The burden of this article is that the problems facing accounting standard-setters are far greater than is, perhaps, apparent to those who consider their endeavours from a practical and pragmatic stance. It indicates some of these problems which either have appeared or are emerging in the U.K. and the U.S. Many of these problems are not yet amenable to analysis and their solutions must await developments in a wide range of disciplines.

The article, therefore, has concentrated on the promise which the use of economic analysis has for the understanding and resolution of these problems. The need to increase the understanding of the basic characteristics of accounting information seems to be paramount. If accounting information can be shown to be a public good then many panaceas currently canvassed are likely to be of little help. This seems equally true of efforts to unearth a generally acceptable conceptual framework for accounting. However, current research is making progress in determining the conditions under which new accounting systems may be introduced without taking into consideration the preferences of all members of the community. The subject of accounting standards is an important and exciting topic for accounting researchers and represents an area where there is some likelihood of success. This promise will be intensified if future researchers are able to approach the problems using a wider range of disciplines than have so far been applied.

References

American Institute of Certified Public Accountants, 'Objectives of Financial Statements', (*Trueblood*) *Report of the Study Group on the Objectives of Financial Statements*. AICPA (1973).

Accounting Standards Committee, 'Setting Accounting Standards: a consultative document', *Accountancy* (November 1978).

Accounting Standards Committee, *Submissions on the Accounting Standards Committee's Consultative Document: Setting Accounting Standards*. ASC (1979). There are two volumes.

Accounting Standards Steering Committee, *The Corporate Report*. ASSC (1975).
Arrow, K. J., *Social Choice and Individual Values*, 2nd ed. Yale University Press (1963).
Arrow, K. J., 'Political and Economic Evaluation of Social Effects and Externalities', in J. Margolis (ed.), *The Analysis of Public Outputs*. National Bureau of Economic Research (1970).
Baxter, W. T., 'Recommendations on Accounting Theory', *The Accountant* (October 1953), reprinted in W. T. Baxter and S. Davidson (eds.), *Studies in Accounting Theory*. Sweet and Maxwell (1962).
Benston, G. J., *Corporate Financial Disclosure in the U.K. and U.S.A.* D. C. Heath and ICAEW (1976).
Blough, Carman, G., 'Development of Accounting Principles in the United States', *Berkeley Symposium on the Foundations of Financial Accounting*. University of California Press (1967).
Bromwich, M., 'The Use of Present Value Valuation Models in Published Accounting Reports', *The Accounting Review* (July 1977).
Bromwich, M., 'Accounting Standards: Criteria Acceptable to Everybody', *Accountancy Age* (May 1979, pp. 18–20).
Bromwich, M., 'The Possibility of Partial Accounting Standards', *The Accounting Review* (April 1980).
Buckley, J. W., 'The FASB and Impact Analysis', *Management Accounting* (USA) (April 1976).
Chambers, R. J., 'Blueprint for a Theory of Accounting', *Accounting Research* (January 1955).
Chatov, R., 'Should the Public Sector Take Over the Function of Determining Generally Accepted Accounting Principles', *The Accounting Journal* (Spring 1977).
Clarke, E. H., 'Multipart Pricing of Public Goods', *Public Choice* (January 1971).
Clarke, E. H., 'Multipart Pricing of Public Goods: An Example', in S. Mushkin (ed.), *Public Prices for Public Goods*. Urban Institute, Washington (1972).
Coase, R. M., 'Business Organisation and the Accountant', *The Accountant* (October/December 1938) reprinted in D. Solomons (ed.), *Studies in Costing*. Sweet and Maxwell (1952).
Cushing, B. E., 'On the Possibility of Optimal Accounting Principles', *The Accounting Review* (April 1977).
Demsetz, H., 'The Private Production of Public Goods', *Journal of Law and Economics* (April 1970).
Demski, J. S., 'The General Impossibility of Normative Accounting Standards', *The Accounting Review* (October 1973).
Demski, J. S., 'The Choice Among Financial Reporting Alternatives', *The Accounting Review* (April 1974).
Edey, H. C., 'Accounting Standards in the British Isles', in W. T. Baxter and S. Davidson (eds.), *Studies in Accounting*. ICAEW (1977).
Edwards, Sir Ronald, 'The Rationale of Cost Accounting', in Sir A. Plant (ed.), *Some Modern Business Problems* (Longman, 1937), reprinted in D. Solomons (ed.), *Studies in Costing*. Sweet and Maxwell (1952).
Edwards, Sir Ronald, 'The Nature and Measurement of Income', *The Accountant* (July/October 1938), reprinted in W. T. Baxter and S. Davidson (eds.), *Studies in Accounting*. ICAEW (1977).

Ekern, S. and Wilson, R., 'On the Theory of the Firm in an Economy with Incomplete Markets', *Bell Journal of Economics* (Spring 1974).

Financial Accounting Standards Board, 'An Analysis of Issues Relating to a Conceptual Framework for Financial Accounting and Reporting: Elements of Financial Statements and their Measurement', *FASB Discussion Memorandum*. FASB (1976).

Fama, E. F., *Foundations of Finance: Portfolio Decisions and Securities Prices*. Blackwell (1977).

Foster, G., *Financial Statement Analysis*. Prentice Hall (1978).

Garner, P., 'Accounting and Auditing Standards', *Proceedings, Asian and Pacific Accounting Convention* 1960, reprinted as 'The Developments of Accounting Principles or Standards' in P. Garner and K. B. Berg (eds.), *Readings in Accounting Theory*. Houghton Mifflin (1966).

Gerboth, D. L., 'Research, Intuition and Politics in Accounting Inquiry', *The Accounting Review* (July 1973).

Gibbs, G., 'Accounting Principles: Generally Accepted by Whom?', *Accounting and Business Research* (Winter 1977).

Gonedes, N. J., 'The Capital Market, the Market for Information and External Accounting', *Journal of Finance* (April 1976).

Gonedes, N. J. and Dopuch, N., 'Capital Market Equilibrium, Information Production and Selected Accounting Techniques: Theoretical Framework and Review of Empirical Work', *Studies in Financial Accounting Objectives*, Supplement to the *Journal of Accounting Research* (1974).

Grossman, S. J., 'The Existence of Future Markets, Noisy Rational Expectations and Information Externalities', *Review of Economic Studies* (October 1977).

Hart, O. D., 'On Shareholder Unanimity in Large Stock Market Economies', *Econometrica* (September 1979).

Hastings, Sir Patrick, 'The Case of the Royal Mail', *Cases in Court* (London, 1949), reprinted in W. T. Baxter and S. Davidson (eds.), *Studies in Accounting*. ICAEW (1977).

Hawkins, D. F., 'Development of Modern Financial Reporting Practices in the US', *Business History Review* (Autumn 1963), reprinted in M. Chatfield (ed.), *Contemporary Studies in the Evolution of Accounting Thought*. Dickenson (1968).

Hawkins, D. F., 'Financial Accounting, the Standards Board and Economic Development', *Emanuel Saxe Distinguished Lectures in Accounting*. Bernard M. Baruch College (1975).

Head, J. G., 'Public Goods and Public Policy', *Public Finance* (September 1962).

Head, J. G., 'Public Goods: the Polar Case' in R. M. Bird and J. G. Head (eds.), *Modern Fiscal Studies*. University of Toronto Press (1972).

Hendriksen, E., *Accounting Theory*, 3rd ed. R. D. Irwin (1977).

Hope, A., 'Accounting Policy: Theory or Pragmatism or Both', *Submissions on the Accounting Standards Committee's Document: Setting Accounting Standards*, Vol. II. ASC (1979).

Horngren, C. T., 'Accounting Principles: Private or Public Sector', *Journal of Accountancy* (May 1972).

Horngren, C. T., 'The Marketing of Accounting Standards', *Journal of Accountancy* (October 1973).

Horngren, C. T., 'Will the FASB be here in the 1980's', *Journal of Accountancy* (November 1976).

Institute of Chartered Accountants in England and Wales, *The History of the Institute of Chartered Accountants in England and Wales 1880–1965 and its Founder Bodies 1870–1880.* Heinemann (1966).

Jensen, M. C. and Meckling, W. H., 'Theory of the Firm: Managerial Behaviour, Agency Costs and Ownership Structure', *Journal of Financial Economics* (October 1976).

Jones, C. J., 'Accounting Standards: A Blind Alley', *Accounting and Business Research* (Autumn 1975).

Kitchen, J., 'Costing Terminology', *Accounting Research* (February 1954), reprinted in W. T. Baxter and S. Davidson (eds.), *Studies in Accounting Theory.* Sweet and Maxwell (1962).

Lafferty, M., 'Why it is Time for Another Great Leap Forward', *Accountancy* (January 1979).

McGuire, C. B., 'Comparison of Information Systems', in C. B. McGuire and R. Radner (eds.), *Decision and Organisation.* North Holland (1972).

McMillan, J., 'The Free-Rider Problem: A Survey', *Economic Record* (June 1979).

McMonies, P. N., 'EEC, UEC, ASC, AISG, ICCAP, IPAC, Old Uncle Tom Cobbleigh and All', *Accounting and Business Research* (Summer 1977).

May, G. O., 'Generally Accepted Accounting Principles', *Journal of Accountancy* (June 1958).

May, R. G. and Sundem, G. L., 'Research for Accounting Policy: An Overview', *The Accounting Review* (October 1976).

Moonitz, M., 'The Basic Postulates of Accounting', *Accounting Research Study No. 1* (AICPA, 1960).

Moonitz, M., 'Why is it so Difficult to Agree Upon Accounting Principles?', *The Australian Accountant* (November 1968).

Moonitz, M., 'Obtaining Agreement on Standards in the Accounting Profession', *Studies in Accounting Research No. 8.* AAA (1974).

Morison, A. M. C., 'The Role of the Reporting Accountant Today', *The Accountant's Magazine* (January and February 1970), reprinted in W. T. Baxter and S. Davidson (eds.), *Studies in Accounting.* ICAEW (1977).

Mueller, D. C., 'Public Choice: A Survey', *The Journal of Economic Literature* (June 1976).

Muiss, J. W., 'Accounting Standards: the Pit and Pendulum', *Accounting and Business Research* (Autumn 1977).

Mumford, M., 'Watts on What's What', *Certified Accountant* (December 1978).

Musgrave, R. A., 'Provision of Social Goods', in J. Margolis and H. Guiton (eds.), *Public Economics.* McMillan (1969).

Ng, D. S., 'An Information Economics Analysis of Financial Reporting and External Auditing', *The Accounting Review* (October 1978).

Ohlson, J. A., 'The Complete Ordering of Information Alternatives for a Class of Portfolio-Selection Models', *Journal of Accounting Research* (Autumn 1975).

Parker, R. H. and Harcourt, G. C., *Readings in the Concept and Measurement of Income.* Cambridge University Press (1969).

Roll, R., 'A Critique of the Asset Pricing Theory's Test, Part I: On Past and Potential Testability of the Theory', *Journal of Financial Economics* (March 1977).

Rowland, S. W., 'Some Modern Difficulties in the Measurement of Profit' in Sir A. Plant (ed.), *Some Modern Business Problems*. Longman (1937).
Samuelson, P. A., 'The Pure Theory of Public Expenditure', *Review of Economics and Statistics* (November 1954).
Samuelson, P. A., 'The Pure Theory of Public Goods', *Review of Economics and Statistics* (November 1969).
Seawell, L. V., 'Corporate Reporting is in Some Respect a Financial Fantasy', *Business Horizons* (Fall 1959).
Sen, A. K., *Collective Choice and Social Welfare*. Holden-Day (1970).
Solomons, D., 'The Politicization of Accounting', *Journal of Accounting* (November 1978).
Spacek, L., 'Professional Accountants and the Public Responsibility', in *A Search for Fairness in Financial Reportings to the Public*. Arthur Andersen (1969).
Sprouse, R. T. and Moonitz, M., 'A Tentative Set of Broad Accounting Principles for Business Enterprises', *Research Study No. 3*. AICPA (1962).
Stamp, E., 'The Public Accountant and the Public Interest', *Journal of Business Finance* (Spring 1969a).
Stamp, E., 'Auditing the Auditors', *The Times* (September 11, 1969b, p. 25).
Stamp, E., 'The Watts Report: an Uncertain Trumpet', *The Accountant's Magazine* (January 1979).
Stamp, E. and Marley, C., *Accounting and the City Code*. Butterworths (1970).
Sterling, R. R. and Harrison, W., 'Discussion of Capital Market Equilibrium, Information Production and Selected Accounting Techniques: Theoretical Framework and Review of Empirical Work', *Studies on Financial Objectives*, Supplement to the *Journal of Accounting Research* (1974).
Stigler, G., 'Free-Riders and Collective Action: An Appendix to Theories of Economic Regulation', *Bell Journal of Economics* (Autumn 1974).
Templaar, A. F., 'Standards have their Dangers', *The Accountant* (22 May 1975).
Watts, R. L., 'Discussion', *Journal of Finance* (April 1976).
Watts, R. L. and Zimmerman, J. L., 'The Demand and Supply of Accounting Theories: The Market for Excuses', *The Accounting Review* (April 1979).
Weetman, P., 'Accounting Standards: A Pause for Reflection', *Accounting and Business Research* (Summer 1977).
Zeff, S. A., *Forging Accounting Principles in Five Countries*. Stripes (1972).

Commentary on 'The setting of accounting standards: the contribution of research'

R J Briston
Reader in Accountancy, University of East Anglia

Professor Bromwich's very comprehensive paper is divided into two main sections and it seems appropriate to discuss it in the same structure, dealing first with the process of setting accounting standards and then with the contribution of research to this process.

His outline of the evolution of accounting standards in the U.S.A. and the U.K. is very thorough, though rather unimaginative. Little attention is paid, for example, to the special factors which have made U.S. accounting standards more inflexible than those in the U.K. These factors include the fear of litigation and of government interference, and the power of the SEC in the field of corporate disclosure. At the same time the power of the international accounting firms, wielded largely from the U.S.A., is likely in the future to bring both U.K. and international accounting standards closer to those of the U.S.A.

The influence of auditors in the standard-setting process is also given scant attention. In both countries, and especially in the U.K., the process is dominated by auditors and by the large accounting firms. As a consequence, the standards tend to reflect what is convenient for auditors to audit rather than what is most useful for those for whom the information is intended. In other words, there is a tendency towards law rather than economics, and towards rigidity rather than judgement. In their enthusiasm for standardization, accountants have ignored the fact that the economic measurement of income in the profit and loss account, and of value in the balance sheet must, of necessity, be subjective. If greater regard had been paid to the fundamental purpose of accounting information in a changing economic environment then the standards might have been more relevant to current economic needs.

Due to the influence of the Companies Acts and the benefits which they have provided over time to the accounting profession the structure of company accounts has not adapted in order to meet the changing needs of users. They are still aimed almost exclusively at shareholders and provide information in a format which has remained relatively static for well over a century. The needs of investment analysts, of employees, of government, and of society at large are all ignored and we have retained a format of reporting which, as research has shown, is not understood by shareholders, and which enables the auditor to discharge his duties with a report which conveys a minimum amount of information.

Professor Bromwich does not consider the needs of other users in any detail. Of particular importance are the requirements of the government at both the micro and the macro level. It seems absurd that so much should be spent on the preparation of annual reports, the value of which to individual shareholders has not been proved, which are of little use for government purposes. In the field of economic planning and in the construction of national accounts the government can place little reliance upon published accounts and has to obtain much of its information from other sources. Furthermore, other sources of information such as details of contracts, industry surveys, company visits by institutional investors and stock-brokers, etc., all influence investor decisions just as much as published accounts, yet, possibly because they are not subject to audit, they do not attract the attention of standard-setters.

In short, it is argued that accounting standards are not nearly so important as many writers suggest; that they are concerned with only a small part of the economic information process; and that even this concern is dominated by the self-interest of the accounting profession in perpetuating a reporting system which meets the needs of the 19th rather than the 20th century.

In his analysis of possible areas of research Professor Bromwich highlights first the costs attached to the provision of accounting information and then the problems involved in the construction of a conceptual framework. The question of the cost of accounting information has attracted much attention in recent years, but there is still much confusion, a great deal of which is caused by the failure to distinguish between economic costs and externally imposed legal costs. The actual cost to a company of preparing information which is useful to its shareholders is minimal, for every listed company will prepare for its own purposes not only a set of final accounts, with fully segmented information, but also a budget for future periods. The cost of providing this information to the shareholders consists partly of printing and postage expenses and partly of 'legal' costs such as the audit fee and the cost of complying with SEC requirements.

As far as most of the above costs are concerned, the shareholder has little discretion, for the law requires that the information should be provided. It would be interesting to discover how many shareholders would prefer to receive a higher dividend rather than the annual report. At least, research suggests that the shareholder receives little benefit from the report and that a commentary upon the accounts in the financial press will probably explain the accounts more clearly than either the directors' report or the auditors' report. Possibly more critical, in the light of the involvement of auditors in the standards-setting process, is the question of the benefits derived either by shareholders or by society from the cost of external audit. The external audit in the U.K. is imposed by law upon all companies and involves a total annual economic cost of well in excess of £500 million. Yet there is no evidence which suggests that the benefits provided by the audit process justify its costs or that the same benefits could not be provided more cheaply, possibly by reorganizing the internal audit system.

Another factor which distorts the analysis of the costs attached to accounting information is the fact that many groups of users are able to require information without payment. The government, workers and major creditors are all able, due either to their economic power or to legal provisions, to obtain information which is not available to shareholders. Only shareholders have to pay for the information which they receive, and even then it is by way of a compulsory charge against the income of their company. Even if the purchase of information by shareholders were placed upon a voluntary basis there would be no way of assessing the value of such information, for its value would only be ascertainable after it had been purchased and would persist only so long as it was not available to other potential users.

Overall, it seems inconceivable that the marginal cost to a company of providing relevant economic, as opposed to legal, information could ever be material, or that a process could be established whereby a price could be set for information. A far more realistic and promising area for research would be an assessment of the relative costs and benefits of the legally-imposed information requirements, such as the audit report and the SEC disclosure provisions. The costs of these, and especially of the audit report, are capable of measurement, and the benefits, though intangible, are at least as measurable as the factors involved in the research studies to which Professor Bromwich refers.

His arguments concerning the difficulty of establishing a conceptual framework are most valid, for there are so many potential users of accounting reports, and so many differing information requirements that their overall needs can, perhaps, only be satisfied by means of a vast multi-purpose report. But does this provide an excuse for consequently limiting the report so that it meets the needs of only a few groups of users and thus becomes more easily capable of standardization? Such a partial, restricted approach has the drawback that the accounting profession, due to understandable self-interest, will tend to favour those groups to which it has traditionally reported rather than those which the public interest would require, and will continue to provide information in a form which is easily audited rather than economically relevant.

Professor Bromwich sees accounting standards as ‘an important and exciting topic for accounting researchers’. I would take issue on this assertion. Accounting standards as they have so far evolved, have encouraged massive research into a series of separate issues and not nearly enough attention has been paid, not only to the fundamental objectives of the reporting process, not as they were one hundred years ago, but as they should be in the modern economy, but also, and more crucially, to the consideration of whether these objectives might not be achieved in a more cost-effective way. In short, the process of reporting annually to a group of uninterested shareholders who often do not understand the information provided, and could not benefit from it even if they did, is only a small part of the subject of accounting, which already attracts far more attention than it deserves, probably because so much published data is available for computer-based doctoral theses. The subject of financial reporting standards should be seen as only a small part of the overall accounting system—a system which involves the collection, processing and communication of information for making, implementing and controlling economic decisions in both the public and the private sector at both the micro and the macro level.

3 Cash flow accounting and corporate financial reporting

T A Lee
Professor of Accountancy and Finance, University of Edinburgh

Approximately 50 writings have been read as preparation for this essay. Three-quarters of them were U.K.-based, and in excess of one-half could be attributed to two U.K. writers—Professors Lawson and Lee. Furthermore, three-quarters of the writings were published in the 1970s. Thus, the subject of cash flow accounting (CFA) is a relatively new one, not attracting many writers to its cause, and being of mainly U.K. interest (at least within the context of corporate financial reporting). However, despite this lack of apparent support in the literature, CFA remains potentially as a serious and viable addition to the corporate financial reporting function, and it is the aim of this essay to review it in order to assess its importance in this context. Inevitably, because of the volume of their contribution to CFA, the work of Lawson and Lee will form the substance of this review. But the work of other accountants will be examined, and a full bibliography is given at the end of the essay.

Nature and Role of CFA

CFA is the term used to denote a system of financial reporting which describes the financial performance of an entity in cash terms. It is based on a matching of periodic cash inflows and outflows, free of credit transactions and arbitrary accounting allocations. Inflows include cash from trading operations and providers of long-term finance; and outflows include payments for replacement and growth investment, taxation, interest, and distributions. As such, it is a measurement and reporting system which avoids time lags and distortions. It concentrates on the liquidity and financial management of the reporting entity, and can be conceived in terms both of actual and forecast cash transactions.

History of CFA

CFA is not a new concept. In fact, as Winjum (1972) has demonstrated, it was the main system of accounting up to the beginning of the 18th century.

Prior to that time, accounting allocations and profit measurements were relatively unimportant; the profit and loss account being used to close off ledger accounts at each period end. However, with the advent of the concept and practice of business continuity, the need grew to produce periodic measures of profit and statements of financial position (Littleton and Zimmerman, 1963). Thus, the basic cash transactions became the foundation for the allocation-based systems of accounting of today.

Although there has been a reasonably sustained interest in funds flow statements (based on allocated accounting data) since the beginning of the 20th century (see Käfer and Zimmerman, 1979), CFA appears to have received little or no support from accountants until the early 1960s. At that time, there was concern over the use of 'cash flow' data in financial analysis—cash flow being interpreted as 'profit plus depreciation' (see Paton, 1963 and Drebin, 1964).[1] The major worry was that such data were being used for decision-making purposes as a substitute for income, and that the cost of durable assets was not being taken into account. Also, at this time, two writers advocated the reporting of pure cash flow data (i.e. CFA)—in the U.S., Coughlan (1960; 1962; 1964) and, in the U.K., Edey (1963).

Coughlan's recommendations were based on a capital budgeting approach involving the reporting of past and expected cash flows as a basis for producing discounted cash flow balance sheets from which measures of income could be derived as a form of internal rate of return. He described these computations of economic income and value as 'industrial accounting', and argued for them because of the distortions caused by conventional accounting allocations, and the need, therefore, to account properly for the influence of time. His pioneering work which, however, appeared to be aimed at internal reporting functions, was apparently not developed further by him.

Edey, on the other hand, advocated the reporting of forecast cash flows because of the difficulties associated with the measurement of profit. He believed such predictive data to be more relevant than profits for the purposes of estimating future dividend levels, evaluating management, and assessing corporate liquidity. Mainly concerned with the provision of relevant information for investors, and with the lack of precision in the meaning of profit, Edey also recommended that investors should be provided with net realizable value-based balance sheets in order to assess potential corporate liquidity, chargeable capacity,[2] and the minimum return to be earned on investment. Edey repeated his recommendations later (1970) but has not developed them since in the literature.

Staubus (1961; 1966) also provided a relatively early contribution to the contemporary CFA debate when reviewing the nature and role of the

1 Confusing CFA with 'cash flow' data which are allocation-based is a common mistake in the accountancy literature—particularly that of the U.S. in the 1960s.

2 Defined as the value of the assets available to act as security for potential borrowings.

funds flow statement for investors. Identifying the importance of assessing corporate liquidity for investment or managerial decisions, he rejected the use of net realizable value data for this purpose and, instead, advocated the reporting of funds statements based on cash or near-cash resources (i.e. including debtors and creditors). In his early work (1961), he envisaged such statements as being of use only to short-term creditors, but in his later writing (1966), he appeared to have widened his views on the relevance of such statements. He particularly emphasized the opinion that cash flow statements ought to distinguish recurrent from non-recurrent flows in order to aid their users in assessing corporate liquidity. Staubus does not appear to have developed his work on CFA since 1966.

Contemporary Contributions

In 1968, Lawson (1968) published his first paper on CFA. Since then he has continued to develop his ideas both conceptually and empirically. Lee (1971) published his first CFA contribution some time later but, together, these writers have provided most of the CFA literature of the 1970s, and this will be examined in detail in later sections. However, Lawson and Lee have not been alone in their support of CFA. In the U.S., the main contributors (other than Coughlan and Staubus) have been Thomas (1969; 1974; 1979), Ijiri (1977; 1978; 1979) and Heath (1978).[3] Briston and Fawthrop (1971), Jones (1975), Climo (1976), and Waldron (1980), have also provided contributions to the CFA debate and literature in the U.K. (in addition to Edey). Their work will be discussed prior to that of Lawson and Lee but, meantime, the U.S. contribution will be reviewed briefly.

U.S. Contributions

Thomas' pioneering work on the frailties of the allocation system in conventional accounting led him to recommend the abandonment of income measurement by accountants, concentrating instead on funds statements using a notion of funds defined in terms of cash plus debtors minus creditors (1969). These net quick asset statements were recommended in addition to statements of monetary and non-monetary assets (1974).

3 The idea of combining CFA and NRVA ought not to be confused with the suggestion by Ronen and Sorter of merging a market rate-determined economic value of the reporting entity with the exit values of its conventionally classified assets and liabilities—see Ronen and Sorter (1972) and Ronen (1974). The Ronen and Sorter proposal was intended to provide investors with (a) means of comparing market values with economic values of the reporting entity and its equity; (b) managerially forecasted cash flows (but in the form of reporting one discounted measure of value); and (c) measurement of the conversion of entity asset economic values into exit values, and vice versa. Nowhere in their system was there a recommendation to specifically disclose either past or forecast CFA data.

However, his relative vagueness with regard to what precise form these statements should take, leaves Thomas' work in a somewhat indeterminate state; he is strongly in favour of reporting allocation-free data (especially related to flow statements) but is less than clear with regard to position statements.[4]

Historic cost accounting is the area for which Ijiri is best known (1967). However, he has recently advocated the use of CFA (1977; 1978; 1979) as a means of enabling the results of managerial decisions to be evaluated on the same basis as they were taken. Ijiri's CFA system, however, is an extension of historic cost, allocation-based accounting. He recommends the reporting of statements reflecting investment flows (changes in historic cost-based assets) and financing flows (changes in sources of finance). The former flows are to be stated before deduction of fixed asset depreciation, and the latter flows are to include such aggregate provisions. Historic costs in this sense are used not to value assets but to describe the entity's investment in them. Ijiri concentrates on what he describes as cash flow recovery (usually profit plus depreciation, interest, and fixed asset sales) and relates this to the total gross investment in assets (before depreciation) in order to determine corporate recovery rates. He recommends these rates as surrogates for discounted cash flow returns in situations where *ex post* measurements of the latter are not possible due to the continuity of the entity concerned. It is not, however, a system which can be regarded as pure CFA; rather, it should be looked upon as an extension of historic cost accounting.

The final U.S. contributor to CFA has been Heath (1978). Writing of the need to provide relevant financial information for investors, creditors and other persons interested in evaluating corporate solvency and liquidity, he has advocated the presentation of a statement of cash receipts and payments (giving a listing of the various sources of cash matched with an equivalent listing of the various uses to which these were put), coupled with a further two statements—one describing the various changes on the assets side of the historic cost-based balance sheet, and the other dealing with the equivalent changes on the liabilities side of the same report. As such, Heath's recommendations do contain an element of CFA but they cannot be taken as advocations of a complete system of financial reporting based on CFA.

U.K. Contributions

A consistent feature of the U.K. accounting literature over the last 10 years or so has been the development of a detailed argument and structure for CFA as a major part of the corporate financial reporting function. Spearheaded by Lawson (1968; 1969; 1970; 1971a; 1971b; 1971c; 1972;

4 In his most recent work, Thomas (1979) advocates cash flow statements coupled with virtually unspecified allocation-free balance sheets.

1973; 1975a; 1975b; 1976; 1978a; 1978b; 1978c; 1979) and Lee (1971; 1972a; 1972b; 1972c; 1974; 1978; 1979a; 1979b; 1979c; 1980a; 1980b), the main argument has been for a logical and coherent reporting framework including statements of past and forecast cash flows, and supported by additional statements concerning, *inter alia*, explanations of variances between actual and forecast data, descriptions of the major assumptions underlying forecast results, audit opinions, and explanations of non-cash transactions. In these respects, the work of Lawson and Lee are reasonably similar, although Lee (1980b) has extended it to include net realizable value-based position statements which relate to the recommended CFA statements.[5]

There have been other contributions to the U.K. debate on CFA. Edey (1963; 1970), as mentioned earlier, provided the initial impetus with his suggestion for the reporting of forecast cash flows. Briston and Fawthrop (1971) also suggested the reporting of such forecasts, supplemented by an audited statement of variances between actual and previously forecast results. Jones (1975) supported the idea of past and forecast cash flow statements as a feasible alternative to the problem of standardizing accounting allocations. The Sandilands Committee on Inflation Accounting (1975), whilst appearing to receive the idea of CFA for corporate financial reporting purposes with some enthusiasm, rejected it on the practical ground that it would not comply with existing company law because of its lack of adherence to statements of profit and financial position.[6] In contrast, Climo (1976) felt that the reporting of CFA data (past and future) would be exceedingly relevant to investors, particularly if the flows concerned were divisionalized, segregated between recurrent and non-recurrent items, and supported by some form of (unspecified) net realizable value-based balance sheet. Waldron (1980) also felt that past CFA reports ought to be supported by forecast data and financial position data—in this case, the former was recommended to be contained in a statement of needs and resources (describing the next 12 months cash receipts and payments), and the latter to take the form of a balance sheet based on (undefined) economic values. On the whole, therefore, these contributions have lent support and added weight to the CFA argument and debate without having the degree of depth and consistency to be evidenced in the work of Lawson and Lee.

The Lawson/Lee Case for CFA

The remainder of this essay is concerned with CFA as advocated by Lawson and Lee. This review will be a general one, examining, first, the

5 The early work on CFA by Lawson and Lee has been reviewed by Ashton (1976), and various similarities and dissimilarities at that time have been examined by him.

6 This appeared to ignore the fact that CFA is usually advocated by its supporters as an addition to the traditional and long-standing system of financial reporting.

structure of the system and, secondly, the considerable advantages which have been claimed for it. References will be made to specific papers when necessary.

Suggested CFA System—Users

The suggestion of a corporate financial reporting system based on cash flows has been underpinned by the fundamental concepts of utility and relevance (Lee, 1971; 1972a; 1972c). This general theoretical base has been operationalized in terms of specific report user groups. Lawson, for example, has been concerned mainly with the use of cash data by investors, CFA containing all the determinants of distributable cash flows—this has characterized most of his writings (as in, for example, 1969; 1971a; 1971b; 1971c; 1972; 1975a; 1978a). However, he has recognized other uses—wage negotiation (1975a; and Lawson and Stark, 1977); bank lending (1978c); and governmental policy-making in relation to corporate taxation (e.g. 1971b; 1973; 1975a; 1975b; 1976; 1978a; 1978c; 1979).

Lee, too, has emphasized the importance of CFA in relation to specific user groups—at first in relation to shareholders (1971; 1972c) but, increasingly, his recommendations for CFA have been given in relation to the needs of a number of specific groups—for example, lenders and creditors, bankers, employees, managers, government agencies, etc. (1974; 1978; 1979b). He has also more recently argued for its general purpose nature in a corporate financial reporting context—i.e. CFA is capable of satisfying a number of different user groups rather than being specifically relevant to a particular group (1980b).

In light of the above comments, as well as a review of the other U.K. papers on CFA, it is clear that such recommendations have been made within the context of an increasing awareness in the 1970s of the need to satisfy the informational needs of corporate report users. Not only is the suggested CFA system seen as being relevant to specific users but is also regarded as having a general relevance. In other words, cash flow data are believed to impinge on most users' behaviour. In this sense, the Lawson and Lee proposals are definitely aimed at aiding user decisions. This underlies all their work, and is made most explicit in their consistent suggestion for the reporting of both past and forecast cash flows. This is not to say that either writer has ignored the use of CFA as a means of making entity management accountable to ownership—the stewardship function (e.g. Lawson, 1975a; and Lee, 1974; 1978). CFA is therefore conceived as a multi-purpose reporting system, compatible with the decision and accountability aims usually associated with the conventional allocation-based reporting systems.

Suggested CFA System—Structure

The system of CFA advocated by Lawson and Lee is all-embracing, containing data related to both actual and predicted business activity, supported (as mentioned previously) by a number of explanatory statements pertaining, *inter alia*, to forecasting assumptions, variances, non-cash transactions, and relevant audit opinions. As his earlier writings indicate (e.g. 1969; 1971a), Lawson has described the reporting entity as a total financial system. Accordingly, his consistent recommendation has been that CFA is an explicit statement of such a system—i.e. the entity receives a net cash flow from its various operational activities (O), and uses this to pay for replacement and growth investment (R), taxation (T), interest on borrowings (I), and distributions to its owners (D). By including new equity receipts (E) and borrowings (B), Lawson's simple tabulated CFA presentation can be reconciled to the periodic change in cash resources of the entity (C). Thus:

$$O - R - T - I + E + B - C = D$$

In other words, the major emphasis is on disclosing the distributed, or distributable, cash flow to the entity's owners and, by deducting E from D, producing a measure of the latter's cash flow which can be used for purposes of discounting to derive a present value of equity. Except for a supplementary statement describing the composition of the operational cash flow, Lawson's system is a relatively simple tabulated one involving 10 years of past data, and between 12 and 18 months of forecast data (1975a). It is also divisionalized, where relevant (1971a).

As will be shown in later sections, the essence of the CFA system described by Lawson is to provide relevant data for a number of measurable tasks—e.g. for determining effective rates of tax, and interest and dividend covers. In other words, he has concentrated on the uses to which CFA could be put rather than on the detail and structure of CFA as a corporate financial reporting system. In contrast, Lee has been mainly concerned with the detail of CFA as a reporting system. Like Lawson, his general recommendations have consistently included the reporting of 10 years of past data, and at least 1 year of forecast data—all suitably audited and supported by a statement of explained variances between actual and forecast results (distinguishing between controllable and uncontrollable differences). However, Lee has also extended this broad framework in a number of ways—first, in relation to statements to support the main CFA data (Lee, 1972c) and secondly, in relation to financial statement data which are compatible with CFA (Lee, 1980b).

Using the above notation, Lee's main CFA statements originally (e.g. 1972c) used the following pattern:

$$O - R - I - T - D + E + B = C$$

This was reasonably similar to that of Lawson above. It assumed that operational cash flows were available to pay, in order of priority, replacement and growth investment (to ensure continuity of the entity), interest on borrowings (deducted before tax as it is allowable for taxation purposes), taxation, and distributions to the entity owners. This would leave a surplus or deficit of cash to be augmented or supplemented by new equity and borrowing receipts. However, as a reporting system, it provided matchings of cash inflows and outflows which suggested new long-term finance was being raised by the reporting entity to pay for dividends (and even taxation) in circumstances where operating cash flows were inadequate to cover these payments in addition to replacement and growth investment. In order to provide a more neutral reporting statement, Lee has recently suggested the formulation (1980b):

$$O - I - T - D + E + B - R = C$$

This effectively leaves the deduction of payments for replacement and growth investment until all available cash resources have been utilized to cover deductions for payments for which some prior commitment or obligation has been recognized by management.

The above basic data in Lee's system are each recommended to be supported by a detailed supplementary statement enabling the report user to comprehend how each figure is composed—e.g. the taxation measure could comprise payments for U.K. and non-U.K. tax; and the replacement and growth investment figure, as well as being derived after making the basic distinction of replacement and growth, could be shown along with receipts for asset disposals and government grants. Furthermore, the operational cash flow statement could be suitably segmented, and all reported statements would require to be audited. A unique feature of Lee's system is the inclusion of a statement to disclose entity transactions which have not involved a cash flow (e.g. the acquisition of assets for equity or loan stock).

Lee (1980b) has extended his CFA system to include statements of financial position based on net realizable values. By combining these potential cash flows with realized cash flows, a measure of total cash flow can be computed. This complete system of CFA can then be tied in with a statement of financial position which describes (in order of realizability) a minimum future cash inflow to be matched against (in order of date of settlement) the various obligations due by the reporting entity. This suggestion is intended as a reasoned answer to the charge that CFA is an incomplete reporting system because it concentrates solely on 'flows' rather than 'stocks'. The combined system appears to provide both, and is, therefore, a practical implementation of the original idea of Edey (1963).

To summarize on the suggested structure of CFA reports, it is clear that there is reasonable agreement in the U.K.—actual and forecast data should be disclosed (segmented where relevant); supplementary disclosure can come from a variety of supporting statements; particular attention ought to be paid to explained forecasting assumptions, and explained variances between actual and forecast results; and auditing of these statements appears to be a priority. Finally, Edey, Climo and Lee (in the U.K.) and Thomas (in the U.S.) have recommended net realizable value position statements in support of CFA. Lee has attempted to implement this suggestion.

However, despite the agreement, there appear to be fundamental differences in the Lawson and Lee proposals. First, Lee conceives of the structure of CFA as an interlocking series of statements for a variety of users. Lawson, on the other hand, is mainly concerned with the provision of cash flow data to improve the information base of investors and financial managers. Secondly, Lawson's system is largely proprietorial in nature because of its attention to distributable flows and investors; Lee's system is enterprise-orientated, intended for a variety of user groups, and concentrating on a reporting of the various cash flows of the entity. The latter approach owes much to the work of Fisher who regarded the entity as a clearing house for various cash flows to creditors, employees, lenders, bankers, government, and owners (Lee, 1979a). This is not to say that Lawson's work has lacked an enterprise approach—his earliest work (e.g. 1969) described CFA as a means of portraying the reporting entity as a total financial system. His later work, however, has concentrated particularly on the needs of investors.

Suggested CFA System—Computation

The computation of CFA data ought to be uncomplicated in an accounting sense. After all, part of its *raison d'etre* is to avoid the complexities and subjectiveness of accounting allocations. Thus, preparing CFA statements from cash transactions should only involve the complications of presentation and disclosure.[7] However, due to the conventional structuring of the credit and allocation-based accounting system, it may not be possible to produce CFA statements directly. In these cases, it should be feasible to take allocated data and, by reversing the effect of the credit transactions and accounting allocations, derive the underlying cash flows. This is particularly feasible when funds statements are available.

Much of the work on adjusting conventional data to their cash flow equivalents is due to the efforts of Lawson (e.g. 1971c; 1976; 1978a; and Lawson and Stark, 1975). By unveiling the hidden cash flows in allocated data, Lawson has been able to highlight the two major shortcomings of the latter, particularly during a period of inflation—i.e. the working capital and depreciation shortfalls in measuring periodic surpluses (e.g. 1975a; 1975b). In conventional accounting, the full cost of working capital is not (and may never be) matched against revenues—e.g. under FIFO systems of stock accounting, there is a base level of stock which will never be

7 There will, of course, also be the problem of forecasting judgements when preparing predicted CFA data.

matched against sales unless the stock is completely consumed (Lawson, 1975b). The same is true of fixed asset costs, assuming continuity of the reporting entity.

Thus, although Lawson's cash flow adjustments to allocated data are, in themselves, relatively obvious and straightforward, his use of them to demonstrate the consistent overstatement of reported entity earnings has been a considerable advance in accounting thinking. In particular, his demonstration that, during periods of inflation, these overstatements become more material, has highlighted the inadequacies of systems of current cost accounting to bridge the gap between the partial costs which are conventionally matched against revenues, and the total costs which, because they have been committed, ought to be so matched (Lawson, 1976; 1978a).

Suggested CFA System—Main Features

CFA has a considerable number of identifiable features which suggest its reporting potential in terms of improving the utility of financial reports. Again, these owe much to the work of Lawson and Lee for their identification. They are given below in no particular order of importance.

1. CFA avoids dubious accounting allocations and thus, unlike periodic income measurements, cash flows provide relatively unambiguous measures of entity financial performance (e.g. Lawson, 1968; 1969; 1970; 1971b; 1971c; and Lee, 1971; 1972c).
2. CFA captures the vital factor in decision-making and valuation of the time value of money; conventional accounting ignores this by allocating data in order to 'smooth' income trends (e.g. Lawson, 1968; 1970; 1971b; 1971c; and Lee, 1971; 1972b).
3. CFA can therefore avoid dubious measures of periodic income which have a variety of meanings depending on the particular measurement contexts and uses to which they are being applied. CFA has a relatively unambiguous meaning, no matter what the measurement context or use is (e.g. Lee, 1974).
4. CFA emphasizes some of the most fundamental and vital features of business activity (cash is the key factor in this long-term issue); the ability of the enterprise to pay its obligations, make distributions, and provide for its future continuity (cash is needed to reinvest, to expand, and to pay for taxation, interest, and distribution commitments, as well as to repay credit and borrowings previously received) (e.g. Lee, 1972c; 1974; 1978).
5. CFA does not require price-level adjustments due to specific inflation as it expresses the cash flow data concerned in the purchasing power of the period in which they were transacted and accounted. However, it may be necessary to convert CFA data of different periods to a base year (by some

form of general price restatement) (e.g. Lawson, 1970; 1971c; 1972; and Lee, 1971; 1978).

6. CFA is capable of producing data which are needed for a variety of decision and control activities both within and without the reporting entity. It, therefore, ought to improve the quality of these matters—e.g. by providing report users with management's views of the future, and data on working capital and depreciation shortfalls, and fiscal drag,[8] there is an argument that the stock market (at least in aggregate) would be more efficient and derive more accurate share values as a consequence (Lawson, 1970; 1971c; 1975a); bankers and lenders would be provided with data relevant to their assessment of the reporting entity's quality of financial (and, particularly, cash) management (Lee, 1980b); and government would learn of the lack of neutrality[9] in its corporate taxation system (Lawson, 1978c; 1979).

7. CFA is the only proper basis for measuring the value of entities as going concerns because of its attention to the time value of money. It is thus capable of providing not only present values of investments but also rates of return which conform with economic principles. CFA is also compatible with Hicksian notions of periodic income and capital valuation (Lawson, 1968; 1969; 1971a; 1978a; and Lee, 1971).

8. CFA as a system of financial reporting is objective, understandable, and simple. It avoids the subjectiveness and language of accounting allocations, and presents the data in a way that is potentially recognizable to its users (Lawson, 1970; and Lee, 1972c; 1974; 1978).[10] It also provides comparable data which are not rendered incomparable because of measurements of different purchasing powers, and subjective allocations (Lee, 1974).

9. CFA conforms to a number of non-accounting theories which, nevertheless, have strong associations with the accounting and reporting function—for example, CFA (as mentioned above) is compatible with economic theories of the time value of money and interest, and of income and capital valuation; it is also consistent with modern capital market theory (Lawson, 1978a).

These are merely a few of the various arguments for, and main features of, CFA which have been highlighted by Lawson and Lee. They cannot really do justice to the case for CFA in financial reporting due to the brevity of description given to each point. Nevertheless, when taken as a whole, they

8 Fiscal drag in this context is the term used by Lawson (1979) to denote the time lag between providing for corporate tax on high levels of accounting profit, and paying for this tax out of considerably smaller cash surpluses in later years (assuming a period of inflation).

9 Tax neutrality is the term used to denote a system of tax which bears equally upon all taxpayers—i.e. it does not favour or discriminate against individual taxpayers.

10 Tweedie (1977), in a pilot study, has produced evidence to suggest that non-accountants may intuitively think of periodic income and financial position in terms of, respectively, cash flows and net realizable values.

provide a formidable case for CFA which is not to be evidenced to such an extent in other systems of financial reporting which have received favour by accountants.

Suggested CFA System—Empirical Evidence

As well as giving conceptual arguments for the introduction of CFA to financial reporting, Lawson and Lee have provided empirical evidence of its utility. In a number of research studies over recent years, both writers have been concerned to back up their assertions with proof of CFA's reporting potential.

In a preliminary study of CFA utility, Lee (1979c) invited shareholders in two medium-sized companies to rank five brewing companies in order of investment preference in accordance with the type of information supplied to them. CFA data comprised one of the information sets provided, and it was found that the companies were ranked considerably differently by shareholders who received CFA data only, compared with those who received historic cost, allocation-based equivalents or a mixture of both. CFA data did not appear to cause any difficulties to its investor-users despite their lack of familiarity with it.

Lee (1980a) has also examined accountants' attitudes towards CFA reporting to external user groups. He evidenced considerable support for the idea—more so for actual cash flow results than for forecast results. CFA data were believed to be useful to most external user groups interested in companies, but especially to bankers and lenders concerned with assessing corporate liquidity. No particular problems were foreseen in preparing past data—several years of audited data being envisaged as the typical reporting format. Forecast statements were not believed to be worthwhile beyond more than one or two years of predicted activity. Most of the respondents' companies utilized CFA systems to a considerable extent for internal management purposes.

Using, alternatively, hypothetical and live data (for individual companies as well as in aggregate), Lawson has documented extensive evidence concerning the utility of CFA data. He has shown that the working capital and depreciation shortfalls for manufacturing companies can be considerable, and can increase substantially as the rate of inflation increases (1975a)—thus, conventional accounting consistently overstates corporate earnings during periods of inflation. He has demonstrated the misleading effects this overstatement may have—e.g. the wisdom of wage claims based on reported income when the effective rates of tax based on CFA are well in excess of the notional rate (Lawson and Stark, 1977).

In more recent times, Lawson has further demonstrated the utility of cash flow data for purposes of economic and financial management. He has revealed (1978c) that, using aggregate data for 1954 to 1976, inclusive, real cash flow returns (net of tax) to shareholders and lenders have typically been negative (particularly between 1964 and 1976). In the same study, Lawson evidences that the market, as a whole, uncovers the cash flows underlying conventional earnings, and impounds these into share prices. His overall conclusions from this data are (a) the market is efficient with regard to cash flow; (b) U.K. companies are consistently paying dividends in excess of cash flow earnings and financing the deficit by borrowings; and (c) company tax rates on a cash flow basis are confiscatory and lack neutrality. These results were further confirmed in a more recent study (Lawson, 1979), although it is not clear that the market is as efficient in unveiling underlying cash flows of individual companies. Suffice to say, however, that Lawson's evidence in the U.K. is of overtaxation, over-distribution, and crisis levels of borrowing to finance this. In this respect, the utility of CFA in the area of corporate taxation has recently been recognized in the report of the Meade Committee (1978), in which it is recommended that company tax in the U.K. be based on measured cash flows. This is the first tangible evidence, other than from the advocates of CFA, of its practical utility and importance.

Conclusions

Although CFA is not as yet a formal part of financial reporting, cash flow data can be derived from conventional allocation-based figures. This can be done relatively easily, and CFA's utility can be reasonably demonstrated at a conceptual level and, increasingly, at an empirical level. A relatively few accountants have achieved this position and, as such, CFA has been argued for at least as consistently as any other system of accounting. Unlike other systems, however, it has not so far suffered from any significant criticism in the published literature.

The argument for CFA has progressed at two levels: conceptually (both in relation to what CFA attempts to describe, and for whom it is addressed); and, more recently, empirically (in terms of utility and feasibility). In other words, CFA is a system which already has a sound theoretical underpinning, a developed measurement and presentation framework, and growing empirical support. Obviously, a great deal of work remains to be undertaken—e.g. in relation to improving the structure and detail of CFA reports (particularly with regard to position statements), forecasting, and avoidance of managerial manipulation of cash flows. Also, there is the very real 'political' problem to be overcome of convincing accounting policy-makers that CFA is a valid, useful and complete reporting system worthy of inclusion in the overall financial reporting package.

That much of this work has been achieved in the U.K. in recent years by so few accountants is a unique contribution to financial reporting. It is to be hoped that their effort will continue to a successful outcome whereby the U.K. can be seen to be the birthplace of the practice of modern CFA for external reporting purposes.

References

Ashton, R., 'Cash Flow Accounting: A Review and Critique,' *Journal of Business Finance and Accounting* (Winter 1976), pp. 63–81.

Briston, R. J. and Fawthrop, R. A., 'Accounting Principles and Investor Protection', *Journal of Business Finance* (Summer 1971), pp. 10–19.

Climo, T. A., 'Cash Flow Statements for Investors', *Journal of Business Finance and Accounting* (Autumn 1976), pp. 3–14.

Coughlan, J. W., 'Contrast Between Financial-Statement and Discounted-Cash-Flow Methods of Comparing Projects', *NAA Bulletin* (June 1960), pp. 5–17.

Coughlan, J. W., 'Accounting and Capital Budgeting', *The Business Quarterly* (Fall 1962), pp. 39–48.

Coughlan, J. W., 'Funds and Income', *NAA Bulletin* (September 1964), pp. 23–34.

Drebin, A. R., ' "Cash-Flowitis": Malady or Syndrome?', *Journal of Accounting Research* (Spring 1964), pp. 25–34.

Edey, H. C., 'Accounting Principles and Business Reality', *Accountancy* (November 1963), pp. 998–1002; (December 1963), pp. 1083–8.

Edey, H. C., 'The Nature of Profit', *Accounting and Business Research* (Winter 1970), pp. 50–5.

Heath, L. C., 'Financial Reporting and the Evaluation of Solvency', *Accounting Research Monograph 3.* American Institute of Certified Public Accountants (1978).

Ijiri, Y., *The Foundations of Accounting Measurement.* Prentice Hall (1967).

Ijiri, Y., 'Corporate Recovery Rate and Cash Flow Accounting', *GSIA Working Paper.* Carnegie-Mellon University (1977).

Ijiri, Y., 'Cash Flow Accounting and Its Structure', *Journal of Accounting, Auditing and Finance* (May 1978), pp. 331–48.

Ijiri, Y., 'A Simple System of Cash Flow Accounting', in R. R. Sterling and A. L. Thomas (eds.), *Accounting for a Simplified Firm.* Scholars Book Co. (1979), pp. 57–71.

Inflation Accounting Committee, 'Inflation Accounting', *Report of the Inflation Accounting Committee,* Cmd 6225 (HMSO, 1975), pp. 156–8.

Jones, C. J., 'Accounting Standards: A Blind Alley?', *Accounting and Business Research* (Autumn 1975), pp. 273–9.

Käfer, K. and Zimmerman, V. K., 'Notes on the Evolution of the Statement of Sources and Applications of Funds', in T. A. Lee and R. H. Parker (eds.), *The Evolution of Corporate Financial Reporting.* Nelson (1979), pp. 133–52.

Lawson, G. H., *Applications of a Business Theory.* University of Liverpool Press (1968).

Lawson, G. H., 'Profit Maximisation Via Financial Management', *Management Decision* (Winter 1969), pp. 6–12.

Lawson, G. H., 'Radical Change in Financial Reports', *Financial Times* (15 July 1970).

Lawson, G. H., 'Measuring Divisional Performance', *Management Accountant* (May 1971a), pp. 147–52.

Lawson, G. H., 'Accounting for Financial Management—Some Tentative Proposals for a New Blueprint', in R. Shone (ed.), *Problems of Investment.* Blackwell (1971b), pp. 36–64.

Lawson, G. H., 'Cash-flow Accounting', *The Accountant* (28 October 1971), pp. 586–9; (4 November 1971c), pp. 620–2.

Lawson, G. H., 'Distributable Profits and Dividends', *Management International Review* (Vol 12 (2–3), 1972), pp. 113–19.

Lawson, G. H., 'Financial Objectives and Annual Financial Targets in the Imputation Tax System', *Journal of Business Finance* (Summer 1973), pp. 1–18.

Lawson, G. H., 'Memorandum Submitted to the Inflation Accounting Committee in July 1974', *Working Paper Series 12* (Manchester Business School, 1975a).

Lawson, G. H., 'The Rationale for Measuring the Cost of Working Capital', *Working Paper Series 15.* (Manchester Business School, 1975b).

Lawson, G. H., 'Initial Reactions to ED18', *Certified Accountant* (December 1976), pp. 357–65 and p. 422.

Lawson, G. H. 'The Rationale of Cash Flow Accounting', in C. van Dam (ed.), *Trends in Managerial and Financial Accounting.* Martinus Nijhoff (1978a), pp. 85–104.

Lawson, G. H., 'The Valuation of a Going Concern on a Cash Flow Basis', *Managerial Finance* (August 1980), forthcoming (1978b).

Lawson, G. H., *Company Profitability and the U.K. Stock Market—An Exercise in Cash Flow Accounting.* Manchester Business School (1978c).

Lawson, G. H., 'The Cash Flow Performance of U.K. Companies: Preliminary Analysis', *paper* to SSRC Conference on Accounting Research (1979).

Lawson, G. H. and Stark, A. W., 'The Concept of Profit for Fund Raising', *Accounting and Business Research* (Winter 1975), pp. 21–41.

Lawson, G. H. and Stark, A. W., 'Does Ford Cash Really Flow?', *Accountancy Age* (12 August 1977), pp. 8–9.

Lee, T. A., 'Goodwill—an Example of Will-o'-the-Wisp Accounting', *Accounting and Business Research* (Autumn 1971), pp. 318–28.

Lee, T. A., 'The Relevance of Accounting Information Including Cash Flows', *The Accountant's Magazine* (January 1972a), pp. 30–4.

Lee, T. A., 'The Nature and Purpose of Cash Flow Accounting', *The Accountant's Magazine* (April 1972b), pp. 198–200.

Lee, T. A., 'A Case for Cash Flow Reporting', *Journal of Business Finance* (Summer 1972), pp. 27–36.

Lee, T. A., 'Enterprise Income: Survival or Decline and Fall?', *Accounting and Business Research* (Summer 1974), pp. 178–92.

Lee, T. A., 'The Cash Flow Accounting Alternative for Corporate Financial Reporting', in C. van Dam (ed.), *Trends in Managerial and Financial Accounting.* Martinus Nijhoff (1978), pp. 63–84.

Lee, T. A., 'The Contribution of Fisher to Cash Flow Accounting', *Journal of Business Finance and Accounting* (Autumn 1979a), pp. 321–30.

Lee, T. A., 'The Simplicity and the Complexity of Accounting', in R. R. Sterling and A. L. Thomas (eds.), *Accounting for a Simplified Firm.* Scholars Book Co. (1979b), pp. 35–55.

Lee, T. A., 'A Test of the Use of Cash Flow Reporting', *Discussion Paper 2.* University of Edinburgh (1979c).

Lee, T. A., 'A Survey of Accountants' Opinions on Cash Flow Reporting', *Discussion Paper 3* (University of Edinbrugh, 1980a).

Lee, T. A., 'Reporting Cash Flows and Net Realizable Values', *Discussion Paper 5*. University of Edinburgh (1980b).

Littleton, A. C. and V. K. Zimmerman, *Accounting Theory: Continuity and Change*. Prentice Hall (1963), pp. 49–71.

Meade Committee, *Structure and Reform of Direct Taxation*. George Allen & Unwin (1978).

Paton, W. A., 'The Cash-Flow Illusion', *The Accounting Review* (April 1963), pp. 243–51.

Ronen, J., 'Discounted Cash Flow Accounting', in J. J. Cramer Jr. (ed.), *Objectives of Financial Statements*. American Institute of Certified Public Accountants (1974), pp. 143–60.

Ronen, J. and Sorter, G. H., 'Relevant Accounting', *Journal of Business* (April 1972), pp. 258–82.

Staubus, G. J., *A Theory of Accounting for Investors*. University of California Press (1961), pp. 134–6.

Staubus, G. J., 'Alternative Asset Flow Concepts', *The Accounting Review* (July 1966), pp. 397–412.

Thomas, A. L., 'The Allocation Problem', *Studies in Accounting Research 3*. American Accounting Association (1969), p. 101 and pp. 108–9.

Thomas, A. L., 'The Allocation Problem: Part Two', *Studies in Accounting Research 9*. American Accounting Association (1974), pp. 119–22.

Thomas, A. L., 'Matching: Up from Our Black Hole', in R. R. Sterling and A. L. Thomas (eds.), *Accounting for a Simplified Firm*. Scholars Book Co. (1979), pp. 11–33.

Tweedie, D. P., 'Cash Flows and Realizable Values: the Intuitive Concepts? An Empirical Test', *Accounting and Business Research* (Winter 1977), pp. 2–13.

Waldron, R., 'Reporting Cash Flow Measurement of Business Achievement and the Statement of Needs and Resources', *Accountancy*, forthcoming.

Winjum, J. O., *The Role of Accounting in the Economic Development of England 1500–1750*. Centre for International Education and Research (1972).

4 The cash flow performance of U.K. companies[1]

G H Lawson
Professor of Business Finance, Manchester Business School

Introduction: Cash Flow Accounting and Summary of Aggregate Data Analysis

This section outlines the rudiments of cash flow accounting and summarizes aggregate data analysis that is reported in detail elsewhere.[2]

The historic cost accounting performance of quoted companies in the U.K. manufacturing sector during the period 1954 to 1976 can be juxtaposed with their cash flow performance as in Table 4.1.

Table 4.1 *U.K. quoted Manufacturing Companies: Weighted Average Profits and Weighted Average Cash Flows 1954 to 1976 (see note (i)).*

	Historic cost	*Cash flows*	
Pre-tax profit	690	407	Entity earnings (see note (ii))
less interest	97	97	*less* interest
Pre-tax profit	593	310	Pre-tax equity earnings
Tax @ 44%	260	260	Effective equity tax burden @ 84% (see note (iii))
Post-tax profit	333	50	Post-tax equity earnings
Dividends (40%)	133	133	Dividends (net of new equity capital)
		26	Liquidity change
Retained earnings	200	(109)	(Debt-financed deficit)

Notes

(i) 23-year averages of profits and cash flows initially restated at base-year prices.
(ii) Operating cash flow minus net capital investment (see identity (2), page 81).
(iii) The effective entity tax burden in this example is 64%, namely, 260/407.

1 I am grateful to Professor J. M. Samuels for his criticisms of the previous draft of this paper which is based on work at the Manchester Business School during 1979 for the Cash Flow Accounting Sub-Committee of The Association of Certified Accountants. The main burden of the individual company analysis reported was undertaken by Keith Thompson and Kian Chin (MBS). Financial support from the SSRC, The Esmée Fairbairn Charitable Trust and The Association of Certified Accountants is gratefully acknowledged.

2 See Lawson (1979).

As virtually all the conclusions which emerge from this paper are concerned with the deviation between pre-tax historic cost profit and entity earnings, it is as well to mention the two components of this deviation at the outset. They are: (a) periodic working capital investment, that is, periodic change in (receivables plus inventories less payables) and; (b) a depreciation shortfall equal to periodic capital investment (net of displacements) *minus* periodic depreciation (including accounting profits or losses on assets displaced). The customary objection that this definition of a depreciation shortfall ignores the unexhausted benefits of periodic capital expenditure is accommodated in the analysis which follows.

In emphasizing that Table 4.1 is a multiperiod caricature of aggregate performance, at least two further qualifications should be entered. First, the twelve months' average time-lag between the charging of corporate taxes and the payment thereof has been ignored in Table 4.1 in order to draw the possible decision-making consequences of the deviation between pre-tax profit and entity earnings into sharper focus. In all analysis which follows this time-lag has been explicitly taken into account.

Secondly, and more important, the effective equity and entity rates of tax on cash flow earnings defined by Table 4.1 are approximations which tend to *understate* the average multiperiod rates of tax on pre-tax equity and entity (cash flow) earnings respectively. Since this proposition has such profound implications from both a corporate and public policy standpoint, and is also pertinent to most of the findings reported here, the basis of the true effective rate of tax on both entity and equity cash flow earnings first needs to be described in detail. It should also be noted that if, as depicted by Table 4.1, dividends persistently exceed post-tax equity earnings, the effective equity tax rate will, typically, be lower than the effective entity tax rate. This follows from the definitions of effective tax rates that are derived later in this section.

Cash Flow Accounting: Cash Flow Statements Expressed in Money Terms

A total cash flow statement for any year j can be expressed as:

$$(k_j - h_j) \pm B_j \pm N_j \pm M_j \equiv (A_j + R_j - Y_j) + F_j + t_j + D_j \pm H_j \qquad (1)$$

that is,

total cash inflows ≡ total cash outflows (including liquidity change)

where, in year j,

$k_j - h_j$ stands for operating cash flow, that is, cash, k_j, collected from customers *minus* cash, h_j, paid out to suppliers of all goods and services other than capital goods;

B_j is new capital received (+) from equity shareholders or repaid (−) thereto;

N_j is new medium/or long-term loans raised (+) or repaid (−);

M_j is the increase (+) or decrease (−) in bank overdrafts and/or short-term loans;

$A_j + R_j - Y_j$ represents net cash outlays on capital investment comprising replacements, A_j, growth investment, R_j, and displacements, Y_j;

F_j represents interest payments;

t_j is the corporate tax payment;

D_j is the dividend paid to shareholders; and,

H_j represents the increase (+) or decrease (−) in liquidity.

Any cash flow concept of periodic earnings must evidently be wholly, or partly, represented by some variant of the basic cash flow identity represented by (1) above. For example, re-arrangement of expression (1) gives

$$(k_j - h_j) - (A_j + R_j - Y_j) - t_j \mp H_j \equiv (F_j \mp N_j \mp M_j) + (D_j \mp B_j) \qquad (2)$$

that is,

$$\begin{matrix}\text{operating} & & \text{net} & & \text{tax} & & \text{liquidity} & & \text{lenders'} & & \text{shareholders'} \\ \text{cash} & - & \text{capital} & - & \text{payments} & \mp & \text{change} & \equiv & \text{cash} & + & \text{cash} \\ \text{flow} & & \text{investment} & & & & & & \text{flows} & & \text{flows}\end{matrix}$$

or,

periodic post-tax entity earnings[3] ≡ total distributions

Alternatively, and by analogy with the equity basis of accounting,

$$(k_j - h_j) - (A_j + R_j - Y_j) - F_j - t_j \mp H_j \equiv (D_j \mp B_j) \mp N_j \mp M_j \qquad (3)$$

that is,

$$\begin{matrix} & & \text{periodic} & & \text{periodic} \\ \text{periodic post-tax equity earnings} & \equiv & \text{shareholder} & \mp & \text{external} \\ \text{adjusted for periodic liquidity change} & & \text{cash} & & \text{debt} \\ & & \text{flows} & & \text{transactions}\end{matrix}$$

For completeness, periodic equity cash flows, $D_j \mp B_j$, that is, dividends minus (or plus) equity capital raised (or repaid) may be defined as:

$$D_j \mp B_j \equiv (k_j - h_j) - (A_j + R_j - Y_j) - F_j - t_j \mp H_j \pm N_j \pm M_j \qquad (4)$$

Cash Flow Accounting: Rates of Return and Effective Tax Rates

Making use of the foregoing identities; the respective 23 year *ex post*

3 Periodic pre-tax entity earnings can obviously take on positive or negative values depending upon the sizes (and signs) of the operating cash flow, $k_j - h_j$, and net investment, $A_j + R_j - Y_j$.

(aggregate) equity (r_e), debt (r_d) and entity (r) rates of return for the period covered by Table 4.1, p. 79, namely, 1954–76, may be defined as:

$$V_{53}^{(e)} = \sum_{j=1}^{23} \frac{D_j \pm B_j}{(1+r_e)^j} + \frac{V_{76}^{(e)}}{(1+r_e)^{23}} \tag{5}$$

$$= \sum_{j=1}^{23} \frac{(k_j - h_j) - (A_j + R_j - Y_j) - F_j - t_j \mp H_j \pm N_j \pm M_j}{(1+r_e)^j} + \frac{V_{76}^{(e)}}{(1+r_e)^{23}} \tag{5a}$$

$$V_{53}^{(d)} = \sum_{j=1}^{23} \frac{F_j \pm N_j \pm M_j}{(1+r_d)^j} + \frac{V_{76}^{(d)}}{(1+r_d)^{23}} \tag{6}$$

and,

$$V_{53}^{(e)} + V_{53}^{(d)} = \sum_{j=1}^{23} \frac{(D_j \pm B_j) + (F_j \pm N_j \pm M_j)}{(1+r)^j} + \frac{V_{76}^{(e)} + V_{76}^{(d)}}{(1+r)^{23}} \tag{7}$$

$$= \sum_{j=1}^{23} \frac{(k_j - h_j) - (A_j + R_j - Y_j) - t_j \mp H_j}{(1+r)^j} + \frac{V_{76}^{(e)} + V_{76}^{(d)}}{(1+r)^{23}} \tag{7a}$$

where,

$$V_{53}^{(e)}, V_{53}^{(d)}, \text{ and } V_{76}^{(e)}, V_{76}^{(d)}$$

represent the end-year 1953 and end-year 1976 aggregate market values of equity and debt respectively.[4]

It follows from the previous five equations, which represent the universally acknowledged methods of calculating (observable) proprietorship rates of return, that the effective *ex post* rates of tax on entity and equity cash flow earnings (for the 23-year period in question) are defined by T and T_e in equations (8) and (9) respectively.

$$V_{53}^{(e)} + V_{53}^{(d)} = \sum_{j=1}^{23} \frac{[(k_j - h_j) - (A_j + R_j - Y_j) \mp H_j](1 - T)}{(1+r)^j} + \frac{V_{76}^{(e)} + V_{76}^{(d)}}{(1+r_e)^{23}} \tag{8}$$

4 The end-year 0 and end-year 23 entity values may be assumed to embody the unexhausted benefits of assets (and outstanding debt) at those respective year ends. This argument is developed at length in Lawson (1979). (See p. 83 *et seq.*).

$$V_{53}^{(e)} = \sum_{j=1}^{23} \frac{[(k_j - h_j) - (A_j + R_j - Y_j) - F_j \mp H_j \pm N_j \pm M_j](1 - T_e)}{(1 + r_e)^j} + \frac{V_{76}^{(e)}}{(1 + r_e)^{23}} \quad (9)$$

The entry and exit values, $V_{53}^{(e)}$ and $V_{76}^{(e)}$, can be regarded as 'net of tax' market values since they represent the (observable) present value of a taxed expected equity cash flow stream at end-years 53 and 76 respectively.[5]

Equation (8) can be re-written:

$$V_{53}^{(e)} + V_{53}^{(d)} = (1 - T) \sum_{j=1}^{23} \frac{(k_j - h_j) - (A_j + R_j - Y_j) \mp H_j}{(1 + r)^j} + \frac{V_{76}^{(e)} + V_{76}^{(d)}}{(1 + r)^{23}} \quad (8a)$$

Substituting $$\sum_{j=1}^{23} [(k_j - h_j) - (A_j + R_j - Y_j) \mp H_j - t_j]\,(1 + r)^{-j}$$

for $$V_{53}^{(e)} + V_{53}^{(d)} - \{V_{76}^{(e)} + V_{76}^{(d)}\}\,(1 + r)^{-23}$$

$$T = \frac{\sum_{j=1}^{23} t_j(1 + r)^{-j}}{\sum_{j=1}^{23} [(k_j - h_j) - (A_j + R_j - Y_j) \mp H_j]\,(1 + r)^{-j}} \quad (10)$$

5 Although not needed for the analysis which follows, the corresponding pre-tax entry and exit values may be defined as:

$$V_{53}^{(e)}/\{1 - \tilde{T}_e^{(53)}\} \quad \text{and} \quad V_{76}^{(e)}/\{1 - \tilde{T}_e^{(76)}\}$$

where $\tilde{T}_e^{(53)}$ and $\tilde{T}_e^{(76)}$ denote expected tax rates as at end-years 1953 and 1976 respectively. This proposition can be elaborated as follows. In the absence of taxes, the observable end-year 0 market value, P_0, of an expected perpetual income stream, $\tilde{x}_1, \tilde{x}_2, \ldots,$ may be defined as:

$$P_0 = \sum_{j=1}^{n} \frac{\tilde{x}_j}{(1 + \tilde{r})^j} + \frac{\tilde{P}_n}{(1 + \tilde{r})^n} \text{ where } \tilde{P}_n = \sum_{j=n+1}^{\infty} \frac{\tilde{x}_j}{(1 + \tilde{r})^j}$$

and $\tilde{r}$ denotes a cost of capital that is commensurate with the risk characterizing the income stream in question. If the expected cash flows, $\tilde{x}_j$, are now assumed to be taxable, the position changes to:

$$V_0 = \sum_{j=1}^{n} \frac{\tilde{x}_j(1 - \tilde{T})}{(1 + \tilde{r})^j} + \frac{\tilde{V}_n}{(1 + \tilde{r})^n}$$

where, $V_0 = P_0(1 - \tilde{T})$ and $\tilde{V}_n = \tilde{P}_n(1 - \tilde{T})$ and $\tilde{T}$ is the expected rate of tax.

Similarly, equation (9) can be re-written as:

$$V_{53}^{(e)} = (1 - T_e) \sum_{j=1}^{23} \frac{D_j \pm B_j + t_j}{(1 + r_e)^j} + \frac{V_{76}^{(e)}}{(1 + r_e)^{23}} \tag{9a}$$

which, after substituting $\sum_{j=1}^{23} (D_j \pm B_j)(1 + r_e)^{-j}$ for $V_{53}^{(e)} - V_{76}^{(e)}(1 + r_e)^{-23}$

yields

$$T_e = \frac{\sum_{j=1}^{23} t_j(1 + r_e)^{-j}}{\sum_{j=1}^{23} (D_j \pm B_j + t_j)(1 + r_e)^{-j}} \tag{11}$$

Generally speaking, the expressions for T and T_e that are defined by equations (10) and (11) are very accurately approximated by:

$$T = \frac{\sum_{j=1}^{23} t_j}{\sum_{j=1}^{23} [(k_j - h_j) - (A_j + R_j - Y_j) \mp H_j]} \tag{12}$$

and,

$$T_e = \frac{\sum_{j=1}^{23} t_j}{\sum_{j=1}^{23} (D_j + B_j + t_j)} \tag{13}$$

This is an important result[6] since it facilitates the calculation of T and T_e when, because of (sufficiently strong) multiple sign-changes, equations (8) and (9) yield multiple or indeterminate real values for r and r_e. In the latter

6 Its robustness can readily be tested by computing equations (10) and (11) for a large range of positive and negative values for r and r_e, respectively. The rare cases in which the values of T and T_e yielded by equations (12) and (13) do not accurately approximate the respective values yielded by (10) and (11) are due to multiple sign changes in cash flows which ultimately result in inconsistencies between the signs of the right-hand sides of equations (10) and (12) and between those of the right-hand sides of (11) and (13).

A clue as to why (12) and (13) are good approximations of (10) and (11) respectively, is to be found in equations (5a) and (7a). Using equation (7a); if $V_{53}^{(e)} + V_{53}^{(d)} = V_{76}^{(e)} + V_{76}^{(d)}$

circumstances, equations (10) and (11) can obviously not be solved for T and T_e.[7]

The effective tax rates T, T_e, of the companies whose performances are reported in this paper are, in fact, computed on two bases. First, as illustrated in Table 4.1 and, thereafter, in accordance with equations (12) and (13) respectively.[8] The tendency for the former method of calculation to understate the latter is ascribable to the fact that the cash flow earnings defined by Table 4.1 ignore periodic liquidity changes, $\pm H_j$. As indicated by equations (8) to (11) (inclusive), such changes should clearly be taken into account.

Aggregate Data: Analysis and Conclusions

If, as is indeed the case, Table 4.1 accurately reflects the main features of the 1954–76 financial performance and financial behaviour of U.K. manufacturing companies then, at this level of aggregation:

(i) effective interest covers were much lower than those perceived by lenders;
(ii) companies suffered enormous fiscal drag;
(iii) dividends were significantly uncovered; and,
(iv) the resultant deficit-financing by lenders caused a substantial increase in debt levels, i.e. debt-equity substitution has taken place.

Other things being equal, the substitution of debt for equity will result in an increase in the value of debt and, tax effects aside, an equal reduction in the market value of equity. The substantial decline in the (real) market value of equity that has taken place in the U.K. since April 1965 has not been offset by an equal increase in the market value of debt.[9] The debt-equity substitution argument therefore needs to be supplemented with something else, for example, a decline in the quality of entity earnings[10] and/or confiscatory taxation.

---

and if $\{(k_j - h_j) - (A_j + R_j - Y_j) \mp H_j\}$ and t_j are all constants then,

$$r = \frac{(k_j - h_j) - (A_j + R_j - Y_j) \mp H_j - t_j}{V_{53}^{(e)} + V_{53}^{(d)}}$$

$$= \frac{[(k_j - h_j) - (A_j + R_j - Y_j) \mp H_j](1 - T)}{V_{53}^{(e)} + V_{53}^{(d)}}$$

whence, $$T = \frac{t_j}{(k_j - h_j) - (A_j + R_j - Y_j) \mp H_j}$$

7 It may also be noted that since (12) and (13) are approximations for (10) and (11) respectively, T and T_e explicitly allow for the unexhausted benefits of capital expenditure.

8 See p. 95.

9 See Lawson and Stark (1981).

10 Lawson (1979).

The enormous deviations between the historic cost and cash flow magnitudes shown in Table 4.1 prompts one to question whether, like lenders, the British Treasury and company directorates, the market has also been fooled by the historic cost accounting model.

The time-series relationship between income gearing[11] and equity earnings on the one hand, and the behaviour of the de Zoete Equity Index (expressed in real terms) on the other, suggests that a combination of low equity earnings and high income gearing is, relatively speaking, usually associated with a low end-year equity index value and vice versa. This raised the presumption that the data may afford at least a rough-and-ready statistical test of the following semi-strong version of the efficient market hypothesis.[12]

In forming its expectations about future dividends, the market uncovers a company's past and current underlying cash flow situation and, using all other relevant known and knowable information, derives estimates of *ex ante* cash flows. This, in turn, leads to the determination of share prices.

To test this hypothesis, the following multiple regression (adaptive expectations) model was used:

$$EI_j = x_1 + x_2\, ECFE_j + x_3\, ECFE_{j-1} - x_4\, CV_{(j,j-3)} \qquad \text{(I)}$$

where,

EI_j denotes the (January 1) level of the de Zoete cost of living-adjusted equity price index for year j;

$ECFE_j$ denotes post-tax equity cash flow earnings as defined by Table 4.1 in year j;[13] and,

$CV_{(j,j-3)}$ represents the coefficient of variation of the past four years equity cash flow earnings about their four-year mean.

The previous year's *ECFE* is used as a proxy for the expected value of equity cash flow earnings estimated by the market in the individual year in question. The coefficient of variation, *CV*, is a proxy for the degree of risk which characterizes expected equity cash flow earnings which, in turn, may be assumed to be a function of the volatility of post-tax entity income and of the expected income gear ratio.

11 Interest divided by entity earnings (as defined in Table 4.1).

12 The test is rough-and-ready because aggregate data are basically unsuitable for the task. Thus, the accounts for each individual company included in the sample are for accounting years which end between 6 April of the year shown and 5 April in the following year. The aggregated accounts for the years shown therefore span a period of 24 months. For example, a company making up its accounts to 10 April 1954 would be included in the year 1954, as would a company reporting on a financial year ending 31 March 1955. Each individual sample year therefore includes accounts for the last nine months of the previous calendar year and for the first three months of the succeeding calendar year.

13 Whereas *EI* is the level of the index on 1 January, *ECFE* denotes earnings aggregated over a two-year period ending three months later (see previous footnote).

A trend in both the *EI* and *ECFE* series could give spurious correlation in the data and lead to misleading statistical results. To avoid this, the raw data were differenced[14] and the resultant series was used for statistical testing. Differencing does not change the model—the model indicates the change over the year which, together with last year's absolute figure, gives this year's actual value for the series.

In that the suggested model explains about 60 per cent of the movements in *EI*, it stands up quite well to the data. The results (using the backshift operator) are:

$$(1-B)EI_j = 3.142 + 0.0744(1-B)ECFE_j + 0.0385(1-B)ECFE_{j-1} - 19.15(1-B)CV_{(j,j-3)}$$

(st. errors)	0.0159	0.0163	15.13
(*t* ratio)	4.675	2.364	1.266

R-squared = 0.6012; Durbin-Watson statistic = 2.043;
Degrees of freedom 18–3; F test = 8.70.

Having established the model, it was further tested on random samples of the data points. The results were encouraging in that only the constant varied substantially (its range was 32 to −4) and the *R*-squared was always above 0.58.

The above cash flow hypothesis may be tested indirectly by regressing an equity price index expressed *in money terms* on the historic cost accounting variables corresponding to those included on the right-hand side of equation (I). Such a model is:

$$EI(\mathrm{m})_j = x_1 + x_2\,HCP_j + x_3\,HCP_{j-1} - x_4\,CV_{(j,j-3)} \qquad \text{(II)}$$

where,

$EI(\mathrm{m})_j$ denotes the level of de Zoete equity price index (on January 1) expressed in money terms for year *j*;

HCP_j stands for actual historic cost profit (i.e. not re-expressed at base year prices) for year *j*; and,

$CV_{(j,j-3)}$ represents the coefficient of variation of the past four years' historic cost profits about their four-year mean.

The results yielded by model II are counter-intuitive. That is to say, the signs preceding the second, third and fourth coefficients are the wrong way

14 Differencing means that the change in the series over the year is used instead of the absolute value. This is represented by the backshift operator, *B*, where $(1-B)X_j = X_j - X_{j-1}$, the difference over the year in series X_j.

about. They are:

$$(1-B)EI(m)_j = 106.94 - 0.085\,(1-B)HCP_j - 0.701\,(1-B)HCP_{j-1} + 777.02(1-B)CV_{(j,j-3)}$$

(st. errors)	0.1955	0.21404	1118.1
(t-values)	0.433	3.276	0.695

R-squared = 0.3162; Durbin-Watson statistic = 2.836;
Degrees of freedom 18 – 3; F test = 3.62.

It is tempting to conclude that cash-flow data re-expressed in terms of a base-year price level constitute highly relevant information for stock market investors, and that historic cost accounts *per se* are apparently ignored by the market whilst being taken seriously by lenders, company directorates and the tax authorities.

Analysis of Individual Company Data

As already noted, the relative orders of magnitude shown in the right-hand column of Table 4.1 reveal the weighted average cash flow performance of U.K. quoted manufacturing companies during 1954–76. The extent of the dispersion about this average across companies is clearly of interest. To reveal dispersion, the accounts of nine of the companies that are included in the F.T. 30 share index were restated on a multiperiod cash flow basis in both money and real terms. The companies selected and the inclusive years covered are:

Blue Circle	(1959–77)	Bowater	(1961–78)	John Brown	(1965–79)
Coats Patons	(1962–78)	Dunlop	(1960–78)	E.M.I.	(1961–78)
I.C.I.	(1961–78)	Plessey	(1963–79)	Tesco	(1960–79)

The analyses of their cash flows, restated at December 1978 prices, are summarized in Table 4.2.

To supplement the individual company (multiperiod) cash flow analyses, their annual (equity) market values were ascertained and, like the cash flows, restated at a base-year price level. The ultimate aim was the formulation of a multiple regression model which, it was hoped, would explain the serial behaviour of a company's equity market value in terms of its equity cash performance.

An indication of the behaviour of the total (real) market values (debt plus equity) of the nine companies over the respective observation periods is provided by Table 4.3, which also shows the real rates of return they generated for their lenders and shareholders.

Digression on the Specification Problem

In formulating a model that is intended to relate a company's stock market performance to its cash flow performance, at least two problems are

Table 4.2 *Average Annual Cash Flow Performance of 9 U.K. Companies Restated at December 1978 Prices*

	Bowater 1961/78 £m	*John Brown 1965/79 £m*	*Coats Patons 1962/78 £m*	*Dunlop 1960/78 £m*	*E.M.I. 1961/78 £m*	*I.C.I. 1961/78 £m*	*Plessey 1963/79 £m*	*Tesco 1960/79 £m*	*Blue Circle 1959/77 £m*	
1. Entity earnings	+21.98	+4.65	+38.97	+30.73	+ 4.79	+203.55	+15.07	+11.79	+26.73	$(k_j-h_j)-(A_j+R_j-Y_j)$
2. *Less* interest	−25.82	−2.74	−10.26	−26.31	− 8.97	− 84.94	− 8.30	− 0.08	− 6.82	F_j
3. Pre-tax equity earnings	− 3.84	+1.91	+28.71	+ 4.42	− 4.18	+118.61	+ 6.77	+11.71	+19.91	
4. Tax paid	−26.90	−2.60	−31.38	−32.89	−18.78	−169.78	−21.41	− 7.87	−19.83	t_j
5. Payments to minorities	− 2.14	−0.49	− 0.47	+ 1.42	− 1.19	− 0.22	+ 0.27	+ 0.18	− 1.19	
6. Post-tax equity earnings	−32.88	−1.18	− 3.14	−27.05	−24.15	− 51.39	−14.37	+ 4.02	− 1.11	
7. Dividend payments*	+ 8.26	−0.70	−12.28	− 1.41	+ 9.22	− 42.83	+ 7.04	− 1.87	− 7.01	$D_j \mp B_j$
8. Increase in cash	− 7.86	−1.72	− 0.51	− 3.27	− 3.58	− 67.72	− 1.73	− 2.75	− 2.65	H_j
9. Deficit(−) surplus(+)	−32.48	−3.60	−15.93	−31.73	−18.51	−161.94	− 9.06	− 0.60	−10.77	
Financed by:										
10. Bank overdraft	+12.82	+2.56	+ 7.85	+14.19	+ 4.06	+136.33	+ 5.06	+ 0.07	+ 3.13	M_j
11. Loan capital	+19.65	+1.07	+ 8.05	+17.55	+14.42	+ 25.66	+ 3.98	+ 0.53	+ 7.65	N_j

* Net of equity capital raised or repaid.

Table 4.3 *Market Values and Internal Rates of Return at December 1978 Prices*

	Opening values			*Closing values*			*Rates of Return*[1]		
	Debt £m	*Equity £m*	*Entity £m*	*Debt £m*	*Equity £m*	*Entity £m*	*Debt*[2] *%*	*Equity*[3] *%*	*Entity %*
Bowater	228	468	696	258	293	551	−5.3	− 5.4	− 5.2
John Brown	0	89	89	12	98	110	*	+ 1.6	+ 0.6
Coats Patons	27	460	487	57	203	260	−8.3	+ 3.0	− 2.4
Dunlop	87	224	311	236	103	339	−2.4	− 3.5	− 2.9
E.M.I.	17	179	196	146	156	302	−5.0	− 6.1	− 5.7
I.C.I.	281	3670	3951	750	2205	2955	−9.9	− 1.3	− 3.0
Plessey	61	230	291	56	195	251	−4.1	− 1.9	− 2.8
Tesco	1	10	10	10	221	231	−6.6	+18.5	+18.0
Blue Circle	8	416	424	86	202	288	−2.6	− 1.4	− 1.6

1. Computed in accordance with equations (5), (6) and (7).
2. Net of tax on interest payments at the rate of 23 per cent.
3. Net of tax on dividend payments at the standard rate of income tax.

* Indeterminate.

encountered which do not appear to arise in the analysis of aggregate data. The one problem concerns the unexhausted benefits of capital expenditure whereas the other relates to the distinction between portfolio risk and individual company risk.

Total Risk and Market Risk

Following the capital-asset pricing model, the total and market risks of the market portfolio (or some sensible proxy therefor) are synonymous. It is reasonable to measure multiperiod market portfolio risk with the (moving) coefficient of variation of its (cash flow) earnings stream (as illustrated by model I above, p. 86) which by definition will not include market value changes. Hence, if this coefficient of variation is seen to change over time, it is being assumed that portfolio risk is changing over time.

In the case of the individual company, the distinction between total risk and market risk is, according to the CAPM, of the essence. Thus, share prices will apparently only compensate for the risk which cannot be diversified away. Now in that a company's market risk (beta) coefficient is dimensionless, i.e. measured in relation to a normalized market portfolio risk of unity, a substantial change in the variance of the returns to the market portfolio may have little effect on a company's beta coefficient.

Recall the CAPM formulation of a company's (single-period) cost of capital, $\tilde{r}_e$, namely:

$$\tilde{r}_e = i + (\tilde{r}_m - i)\beta_e$$

where (everything measured in real terms)

i is the single-period risk-free interest rate,

$\tilde{r}_m$ is the expected one-period rate of return on the market portfolio, and,

β_e is the covariance of the rates of return on the market portfolio and company e divided by the variance of the expected rate of return on the market portfolio.

It would therefore appear that a change in the market portfolio risk will primarily affect an individual security's risk and, therefore, its price, by changing the magnitude of the excess return, $\tilde{r}_m - i$. This mechanism would involve a change in the level of share prices in response to the market's view that earnings had undergone a quality change and, in turn, would, given the market portfolio expected earnings stream, result in a change in the expected rate of return on the market portfolio.

Whereas the derivation of 'moving' coefficients of variation from *ex post* market portfolio earnings data is realistic, the derivation of a sequence of excess returns, $r_m - i$, is not. Portfolio price adjustments in response to continuous serial changes (in the same direction) in portfolio earnings risk result in *ex post* periodic rates of return, r_m, which are seemingly perverse. Hence, *ex post* values of $r_m - i$ ought not to be used for proxying $\tilde{r}_m - i$. A way around this problem does, however, suggest itself.

In that the expected excess, $\tilde{r}_m - i$, is a function of market portfolio risk, the coefficient of variation of market portfolio earnings can reasonably be used as a proxy therefor. This still leaves the question of what to do about the company's beta coefficient itself. If betas are stable over time, there would appear to be no problem. Here we use the betas that are published by the London Business School (1979).

Unexhausted Benefits of Capital Expenditure

The unexpired benefits of capital expenditure are apparently ignored when, as in Table 4.1, equity cash flow earnings, $ECFE_j$, are defined either as:

$$ECFE_j = (k_j - h_j) - (A_j + R_j - Y_j) - F_j - t_j$$[15]

or in accordance with identity (3), p. 81, *ante*.

The unexpired benefits of capital expenditure are expectations which can be assumed to be impounded in the market values of a company's debt and equity. In measuring multiperiod *ex post* performance on a cash flow basis the latter values should therefore be taken into account.[16] In using an adaptive expectations model to explain the serial relationship between cash flow performance and market value, growth capital expenditure, R_j, is an

15 These symbols were defined earlier in section 1.

16 As already noted, equations (5) to (9) (inclusive) exemplify rate of return calculations which account for the unexpired benefits of capital expenditure via entry and exit values. Corresponding absolute performance measures are elaborated in Lawson (1979), which contains a fuller discussion of the treatment of capital expenditure in cash flow accounting.

appropriate proxy for the effect on market value of the unexpired benefits of capital expenditure. Thus, it can be argued, replacement expenditure, A_j, is primarily intended to maintain existing earning power intact whereas growth expenditure creates additional earning power. If R_j is invested in new projects promising positive net present values, a company's market value will, in efficient stock markets, respond immediately thereto.

At the aggregate level, the distinction between A_j and R_j is possibly of much lesser importance because total capital expenditure is, under the effect of cross-section averaging, much more stable over time.

Individual Company Regression Model

In attempting to explain an individual company's share price behaviour in terms of its cash flow performance, whilst allowing for both risk and unexpired capital expenditure, models III and IV were used.

$$P_j = x_1 + x_2 ECFE_j + x_3 ECFE_{j-1} - x_4 CV^{(m)}_{(j,j-3)} \cdot \beta_e \pm x_5 H_j + x_6 R_j \qquad \text{(III)}$$

where,

P_j is the level of the company's share price in year j restated at a base-year price level;

$ECFE_j$ denotes the company's cash flow earnings for year j;

$CV^{(m)}_{(j,j-3)}$ represents the coefficient of variation of the past four years' 'market portfolio' equity earnings about their four-year mean;

β_e stands for the beta coefficient of the individual company in question;

H_j denotes change in the company's cash balance in year j; and

R_j represents the company's growth capital expenditure in year j which was in turn estimated from $A_j + R_j - 1.25\ L_j$, where L_j is the depreciation charge published in year j.

The results for I.C.I. derived from model III are:

variable	*coefficient*	*st. errors*	*t ratio*
$ECFE_j$	0.031	1.45	0.02
$ECFE_{j-1}$	−1.743	1.24	−1.40
$CV^{(m)}_{(j,j-3)}\beta_e$	−1.42	48.09	−2.98
H_j	−0.371	1.76	−0.211
R_j	0.462	1.30	0.357
constant	1713.8	116.94	14.655

R-squared 0.39; Durbin-Watson statistic 1.183
degrees of freedom 16; F test = 3.04.

These results show that only the constant and the coefficient of variation were significant and even then the R^2, Durbin-Watson and *F*-values suggest that their relevance may be slight.

As both $CV^{(m)}_{(j,j-3)}$ and P_j display trends that are strong enough to render the series unusable for statistical purposes, it was necessary to introduce a dummy variable (0 to 1972 and 1, thereafter) to cause P_j to be stationary. The H_j, $ECFE_j$ and R_j series are sufficiently stationary and need not be transformed. The results with the dummy variable were:

variable	*coefficient*	*st. errors*	*t ratio*
$ECFE_j$	0.588	1.23	0.48
$CV^{(m)}_{(j,j-3)}\beta_e$	−28.4	85.54	0.34
H_j	2.06	1.38	1.497
R_j	0.704	1.03	0.69
constant	1709.3	87.03	19.64
dummy	−764.6	246.35	3.104

R-squared 0.59; Durbin-Watson statistic 1.691.

These results represent no improvement and the $CV^{(m)}_{(j,j-3)}$ has become virtually unimportant.

Model IV was the same as model III except that $CV^{(m)}_{(j,j-3)}$ was replaced with the corresponding coefficient of variation for the individual company in question. In this case, all series were stationary except the P_j series itself.

As with model III, the regressions were tried with and without dummy variables in an attempt to reveal the effects of non-stationarity. The results are:

without dummy: R-squared = 0; Durbin-Watson statistic = 0.834; all t-values less than 1.

with dummy:

variable	*coefficient*	*st. errors*	*t ratio*
ECF_j	0.967	1.29	0.752
$CV^{(m)}_{(j,j-3)}\beta_e$	−0.312	14.33	0.022
H_j	1.427	1.22	1.165
R_j	0.857	1.12	0.765
constant	1719.0	116.21	14.792
dummy	−777.9	169.38	4.59

R-squared 0.60.

The low t-values indicate that the model is unusable in its present form. This being the case, it was not tested with the data for the other companies.

Alternative specifications are to be tried in the future. As there is a stronger visual correlation between the equity cash flows of individual companies and their equity market values than between the latter and historic cost profits, there is a presumption that the appropriate model will be a cash flow specification. But if any model is to provide a convincing explanation of the relationship between performance measured in accordance with some accounting method and stock market performance, it will need to take cognizance of post-tax earnings, risk and debt-equity substitution.

Financial Analysis of the Data

Interest Cover

The interest cover ratios (reflecting legal commitments to lenders) that may be derived from Table 4.2 show that, over the periods in question, effective interest covers fell well short of what is regarded as normality among lending institutions (see Table 4.4, below). To the extent that the decisions to lend to the nine companies in question were based on historic cost interest cover yardsticks, this outcome was virtually inevitable.

In that the stock appreciation tax reliefs that were introduced in November 1974 have lessened the pressure on corporate financial viability, the interest cover ratios that have emerged since that date are of particular significance. These are separately indicated in Table 4.4.

Table 4.4 *Interest Cover Ratios*

Inclusive years		*% of Interest Covered (see note)*	*% of Interest Covered since 1974*
1961–78	Bowater	85	159
1965–79	John Brown	170	280
1962–78	Coats Patons	380	482
1960–78	Dunlop	117	105
1961–78	E.M.I.	53	158
1961–78	I.C.I.	240	204
1963–79	Plessey	182	304
1960–79	Tesco	∞	∞
1959–79	Blue Circle	392	528

Note
Derived from Table 4.2 (row 1 divided by row 2).

In six of the nine cases, interest cover ratios have strengthened since 1974. Those of I.C.I. and Dunlop have deteriorated. Except for Coats Patons and Blue Circle, the post-1974 values shown in Table 4.4 are much lower than the conventional interest cover yardsticks derived from the published accounts. Moreover, as discussed in the concluding section, the joint effect of interest and tax commitments is the crucial consideration in assessing a company's financial viability.

Effective Tax Rates

As the analysis outlined at the beginning implies, (effective) corporate tax rates may reflect either equity or entity concepts of cash flow income. The equity approach treats interest payments as a tax-deductible expense and, holding clearly in view the legal nature of loan commitments, provides some indication of the effect of taxes on corporate financial viability.

Columns (2) and (3) of Table 4.5 show the average effective rates of tax (calculated in accordance with Table 4.1 and equation (13) respectively) on

Table 4.5 *Effective Rates of Tax on Equity Earnings*

				Since 1974	
(1) Inclusive years		*(2) (see note i) %*	*(3) (see note ii) %*	*(4) (see note iii) %*	*(5) (see note iv) %*
1961–78	Bowater	∞	144	177	109
1965–79	John Brown	136	79	16	1766
1962–78	Coats Patons	109	72	66	76
1960–78	Dunlop	744	96	1816	104
1961–78	E.M.I.	∞	196	282	140
1961–78	I.C.I.	143	80	146	94
1963–79	Plessey	316	149	91	89
1960–79	Tesco	67	81	51	59
1959–79	Blue Circle	100	74	53	71

Notes

(i) Computed in accordance with Table 4.1 and derived from Table 4.2 (row 4 ÷ row 3).

(ii) Computed in accordance with equation (13) and derived from Table 4.2 [row 4 ÷ (row 4 + row 7)].

(iii) Computed as in column (2) above using only the post-1974 data included in Table 4.2.

(iv) Computed as in column (3) above using only the post-1974 data included in Table 4.2.

the equity cash flow earnings of the nine companies in the sample for the inclusive years indicated in column (1). Columns (2) and (3) both suggest that the U.K. corporate tax system virtually confiscated equity earnings.[17] If so, dividends (net of new equity raised) could only have been paid out of new debt.

Although the tax burden on equity cash flows may have fallen slightly since 1974, it still appears to be confiscatory at the equity level in the cases of Bowater, Dunlop, E.M.I. and I.C.I.

It is arguable that if company cash flow performances are restated at a base-year price level, i.e. in real terms, the (gross) interest payments

17 In that all nine companies generated a significant proportion of their income abroad, this proposition should be qualified accordingly.

disclosed in Table 4.2 mainly represent the repayment of lenders' capital. Thus, leaving aside the fact that corporate debt is not risk free and that interest payments therefore embody a risk premium, corporate taxable capacity should, so the argument runs, be measured on an entity basis. There is, however, a counter-argument, namely, that an effective equity tax rate calculated in accordance with equation (11) fully allows for repayments of lenders' capital which amounts are reflected in share values.[18] Be this as it may, an entity concept of taxable capacity is justifiable in its own right. That is to say, an undertaking's taxable capacity ought to be independent of the manner in which that undertaking is financed.

The proposition that (gross) interest payments represent the repayment of lenders' capital should be qualified in respect of personal taxes. The evidence suggests that lenders shift their personal taxes forward into the interest rate.[19] If so, such taxes become a charge on entity earnings and should be added to corporate tax payments. Such an adjustment, using a 23 per cent personal tax rate, is included in Table 4.6.[20]

Table 4.6 *Effective Rates of Tax on Entity Earnings (Corporate Tax adjusted for Tax on Interest)*

				Since 1974	
(1) Inclusive years		*(2) (see note i) %*	*(3) (see note ii) %*	*(4) (see note iii) %*	*(5) (see note iv) %*
1961–78	Bowater	149	233	80	95
1965–79	John Brown	69	110	19	352
1962–78	Coats Patons	86	88	57	63
1960–78	Dunlop	127	142	105	143
1961–78	E.M.I.	435	1723	118	143
1961–78	I.C.I.	93	139	86	146
1963–79	Plessey	155	175	68	80
1960–79	Tesco	67	87	51	76
1959–79	Blue Circle	80	89	47	72

Notes

(i) Computed in accordance with Table 4.1, note (iii), and derived from Table 4.2, i.e., [row 4 + (0.23) (row 2)] ÷ row 1.

(ii) Computed in accordance with equation (12) and derived from Table 4.2, i.e., [row 4 + (0.23) (row 2)] ÷ (row 1 – row 8).

(iii) Computed as in column (2) above using only the post-1974 data included in Table 4.2.

(iv) Computed as in column (3) above using only the post-1974 data included in Table 4.2.

18 See Lawson (1979).

19 Stapleton and Burke (1978).

20 Judging from the evidence cited in Stapleton and Burke, 23 per cent is a conservative estimate of the tax shifted forward into interest rates.

The effective entity tax rates shown in columns (2) and (3) of Table 4.6 provide compelling evidence of the confiscatory character of the corporate tax regimes that have operated in the U.K. in the last two decades. Moreover, the values in columns (4) and (5) of this table strongly contradict the new conventional wisdom to the effect that the 1974 stock appreciation relief has roughly eliminated the effects of inflation on taxable earnings.[21]

In concluding this discussion of corporate taxes, reference is made to the popular view that the only corporation tax paid by companies is the advance corporation tax that is simultaneously payable with dividends. As Table 4.2 suggests, and as is confirmed by an examination of the individual years' data since 1974, the ACT paid by all nine companies has represented only a small fraction of their total corporate tax burdens.

Dividend Cover

A comparison of lines 6 and 7 in Table 4.2 suggests that Tesco alone succeeded in covering its average dividend payment over the years in question. The shareholders of Bowater, E.M.I. and Plessey were net cash flow contributors over the respective 18-, 18- and 17-year periods analysed. Assessing dividend cover on the assumption that 77 per cent of interest paid represented the repayment of lenders' capital, John Brown and Tesco covered their dividends from internally-generated finance.

In assessing the degree of debt-equity substitution that resulted from uncovered dividends, periodic liquidity changes are also a pertinent consideration. To the extent that periodic liquidity changes reflect transactions and precautionary motives, they constitute an investment (or disinvestment) of the same character as inventory changes. Like the unexhausted benefits of capital expenditure, inventories and cash balances can be assumed to be impounded in a company's market value. It may, therefore, be contended that liquidity changes should be accounted for in a multiperiod cash flow statement in much the same manner as capital investment. On this argument, all nine companies engaged in (dividend-induced) debt-equity substitution (on average every year) over the respective periods considered and, except for Tesco, whose average dividend was only 32 per cent debt-financed, wholly financed their dividends with debt.[22] If dividend policy is an active decision variable and is based on historic cost profits, such debt-equity substitution is the predictable outcome mentioned at the outset. Whilst the level of debt-raising was trivial in Tesco's case, the changes in the relative market values of debt and equity (shown in Table 4.3 above) are generally consistent with a signifi-

21 This view was recently reiterated by the Governor of the Bank of England (1979).

22 Treating 77 per cent of interest as the repayment of lenders' capital and taking dividends net of new equity raised.

cant degree of debt-equity substitution stemming from uncovered dividend payments.

Since 1974, the shareholders of Bowater, John Brown, Dunlop and E.M.I. have been net cash contributors and these companies have, on average, also raised debt in each year during the period. The dividends paid to the shareholders of Coats Patons, I.C.I., Plessey, Tesco and Blue Circle were debt-financed to the extent of 29, 100, 100, 41 and 89 per cent respectively.

Market Values

The entity market values of Bowater, Coats Patons, I.C.I., Plessey and Blue Circle declined in real terms over the periods considered. In the cases of Coats Patons, I.C.I. and Blue Circle real debt levels rose significantly causing a reverse leverage effect on their equity market values. The percentage declines in the latter were 28, 54 and 40 per cent for Coats Patons, I.C.I. and Blue Circle respectively. Notwithstanding net cash flow contributions from their respective shareholders, there were real declines in the market values of both debt and equity in the cases of Bowater and Plessey.

The real increase in the entity market value of E.M.I. must be qualified by the fact that its shareholders were net cash contributors over the 18 year observation period. Notwithstanding this equity cash injection, its equity market value declined by 13 per cent in real terms.

The entity market values of the three remaining companies, namely, John Brown, Dunlop and Tesco, increased in real terms. In the cases of John Brown and Tesco, the real market values of both debt and equity showed increases. In Dunlop's case, an increase in entity market value was associated with a 271 per cent increase in the market value of its debt and a 54 per cent decline in the market value of its equity which, in 1978, constituted 30 per cent of its total market value.

Taking cognizance of the debt ratios of Bowater, Dunlop and E.M.I., expressed on a market value basis, it is reasonable to question whether these companies may not be geared to precarious levels. Their debt levels constituted 47, 70 and 48 per cent of their respective entity values at their 1978 financial year ends.

Implicit in the foregoing paragraphs, and in the discussion in the earlier sections, is the proposition that (real) multiperiod cash flow analyses and (real) changes in market values are integrally related. Viewed on its own, the multiperiod cash flow analysis understates the financial performance of four of the companies in the sample and overstates it in the case of the other five. The degree of profitability achieved by the nine companies over the respective (roughly 18-year) periods considered is more decisively indicated by the real rates of return shown in Table 4.3 above. On these criteria, shareholders did slightly better than lenders, and only Tesco and John Brown were profitable as entities over the period as a whole.

Conclusions

It should finally be questioned whether the combination of interest and taxes that is borne by U.K. companies is a dangerous threat to their financial viability. Notwithstanding the obligation under debt contracts to pay interest payments which effectively provide for the return of lenders' capital *as a prior charge on equity cash flow earnings*, the interpretation of Table 4.2 represented by (row 1, minus 23 per cent of row 2, minus row 4), provides the most appropriate statement of corporate financial viability in a fundamental economic sense. Over the respective (roughly 18-year) observation periods, four companies, namely, Bowater, Dunlop, E.M.I., and Plessey were, judged by the latter criteria, not financially viable.

Since 1974 the position has improved. Only Dunlop and E.M.I. seem, on average, to have satisfied the above definition of corporate bankruptcy.[23] It is, however, noteworthy that both these companies generated positive pre-tax entity earnings in three of the four years between 1974 and 1978. Their annual averages for this four-year period were £39.2m and £23.45m respectively compared with the £30.73m and £4.79m shown in Table 4.2 (for periods of 19 and 18 years, respectively). It may therefore be concluded that the U.K. corporate tax system still lacks the inbuilt safeguards that would prevent it from converting financial viability into corporate bankruptcy.[24]

It must also be added that companies cannot rely on the possibility that lenders will always modify debt contracts in accordance with the above notion of 'corporate financial viability in a fundamental economic sense', and will usually be more impressed by lines 1 and 2 of Table 4.2. When gross interest payments exceed adjusted taxes, financial viability is obviously more stringently evaluated by this comparison.

There is also the point that taxable capacity is measured independently of cash flow interest cover. Thus, the combined, legally-enforceable, burden of interest and taxes may be potentially overwhelming in many cases in practice. If Table 4.4 (column 4) is anything to go by, this would appear to be true of Bowater, Dunlop, E.M.I., I.C.I. and Plessey. It says much (or little) for the U.K. lending mechanism that such companies do not encounter serious financial trouble.

Finally, one may question the implications of the results presented in this paper for the formation of expectations by businessmen. If, intuitively or

23 See Table 4.6, column (4).

24 As shown elsewhere (see Lawson (1979)), the U.K. system of corporation tax also increases the volatility of post-tax company earnings.

otherwise, businessmen are aware of the effect of a hostile fiscal environment on the returns to investment they will respond accordingly. There seems little point in examining the efficiency of the U.K. lending mechanism in seeking explanations for a low level of investment in circumstances in which dividends are habitually debt-financed because the returns to equity investment are confiscated by the tax system.

References

Henfrey, A. W., Albrecht, B. and Richards, P., 'The U.K. Stockmarket and the Efficient Market Model: A Review', *The Investment Analyst* (No. 48, 1977).

Ijiri, Y., 'Cash-Flow Accounting and Its Structure', *Journal of Accounting Auditing and Finance* (1978, No. 4).

Lawson, G. H., 'Accounting for financial management: some tentative proposals for a new blueprint' in Sir Robert Shone (ed.), *Problems of Investment*. Blackwell (1971).

Lawson, G. H. and Stark, A. W., 'The Concept of Profit for Fund Raising', *Accounting and Business Research* (Winter 1975).

Lawson, G. H., 'The Rationale of Cash Flow Accounting' in Cees van Dam (ed.), *Trends in Managerial and Financial Accounting*. Martinus Nijhoff, Leiden/Boston (1978).

Lawson, G. H., *Company profitability and the U.K. stock market—an exercise in cash flow accounting* (Manchester Business School, Research Report, March 1979).

Lee, T. A., 'A Case for Cash Flow Reporting', *Journal of Business Finance* (Summer 1972).

Lee, T. A., 'The cash flow accounting alternative for corporate financial reporting' in Cees van Dam (ed.), *Trends in managerial and financial accounting*. Martinus Nijhoff, Leiden/Boston (1978).

Lawson, G. H. and Stark, A. W., 'Equity values and inflation: dividends and debt financing' *Lloyds Bank Review* (January 1981, No. 138).

London Business School, *Risk Measurement Service*. LBS Financial Services (January–March 1979).

Richardson, G., The Rt. Hon., 'Companies, Inflation and Taxation', *Bank of England Quarterly Bulletin* (December 1979).

Stapleton, R. C. and Burke, C. M., *Tax Systems and Corporate Financing Policy*, Monograph Series in Finance and Economics, N.Y.U. (1978).

Commentary on
Papers by Professors Lawson and Lee

J Samuels
Professor of Business Finance, University of Birmingham

We are fortunate to have in the U.K. the two leading researchers on cash flow accounting, namely Professors Lawson and Lee. It is now rare for the U.K. to lead the U.S.A. in academic research, but in this one area we do have a clear lead. The ideas of the professors did not receive a great deal of support in the 1970s and it was not until the Meade report that their efforts received some recognition.

The accounting profession has ignored the possibilities of cash flow reporting, and, instead, has embarked on an experiment at great expense which seems more designed to show the general public how clever we accountants can be than to present meaningful figures that can be understood by readers. For a long time I was critical of cash flow reporting and it was not until I became involved in the manipulation of numbers which is required to produce current cost accounting figures that I became convinced that cash flow reports had a lot to offer. If one looks at accounting standards as being influenced more by political considerations than accounting theory and practice, then the support of CCA over cash flow reporting is understandable. If a committee and a large secretariat work for a number of years to produce an acceptable standard, then some sort of proposal which minimizes opposition will no doubt emerge. By comparison, the political support for two academic researchers will be far less weighty. Perhaps, having produced CCA reports for three years, the profession may welcome the simplicity of cash flow accounting.

One surprise to me is that businessmen have not embraced cash flow accounting ideas. As Lawson's paper clearly shows (and as his papers have clearly shown for many years) the technique produces evidence which supports the point that many businessmen have been making with regard to the demands of taxation and working capital needs.

Now for some detailed points regarding Lawson's work. I have always felt that he has oversold the technique. Over time he has met the points made by his critics and now his model is very hard to attack. For example, he now allows for time lags in the payment of taxation. Nevertheless, I still feel he oversells the political side in his writings and this does not help with the acceptance of the technique. In this particular paper, he makes a strong point concerned with the substitution of debt for equity funds. That this has happened cannot be denied but it could be that it is not, as he suggests, a bad trend. At the commencement of his period of study, the 1960s, debt levels in the U.K. were extremely low, and so, perhaps, it is not unfortunate that they have increased. Lawson refers to the alarming rate of substitution of debt for equity, but is it alarming? We are still nowhere near the debt levels to be found in Germany and Japan and the economic performance of these two economies does not seem to have suffered from their levels of borrowing.

Lawson refers to the low levels of interest cover that have existed recently in the U.K., and when looking at the situation in a number of leading companies he makes the point that effective interest cover now often falls short of what is regarded as normal among lending institutions. Lending institutions are, however, quite capable of working out cash flow statements for themselves, and the fact that they have continued to lend to the companies examined in the study, indicates, perhaps, not that they are using the wrong accounting techniques to measure risk, but that we, as outsiders, are out of date in what we regard as normal acceptable levels of cover. Advanced industrial societies have perhaps moved to a state where companies do rely heavily on debt financing, and equity financing, at least externally raised equity-financing, is of less importance. It is agreed that equity-financing is needed for high risk situations, but when companies grow to the size of those examined by Lawson, then society and financial institutions will continue to support them since they are important for the well-being of the economy. The old idea of risk and uncertainty in large individual companies perhaps needs to be re-examined.

A cash flow analysis of the situation in Japan and Germany would throw interesting light on this question. In Japan companies continue to borrow and to produce goods even when demand for their products falls. They produce for inventory in order to avoid laying off workers and causing instability in the economy. Ideas of short-term interest cover do not dominate in bankers' minds, but rather the long-term strength of industry and the economy is considered to be of more importance. It must be appreciated, however, that the attitude of banks, companies and employees differs as between the U.K. and Japan. Banks in the U.K. do not seem to have suffered, in terms of their own profitability, when lending to industry.

The cash flow analysis clearly shows the decline in equity returns. One point that perhaps Lawson could look at, is the differential effects of the change from equity finance to debt finance on an industry by industry basis. It is agreed that equity investment in certain industries has suffered. For example, investment in capital intensive industries, but trading and service companies may well have benefited from this swing.

Another point that can be made is that the period which Lawson has studied can be divided up into a number of separate periods, and it is quite noticeable from Table 4.2, p. 89, that in the last 2 years the composite tax rate dropped dramatically to be in the region of 50 per cent. This can be compared with the early part of his period, in the mid-1950s, when it was in the region of 100 per cent. Perhaps Lawson's message has been accepted and some of the figures he produces such as those in Table 4.1, p. 79, are really only dramatic because they are weighted heavily in terms of the early period.

Lee's approach to cash flow accounting is somewhat more restrained than that of Lawson. He is not attempting to convince the reader that an injustice has taken place, which could not be seen from considering the traditional accrual accounting approach, but which is obvious when cash flow is considered. Lee has shown in his many writings on the subject that it is perfectly possible to produce an annual cash flow statement for a company which is useful to investors and is meaningful, or more meaningful than the traditional statements.

Lee's paper is mainly a review of the literature which will be extremely valuable to those not familiar with the history of the subject. He is now undertaking work which appears to show that the type of financial information given to investors affects the way in which they rank companies in terms of expectations. Clearly, cash flow accounting will give some investors a different impression of the company's performance than the traditional annual financial statements and the newer type of current cost report.

To conclude, I must congratulate the two researchers on their contribution to the subject over the last 10 years. This reviewer looks forward to the day when cash flow statements are produced as supplementary statements in the annual report. I would be concerned at seeing them as the primary statement, however, as they need to be interpreted with as much caution as any set of accounts based on one single set of ideas.

5 Empirical research in financial accounting

K V Peasnell
Wolfson Professor of Accounting and Finance University of Lancaster

Introduction

The achievements of the natural sciences exercise a powerful hold on the popular imagination. Scientists are able to explain and predict the behaviour of an amazingly wide variety of natural phenomena. The achievements of social scientists are puny in comparison. It is, therefore, hardly surprising that questions of the following sort are frequently asked in social science circles: 'Why does my field fail to move ahead in the way that, say, physics does? What changes in technique or method or ideology would enable it to do so?' (Kuhn, 1970, p. 60). Consequently, great enthusiasm is being displayed in most of the social sciences for the hypothetico-deductive-positive methods of the physical sciences. An upshot of this is that considerable emphasis is placed on the acquisition of statistical-cum-experimental skills in the education of modern social scientists; academic journals in economics, for example, contain numerous articles devoted to the mathematical elaboration and statistical testing of hypotheses, articles which are virtually incomprehensible to older generations of economists.

Accounting has not remained unaffected by these intellectual influences. Academic accountants have been quick to embrace the scientific methods of other social sciences—particularly American academics. Indeed, enthusiasm for scientific approaches to the study of accounting problems, particularly ones placing primary emphasis on empirical investigation, has reached such a pitch there as to cause one reviewer of empirical research achievements in the 1960s to note the prevalence of '. . . the view that a researcher in the social sciences is not worthy of the name unless he has completed a successful empirical study' (Hakansson, 1973, p. 137). More recently, concern has been expressed in the U.S. about the tendency to use 'research and publication' as the sole criterion for promotion, and moreover that 'this sole criterion is being interpreted even more narrowly as "publication of empirical research in refereed journals"' (AAA, 1979, p. 1). Casual inspection of U.S. academic accounting journals suggests that a lot of effort is now being put in accounting PhD programmes into the production of academics capable of conducting rigorous empirical investigations, in much the same way as it is in other areas of the social sciences.

In contrast, Britain has been very slow off the mark. Until fairly recently the number of academic accountants has been small and their resources meagre. Whilst the U.K. has long been plentifully supplied with accounting journals in which academics could publish the results (but not the body) of their researches, it is only with the starting up of *Accounting and Business Research* and the *Journal of Business Finance* (now the *Journal of Business Finance and Accounting*) in the last decade that there became available a domestic journal outlet for empirical studies. (*Accounting Research* existed for a short while as an outlet, of course, but at a time when there were very few accounting academics.)

The time is ripe for an analysis of the contributions which empirical research in particular, and the modern scientific approach in general, have made, and are likely to make to the development of accounting thought. This is the task of the present paper.

The scope of the paper is restricted in three ways. First, attention is restricted to financial accounting, which term is taken to include the many sorts of statements published by corporate business enterprises in addition to balance sheets and income statements, but to exclude financial reports purely intended to be used for internal decision-making and control purposes. It consists of the part of accounting concerned with financial reporting to outsiders. Secondly, the groups of outsiders deemed to be users are limited to the traditional ones, viz. owners and creditors—mainly in order to avoid discussion of 'societal' accounting which involves very different issues, and problems of sufficient complexity to warrant a separate paper. Thirdly, theory is eschewed, attention being concentrated, more or less exclusively, on empirical research.

The first two restrictions are convenient but arbitrary (Mattessich, 1971); the third is more problematical. One of the functions of empirical research is to attempt to falsify theory; what is needed are (a) hypotheses couched in refutable form and (b) empirical studies which do justice to theory, i.e. do not distort theory out of all recognition. Empirical investigations can also help (*a là* Darwin) in the *formulation* of theories.

The paper is divided into two main parts. The first considers the scope for empirical research in financial accounting, the main questions considered to date, methods employed and directions research might take. The next section analyses past and current empirical research efforts in the U.K.

An Overview of Empirical Research

A number of useful reviews of empirical research in financial accounting have already appeared in the literature and it is not proposed to go over ground covered so ably elsewhere. See, e.g., Hakansson (1973), Gonedes and Dopuch (1974) and Beaver (1976). See also the survey of theory and empirical work undertaken recently by a committee of the American Accounting Association (AAA, 1977). Instead, I shall examine briefly what seem to be the main features of empirical work to date.

Empirical research cannot take place in a vacuum. There must be agreement as to which accounting issues are deemed to be important; to what sets of empirical phenomena one might have recourse in resolving disputes; and to what scientific criteria one can legitimately appeal in evaluating the empirical evidence (AAA, 1977). It is likely that the vast majority of accountants have not even heard of the principle of falsifiability, much less committed themselves to it. As in other discipline areas of the social sciences, accounting disputes are often conducted on a metaphysical plane—no attempt is made to couch assertions in refutable form, rather the opposite. All of which makes it extremely difficult to get agreement on what is to be viewed as good or bad empirical research.

Theory cannot be avoided. Starting from basics, most accountants are likely to agree that accounting is not a costless activity, and therefore that the imposition of disclosure requirements on firms is only warranted if the (social and/or private) benefits are expected to exceed the costs. In the broadest sense, the relevant costs and benefits are those falling on society in general, the determination of which requires agreement about a social-preference function. At a more operational level, there is likely to be broad agreement that knowledge is needed concerning: the benefits to users (direct and indirect) of financial statements utilizing various alternative accounting disclosure policies; the behaviour of firms likely to be 'induced' by different policies (Prakash and Rappaport, 1977); the impact of accounting policies in areas of public or government concern (e.g. aggregate investment, taxation, pollution control, corporate honesty); the sophistication required of readers of published financial statements; the feasibility, timeliness and cost of alternatives. All of these areas of concern are, in principle at least, capable of being scientifically investigated if and only if the issues can first be cast in the form of (potentially) refutable hypotheses.

The possible programme of work is considerable, the total achievements to date, rather limited. There is no sign of agreement being reached on what constitutes 'society's' preferences, nor is there likely to be any such agreement. (If agreement were to be reached, the social sciences would have finally broken away from the humanities and would be 'moral sciences' no more.) We must content ourselves with lower-order, more operational, questions.

It has long been recognized by many accountants, at least implicitly, that the contents of published financial statements should be relevant to the decision needs of users. It does not necessarily follow, of course, that accounting policy decisions should or will be reached on usefulness grounds alone (ignoring cost and feasibility considerations for the moment)—merely that it is likely to be widely recognized that usefulness is a necessary but not sufficient criterion in accounting policy decision-making. It is no exaggeration to say that the determination of (perceived and actual) usefulness of existing and proposed elements of financial statements has been the primary (almost exclusive?) concern of empirical researchers during the last decade.

Studies have generally taken one of two courses of action. They have either (a) tried directly to determine the usefulness of different types of disclosure, or (b) concentrated on subsidiary, component aspects of usefulness, such as whether or not accounts are relevant, readable/understandable, timely, and/or comparable.

The empirical data sets used to test accounting hypotheses have been varied. Attempts have been made: (a) to observe the impact of accounting messages on actual decisions and on simulated 'game' decisions; (b) to inquire directly of users about the uses they make of extant accounting, what use they would make of various proposed disclosures, and the preferences they might have between disclosure alternatives; (c) to examine the contents and timing of published accounts; (d) to evaluate the cross-sectional and time-series properties of accounting numbers; (e) to ascertain the 'predictive ability' of various types of accounting disclosures; (f) to determine the feasibility and reliability of proposed accounting alternatives including entirely new reporting materials (e.g. 'social impact' data); (g) to estimate the extent to which managers attempt to 'manipulate' or 'smooth' reported earnings and the degree to which users are 'fooled' by the same; (h) to measure the impact on reported accounting numbers (and the rankings of firms by the same) of changes in accounting methods.

This complex variety of phenomena can be reduced to three empirical domains: (a) accounting numbers and other data (which might be) included in financial statements, (b) the actions of individuals (behaviour of decision-makers), and (c) socio-economic aggregates. Domain (a) has long been of interest to accountants—to that extent the profession has always been interested in empirical research, while (b) is undoubtedly a more recent concern.

Accounting researchers have been willing (found it necessary?) to employ a considerable variety of research methods. These include: econometric estimation of the aggregate market-level impact of accounting disclosures on investors; laboratory-type experiments to simulate the impact of disclosure variations on decision-makers; postal mail and interview surveys of the behaviour and opinions of investors, managers and others; statistical time-series model-fitting, prediction of corporate failure using discriminant analytic methods, and the like.

Perhaps the most intellectually impressive area of empirical research has been that concerned with the study of market-wide user behaviour, sometimes referred to as 'efficient markets' research. For details see Dyckman *et al.* (1975) and Gonedes and Dopuch (1974). The research is impressive for three reasons: (a) the research activity does not consist of unco-ordinated, 'one-off' exercises, but is part of a highly-developed research programme with its own supporting theories capable of generating interesting hypotheses that are potentially testable; (b) the research programme makes clear why it is important to look at actual aggregate-market responses, incentives, and user-interactions to accounting disclosures rather than simulated individual responses (because of the existence of competing information sources) and how one can interpret the results (private value of information); (c) there is an impressive economic-statistical methodology for controlling for confounding variables the like of which is not to be found elsewhere in accounting. Not only is the efficient markets research programme intellectually impressive, but also the studies to date have had a considerable impact on the deliberations of accounting policy-makers in the U.S. (FASB, 1976).

The efficient markets approach has its limitations, however. These include the following:

(1) It cannot be used to test hypotheses concerning the private information value of undisclosed alternatives which means that the method cannot be brought to bear on a wide class of important disclosure disputes.

(2) There is ambiguity surrounding the interpretation of 'no reaction' results. Accounting messages which do not bring about changes in expectations (and hence portfolio revisions resulting in observable price changes) are treated as having zero information content. There is a distinction, though, between messages which are viewed as being irrelevant and those which are in line with expectations. Confirmatory messages might reduce systematic risk; but this confirmatory role is ignored in the tests. See Peasnell (1974a), Findlay (1976), Taylor (1979). The results of Morris' (1975a) U.K. study of the market reaction to general price-level adjusted data, for example, is subject to just this ambiguity of interpretation. Findlay (1976) goes so far as to hypothesize that the favouring of accounting disclosure options associated with strong market reactions would increase the instability of the resource allocation process.

(3) There are technical and theoretical problems regarding the Abnormal Performance Index (API) employed in the empirical studies. Studies based on the API metric are critically dependent on the implied assumption that equilibrium share prices can be 'explained' (i.e. represented) by the Capital Asset Pricing Model (CAPM); see Ohlson (1977). Basically, a non-zero API can be regarded as evidence against the CAPM rather than evidence of 'market reaction'. It has recently been argued that the CAPM is untestable (Roll, 1977) and hence there are serious doubts about the positive-scientific status of the model. In consequence, there is now considerable ground for doubt concerning the feature of the efficient-markets studies which has been accorded most prominence, viz. the way in which the API metric reflects market reactions purged of the confounding influence of risk differences. The method of controlling for risk is not

arbitrary in that it is supported by an economic theory of pricing of risky assets; unfortunately, there is no real way in which this theory can be said to have been scientifically tested, contrary to what was previously believed. It is therefore perfectly possible that the use of a different API metric, i.e. of risk-adjustment procedures derived from a different economic theory, might yield quite different results. In this regard, it is interesting to note some recent findings of the effect of using different risk-adjustment procedures to assess the performance of unit trusts in the U.K. Application of CAPM-based metrics has been widespread with near-universal agreement that unit trust managers are incapable of consistently outperforming the market as a whole due allowance being made for risk. See Peasnell *et al.* (1979) for details of some of the studies' findings. However, a recent empirical study (Saunders *et al.*, 1980) using stochastic dominance tests suggests that trusts as a group *have* generally outperformed the market; the authors note that 'mean variance models which ignore the higher moments of the distribution of trust returns may well have biased downwards the performance of unit trusts relative to the market'. It would be interesting to see the effect of using stochastic dominance methods to evaluate the impact of accounting messages.

(4) The tests assume that it is legitimate to treat all the (risk-adjusted) share price changes around the date of release of a particular accounting message as being a consequence of the information content of that message; whereas it is the interaction of the message with beliefs formed from other sources and past messages which causes the observed portfolio revisions (see Anderson, 1975). For an empirical demonstration of this effect, whereby returns change for firms contemporaneously with the reporting of the results of *other* firms, see Firth (1976). In order to justify such an allocation it is necessary to assume that the market is 'semi-strong' efficient (Fama, 1970), i.e. that the share price of a firm reflects all relevant published information. However, in order to test the 'efficient market hypothesis' it is necessary to make assumptions about the relevance of certain types of information. Consequently, some studies have been interpreted twice-over, both as tests of market efficiency and as tests of market reaction. See Anderson and Meyers (1975).

(5) Researchers have been unable to provide an unambiguous social cost-benefit interpretation of the findings of the research programme, for the costs of mandatory accounting disclosures are not borne by the investors who are responsible via their portfolio revision decisions for impounding the information content of the resultant accounting messages in the (equilibrium) structure of security prices. As accounting involves external effects it is not reasonable to interpret the API metric as an index of social desirability (see May and Sundem, 1973).

Clearly, the aggregate-user studies have their deficiencies. The main justification for the above somewhat lengthy treatment of the limitations of this type of research is that there is a need to temper the excessive enthusiasm which one sometimes encounters for studies of this type. One should not make the contrary error of dismissing the aggregate-user research programme out of hand. The studies have been very effective in drawing attention to the importance of the accounting profession devoting more effort to 'substantive' disclosure issues and less to matters of mere 'form' and questions of the 'where to locate items' (e.g. in the main body of the accounts or in footnotes) variety (Beaver, 1972). The evidence supporting the hypothesis that the market is not 'fooled' by easy-to-correct variations in accounting methods (e.g. see Kaplan and Roll, 1972) and can distinguish such changes in methods from those which alter future cash flows (Sunder, 1973) is strong.

The aggregate-user research programme takes as its starting point the assumption that the stock market is semi-strong efficient and hence that investors in aggregate 'know best', the logical implication of which is that observation of market price changes is necessary and sufficient to determine the information effect of published financial statements. The counterpart of this approach at the individual-user level involves the observation of the decisions reached by individuals consequent to the receipt of particular types of accounting messages.

I know of no studies which entail the observation of *actual* individuals' reactions to accounting messages. Clarkson (1962) conducted a study which indicates how this type of research might proceed. He developed a computer model of the investment decision-making procedures employed by a particular trust investment officer. It would be very interesting to observe how an investment analyst, say, uses the published accounts of companies in making a forecast or in arriving at buy/sell recommendations. Of particular contemporary value would be attempts to model behaviour in instances where the historical cost profit trend points in a different direction to the trend in the comparative current cost data (where reported).

There have been a number of studies of the impact of accounting messages on individuals' investment choices in *simulated* decision problems. One of the best organized examples of this type of research is the study by Dyckman (1969) of the impact on financial analysis of switching from an historical cost to a general price-level basis of accounting. Randomly selected financial analysts were sent financial statements through the mail, prepared on one or both of these bases for two hypothetical companies, and asked to estimate the share price of each company. The data were so constructed as to favour one firm on the historical cost basis and the other when general price-level figures were used.

This simulation method of selecting samples of actual decision-makers and sending to them a hypothetical investment problem, the data in which have been 'rigged' in order to test an accounting hypothesis has proved to be a popular one, particularly amongst PhD students in the U.S.—if only because it has the advantage of being relatively cheap. The advantage claimed for the method is that it can be used to test hypotheses about accounting and reporting methods not currently to be found in practice. A recent application of the simulation approach is the study of the effect of qualified auditors' opinions on bankers' lending decisions by Estes and Reimer (1977).

A variant of the above simulation method is where the 'experiment' is carried on in a 'controlled' environment, i.e. where the experiment is personally administered by the researcher or his assistants rather than being sent through the mail. This enables the researcher to guarantee that the task is taken seriously (the subject is not doing it whilst watching television); also the task can be made 'real' by offering some kind of reward, thereby inducing the appropriate state of psychological awareness. The main problem encountered is that it is not always or even usually possible to use 'real people', i.e. businessmen, financial analysts and the like. There are good grounds for wondering how safe it is to generalize from studies of the reactions of student volunteers to the wider business world. See Copeland *et al.* (1973) and also Birnberg and Nath (1968) for details.

The simulation approach has come in for a considerable amount of criticism in recent years (e.g. see Gonedes and Dopuch, 1974) and it is now rare to find the results of such studies written up in the leading American journals. The problems involved in designing and executing simulation studies with 'external validity' (i.e. where the results are capable of generalization to real business settings) are, indeed, immense. Nevertheless, the simulation approach should not be dismissed too readily. The approach has great 'internal validity' (ability to control for confounding factors). Psychologists have shown that it is possible to use the method to good effect and are a lesson to us all in how it is possible, with the exercise of ingenuity, to design experiments often bearing little or no resemblance to the normal situation yet which invoke the correct responses from the subject (e.g. see Brown, 1970, pp. 736–44). Properly done, the method has potential value in throwing light on users' reactions to currently undisclosed accounting alternatives.

Another way of determining how useful alternative accounting disclosures are likely to be to individual decision-makers is simply to ask them. There is a long history of using interview and postal survey techniques in accounting. For an early example, see Roper (1948). Again, one has to be careful in generalizing from the results of such studies. Survey methods are particularly valuable in testing hypotheses concerning how and to what extent accounts are actually read. It is interesting to know, for example, the relative usage of, and perceived importance of, financial statements to different types of users; for survey evidence on this point, see (among others) the surveys by Edwards *et al.* (1972), Baker and Haslam (1973),

Peasnell (1974b), Fisher (1974) and Lee and Tweedie (1975a). In accounting policy decision-making, as carried out by the Financial Accounting Standards Board in the U.S. and the Accounting Standards Committee in the U.K., it is important to know about the views of the various user and managerial groups, no matter however non-sensical those opinions may be; their views might decide the success, or otherwise, of the accounting standards programmes of those bodies.

The three types of empirical research considered above—aggregate-user studies, investigations of individual user reactions, and opinion surveys—all assume that 'users' views count' (consumer sovereignty). It is the behaviour/attitudes of decision-makers which is the object of inquiry.

There is another approach to the empirical investigation of the decision-usefulness of published financial statements. This places emphasis on determining what are the 'best' (or better) methods of financial reporting—rather than on finding out what investors and other decision-makers (act as if they) view as the best methods. Attention is shifted from the accounting data to determining which accounting data and methods give the best predictions of the events in the future of relevance to a particular type of decision. Strictly speaking, most forms of accounting data (managerial forecasts being the exception) do not 'give' predictions; predictions are obtained by putting the data into a model. Therefore, 'predictive ability' tests of accounting data are tests of a joint hypothesis, that the data and model *combined* have predictive value.

There are two main types of predictive value tests: (a) tests of the ability of model/data to predict future events of *basic* interest to a particular class of decision-makers; and (b) tests of ability to predict *surrogates* for those basic events. In order to conduct type (a) tests it is necessary for the researcher to develop (or find in the literature) a theoretical *model* of the decision process before it is possible to ascertain just what it is about the future which is (to be deemed to be) of interest to particular types of decision-makers.

In the case of the investors, it is generally agreed that relevant future events are either cash flowing to equity holders (dividends) and/or the cash flows out of which such dividends can be paid. Reference is frequently made to the CAPM in order to determine the relevant aspects of those uncertain future cash flows. See Lev (1974), Revsine (1973), Carsberg *et al.* (1974) and Arnold and Hope (1975) for details of the predictive ability criterion in this context.

There have been a number of attempts to measure the contemporaneous association between (a) extant accounting numbers and ratios, and (b) sample estimates of betas calculated from share price data. See, e.g., the studies by Ball and Brown (1969), Beaver and Manegold (1975), Belkaoui (1978a) and Bildersee (1975). The methods employed include: (a) estimation of the correlation between market betas and accounting analogues of the same; (b) correlating market betas with accounting risk measures (e.g.

earnings variability, current ratios, leverage ratios); (c) multivariate regression of market betas on a number of accounting risk ratio measures at once. The amount of beta variation 'explained' by contemporaneous variation in accounting ratios based on extant reporting methods seems to be rather limited.

Studies of contemporaneous association can hardly serve to measure the usefulness of accounting data to investors. What is needed is a demonstration of the way in which one could use *past* accounting data to predict market betas in the future. Research to date indicates that extant accounting data have some, fairly minimal, forecast value (see Beaver *et al.*, 1970, Rosenberg and McKibben, 1973, and Barefield and Comiskey, 1979).

Attempts to measure the relative power of alternative reporting methods to predict future cash flows are extremely thin on the ground. Staubus (1965, 1967, 1968) correlated selected accounting variables with future discounted returns to shareholders in order to see if conventional depreciation, inventory adjustments, and the like had predictive value. Unfortunately, there is no way of telling whether or not his failure to allow for differences in risk affected his results.

The predictive ability and aggregate-user approaches share a common problem—data shortages. Most of the really interesting controversies in financial accounting involve comparisons of the merits of as yet unused accounting methods with extant ones. Unfortunately, it is impossible to measure the market's 'reaction' to accounting messages which it has not received; and it is fiendishly difficult (although not impossible, in principle) to estimate the predictive value of undisclosed alternatives.

Practical difficulties can arise with the predictive-value approach over the need to predict consequences far into the future. For example, it is assumed in corporate finance theory that investors are interested in forecasting future cash flows up to and including an indefinite horizon date (infinity). There is a limit, though, to the length of the 'future' cash flow time-series that the empirical researcher can actually observe; it will be necessary to include a terminal receipt (proceeds from sale of shares) in the series. If the time-series is very short then the terminal receipt will be more important than the dividends.[1] In which case what is being tested is the

1 It can easily be shown that the sale-proceeds elasticity of share value is given as the ratio of discounted sale-proceeds to share value:

$$\frac{S_N}{V} \cdot \frac{\delta V}{\delta S_N} = \frac{S_N(1+i)^{-N}}{V}$$

where V is the discounted present value of future receipts, S_N is the sale-proceeds at horizon date N and i is the (assumed constant) rate of discount. The result is unaffected by the constant discount rate assumption. If it is assumed for simplicity that a constant dividend D is to be paid in perpetuity, then $V = S_N = i^{-1}D$ and the elasticity becomes

$$\frac{S_N}{V} \cdot \frac{\delta V}{\delta S_N} = \frac{1}{(1+i)}N$$

Thus at i = 10 per cent and N = 5 years, the impact of a 20 per cent increase (decrease) in sale-proceeds will be a 12½ per cent increase (decrease) in present value.

ability of the accounting numbers to forecast how investors will subsequently value the company—which with *extant* accounting data reduces to a test of the semi-strong version of the efficient markets hypothesis.

These difficulties do not arise in studies of the usefulness of accounting data in predicting corporate bankruptcies. It is, therefore, not surprising that this is the area in which most predictive value studies have been carried out. The studies can be broken down into two types: (a) univariate studies where a single accounting variable (ratio) is used at a time to predict bankruptcy; and (b) multivariate (discriminant analysis) studies in which more than one variable can be used at a time for prediction purposes. In both cases it is assumed that the (joint) probability distribution of the accounting variable(s) for firms which fail differs systematically from the (joint) distribution of the variable(s) for the firms which survive and that these differences can be exploited for prediction purposes. The aim is to develop a model with which to classify firms: if the observed ratio (z-score in the case of discriminant models) is below a certain point then predict failure.

These predictive value studies appear to have been very successful, on first sight, at least. According to studies published to date, historical cost data have excellent predictive ability. See, e.g., the studies by Beaver (1966) and Altman (1971). From an accounting viewpoint, the recent study by Norton and Smith (1979) is even more interesting: general price-level data were found to be consistently neither more nor less accurate than historical cost data for predictions of bankruptcy. This is not so surprising when one notes the degree of predictive power of these latter models; there is not much room for improvement.

There is a problem with this area of research. Bankers often require firms to maintain current ratios above a certain level; there are similar restrictive covenants in many debenture deeds. Failure to meet these requirements can precipitate bankruptcy. Similarly, credit-rating agencies pay close attention to accounting data when classifying companies. It is, therefore, hardly surprising that accounting ratios have predictive power; a cause and effect relationship exists.

The second type of predictive value test involves not the prediction of a future event of basic interest to the decision-maker, such as future cash flows, betas or failure, but a *surrogate* for that event. For example, investors may be content to forecast the accounting profits to be published in future periods, perhaps by looking at the behaviour through time of the numbers. A considerable number of studies have been made of the stochastic time-series properties of accounting numbers. See, e.g., the analysis by Beaver (1970), Ball and Watts (1972) and Ball *et al.* (1973). The evidence to date suggests that the time-series behaviour of reported profits is more or less consistent with a random walk model or a submartingale model.

It is not very clear from the literature what is the value of this kind of time-series research to accounting policy-makers and accounting theorists. For example, evidence that historical cost profits follow a random walk whereas operating cash flows are mean-reverting (say) would give little help in deciding on which basis to report to investors. It is difficult not to conclude that this area of empirical research has paid little heed to the theoretical accounting literature. Of course, the research is useful to financial analysts and investors interested in finding the most accurate earnings time-series forecasting models. What some argue would be of great help from an accounting rather than financial statement analysis perspective is empirical work concerning the impact on time-series of changes in accounting techniques. It has been suggested by Revsine (1973) that one technique selection criterion that accounting policy-makers could adopt is extrapolation accuracy of the resultant series. Of course, the logical implication of this criterion is that techniques should be chosen such that a *constant* earnings figure is reported resulting in a perfectly predictable series (Peasnell, 1974c)!

There have been a number of studies of the extrapolation accuracy of different accounting models. See, e.g., Frank (1969) and Buckmaster *et al.* (1977). This type of time-series research is more directly concerned with investigating the usefulness of accounting numbers than is the stochastic model-fitting work described above; but it is just as difficult to see how accounting policy-makers are to make use of the results (for the reasons set out in the previous paragraph).

The above examination of empirical work is illustrative, not exhaustive. There are many more interesting studies in each of the areas listed than it has been possible to cite. Numerous other areas of research could be quoted. For example, other empirical studies include: Benston's (1976) comparative study of the economic impact of the regulatory environments governing corporate disclosures in the U.K. and the U.S.A.; the managerial motives behind and the organizational structures determining changes in and choice of accounting methods (Archibald, 1967, Salamon and Smith, 1979); the availability of current price data (Peasnell and Skerratt, 1976, Wolnizer, 1977); the objectivity of exit-price measurements relative to historical cost ones (Sterling and Radosevich, 1969, McKeown, 1971); the readability of financial statements (Smith and Smith, 1971, Adelberg, 1979).

Empirical Research in the U.K.

Generally speaking, the British coverage of the 'go-go' areas in U.S. research is rather poor, particularly in the area of aggregate-user research. Morris (1975a) has studied the stock market's reaction to the publication of general price-level data. Firth (1976) has examined the share price reaction to the earnings announcements of *other* firms in the same industry and has also investigated impact of qualified auditors' reports on the stock market (1978). These are the only British accounting studies based on the API metric known to the author.

My survey[2] of the British literature does not encourage the opinion that there is a major form of empirical enquiry, research programme, in which Britain can be said to be setting an example to the rest of the world. Where, on the face of it, Britain would appear to have an advantage is in empirical research concerned with inflation accounting; in reality, though, inflation accounting is more talked about than practised in Britain, and there is a paucity of accounting data prepared on bases other than historical cost. Morris' (1975a) study has already been noted. Lawson and Stark (1975) report aggregate data on a cash flow basis. Wanless (1976) restates the accounts of twenty-nine Scottish firms. Gray (1976) provides a case study implementation of exit-price accounting. Bourn *et al.* (1977) and Peasnell and Skerratt (1976, 1977a, 1977b) examine the heterogeneity of replacement cost indices. Peasnell and Skerratt (1978b) test the hypothesis that the concept of general price level inflation is meaningless because it is different for different individuals. Mason (1978) examines the support around the world for current attempts to harmonize accounting standards, particular attention being paid to the possibility of increased disharmony resulting from the disjointed efforts in different countries to develop inflation standards. All in all, the research effort being put into the inflation accounting area is substantial in Britain but it hardly merits the title of 'research programme' (Blaug, 1976) in the same way that the efficient markets research does.

Where Britain does seem to offer empirical researchers an environmental advantage over the U.S. at the moment is in the availability of published corporate financial forecasts. Until recently, the Securities and Exchange Commission forbade the publication of forecasts; so it is only possible there to conjecture about the usefulness of such forecasts to investors. This is not so in the U.K. Dev has made a useful contribution to current knowledge in compiling evidence about the form and character of

2 As a first step, the contents of *Accounting and Business Research* (ABR), *Journal of Business Finance* (JBF) and *Journal of Business Finance and Accounting* (JBFA) were analysed in detail. There are of course many other outlets for scholarly articles; British accounting academics can and do publish in other British business and economics journals (e.g. theoretical and/or empirical articles have appeared in *Omega* and *Economic Journal*), in the professional magazines and press, in the Occasional Paper series of Lancaster University's International Centre for Research in Accounting and of the Research Sub-Committee of the Institute of Chartered Accountants in England and Wales, or in the North American journals. Nevertheless, *ABR* and *JBFA* include the lion's share of the pool and can be conveniently analysed.

It is not possible, for space reasons, to report the results of this survey. However, all the 61 empirical studies uncovered are included in the list of references given at the end of this article. Readers may be interested to note that of the 61 articles, 37 employed U.K. data, 15 U.S. and 9 other. Further details can be obtained from the author on request.

the corporate profit forecasts appearing in company accounts and prospectuses (Dev, 1973, 1974) and in investigating the accuracy of such forecasts (Dev and Webb, 1972). The managers do not appear to be able (or willing) to publish very accurate forecasts; on the other hand, the forecasts are not as inaccurate as one is sometimes led to believe. Interestingly, Dev and Webb found that forecast accuracy did not vary very much with the number of remaining months being forecast. Ferris (1975) conducted a questionnaire survey of thirty-one U.K. firms which had published prospectus forecasts; he concluded that 'managers tend to underestimate the prospectus forecast; where managerial forecast deviations occur, managers tend to resort to the use of discretionary actions, and, occasionally, to accounting adjustments, to reduce those deviations'. Ferris (1976) also considered the question of forecast accuracy, his sample consisting of 283 forecasts for the years 1971 to 1974, confirming that there was a pessimistic bias in forecasts.

It is not clear to what extent these results concerning the accuracy of forecasts can be generalized to all British companies. Few British managements provide quantitative profit forecasts except when they have to, in contested takeovers and prospectuses. Many company chairmen do, however, include 'views' of what they expect to happen to their company's profits next year; but the 'forecasts' are almost invariably couched in imprecise terms. In order to assess the usefulness of these statements, Steele (1979) examined the annual reports of a hundred companies covering the period 1969–78. All the qualitative statements were classified into one of the following profit categories: 'much improved', 'slightly improved', 'similar', 'slightly lower', 'much lower', etc. A quality index based on mathematical information theoretic concepts was employed to evaluate the accuracy of such statements. Steele found that on average an optimistic forecast marginally improves the chances of subsequently observing an increase in profits while a pessimistic forecast improves the odds of observing a decrease by 2½ times. Strong evidence was found to support the view that in a particular year that had experienced a profit down-turn, chairmen make pessimistic predictions of the next year's profits.

It is important to note that all the forecasting studies cited above deal with the question of forecast accuracy in an absolute sense. No attempts have been made in the U.K. to compare forecast accuracy with a naive benchmark such as no change in earnings. Even less has there been an assessment of the *utility* of forecasts to investors and other users (accuracy is a subordinate issue).

Forecasting is not the only area of special activity in the U.K. A lot of attention has been devoted—at Manchester University in particular—to the possibility of providing a major input into the policy process of choosing accounting methods by empirically investigating the predictive ability of alternatives. The main kinds of predictive value studies have already been noted in section two. Hope (1974) has examined the time-series trend in the profits of a particular British company, profits being calculated on a variety of bases. Building on extensive earlier British research into the time-series properties of historical cost profit figures, Jones *et al.* (1976) have investigated the extent to which it is possible to capitalize on the tendencies of earnings per share to regress to the mean in developing a portfolio selection model. (This study can just as easily be interpreted as a test of the semi-strong version of the efficient markets hypothesis; see Peasnell and Skerratt, 1978a.) Skerratt has undertaken as yet unpublished researches at Lancaster University into the nature of the time-series processes of annual historical cost profit figures of a large sample of British companies for the years 1948–72 using sophisticated Box-Jenkins techniques. As in the U.S. the random walk (with or without upward drift) model fits the great majority of the companies. Interestingly, he has also done the same analyses on annual cash flow figures and found that these flows are not usually explained by random walk models.

Some of the problems with the predictive value approach were noted in the second section of this paper. One way of dealing with these problems is not to attempt empirical studies but to resort to computer-based simulation methods. (Strictly speaking, computer simulations are not classifiable as empirical research *unless* the computer simulations are based on real-world data, in the sense of including empirically estimated parameters, i.e. are models of real systems.) Simmons and Gray (1969) used this method in the U.S.A. to investigate the extrapolation properties of alternative accounting models. The limits to extrapolation power as a predictive value criterion have already been noted. In the U.K. Arnold and El-Azma (1978) have used the simulation model-building approach not in this fashion but to test the usefulness of six different accounting models in predicting future dividends payable to shareholders. In general, they found that the inclusion of any form of capital maintenance adjustments reduces the predictive value of the series. When no explicit capital maintenance adjustment is made current cost measures generally give better results.

A problem with predictive value studies is that an income series is only likely to be as good as the model for which it is to be an input; yet there is no totally satisfactory procedure available for finding the best model (Peasnell, 1974). Another problem is how to weigh errors one against another without recourse to the loss-functions of particular users; different users might have different loss-functions. Put differently, different users value information differently. Arnold and El-Azma (1978) do not get hung up on such problems. By a somewhat heuristic process of reasoning they argue that investors would be more or less as well served by being given the figure of 'true' economic income as they would by 'correct' (i.e. 100 per cent accurate) forecasts of future dividends; forecast accuracy is measured by them by (a) the coefficient of determination (r^2) between accounting profit and economic income and (b) mean absolute relative error (MAR) of the same. The choice of economic income as a 'benchmark' implies a model in which more than one future dividend is being forecasted and the dividends are geometrically weighted (i.e. discounted). The r^2 accuracy measure is equivalent to fitting a linear regression model for prediction purposes which is consistent with earlier references by Arnold and El-Azma to the CAPM (in turn derivable from quadratic utility functions) as the investors' decision model; but MAR is not consistent with CAPM. These methodological aspects of the predictive value approach need to be given more thought.

Another area in which British researchers have made a valuable contribution is in the investigation of the comprehensibility of financial statements to ordinary users. Lee and Tweedie's (1975a, 1975b, 1976, 1977) efforts in this direction are particularly noteworthy here. The recent study by Hussey (1979) of the readability of financial statements by union officers and shop floor operatives is an interesting extension of this theme. The exclusive concern in accounting research with the information needs of investors and creditors may make sense in the U.S., but less so in Britain. All investigators seem agreed that a lot can be done to make accounts more comprehensible to lay readers. There are serious dangers to accountants in simplifying financial statements, e.g. by giving a misleading impression of concreteness and one-dimensionality to accountants' measures of profit and financial position. Lee and Tweedie (1977) seem to make light of these dangers (see Stamp, 1978, for more details). Tweedie's (1977) 'game' experiments with student subjects suggests that the answer might not be in the direction of greater simplification as such, but in the adoption of more intuitively comprehensible accounting measures (cash flows in the income statement and exit-prices in the balance sheet for example).

One question which needs to be considered is whether empirical research in Britain is being hampered by a lack of suitable data banks. There is no doubt that until recently there were no conveniently available machine-readable sources of share price and company accounting data, and those which did exist were effectively private property. This problem no longer exists, so a number of market reaction type studies can be expected to appear in the literature. There is the problem that share price data are of very poor quality in Britain, owing to the somewhat haphazard way in which the Stock Exchange records prices; however, this does not seem to be causing any great difficulty to finance researchers.

It could be argued that any short-comings in the U.K.'s empirical research effort in the financial accounting area has to be laid at the door of our universities, viz. in the lack of research skills of the researchers, lack of motivation and/or institutional barriers. One indication of the empirical research skills of British academics relative to their U.S. counterparts can be obtained by comparing the empirical articles of U.K. and U.S. origin in *ABR* and *JBFA*. In the main, there is little doubt that the latter are the more technically sophisticated. This impression is greatly strengthened by an examination of the contents of *Accounting Review* and *Journal of Accounting Research.* U.S. researchers seem to have a greater appreciation of the wide range of statistical techniques which can be brought to bear on financial accounting problems; e.g. multiple regression and multivariate methods (factor analysis, discriminant analysis, clustering techniques) have all been employed, whereas the British studies (with some notable exceptions) tend to stick to much cruder techniques. Moreover, it is clear from the U.S. articles that American researchers generally have a much better appreciation of the limitations of the techniques. For example, they are far more likely to pay attention to the following types of problems: the seriousness of violations of the assumptions (multicollinearity, autocorrelation, homoscedasticity, errors in variables) underlying the regression model and the ways in which this can bias tests of the fit of the model and the significance of the parameter estimates; the need to conduct, at a minimum, hold-out tests in discriminant analysis in order to assess the predictive power of the model, and to consider the effects of unequal dispersion matrices and violation of the normality assumption. All in all, there is little sign to date that more than a handful of British academics have anything like the command of empirical research techniques which are ordinarily required of graduates of U.S. accounting PhD programmes *whether or not* these entrants to the academic profession intend to undertake empirical research studies in the future.

As it is, the majority of academics in Britain are completely lacking in training in empirical research methods. The typical education and training prior to taking up a teaching post is a professional qualification followed by a taught master's degree; entrants might or might not possess a first degree (sometimes in accounting, often not). Few possess a doctorate. If lucky, he/she will have a first degree in a quantitative subject; but such individuals usually seem to turn to finance rather than financial accounting.

There is little sign that the situation is improving. Indeed, it may be getting worse, given the current serious difficulties which departments offering taught master's degrees in accounting are experiencing in attracting students of the requisite quality. The main problem seems to be one of opportunity cost, the enormous and growing disparity between the salaries which accounting graduates and newly qualified accountants can earn in the profession and industry, and that which they will receive in universities; matters are being made worse by the rapid rate of expansion in the provision of university instruction in accounting. This latter point is of additional relevance in that not only is it becoming increasingly difficult to get future academics to 'invest' in higher degrees but also it is bringing about the rapid promotion of young academics with attendant loss of time for and motivation to do empirical research. Empirical research is a type of research which is both time-consuming in execution and requires the prior devotion of time to the study of methods.

The state of affairs is not hopeless. Growth-induced pressures will ease eventually. Competition in the marketplace will decline as the numbers of accounting graduates seeking employment grows. The example set by empirical researchers in the U.S.A. will continue to excite the interest of young British academics some of whom will have sufficient scholarly interest and competitive instinct reinforced by institutional pressure ('publish or perish') to seek to emulate and even surpass their American counterparts.

Concluding Comments

The review of empirical research in financial accounting concludes with some observations on the role of empirical investigation in accounting theory and policy development.

The implicit assumption that has been made throughout the paper is that empirical research is a 'good thing'. This accords with the statements that one hears being made at academic conferences and reads in journal articles (e.g. see Nelson, 1973). It is only a small step to take to assume that anything which can be done to further the development of a greater quantity of and more excellence in empirical research must also be a good thing, other things being equal.

The possibility must be recognized, though, that in putting a major emphasis on improving the quantity and quality of empirical research in financial accounting there is a danger of creating a generation of accounting academics and teachers who have more in common with fellow empirical researchers in economics, psychology and other social sciences than with practising accountants. The result could be a 'schism' between academic accountants and practising accountants to the detriment of the long run interests of both. Some believe this schism already exists in the U.S.A.

There is not much danger of such a schism occurring in the U.K. at present. (There may indeed be one in the U.K. but it has a different origin, in the non-graduate nature of the English—but not Scottish—profession.) British accounting academics tend to be long in experience and short in research training relative to their U.S. counterparts. A consequence of this has been a willingness amongst British academics—not always reciprocated by the profession—to engage in and communicate the results of *a priori* studies of the 'what should be the contents of financial statements?' type best exemplified by the efforts put into the development of inflation accounting methods in the past decade (see Whittington, 1980). These are problems much closer to the hearts of practitioners than are the early U.S. studies of the market's reaction to historical cost profit data (tests of the 'can the bumble-bee fly?' variety).

British empirical research achievements to date might not be very significant; by the same token, it could be argued that the *a priori* research efforts of British academics have had as much if not more impact on accounting practice (*vide* the proposals in Sandilands and *The Corporate Report*) than have the more intellectually impressive empirical research programmes in the U.S. This may be partly due, it has to be admitted, to the different regulatory environments which the two professions face; it may also be due to a lack in Britain of the methodology-induced schism referred to above.

On the subject of empirical research, an interesting feature of British empirical research has been a willingness to test the truth of assumptions made in *a priori* research. See, e.g., the Peasnell and Skerratt (1978b) study of the assumption made by a number of accounting theorists that different individuals experience different rates of inflation; or the test of the assumption that the conventional rule of excluding anti-dilution situations from earnings per share calculations implies zero-probability of conversion (Skerratt and Peasnell, 1975). U.S. researchers, on the other hand, have shown little interest in conducting studies of this kind.[3]

References

Abdel-Khalik, A. R. and Keller, T. F. (eds.), *Financial Information Requirements for Security Analysis*. Graduate School of Business Administration, Duke University (1976).

Accounting Standards (Steering) Committee, *The Corporate Report: A Discussion Paper*. ASSC (1975).

Adelberg, A. H., 'Narrative Disclosures Contained in Financial Reports: Means of Communication or Manipulation?', *Accounting and Business Research* (Summer 1979).

Altman, E. I., *Corporate Bankruptcy in America*. Lexington (1971).

American Accounting Association, Committee on Concepts and Standards for External Financial Reports, *Statement on Accounting Theory and Theory Acceptance*. AAA (1977).

American Accounting Association, 'Committee on Promotion Criteria', *Accounting Education News* (October 1979).

Anderson, J. A., 'Information Interactions and Accounting Information User Reactions', *Accounting Review* (July 1975).

Anderson, J. A. and Meyers, S. L., 'Some Limitations of Efficient Markets Research for the Determination of Financial Reporting Standards', *Abacus* (June 1975).

Archibald, T. R., 'The Return to Straight-Line Depreciation: An Analysis of Change in Accounting Methods', *Journal of Accounting Research* (Supplement, 1967).

Arnold, J. and El-Azma, M., ICAEW Research Committee Occasional Paper No.

3 A noteworthy exception is Beidleman's (1974) study of the determinants of price changes in second-hand plant and machinery. See Peasnell (1977).

13, *A Study of the Relative Usefulness of Six Accounting Measures of Income.* ICAEW (1978).

Arnold, J. and Hope, A., 'Reporting Business Performance', *Accounting and Business Research* (Spring 1975).

Baker, H. K. and Haslem, J. A., 'Information Needs of Individual Investors', *Journal of Accountancy* (November 1973).

Ball, R. and Brown, P., 'Portfolio Theory and Accounting', *Journal of Accounting Research* (Autumn 1969).

Ball, R., Lev, B. and Watts, R., 'Income Changes and Balance Sheet Compositions', *Journal of Accounting Research* (Autumn 1973).

Ball, R. and Watts, R., 'Some Time Series Properties of Accounting Income', *Journal of Finance* (June 1972).

Barefield, R. M. and Comiskey, E. E., 'The Differential Association of Forecast Error and Earnings Variability With Systematic Risk', *Journal of Business Finance and Accounting* (Spring 1979).

Beaver, W. H., 'Financial Ratios as Predictors of Failure', *Journal of Accounting Research* (Supplement, 1966).

Beaver, W. H., 'The Time Series Behaviour of Earnings', *Journal of Accounting Research* (Supplement, 1970).

Beaver, W. H., 'The Behavior of Security Prices and its Implications for Accounting Research (Methods)', Report of the American Accounting Association Committee on Research Methodology in Accounting, chapter II, *Accounting Review* (Supplement, 1972).

Beaver, W. H., 'The Implications of Security Price Research for Disclosure Policy and the Analyst Community', in A. R. Abdel-Khalik and T. F. Keller (1976).

Beaver, W. H., Kettler, P. and Scholes, M., 'The Association Between Market-Determined and Accounting-Determined Risk Measures', *Accounting Review* (October 1970).

Beaver, W. H. and Manegold, J., 'The Association Between Market-Determined and Accounting-Determined Measures of Systematic Risk: Some Further Evidence', *Journal of Financial and Quantitative Analysis* (June 1975).

Beidleman, C. R., 'Determinants of Second-Hand Asset Values', *Accounting and Business Research* (Spring 1974).

Belkaoui, A., 'The Entropy Law, Information Decomposition Measures and Corporate Takeover', *Journal of Business Finance and Accounting* (Autumn 1976).

Belkaoui, A., 'Accounting Determinants of Systematic Risk in Canadian Common Stocks: a Multivariate Approach', *Accounting and Business Research* (Winter 1978a).

Belkaoui, A., 'Financial Ratios as Predictors of Canadian Takeover', *Journal of Business Finance and Accounting* (Spring 1978b).

Benjamin, J. J. and Stanga, K. G., 'Differences in Disclosure Needs of Major Users of Financial Statements', *Accounting and Business Research* (Summer 1977).

Benston, G. J., *Corporate Financial Disclosure in the U.K. and the U.S.A.* Saxon House 1976).

Bildersee, J. S., 'Market-Determined and Alternative Measures of Risk', *Accounting Review* (January 1975).

Bird, R. G. and McHugh, A. J., 'Financial Ratios—An Empirical Study', *Journal of Business Finance and Accounting* (Spring 1977).

Birkett, W. P. and Walker, R. G., 'Accounting: A Source of Market Imperfection', *Journal of Business Finance and Accounting* (Summer 1974).

Birnberg, J. G. and Nath, R., 'Laboratory Experimentation in Accounting Research', *Accounting Review* (January 1968).

Blaug, M., 'Kuhn versus Lakatos, or Paradigms versus Research Programmes in the History of Economics', *History of Political Economy* (January 1976).

Bourn, M., Stoney, P. J. M. and Wynn, R. F., 'Price Indices for Current Cost Accounting', *Journal of Business Finance and Accounting* (Autumn 1976).

Briggs, D. H., 'Information Requirements of Users of Published Corporate Reports—Unit Trusts', *Accounting and Business Research* (Winter 1975).

Briscoe, G. and Hawke, G., 'Long-term Debt and Realisable Gains in Shareholder Wealth: an Empirical Study', *Journal of Business Finance and Accounting* (Spring 1976).

Brown, R., *Social Psychology* (2nd edn.). Collier-Macmillan (1970).

Buckmaster, D. A., Copeland, R. M. and Dascher, P. E., 'The Relative Predictive Ability of Three Accounting Models', *Accounting and Business Research* (Summer 1977).

Carsberg, B., Hope, A. and Scapens, R. W., 'The Objectives of Published Accounting Reports', *Accounting and Business Research* (Summer 1974).

Carsberg, B., Hope, A. and Scapens, R. W., 'The Objectives of Published Accounting Reports: Reply to a Comment', *Accounting and Business Research* (Spring 1975).

Chenhall, R. H. and Juchan, R., 'Investor Information Needs—An Australian Study', *Accounting and Business Research* (Spring 1977).

Clarkson, G. P. E., *Portfolio Selection: A Simulation of Trust Investment.* Prentice-Hall (1962).

Copeland, R. M., Francia, A. J. and Strawser, R. H., 'Students as Subjects in Behaviorial Business Research', *Accounting Review* (April 1973).

Courtis, J. K., 'Relationships between Timeliness in Corporate Reporting and Corporate Attributes', *Accounting and Business Research* (Winter 1976).

Dev, S., 'Problems in Interpreting Profit Forecasts', *Accounting and Business Research* (Spring 1973).

Dev, S., 'Statements of Company Prospects', *Accounting and Business Research* (Autumn 1974).

Dev, S. and Webb, M., 'The Accuracy of Company Profit Forecasts', *Journal of Business Finance* (Autumn 1972).

Devon, P. C. and Kolodny, R., 'Price-Level Reporting and its Value to Investors', *Accounting and Business Research* (Winter 1978).

Dhaliwal, D. S., Spicer, B. H. and Vickrey, D., 'The Quality of Disclosure and the Cost of Capital', *Journal of Business Finance and Accounting* (Summer 1979).

Dopuch, N. and Revsine, L. (eds.), *Accounting Research 1960–1970: A Critical Evaluation.* Center for International Education and Research in Accounting, University of Illinois (1973).

Dyckman, T. R., *Investment Analysis and General Price-Level Adjustments.* Studies in Accounting Research No. 1. American Accounting Association (1969).

Dyckman, T. R., Downes, D. H. and Magee, R. P., *Efficient Capital Markets and Accounting: A Critical Analysis*. Prentice-Hall (1975).

Edwards, J. W., Dominiak, G. F. and Hedges, T. V., *Interim Financial Reporting*. National Association of Accountants (1972).

Elgers, P. and Clark, J. J., 'Inclusion of Budgets in Financial Reports: Investor Needs v. Management Disclosure', *Accounting and Business Research* (Winter 1972).

Emmanuel, C. R. and Gray, S. J., 'Segmented Disclosures and the Segment Identification Problem', *Accounting and Business Research* (Winter 1977).

Estes, R. and Reimer, M., 'A Study of the Effect of Qualified Auditors' Opinions on Bankers' Lending Decisions', *Accounting and Business Research* (Autumn 1977).

Estes, R. and Reimer, M., 'An Empirical Study of the Differential Effect of Standard and Qualified Auditors' Opinions on Investors' Price Decisions', *Accounting and Business Research* (Spring 1979).

Fadel, H., 'The Predictive Power of Financial Ratios in the British Construction Industry', *Journal of Business Finance and Accounting* (Autumn 1977).

Fadel, H. and Parkinson, J. M., 'Liquidity Evaluation by Means of Ratio Analysis', *Accounting and Business Research* (Spring 1978).

Falk, H. and Heintz, J. A., 'The Predictability of Relative Risks Over Time', *Journal of Business Finance and Accounting* (Spring 1977).

Fama, E. F., 'Efficient Capital Markets: A Review of Theory and Empirical Work', *Journal of Finance* (May 1970).

Fama, E. E., *Foundations of Finance*. Blackwell (1976).

Ferris, K. R., 'Profit Forecast Disclosure: The Effect on Managerial Behaviour', *Accounting and Business Research* (Spring 1975).

Ferris, K. R., 'The Apparent Effects of Profit Forecast Disclosure on Managerial Behaviour: An Empirical Examination', *Journal of Business Finance and Accounting* (Autumn 1976).

Financial Accounting Standards Board, *Tentative Conclusions on the Objectives of Financial Statements*. FASB (1976).

Findlay, M. C., 'Corporate Finance and Normalised Price', *Journal of Business Finance and Accounting* (Summer 1976).

Firth, M., 'The Impact of Earnings Announcements on the Share Price Behaviour of Similar Type Firms', *Economic Journal* (June 1976).

Firth, M., 'Qualified Audit Reports: Their Impact on Investment Decisions', *Accounting Review* (July 1978).

Fisher, J., 'Financial Information and the Accounting Standards Steering Committee', *Accounting and Business Research* (Autumn 1974).

Flink, S. J., Birati, A. and Ungar, M., 'The Impact of Inflation on the Profits of Listed Firms in Israel', *Accounting and Business Research* (Autumn 1978).

Frank, W., 'A Study of the Predictive Significance of Two Income Measures', *Journal of Accounting Research* (Spring 1969).

Garsombke, H. P., 'The Relationship between Corporate Disclosure and Firm Risk', *Journal of Business Finance and Accounting* (Spring 1979).

Gilling, D. M., 'Timeliness in Corporate Reporting: Some Further Comment', *Accounting and Business Research* (Winter 1977).

Gonedes, N. J. and Dopuch, N., 'Capital Market Equilibrium, Information Production, and Selecting Accounting Techniques: Theoretical Framework and

Review of Empirical Work', *Journal of Accounting Research* (Supplement, 1974).

Gray, S. J., 'Accounting for Price Changes: A Case Study of a Multinational Company', *Journal of Business Finance and Accounting* (Spring 1976).

Grinyer, J. R., 'Holding Gains on Long-Term Liabilities—an Alternative Analysis', *Accounting and Business Research* (Spring 1978).

Hakansson, N. H., 'Empirical Research in Accounting, 1960–70: An Appraisal', in Dopuch and Revsine (1973).

Hakansson, N. H., 'Information Needs for Portfolio Choice: Some Normative Aspects', in Abdel-Khalik and Keller (1976).

Henderson, S. and Pierson, G., 'Does Accounting Research Matter?', *Accounting and Business Research* (Winter 1978).

Hope, A., ICAEW Research Committee Occasional Paper No. 4, *Accounting for Price Level Changes—A Practical Survey of Six Methods.* Institute of Chartered Accountants in England and Wales (1974).

Hussey, R., *Who Reads Employee Reports?* Touche Ross (1979).

Johnson, W. B., 'The Cross-Sectional Stability of Financial Patterns', *Journal of Business Finance and Accounting* (Summer 1978).

Jones, C. J., Tweedie, D. P. and Whittington, G., 'The Regression Portfolio: A Statistical Investigation of a Relative Decline Model', *Journal of Business Finance and Accounting* (Summer 1976).

Kaplan, R. S., 'Discussion of Capital Market Equilibrium, Information Production, and Selecting Accounting Techniques: Theoretical Framework and Review of Empirical Work', *Journal of Accounting Research* (Supplement, 1974).

Kaplan, R. S. and Roll, R., 'Investor Evaluation of Accounting Information: Some Empirical Evidence', *Journal of Business* (April 1972).

Kuhn, T. S., *The Structure of Scientific Revolutions* (2nd edn.). University of Chicago Press (1970).

Lawson, G. H. and Stark, A. W., 'The Concept of Profit for Fund Raising', *Accounting and Business Research* (Winter 1975).

Lee, T. A., 'Accounting for and Disclosure of Business Combinations', *Journal of Business Finance and Accounting* (Spring 1974).

Lee, T. A. and Tweedie, D. P., 'Accounting Information: An Investigation of Private Shareholder Usage', *Accounting and Business Research* (Autumn 1975a).

Lee, T. A. and Tweedie, D. P., 'Accounting Information: An Investigation of Private Shareholders' Understanding', *Accounting and Business Research* (Winter 1975b).

Lee, T. A. and Tweedie, D. P., 'The Private Shareholder: his Sources of Financial Information and his Understanding of Reporting Practices', *Accounting and Business Research* (Autumn 1976).

Lee, T. A. and Tweedie, D. P., *The Private Shareholder and the Corporate Report.* Institute of Chartered Accountants in England and Wales (1977).

Leech, S. A., Pratt, D. J. and Magill, W. G. W., 'Company Asset Revaluation and Inflation in Australia, 1950 to 1975', *Journal of Business Finance and Accounting* (Winter 1978).

Lev, B., *Financial Statement Analysis: A New Approach.* Prentice-Hall (1974).

Mason, A. K., ICRA Occasional Paper No. 17, *The Development of International Financial Reporting Standards.* International Centre for Research in Accounting, University of Lancaster (1978).

Mattessich, R., 'The Market Value Method According to Sterling: A Review Article', *Abacus* (December 1971).
May, R. G. and Sundem, G. L., 'Cost of Information and Security Prices: Market Association Tests for Accounting Policy Decisions', *Accounting Review* (January 1973).
McKeown, J. C., 'An Empirical Test of a Model Proposed by Chambers', *Accounting Review* (January 1971).
Morris, R. C., 'Evidence of the Impact of Inflation Accounting on Share Prices', *Accounting and Business Research* (Spring 1975a).
Morris, R. C., 'The Comparability of Oil Company Accounts: A Comment', *Accounting and Business Research* (Winter 1975b).
Morris, R. C. and Breakwell, G. H., 'Manipulation of Earnings Figures in the U.K.', *Accounting and Business Research* (Summer 1975).
Most, K. S., 'A Comparative Study of the Accounts of Seven Major Oil Companies', *Accounting and Business Research* (Autumn 1974).
Most, K. S., 'Oil Company Accounting: Not so Comparable? A Reply', *Accounting and Business Research* (Winter 1975).
Mumford, M., 'The End of a Familiar Inflation Accounting Cycle', *Accounting and Business Research* (Spring 1979).
Nelson, C. L., '*A Priori* Research in Accounting', in Dopuch and Revsine (1973).
Norton, C. L. and Smith, R. E., 'A Comparison of General Price Level and Historical Cost Financial Statements in the Prediction of Bankruptcy', *Accounting Review* (January 1979).
Ohlson, J. A., 'On the Theory of Residual Analyses and Abnormal Performance Metrics', unpublished manuscript, School of Business, University of California at Berkeley (March 1977).
Peasnell, K. V., ICRA Occasional Paper No. 1, *The Usefulness of Accounting Information to Investors*. International Centre for Research in Accounting, University of Lancaster (1974a).
Peasnell, K. V., *The Fundamental Nature and Purposes of Published Accounts of Companies, with Particular Reference to the Needs of Users and Potential Users*. PhD thesis, University of Lancaster (1974b).
Peasnell, K. V., 'The Objectives of Published Accounting Reports: A Comment', *Accounting and Business Research* (Winter 1974c).
Peasnell, K. V., 'The CCA Depreciation Problem—An Analysis and Proposal', *Abacus* (December 1977).
Peasnell, K. V. and Skerratt, L. C. L., ICRA Occasional Paper No. 8, *Current Cost Accounting: The Index Number Problem*. International Centre for Research in Accounting, University of Lancaster (1976).
Peasnell, K. V. and Skerratt, L. C. L., 'Price Indices for Current Cost Accounting—A Reply and Some Further Evidence', *Journal of Business Finance and Accounting* (Spring 1977a).
Peasnell, K. V. and Skerratt, L. C. L., 'How Well Does a Single Index Represent the Nineteen Sandilands Plant and Machinery Indices?', *Journal of Accounting Research* (Spring 1977b).
Peasnell, K. V. and Skerratt, L. C. L., 'Performance of a Relative Decline Model: An Efficient Markets Interpretation of Some Results of Jones, Tweedie and Whittington', *Journal of Business Finance and Accounting* (Summer 1978a).
Peasnell, K. V. and Skerratt, L. C. L., 'Income-Group Inflation Rates and General

Purchasing Power Adjustments: An Empirical Test of the Heterogeneity Hypothesis', *Accounting and Business Research* (Winter 1978b).

Peasnell, K. V., Skerratt, L. C. L. and Taylor, P. A., 'An Arbitrage Rationale for Tests of Mutual Fund Performance', *Journal of Business Finance and Accounting* (Autumn 1979).

Perks, R. W. and Butler, L., 'Accountancy Standards in Practice: the Experience of SSAP2', *Accounting and Business Research* (Winter 1977).

Prakash, P. and Rappaport, A., 'Information Inductance and its Significance for Accounting', *Accounting, Organizations and Society* (January 1977).

Revsine, L., *Replacement Cost Accounting.* Prentice-Hall (1973).

Roll, R., 'A Critique of the Asset Pricing Theory's Tests, Part I: On Past and Potential Testability of the Theory', *Journal of Financial Economics* (March 1977).

Roper, E., *A Report on what Information People want about Policies and Financial Conditions of Corporations.* Controllers Institute Foundation (1948).

Rosenberg, B. and McKibben, W., 'The Prediction of Systematic and Specific Risk in Common Stocks', *Journal of Financial and Quantitative Analysis* (March 1973).

Ruland, W., 'The Time Series of Earnings for Forecast Reporting and Non-reporting Firms', *Journal of Business Finance and Accounting* (Summer 1979).

Salamon, G. L. and Smith, E. D., 'Corporate Control and Managerial Misrepresentation of Firm Performance', *Bell Journal of Economics* (Spring 1979).

Saunders, A., Ward, C. and Woodward, R., 'Stochastic Dominance and the Performance of U.K. Unit Trusts', *Journal of Financial and Quantitative Analysis* (June 1980).

Simmons, J. K. and Gray, J., 'An Investigation of the Effect of Differing Accounting Frameworks on the Prediction of Net Income', *Accounting Review* (October 1969).

Skerratt, L. C. L. and Peasnell, K. V., 'Anti-Dilution of Earnings per Share', *Accounting and Business Research* (Winter 1975).

Smith, J. E. and Smith, N. P., 'Readability: A Measure of Performance of the Communication Function of Financial Reporting', *Accounting Review* (July 1971).

Spicer, B. H., 'Market Risk, Accounting Data and Companies' Pollution Control Records', *Journal of Business Finance and Accounting* (Spring 1978).

Stamp, E., 'Review of "The Private Shareholder and the Corporate Report"', *Accounting and Business Research* (Autumn 1978).

Staubus, G. R., 'The Association of Financial Accounting Variables with Common Stock Values', *Accounting Review* (January 1965).

Staubus, G. R., 'Statistical Evidence of the Value of Depreciation Accounting', *Abacus* (August 1967).

Staubus, G. R., 'Testing Inventory Accounting', *Accounting Review* (July 1968).

Steele, A., 'Forecasts in Accounts: An Investigation', unpublished master's dissertation, University of Lancaster, 1979.

Sterling, R. R. and Radosevich, R., 'A Valuation Experiment', *Journal of Accounting Research* (Spring 1979).

Still, M. D., 'The Readability of Chairmen's Statements', *Accounting and Business Research* (Winter 1972).

Sunder, S., 'Relations Between Accounting Changes and Stock Prices: Problems of

Measurement and Some Empirical Evidence', *Journal of Accounting Research* (Supplement, 1973).

Taylor, P. A., 'The Information Content of Dividends Hypothesis: Back to the Drawing Board?', *Journal of Business Finance and Accounting* (Winter 1979).

Trueman, J. W. H., 'Oil Company Accounts; Not So Comparable', *Accounting and Business Research* (Spring 1975).

Tweedie, D. P. (1977), 'Cash Flows and Realisable Values: the Intuitive Accounting Concepts? An Empirical Test', *Accounting and Business Research* (Winter 1977).

Wanless, P. T., 'Inflation and the Comparability of Accounts', *Journal of Business Finance and Accounting* (Spring 1976).

Wolnizer, P. W., 'Primary Production Inventories under Current Value Accounting', *Accounting and Business Research* (Autumn 1977).

Whittington, G., 'The British Contribution to Income Theory', Chapter 5 in this volume.

Commentary on 'Empirical research in financial accounting'

Geoffrey Whittington
Professor of Accounting and Finance, University of Bristol

What is Empirical Research?

Part I of the paper gives a brief introduction without actually defining what is meant by 'empirical research'. It might have been worth spelling out the role of empirical studies in accounting research, because a superficial reading of some of the U.S. literature (such as Gonedes and Dopuch, 1974) might give the false impression that accounting research is all about empirical testing, with no role for *a priori* theorizing. In practice, *a priori* theorizing and empirical observation should be complementary activities. The assumptions which theorists make are usually based upon piecemeal empirical observation. Hence, Chambers (1973) can justifiably claim to have done empirical work, and so might a number of British writers who are not credited (or debited!), in this paper, with having done any empirical research.

However, a theory which claims to explain events in the real world[1] must

1 This qualification is important because even in accounting there is scope for abstract theory, such as Ijiri's (1967) axiomatization of accounting measurement, the validity of which stands or falls by its logical consistency alone.

yield empirically testable propositions if it is to pretend to scientific status. This stage of testing is usually more sophisticated than piecemeal empiricism, and 'empirical research in accounting' has (perhaps because of the contents of the *Journal of Accounting Research Supplements* bearing this title) become associated with the sophisticated statistical testing of hypotheses, usually derived from efficient markets theory (although the *Concise Oxford Dictionary* defines 'empirical' as 'based or acting on observation or experiment, not on theory' and 'deriving knowledge from experience alone', i.e. it associates empiricism with induction rather than deduction or hypothesis-testing).

This point is not merely academic. It is crucial for the proper development of accounting research that theorists pay attention both to the empirical basis of their assumptions and the empirical testability of the inferences of their theories[2]: this was the point of Nelson's (1973) critique. Equally, empirical researchers must be aware of the theoretical assumptions underlying their work. In particular, it would be naive in the extreme to assume that empirical research is somehow value-free whereas theoretical or *a priori* research is uniquely burdened with value-laden assumptions which mean that it is doomed to satisfy what Watts and Zimmerman (1979) describe as 'the market for excuses'.

The Current State of Empirical Research

Part II of the paper gives a concise overview of the main areas of empirical research as they have developed during the last decade or so. The author refers to four more detailed surveys which supplement his paper. Recent works by Basu (1977), Dyckman *et al.*, and Kaplan (1978) can also be recommended.

The author quite correctly gives pride of place to the 'efficient markets' research. This has certainly provided a valuable framework for the first systematic empirical 'research programme' to be conducted in accounting. The author gives a balanced account of the limitations of this approach, but it might be worth stressing the important role of assumptions in this work. The fact that the Capital Asset Pricing Model has to be held as a maintained hypothesis in this type of work is an important limitation (see Jensen, 1978)[3]. However, a more fundamental problem from the point of view of evaluating accounting information from the point of view of society

2 Stone (1966), in an admirable account of the interaction between *a priori* and empirical research in economics, points out that even the solution to the well-known statistical problem of estimating the outcome of successive tosses of a coin is crucially dependent upon the empirical assumptions made.

3 Apart from the empirical difficulty of testing the CAPM, its restrictive assumptions include homogeneous expectations across all investors, concerning the distributions of the returns on all assets in the market, and a common, single-period time-horizon for all investors.

is that the efficient markets model has nothing to say about real resource allocation in the economy (a point made by Anderson and Myers, 1975, Boatsman, 1977, and Whittington, 1978). The efficient markets approach confines itself to the question of how information affects stock market prices, and does not consider whether those prices are conducive to an optimal allocation of resources from the standpoint of the whole economy. The purpose of stressing this is not to belittle the achievements of efficient markets research but to show that it has limitations which should temper the manner in which some of its adherents (such as Gonedes and Dopuch, 1974) dismiss competing lines of research.

Efficient markets research is at present undergoing a reappraisal. If it is to be supplanted by a new research programme (possibly derived from agency theory, see Watts and Zimmerman, 1979) it is to be hoped that the adherents of the new approach will show due humility (of which there is little sign in the Watts and Zimmerman paper). Perhaps the best development for the future of the subject would be the emergence of a number of competing models. Testing the null hypothesis may be a deceptively encouraging pastime where there is no competing model to explain events. A good example in economics is the problem of distinguishing empirically between 'monetarist' and 'Keynesian' models of macroeconomic behaviour (see Walters, 1971). Either model is 'statistically significant' when set against the 'man of straw' null hypothesis that its parameters are zero, but when the two models are compared we face the difficult problem of discriminating between them (Pesaran, 1974). This problem does not seem to have arisen in empirical testing in accounting, presumably because of the rudimentary state of development of testable theories. In particular, the efficient markets framework has been predominant during the past decade.

The British Contribution

The third part of the paper struggles against overwhelming odds to identify a distinctive British contribution to empirical research in accounting. It is quite clear that there really has been no such contribution, although various individuals have made useful additions to the literature. This leads to an important discussion of the reasons for this state of affairs. The reasons suggested are undoubtedly important: lack of training in research techniques; lack of motivation; and lack of time. There is, however, one other aspect of empirical work which is important: it is very labour intensive and often requires team-work (e.g. see the multiple authorship of the typical American empirical paper). Such team-work requires, ideally, an experienced leader with time to devote to the project, and a number of collaborators with a range of complementary skills. This situation is most likely to be found in a reasonably large department with a relatively light teaching load, and a number of senior staff with good past experience of empirical work and good research infrastructure (such as computer support). For historical reasons, such departments do not exist in Britain (and they are by no means common in the U.S.A.) so it is not surprising that *a priori* work, which requires little more than a pencil, paper and a library is a rather more fashionable route to publication and promotion.

However, the present situation should be put in its historical context. Twenty years ago, there was virtually no empirical research, and now there is some. Experience is slowly being accumulated, and so is the infrastructure. For example, the London Business School Share Price Data Bank and the Cambridge/Edinburgh Data Bank of Company Accounts[4] now provide excellent bases for empirical research in financial accounting, and the number of academic users is increasing, albeit slowly. It is hoped that these two data banks will be a focus for future empirical research, eliminating some of the more tedious and time-consuming aspects of data preparation, just as COMPUSTAT data has been in the U.S.A.

References

Basu, S., *Inflation Accounting, Capital Market Efficiency and Security Prices*. The Society of Management Accountants of Canada, Hamilton, Ontario (1977).

Boatsman, J., 'Why are there Tigers and Things?', *Abacus*, Vol. 13 (1977) pp. 155–67.

Chambers, R. J., *Securities and Obscurities* Gower Press, Melbourne (1973).

Dyckman, T. R., Gibbins, M. and Swieringa, R. J., 'Experimental and Survey Research in Financial Accounting: A Review and Evaluation' (1978) pp. 48–105 of Abdel-Khalik and Keller (see Kaplan, 1978).

Ijiri, Y., *Foundations of Accounting Measurement*. Prentice-Hall (1967).

Jensen, M. C., 'Some anomalous evidence regarding market efficiency', *Journal of Financial Economics* (June/Sept. 1978) pp. 95–102.

Kaplan, R. S., 'The Information Content of Financial Accounting Numbers, a Survey of Empirical Evidence', pp. 134–69, in Abdel-Khalik, A. R. and Keller, T. F. (eds.), *The Impact of Accounting Research on Practice and Disclosure*. Duke University Press (1978).

Pesaran, M. H., 'On the General Problem of Model Selection', *The Review of Economic Studies*, Vol. XLI (1974) pp. 153–71.

Stone, J. R. N., 'The *a priori* and the empirical in economics', in *Mathematics in the Social Sciences*. Chapman and Hall (1966).

Walters, A. A., *Money in Boom and Slump*, Hobart Paper No. 44, Institute of Economic Affairs (1971).

Watts, R. L. and Zimmerman, J. L., 'The Demand for and Supply of Accounting

4 Both were prepared with substantial SSRC support on the understanding that they would be made available to the academic research community.

Theories: The Market for Excuses', *The Accounting Review* (April 1979) pp. 273–305.

Whittington, G., 'A Comment on the Efficient Markets Interpretation of a Relative Decline Model', *Journal of Business Finance and Accounting* (Summer 1978) pp. 269–73.

6 Accounting research from the perspective of practice

David Flint
Professor of Accountancy, University of Glasgow

and John C Shaw
Johnstone Smith Professor of Accountancy, University of Glasgow

> 'It seems extraordinary that so many people who like to think of themselves as plain, down-to-earth, practical men should dismiss the critical examination of models as an unpractical activity. If you don't drag out into the light the pre-suppositions of your thinking you remain simply the prisoner of whatever the reigning orthodoxy in the matter at issue happens to be. Thus the model of your age, or the model of your day, becomes your cage without your even realizing it.' Magee (1978)

The objective of this paper is to make some suggestions as to what is the perspective towards research which practitioners can reasonably be expected to develop, and which researchers, accordingly, must address if they seek to have research achieve some impact on practice. In the introductory section, which follows, an examination is made of the terms of reference prior to reviewing the objectives of accounting research and the research environment. Thereafter, in the principal section of the paper, the critical issues of relevance, authority and communication are examined from the perspective of practice.

Introduction

The general premise on which this paper is prepared is that all accounting research should have a relevance to practice or, in view of the uncertainty of any research result, a potential relevance to practice. Accounting has been variously defined but for the present purpose has been taken to include the practice of accounting on the widest possible basis in terms of the current conventional interpretation of what accounting is about, including the social and political implications of that practice, but stopping short of embracing those propositions which would take a comprehensive sociological view of accounting and accountability, which is far removed from any currently accepted understanding of what accounting practice constitutes. At the same time, it is not intended that the scope should be constrained by the limit which would be imposed by defining accounting practice as what the accountancy profession presently does. Particularly in relation to research, that would be too confining. It is believed that within the general boundaries which have been set, and without embarking into more controversial areas, an examination of the interaction of research and practice includes the extension and development of that practice, better to fulfil the presently perceived role of accounting. The field of knowledge with which the paper is concerned includes all that is involved in the creation and the communication for the relevant individuals and groups in society, of information which is measured and expressed in monetary terms about economic activity and economic resources in units of organization, or about the impact on economic resources of other activities, retrospectively, currently and prospectively, which is perceived from time to time to be necessary for the exercise of control within the organization and of the organization, including social control; for the purpose of informing the process of rational decision taking, within and external to, but affecting the organization; and about the provision and the management of the financial resources for all units of organization. There is no type of organization or individual or interest group excluded from the frame of reference, but it stops short of the macro accounting necessary for national economic and social policy-making and decision.

Objective of Accounting Research

Accounting from its origin has been concerned with the systematic recording in money terms of events, actual and potential, with economic significance, of individuals and of organizations whether commercial, industrial, social, administrative or governmental. As the events, and the organizations and the societies in which they take place, have become more complex, so has the accounting for them. The development has been essentially pragmatic and, in a strict interpretation of the word, unsystematic (or, non-systematic). This is not surprising, and is a normal evolutionary pattern for a craft skill which has progressed to a professional service, as the education and training necessary to equip practitioners with the capability to provide the service has increased in intellectual demand at the same time as the extent of the judgmental element in the exercise of the acquired skills has expanded.

Accounting endeavours to model economic phenomena, and in doing so, to interpret or to reflect societal rights and interests in income, wealth and property as determined both by law and social philosophy and to influence the application, use and consumption of economic resources. By its nature and function in society accounting must be culturally dependent and conditioned by the organizational framework in which it operates and by the individual behavioural responses which it generates or is designed to do. It is perhaps no more than an extension of the acceptance of such a proposition to say that accounting objectives, methods and procedures will derive from the social values and standards of society (this is part of the 'culture' in the sense in which that term is being used). Accounting is, therefore, interactive with not only political economy but also law, social philosophy, industrial sociology, political theory, administrative theory, organizational theory and psychology. The development of research must recognize this interaction and the need for an understanding of these fields of knowledge in addition to accounting if it is to provide new insights in the field of accounting itself.

Accounting also, as a field of knowledge, is, like any other social science, a continually changing one, as it reacts with the changes in its environment and evolves to meet the changing expectations of its society. Research activity must take account of this continual change, as well as being sensitive to the implications of growth in knowledge and understanding of the disciplines with which accounting interacts.

Against this background, the objectives of research in accounting are perceived to be:

(a) to enable a better understanding—
(i) of what accounting is, that is, of the means or process of creating and communicating accounting information;
(ii) of what accounting is about, that is, of those resources and activities which are the subject of accounting information, of those issues of control or decision about which accounting information is concerned, and of those individuals or interest groups who are involved; and
(iii) of what and how external influences affect accounting; contributing to the development of a meta-theory of accounting;

(b) to put existing practice into historical perspective and current context, identifying the social expectations, the legal constraints and the cultural factors which, together with the organizational and behavioural influences, have brought that practice to its present state by pragmatic development;

(c) to isolate those areas or instances of practice in which this unsystematic development has resulted in misinterpretation of needs, inconsistency, illogicality or lack of soundness and failures to take advantage of or to apply new knowledge or new technology, to recognize the need for change or to perceive emergent new expectations, new influences or new organizational structures; and, not least,

(d) to gain an early perception of emergent new applications for accounting practice and to recognize the applicability of new knowledge in other fields to existing accounting practice, by analysis and interpretation of the trends in the environmental factors, to which reference has already been made.

The impact, or potential impact, of research on practice may be more or less remote or more or less immediate, dependent on the objectives and results of that research, and this will have some relevance in considering its significance from the perspective of practice.

Classifying Accounting Research

The nature of scientific research has been conveniently classified according to its objectives into pure research, applied research and development (see the OECD definitions of scientific research adopted for SSAP13), and although accounting research follows a pattern which is parallel to this model, because of the nature of accounting, and consequentially of the matters which can be the subject of accounting research, the emphasis is inevitably towards specific practical aims or objectives, even in what might be thought to be approaching pure research.

It should be recognized, however, that because of its interaction with other disciplines accounting research may yield or contribute to new insights of more general significance. Accounting is one of the primary means of communication about progress, achievement and accountability of organizations and of individuals, of explaining the functioning of organizations by means of the models or constructs that it furnishes, or of effecting social control by its facility to demonstrate adherence to a society's laws and conventions in the recognition of economic rights and the allocation and distribution of income and wealth. Accordingly, to a greater extent than has perhaps been appreciated, research in accounting is capable of contributing to research in other disciplines, in producing an understanding of the behaviour and means of direction and control of social institutions and of human behaviour, needs and aspirations.

Suggestions for classification of accounting research have included: basic, applied and usable (Miller, 1977); empirical, formal and philosophical (Tricker, 1978); *a priori* and empirical (Wolk and Briggs, 1975); and fundamental and technical (Carey, 1965). Miller uses 'basic research' to describe inquiries at the frontier of knowledge, discovering a new problem or developing a new theoretical approach to solve previously known problems; whereas, 'applied research' is concerned with 'real world' problems, usually involving the testing of new solutions to well recognized problems and frequently building on a foundation created by basic research. Miller's category of usable research is not research in the accepted sense; it does not involve expanding or testing knowledge; its purpose is to disseminate information about basic and applied research so that new ideas can be brought to bear on old problems.

Wolk and Briggs (1975) suggests that *a priori* research is related to tool and model building and hypothesis construction, and empirical research is concerned with hypothesis testing and validation. Bedford (1971 and 1975) also refers to *a priori* models as an area of accounting research. Tricker quotes from a television talk by Sir Isaiah Berlin which analysed the nature of questions to be answered. Empirical questions are about the way things are; they involve observation and measurement. Formal questions are about rules and logic. Philosophical questions cannot be answered by science or logic, but concern presuppositions in our thinking, our values, our notions of justice, right and wrong. The question 'what is the objective of financial statements' is essentially a philosophical one in this classification; this perhaps explains why empirical research on user perception and comprehension has not been able to produce an answer, although it does yield interesting and valuable information.

Basic research can be concerned either with the development and testing of normative hypotheses concerned with what 'ought to be' or with descriptive hypotheses which will explain and validate, or perhaps expose inherent inconsistency in, the practice of accounting 'as it is'. A series of normative hypotheses regarding the measurement of business success on the basis of alternative definitions of capital maintenance could be established by formal logical reasoning. These would, at least potentially, be equally persuasive but not wholly compelling; empirical testing would be necessary to establish that in relation to a defined objective one was superior to the others. This would be basic research. Research to validate hypotheses that budgetary control and standard costing had behavioural implications well understood by psychologists, or that financial management and control systems made assumptions about organizational structure and behaviour which had already been studied by scholars in that field, would also be basic research, and so on. This type of research is fundamental to the what, how and who of accounting; the propositions and issues which they examine go to the very roots of existing practice. While applied research is appropriately used to describe inquiry designed to produce improvement in methods or procedures in use, or new methods and procedures for old or new applications of accounting, the dividing lines from pure research at one end, and technical development at the other, are by no means clearly defined. The classification in this spectrum from pure (or basic) research to development is not so important, however, as the recognition that the questions to be asked or issues to be explored include the philosophical, the empirical and the formal, that the hypotheses to be tested include both the normative and the descriptive, and that the choice of methodology is important and will be determined by the questions, the hypotheses or the objectives in each case.

The Research Environment

While the purpose of accounting research may be the advancement of knowledge and improvement of practice, the motivation to engage in research and the choice of research topic may be dependent on different considerations. With the exception of the more problem-oriented technical research, some of which may be done by practitioners, research is an academic activity. It is an activity which is important to the academic for advancement and career development, and to establish status, reputation and recognition among his peers. As a generalization, there is an understandable tendency, which has become marked in the U.S.A. over the last 15 or so years as the volume of activity has grown, to prefer topics requiring highly sophisticated methodology primarily as a vehicle for demonstrating the intellectual excellence of the researcher without too much regard for the interest or value of the issue which is being explored (Tricker, 1978; Dopuch, 1975; Miller, 1977). This, of course, contrasts acutely with the approach of the practitioners who regard themselves as consumers in this market place with a right to get exactly what they want (Miller, 1977). (There is, of course, no intention to criticize the use of sophisticated methodology *per se*. As has already been stressed, choice of the appropriate methodology is important and some research objectives will only be achieved by use of complex techniques. Choice of objective should, however, be the dominant factor.)

A very relevant factor in the U.K. is that the academic capability for research in accounting is not great in numbers and is of relatively recent origin. This is simply a reflection of academic development; most posts in accounting in British universities having been created in the last 10 to 15 years. Such research in accounting as was carried out prior to this period was mainly practitioner-based, falling within the 'applied' or 'usable' categories. It is not to be wondered at, therefore, that it is only in recent years that practitioners could have been expected to perceive the need to develop a different philosophy or change of attitude, and to adjust or adapt to the possibility that there may be a research input to deciding what, how, and for whom accounting is done. However, established attitudes change slowly. It is not surprising that the conviction of academic researchers in their views is not sufficient authority on its own to convince practitioners who have been accustomed to resolve their own problems, particularly when some other academics may equally vigorously advance one or more different views. Although academic research in accounting in the U.S.A. is of longer standing, the major thrust probably goes back no further than another 10 years. Henderson and Pierson (1978) recognized three time periods in the evolution of accounting research: 1801–1955 (explanatory hypotheses: empirical research); 1956–70 (normative hypotheses: logic); 1970 to the present (descriptive hypotheses: empirical research). A first major review of accounting research in the U.S.A. embraced the period 1960–70 (Dopuch, Nicholas and Revsine, 1971). In spite of the earlier start and the greater volume in the U.S.A., even now, evaluations of the research efforts show dissatisfaction with what is being done and what is being achieved. There is dissatisfaction among academics because such research as might be entitled to recognition and to influence practice has a limited and disappointing impact on the way things are done; and, practitioners of accounting are not receiving support in the form of the sustained and relevant research that a public profession needs and is entitled to expect.

It would be unrealistic to suggest that all, or even a majority of practitioners, took an interest in research activity. Carey (1965), developing the theme that the emergent profession comes to recognize the need for research as a means of improving its knowledge and its performance, qualifies this by saying: 'to be more accurate, its leaders recognize the need. The rank and file of all professions show little interest in research and innovation'. There is, of course, some substance in the claim that academic researchers write for other academics on issues which are far removed from the problems which the practitioner has to deal with today, and in a language which only academics understand; and that the practitioners' most pressing need is for straightforward answers to operational questions. 'If a publication does not offer the practitioner a usable suggestion, then it is not worth reading' (Miller, 1977). This practitioner view is reflected in the nature of 'research' activity in accounting firms which Hicks (1972) correctly discerns as being largely 'geared to keeping track of what is happening. The objective is to be attuned to the state of generally accepted accounting principles. . . . This is essentially an information-retrieval activity, in which information is classified under subject headings, stored and, when needed, retrieved'.

In U.K. current terminology, the objective is to keep up to date on the state of play on draft SSAPs and on interpreting the detailed applicability of promulgated SSAPs. There is another aspect to this work of 'keeping track of what is happening' in relation to exposure drafts and new Standards, which represents an important and more constructive role of practitioner research. The practitioner investigates proposals and tries to come to some sort of conclusion about the practical implications for any particular interest group. The academic may be sceptical about the merits of this research because of this 'political' aspect, but research which leads to political solutions does have direct relevance for accounting practice. Klaasen and Schreuder (1979) developed this idea by drawing attention to the need to identify separately 'tool-making'—a professional responsibility, and 'rule-making'—a political activity. 'The main contention . . . is that an important source of the present methodological confusion in the field of accounting research is the insufficient understanding and subsequent delineation of the political (rule-making) and the actual (tool-making) spheres of accounting'. The inter-relationship between the two elements in the 'accounting domain' is represented by Klaasen and Schreuder in the diagram below: In their words, '. . . arrow I would indicate rules emanating from the accounting policy process and arrow II pressures for rule-reorientation springing from accounting practice'. This classification of accounting research into aspects which are directed towards 'rule-making' and those towards 'tool-making' may be

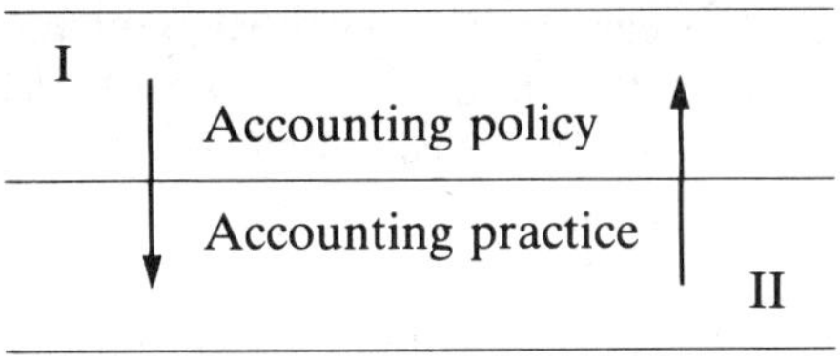

The two elements of the accounting domain.

helpful in reaching an understanding of the practitioner-stance in this matter.

There is a danger, however, if the greater part of the research effort by practitioners is directed as Hicks (1972) suggests. Efforts largely geared to keeping track of what is happening may result in the perpetuation of existing practices and a tendency to reinforce the apparent validity of existing practices. If one way towards the construction of theory is through the observation of practice and the abstraction of assumed principles from such observations, then any resulting statement of principles will reinforce the apparent validity of the practices observed. 'Beliefs may harden into dogma.'

Such research activities are, however, not only important for practitioners—not only those in practice firms but also those in industrial and commercial firms where a large volume of this kind of research work is done—but essential for survival; and while practitioners may engage the assistance of academic researchers in this work, it is an area in which the practitioner is likely to be more effective. This is the area of research which is individually and institutionally most readily comprehended by practitioners. The practitioner, beset by problems and increasingly subject to public criticism, is conscious of the need for help and guidance but is likely to look primarily to the professional society for assistance; the pressures of accommodating conflicting interests to produce a workable solution acceptable to fellow practitioners, and perhaps also to the censorious media, or some regulatory authority, can have an irresistible urgency. The professional society, in its turn, also under pressure, in its case from its members, on the one hand, and from a variety of external interest groups on the other, must demonstrate its capacity to respond in a practical manner within a reasonable, but essentially short, time.

These are not the circumstances in which academic research addressed to longer term and more fundamental issues, particularly if expressed in an obscure and unfamiliar language, is universally seen to be relevant. The fact that such research is not irrelevant is, of course, not completely unappreciated by the practitioners or the professional societies. Generalizations are liable to be misleading and accounting practitioners like any other group are diverse in their characteristics. While there are certainly some who are totally unprepared to see purpose and value in research in accounting, which is to them wholly a matter of practice and experience, there are others who seek the insights of research for the improvement and development of practice. The difficulty for this latter group is in relating research results, as they are reported, to the practical situation as they experience it, or in judging the merit or persuasiveness of proposals for changes in practice based on research.

The accounting practitioner is not alone in his difficulty of comprehending the nature, relevance and value of research activity beyond the limits of what he does himself. It is a more general and serious issue as the following extract from a television series about modern philosophers and philosophy demonstrates. The first programme of the series, broadcast in 1978, consisted of a dialogue between Sir Isaiah Berlin and Brian Magee on 'An Introduction to Philosophy'. In response to Magee's question: 'We're all of us made uncomfortable by having our presuppositions probed beyond a certain point, and beyond that point we all resist it. Why are we like that?' Berlin replies: 'Partly, I suppose, because people don't like being over-analysed—having their roots laid bare and closely inspected—and partly because the need for action itself precludes this kind of thing. If you are actively engaged in some form of life, then it is inhibiting and, perhaps, even in the end paralysing, if you are constantly being asked: "Why do you do this? Are you sure that the goals you are pursuing are true goals? Are you certain that what you are doing does not in some way contravene moral rules or principles or ideals which you would say that you believed in? Are you sure that some of your values are not mutually incompatible, and that you are failing to admit this to yourself?" . . . Too much of this daunts people or irritates them, undermines their confidence and naturally creates resistance'.

The sort of questions which Berlin is suggesting as being inhibiting or paralysing are very much the sort of questions which accounting practitioners find extremely uncomfortable. He goes on, however, to offer a very clear explanation of why such exploration and confrontation is essential: '. . . Yet if presuppositions are not examined, and left to lie fallow, societies may become ossified; beliefs harden into dogma, the imagination is warped, the intellect becomes sterile . . .'. This is the challenge to the intellect to which accounting practitioners must respond in developing their responsible perspective of accounting research.

A review of the research environment would be incomplete without some reference to the accounting research which is being done by practitioners in practice firms, in industrial and commercial firms and in organizations in government and the public sector. Without conducting a survey it is not possible to know for certain, but it seems likely, that in the U.K. the number of individuals who are engaged in research and technical development related activities in accounting, and the value of resources so devoted, in the firms and organizations referred to, greatly exceed the academic staff and financial resources so employed. The work, of necessity, is mainly directed to immediate improvement of practice by finding out better ways of carrying out present tasks, or solving present problems, for example, in management planning, decision-making and control, and in management systems development, as well as in financial reporting. A major input is certainly being made in the preparatory work of the Accounting Standards Committee and the Auditing Practices Committee of the CCAB, the Technical Committees of UEC, the International Accounting Standards Committee and the International Auditing Practices Committee of the International Federation of Accountants. This is the area of 'usable' research or technical development in which it is to be expected that the practitioners' contribution can best be made. Unfortunately, to too great an extent, the work is not based on well-tested basic research but is, of necessity, a formulation, rationalization or codification of existing or evolving practice, or authoritative reaction to perceived problems or criticisms.

Practitioner involvement in applied research and in development aimed at implementing changed techniques as a result of research results is, however, of much longer standing than this more recent activity. Many aspects of the practice of accounting, now taken for granted, were originally the results of individual research efforts by practitioners. A few examples will illustrate the point. In external reporting there is the development of the concepts of group accounts and the detailed techniques of preparing consolidated accounts. In the 1930s the pioneers of those concepts and techniques, dissatisfied with the then current conventions by which results and resources of an economic grouping of legal entities were portrayed, analysed the deficiencies and developed improved methods of reporting to overcome them, before they were perceived as generally relevant and incorporated in legal requirements. The widespread introduction of standard costing techniques in the 1940s and early 1950s resulted substantially from the reports of working parties and missions of practitioners who carried out research into the way such techniques were being applied in the U.S.A. During the late 1950s and 1960s practitioners in industry and commerce came to grips with the impact of computer technology on the organization of data collection and data utilization within the enterprise; and substantial work has been done by accountants in adapting financial measurement and reporting procedures to exploit the volume-handling and speed capabilities of computers and extend the practical application of management techniques based on mathematical principles. Investment analysts, embraced within the definition of practitioners, have, during the 1960s and 1970s, developed a number of techniques for recording and assessing significant indicators of financial performance. The accounting research units of some of the large U.K. based companies are engaged directly in researching the most appropriate ways of measuring and disclosing the results of management decisions as well as exploring how best to assist management to take decisions. These research groups also develop on behalf of the company its responses to political pressures—the feed-back into policy-making of the pressure from practice to reorientate the rules (identified by Klaasen and Schreuder).

Understandably, the motivation for research by practitioners is likely to be different from that of academics. While, as a matter of principle, on reflection, they may accept there is a social duty, practitioners, generally, will tend to look upon research as a means of improving their own performance. As a result of his research effort the practitioner hopes, for example, to be able to assist his management to a better decision, to provide better quality information to report the results of decisions, or to provide more successful investment advice; or to be able to achieve an audit opinion at less cost, or with less risk of audit failure. At a loftier level, practitioners aim to enhance the status of their profession by research. This leads them from time to time to attempt to discern future developments in the areas in which they practice, so that they can acquire the necessary technical and organizational resources needed to ensure the maintenance of their professional status. This type of research will be less immediately related to short-term technically-orientated goals.

It is not claiming too much to suggest that there have always been accounting practitioners of vision and understanding with a scholarly approach to the analysis of problems, but they have been too few. There are now within the accountancy profession a larger and important group of relatively young practitioners who have experienced full-time academic study and have observed the results of exploration of some of the fundamental issues of accounting. These 'one-eye' practitioners who have been exposed to the academic process will not be content to reinforce their existing prejudices by observing with satisfaction that many of their fellows are blind. They are aware, in a general way at least, of the contribution which academic research can make to providing the professional accountancy societies with the intellectual self-confidence to confront the political and social problems of the late 20th century. Instead of reacting with the defensive and conservative response of 'this is how things are because this is how we do them' these practitioners are likely to have the intellectual self-confidence to be able to say 'we cannot yet solve this problem because it is a difficult problem; here are some of the difficulties'.

Relevance, Authority and Communication

On the basis of some review and observation of the research experience and a knowledge, or perhaps more correctly a well-informed impression, of the practitioner attitude, it does appear that, in the consideration of accounting research from the perspective of practice, there are three major areas for attention, namely: relevance; authority; and communication.

Relevance

Attention has already been drawn to the fact that the academic recognition and reward system may have the result that relevance to society's needs and, in particular, the practitioners' needs may not rank very high in the academic researcher's priorities in selecting a topic for research. Insufficient contact between researcher and practitioner may be a further factor resulting in a failure on the part of the researcher to understand, in all their complexities, the issues with which accounting is faced. Academic researchers understandably have limited access to practical situations and practitioners are notably poor at communicating the circumstances of interesting cases, or at rationalizing and conceptualizing from the generality of their experience. Yet, academic researchers and practitioners have interdependent responsibilities. The researchers' job is to produce a viable body of research that constructively criticizes and helps to improve accounting practice; complementarily, the practitioners have the responsibility of attempting constantly to improve accounting practice by evaluating and utilizing the best ideas emanating from the research literature. However, it would be wrong to suggest either that academic researchers should be circumscribed by what is of immediate operational relevance, or that practitioners should not be expected to have a perspective with a more distant horizon than the present day. Relevance for research is not simply whether the research result will help the practitioner do a better job today for his client, or his employer, or society, but embraces also the wider question of whether it will be of value to accounting policy-makers in deciding how and what accounting should be done. Accounting policy-making is a social process and accounting policy-makers include not only the ruling bodies of the accountancy profession but also all those institutionally or individually involved in that social process. The ruling bodies may be the final instrument of giving the policy expression and should be the leaders in developing accounting policy, but in social terms, they are not uniquely the accounting policy-makers. Significance for accounting policy-making is just as much, and probably more frequently, a criterion of relevance from the perspective of practice, as is immediate applicability to dealing with a problem or to changing an established method or procedure. The essential requirement of the researcher is that in formulating the research objective and framing the research design he should have established to his satisfaction that there are implications for practice in what he proposes of sufficient importance to justify the research effort.

Much of the literature examining the subject of accounting research appears to relate solely or primarily to matters of financial reporting, particularly for the securities market. It is important, therefore, to emphasize that from a research standpoint this is only part of the field and, especially from the perspective of the practitioners embraced within a definition of all who practice accounting whether in public practice, industry, commerce or the public sector, and, having regard to the potential scope for accounting in an evolving society, it may not be the most important. Research which examines and explains the behavioural implications, the organizational implications, or the social and political implications, of accounting is all relevant; as is research which relates systems theory or decision theory to accounting theory; or research which seeks to extend the concepts for recognition of events which come within the scope of accounting. These are only some illustrations of accounting research which is at the frontier of knowledge but which is just as relevant as, for example, research which endeavours to explain the origins in custom and/or reason for accepted precepts; or research which tests the information quality or effectiveness of accounting data; or research which examines the complexities of measurement and valuation rules, in that the research results have implications for practice. From the perspective of practice, practitioners, however they are employed, ought to be able to look to the research literature for insights as to how what they do is affected by new knowledge, by a changed social, economic or political environment or by changed or additional accounting information expectations or requirements. Practitioners have a great familiarity with, and wealth of experience of, accounting as it is. The research responsibility is to alert them to prospective development so that they can prepare; and, particularly, to support and to inform those practitioners who have shown sensitivity to the signs of change and to seek a knowledge which they do not have time to obtain for themselves. With a proper relationship between researcher and practitioner, the more relevant the research and the more pertinent and specific the research results, the more trust and confidence between the two groups will grow. It would be unrealistic to suggest that there can be discerned more than the first signs of a kind of research approach or attitude which would foster and promote such a relationship.

Authority

Looked at from the perspective of practice, adoption of change or innovation based on research findings is a departure from the known and familiar and entry into the unknown. The decisions which are taken on the basis of accounting have consequences for individuals, for organizations and for society as a whole. The public responsibility, or the corporate duty, of the practitioner, apart from the natural instinct of self-preservation, is to seek authority for the soundness of any new proposal or development before bringing it into operation. The analogy with medicine is striking. The medical profession would not contemplate introducing, and indeed would not be permitted to introduce, new drugs without the most stringent laboratory testing followed by controlled field tests designed to establish confidence; and subsequent use and effect continue to be carefully monitored. Accounting practice may not be quite so dramatically, or obviously, a matter of life and death, but certainly in the longer run, and perhaps even sometimes in the shorter run, the consequences for wealth, welfare, standard of living and social justice in a society, of misallocation of resources or maladministration based on inadequate accounting may be just as serious.

Accordingly, not only is the quality of accounting research and of research findings important, but also that quality must be susceptible to appraisal by practitioners. The authority and appropriateness for adoption must be established by criteria which are well understood by them. Indeed, it could be represented that the practitioners' responsibility to society is to ensure that research ideas are thoroughly tested and proved before being brought into use. A change in accounting method is likely to have social consequences, for example, investment decisions affecting the allocation of resources or share price movements affecting personal or corporate wealth, and so on.

Authoritative commentary on accounting research criticizes much of the work as being inadequate to command authority or to have the right to expect to influence practice. How true that is may be a matter of opinion but it cannot be denied that research conclusions will be of limited value in the advancement of knowledge and understanding, and may be dangerous for their influence on practice if the research design is poor and the methodology inadequate or inappropriate. For example, conclusions derived from a poor survey or a badly constructed questionnaire, producing data with limited statistical significance, the interpretation of which is unsound, are of no value to the practitioner; and it would not be impossible for such conclusions to gain spurious authority by finding their way into the literature by citation in some other academic work. Although concern has been expressed about the fact that academics write for academics in a language which only they understand, it is vitally important that they continue to do so, particularly in the more basic research areas.

The practitioner cannot be expected to test the validity of research findings and must be able to rely on rigorous testing by scrutiny and debate of one academic researcher's work by others, exploring shortcomings and limitations in the hypotheses, the methodology, the logic or the mathematics. Scrutiny, debate and the replication of the research and the findings are essential parts of the process to induce confidence in the research conclusions and their implications for practice. Without an efficient forum in which academic researchers are required to defend their findings the judgment holds good that 'without a set of standards for research approach and methodology, and without review by competent experts, research conclusions—no matter how costly nor how diligent the efforts of the researcher have been—tend to remain not much more than one man's opinion; and thus they remain unconvincing to anyone who, for any reason at all prefers to think otherwise' (Mautz and Gray, 1970). On the other hand, 'practitioners applaud a trend . . . towards the development of standards by which the adequacy of research may be measured. If such standards were generally accepted and if research were stated to have been performed in accordance with them, the influence of the findings on persons who are not qualified to appraise the research, or are unwilling to do so might be enhanced' (Hicks, 1972). Chambers (1972) also makes the case for better standards, arguing that 'there would be more disciplined research if practitioners refused to take notice of research work unless or until the products of enquiry had been thoroughly debated by researchers themselves, or substantially supported by evidence and were in the form of tightly constructed and well-defined proposals'.

Much of the research work in accounting must, by its nature, be inconclusive. Like most work in the social sciences, controlled experiments to replicate conditions and test conclusions are frequently not possible. The validity of conclusions is, in turn, dependent on the validity of preliminary assumptions which themselves must be researched. There is almost universal agreement that the framework of financial reporting for corporate enterprise involving measurement and valuation is dependent on the objectives of the financial statements and the decision models and information needs of the users, a knowledge of which is negligible and research into which is minimal. Academic debate on the respective merits of different concepts of capital maintenance for profit measurement falls within Chambers' (1972) condemnation that 'there is too great a tendency to rely on argument rather than evidence'. Such a question can only be resolved by giving users the opportunity to use alternative information in full knowledge and understanding of its meaning and finding out which produced the 'best' decision. The enormity of the practical obstacles to be overcome in such experimental work is well appreciated. It is considerably daunting, but it would be preferable and certainly academically and intellectually more honest to admit to it than for individuals to advocate a preferred method as if they had uncovered an ultimate truth, and for accounting policy-makers to be encouraged to promulgate definitive solutions to imperfectly defined problems. Similarly, for example, in some research areas it must be recognized that insufficient is known about managerial decision processes; and the formulation of research hypotheses on the accounting information needs and expectations of representative employee groups inevitably subsumes certain social and political factors for which there is a number of models.

This is the perspective of practice. Practitioners are not a homogeneous group, and the variety of possible models for research hypotheses will be paralleled by the experience of practitioners; their preparedness to accept the reliability of research conclusions will be conditioned by their identification of any recognizable fundamental defect in research design. In a word, accounting research has to be demonstrated to be sound to command authority and to be of value to practice. The practitioners' test of some recognizable 'seal of approval' may to the academic researcher appear to be a simplistic one but from his standpoint it is an imperative one.

It is doubtful whether in the U.K. the academic research community is large enough or has sufficient time or sufficient resources to create the forum which will challenge and accept or reject the research which is carried out. It is certain that it is neither large enough nor possessed of sufficient time and resources to carry out the research which the needs and expectations of society require. Research is, of course, international, and advance in knowledge in this, as in other fields, is not limited to what can be done in the U.K. alone. However, while theoretical concepts and the principles established by basic research may have universal relevance, differences in the cultural and institutional environment may prevent the results of empirical research having the same universality. These differences also mean that solutions and applications are not necessarily readily transferred without modification from one country to another. To the extent that accounting, international in character as it is, is culturally, socially and politically dependent, some research must have specific regard to the peculiar circumstances in the U.K. Until this research is carried out and tested on a sufficient scale, the perspective of the U.K. practitioner is likely to remain a sceptical one.

Communication

The traditional concept of the academic researcher patiently exploring, seeking out and examining evidence, ideas and argument in pursuit of the truth unhampered by material or practical considerations may be an attractive one in some fields of knowledge such as the natural sciences, but it is simply not applicable in accounting. Accounting is not dealing in natural phenomena, the nature and inter-relationship of which are fixed and constant, which will yield to research inquiry and experiment and the significance of which will only become known on interpretation of the research results. Accounting does not have an existence beyond what is justified by its value in social intercourse. In primitive society all the natural elements are there although they may not be understood and they will not change; there is no accounting because it is not necessary. Accounting research, therefore, is not the pursuit of some ultimate truth but is concerned to increase knowledge and understanding in order to improve and extend the practice of accounting. Research can have no purpose, therefore, unless it can have an impact on practice and this means there needs to be effective communication of research results from researchers to accounting policy-makers and practitioners. It has already been recognized that for some part of accounting research, particularly basic research, academic researchers will write, and must properly be expected to write, in a language which many, and in most cases the majority of, or all practitioners will not understand. However, from the perspective of practice, once the status and authority of the research findings have been established the means have to be found to enable the findings to become operational.

It is not an infrequent complaint of academic researchers that in spite of the increasing volume of research it is not perceived as having much impact on practice. There could be a number of reasons for this. The process of accounting policy-making is itself an urgent one for research. The reason for the limited impact of research on practice may be a question of lack of relevance or of insufficient authority; and, it is suggested by some writers that accounting policy-making is subject to political constraints and not based solely on rational argument and theoretical justification. There may be some substance in these points, but there is no doubt that there is a communication gap which from the perspective of practice has to be bridged to enable practitioners to draw on research results and to enable society to have the benefit of research to which it is entitled. Sterling (1973) draws an alarming picture of lack of congruence and at the same time lack of conflict between research and education and practice because of the isolation of research from the other two activities. Yet a fundamental principle of university teaching is that it should be enlivened and refreshed by contact with research and with emergent new knowledge. Sterling properly advocates that educators should teach research results as the desired state and teach accepted practice as the current state, recognizing that students should not only be acquainted with the most advanced state of knowledge but also be prepared for the world as it is. In this process it is important, of course, that only research results of sufficient authority should find their way into teaching; accordingly, adherence to research standards is critical.

Communication through teaching, while important, is both indirect and longer term. There also is a need for networks of communication explaining, interpreting and adapting for operational use the results of research. In certain areas, the responsibility of research may be to produce alternatives to give a choice to accounting policy-makers; where results are definitive, practical exigencies may necessitate modification for practice; where conclusions are uncertain a period of practical experiment may be desirable; and so on. What is apparent is that dialogue is necessary between researchers and practitioners to produce the conditions in which research can have an impact on practice. There is an area of research, whether it is classified as 'applied', or 'usable', or even technical development, which only academic researchers can fill, rewriting research results, which have survived the testing forum discussed above, in a language and a context which practitioners can understand and use. Converting research results into accounting practices may be an area for co-operation and joint work between researchers and practitioners, although in many instances, dependent on the issue, competent practitioners ought to be able to do this individually, collectively or institutionally.

From the perspective of practice the crucial issue is that communication requires positive action on the part of the research community. Practitioners must be receptive to new ideas but it is unrealistic of researchers to expect that practitioners will in all cases have the knowledge, the expertise or the time to understand and to use research results in the form in which they are first developed with all the academic rigour which the situation requires.

Research Needs

From the perspective of the needs of practice, accounting research in the U.K. is so desperately inadequate that a major initiative is necessary.

The substantial input of resources by firms in public practice, industrial and commercial firms, public corporations and boards and, not least, institutionally by the accountancy professional societies is not underrated but these are devoted almost exclusively to attacking the most pressing problems of current practice. It is at the most operational end of applied research or usable research and technical development and it does not begin, understandably, to tackle basic research, particularly of an interdisciplinary nature or directed towards analysis of the needs of a future society.

The initiative of the Social Science Research Council in recent years leading first to commissioning the Tricker Report (1975) and then to the specific research initiatives, comprising, the information disclosure projects, the study groups on social and political implications of accounting and on management accounting, the research conferences and the inflation accounting research fellowship, is a most welcome indication of concern by scholars and researchers in cognate disciplines to stimulate activity in a neglected field. An earlier initiative, made possible by the generosity of private benefactors, was the founding, in 1971, in the University of Lancaster, of the International Centre for Research in Accounting. The purpose was to create a research community, to stimulate research and to provide a centre for visiting scholars from throughout the world. The most significant achievements include nearly twenty occasional papers and a number of other publications, research seminars and contributions by written submissions, oral testimony and lecturing, in the development of accounting thought.

However, in relation to total needs all these are modest efforts.

The accounting research capability in the U.K. is alarmingly small in terms of numbers; and obstacles (principally a major commitment to teaching) in the way of competent researchers devoting substantial sustained time to research are considerable. The scope for increasing the number of competent researchers is not great and the financial and other rewards for research activity are not particularly attractive. Yet, accounting is so important for society that the present situation requires the dedication of some of the most experienced and highly intellectually gifted accountants to research to give the necessary dynamic thrust to this neglected activity. What the situation requires is the creation of a national accounting research body with the backing of the accountancy profession, industry, commerce, the related professions, the financial institutions, the financial markets, the trade unions, the management organizations, the universities, the business schools, the polytechnics and the government, in no way supplanting, or in conflict with, the universities or any other existing institution or research activity, but with the role of formulating an overall national research strategy and the task of remedying deficiencies, fostering the creation of a research community, ensuring there is a satisfactory reward and compensation structure, identifying research projects, generating financial support, stimulating networks of communication at all levels of research and with practitioners, and generally creating the environment in which accounting research can flourish. (See also proposals by Mautz (1974) and by the Report of Task Force 2000 of the Canadian Institute of Chartered Accountants (1970).)

The importance of accounting to society and the increase in its scope make the quality of accounting a matter of even greater concern than has been the case in the past. From the perspective of practice, a highly qualified research community and dynamic, penetrating research activity are essential complements to an efficient, socially responsible accountancy profession.

References

Abdel-Khalik, A. Rashad, *Research Methods and Accounting Research* (unpublished lecture notes for A.A.A. Seminar on Research Appreciation).

Barden, Horace, G., 'The Trouble with Accounting Research', *Journal of Accountancy* (January 1975).

Beaver, W. H., *Current Trends in Accounting Research* (unpublished paper, Graduate School).

Bedford, Norton M., 'The Need for an Evaluation of Accounting Research', in Nicholas Dopuch and Lawrence Revsine (eds.), *Accounting Research 1960–1970: A Critical Evaluation*. Center for International Education and Research in Accounting, Illinois (1971).

Bedford, Norton M., 'The Impact of A Priori Theory and Research on Accounting Practice', in A. Rashad Abdel-Khalik and Thomas F. Keller (eds.), *The Impact of Accounting Research on Practice and Disclosure*. Duke University (1975).

Berlin, Isaiah and Magee, Brian, 'An Introduction to Philosophy', in Brian Magee (ed.), *Men of Ideas*. BBC (1978).

The Canadian Institute of Chartered Accountants, *Report of Task Force 2000, A Study of the Future Roles of the Accountancy Profession* (1970).

Carey, J. L., *The C.P.A. Plans for the Future*. A.I.C.P.A. (1965), Chapter 15.

Carsberg, Bryan, 'Directions into the Future, the prospects for research', in Bryan Carsberg and Tony Hope (eds.), *Current Issues in Accounting*. Philip Allan (1977).

Caws, Peter, 'Accounting Research—Science or Methodology', in Robert R. Sterling (ed.), *Research Methodology in Accounting*. Scholars Book Co. (1972).

Chambers, R. J., 'The Anguish of Accountants', *Journal of Accountancy* (March 1972).

Chan, James L., 'Research Output Indicators', *Accounting Review* (April 1978).

Chenok, Philip B., 'A Practitioner's View of Accounting Research', in Robert R. Sterling (ed.), *Research Methodology in Accounting*. Scholars Book Co. (1972).

Davidson, H. J., 'Research in Accounting', *Journal of Accountancy* (September 1968).

Dopuch, Nicholas, 'The Impact of Research on Practice—A Synthesis', in A. Rashad Abdel-Khalik and Thomas F. Keller (eds.), *The Impact of Accounting Research on Practice and Disclosure*. Duke University (1975).

Dopuch, Nicholas and Revsine, L. (eds.), *Accounting Research 1960–70: A Critical Evaluation*. Center for International Education and Research in Accounting, Illinois (1971).

Henderson, Scott and Pierson, G., 'Does Accounting Research Matter?', *Accounting and Business Research* (Winter 1978).

Hicks, E. L., 'Accounting Research, The Why, The How, The Who', in Robert R. Sterling (ed.), *Research Methodology in Accounting*. Scholars Book Co. (1972).

Ijiri, Yuji, 'The Nature of Accounting Research', in Robert R. Sterling (ed.), *Research Methodology in Accounting*. Scholars Book Co. (1972).

Ijiri, Yuji, '*A Priori* Research in Accounting: A Critique', in Nicholas Dopuch and Lawrence Revsine (eds.), *Accounting Research 1960–70: A Critical Evaluation*. Center for International Education and Research in Accounting, Illinois (1971).

Larson, Kermit D., 'A Commentary on *a Priori* Research in Accounting', in Nicholas Dopuch and Lawrence Revsine (eds.), *Accounting Research 1960–70: A Critical Evaluation*. Center for International Education and Research in Accounting, Illinois (1971).

Klaasen, J. and Schreuder, H., *Accounting Research: The Unhappy Marriage of Rule Making and Tool Making* (unpublished paper presented at the European Accounting Association Congress, 1979).

Magee, Brian, *Men of Ideas*. BBC (1978).

Mautz, R. K. and Gray, Jack, 'Some Thoughts on Research Needs in Accounting', *Journal of Accountancy* (September 1970).

Mautz, R. K., 'Discussants' Response to Facts and Foibles in Auditing Research', *Symposium on Auditing Research*. University of Illinois (1974).

Mautz, R. K., 'Some Thoughts on Applied Research', in Gary John Previts (ed.), *Accounting Research Convocation*. University of Alabama (1975).

May, R. G. and Sundem, G. L., 'Research for Accounting Policy: An Overview', *Accounting Review* (October 1976).

Miller, P. M. W., 'What is Accounting Research supposed to do?' *Management Accounting* (U.S.A.) (December 1977).

Nelson, Carl L., '*A Priori* Research in Accounting', in Nicholas Dopuch and

Lawrence Revsine (eds.), *Accounting Research 1960–70: A Critical Evaluation*. Center for International Education and Research in Accounting, Illinois (1971).

Roy, Robert H. and Macneill, James H., *Horizons for the Profession*. AICPA (1967), Chapter 6.

Sterling, Robert R., 'Editor's Introduction', *Research Methodology in Accounting*. Scholars Book Co. (1972).

Sterling, Robert R., 'Accounting Research, Education and Practice', *Journal of Accountancy* (September 1973).

Sterling, Robert R., 'Accounting at the Crossroads', *Journal of Accountancy* (August 1976).

Tricker, R. I., *Research in Accountancy, a Strategy for Further Work*. SSRC (1975).

Tricker, R. I., *Research in Accounting, Purpose, Process and Potential*. University of Glasgow Press (1978).

Wolk, H. I. and Briggs, R. W., 'Accounting Research, Professors and Practitioners: A Perspective', *International Journal of Accounting Education and Research* (Spring 1975).

Zeff, Stephen A. and Hofstead, Thomas R., 'A Communications Gap: The Researchers and the Practitioners', *Accountants Magazine* (January 1974).

7 The British contribution to opportunity cost theory

J Arnold
Professor of Accounting, University of Manchester

and R Scapens
Senior Lecturer in Accounting, University of Manchester

(The authors wish to express their gratitude to Diane Berry for her help in the literature search that preceded the writing of this paper.)

The British contribution to costing theory may be regarded as either substantial or relatively insignificant depending on where one chooses to draw the boundaries of the subject. This paper concentrates on those elements of costing where the development has been heavily influenced by British contributions. These elements may be described loosely as the areas of 'opportunity cost' or the determination of costs for decisions. No attempt has been made at an exhaustive review of the international literature, which would have involved a much longer paper. Rather we have tried to identify and evaluate major British writings and relate them to developments elsewhere.

The paper is divided into three main sections. The first rehearses the major areas of difference between 'conventional' cost accounting procedures and opportunity cost ideas in providing costs for decisions. The development of opportunity cost is traced from the late 19th century to the mid 20th century. Much of the development of the basic concepts of opportunity cost was undertaken by British academics, both economists and accountants. A particularly strong contribution came from the Economics Department at the London School of Economics during the 1930s. The second section discusses three areas in which opportunity cost concepts have been applied: the use of mathematical programming techniques; the application of dual prices to the problem of determining transfer prices; and the role of residual income. Although much of the writing in these areas has been undertaken by overseas academics, there have been significant contributions from British writers. Indeed, the third area has involved a debate which has been almost exclusively British. In the last section, some suggestions are made for research which might fruitfully be conducted to identify more clearly the nature, role and usefulness of opportunity cost concepts.

Although most of the paper is devoted to an evaluation of past British contributions we, at least, believe in the irrelevance of sunk costs! In consequence, one of our major purposes is to suggest ways in which the long British tradition in the opportunity cost field may be extended.

The Development of Opportunity Cost

The opportunity cost approach to decisions is now standard fare in many U.K. undergraduate degree courses and textbooks. In this section the current state of opportunity cost ideas is discussed and their (largely British) origins traced. Decisions may be categorized broadly as either accept/reject decisions or ranking decisions. The choice of a particular course of action under both accept/reject decisions and ranking decisions involves foregoing alternatives—alternative uses of resources for accept/reject decisions and alternative projects for ranking decisions. (The distinction between accept/reject and ranking decisions, and the consequent distinction between opportunities foregone is somewhat artificial, but useful for the subsequent discussion of the development and role of opportunity cost.) Recognition of the inevitability of having to forego alternatives in any decision is the backbone of opportunity cost.

The Opportunity Cost Approach

The opportunity cost approach can be illustrated by taking a simple example of two mutually exclusive contracts. The significant figures are as follows:

	Contract A	Contract B
	£	£
Contribution	38,000	30,000
Alternative contribution foregone (as a result of resource scarcity)	30,000	38,000
Surplus/(Deficit)	8,000	(8,000)

The contribution figures show the incremental effect of each contract on the cash flows of the company, and reflect one part of the opportunity cost involved. The surplus/(deficit) figures show how much better (or worse) each contract is than the alternative contract, and reflect the other part of opportunity cost, the contribution foregone on alternative projects. This latter part of opportunity cost has been criticized on the grounds that it cannot be calculated until sufficient information is already available to proceed to a decision (see Gould, 1974 and 1977). In our example, a choice could be made by comparing the contributions of the two contracts. Nevertheless, a further calculation does have the advantage that it results in 'profit' figures which may be interpreted in isolation against a benchmark of zero. The positive 'profit' implies that the alternative not only adds to a company's net cash resources but is better than competing alternatives. Although this information may, in some cases, be superfluous it may, in others, enhance the role of the accountant as a communicator of information for decisions.

A Comparison with the 'Conventional' Accounting Approach

The essence of the opportunity cost approach is that only the differential effects of decisions are relevant; the decision-maker should take account of all changes in cost and benefit streams expected if a particular course of action is pursued. This approach is often inconsistent with that implied by the application of conventional accounting principles, based on recording and reporting past transactions, and on matching historical costs with actual revenues.

It is probable that many decision-makers now recognize the limitations of conventional accounting measures of cost for decision purposes (although, as pointed out later, this is an area in which empirical evidence is still sparse). Broadly speaking, the conventional approach involves matching the original costs of the resources actually used on a project against its revenues, and may result in profitability statements that differ from those prepared using opportunity costs in three main respects. The first concerns the treatment of historical costs. The application of conventional practice involves charging resources to particular projects at their original cost. Under the opportunity cost approach relevant cost depends on the currently available alternative uses of the resources and will equal historical cost only by accident. As will be discussed later, the cost of using capital assets is an extension of this area of difference.

The second area of difference concerns fixed costs. Costs that are fixed regardless of the decision under consideration are irrelevant under the opportunity cost approach. In conventional accounting practice, however, they are often allocated to available opportunities. It has become widely accepted, at least in the academic literature, that such allocations are arbitrary and misleading. Despite this, some writers argue that the allocation of fixed costs may be sensible in practice. This view is discussed further in the last section.

The final main area of difference relates to the impact of a project on a firm's other activities. In our example, resource scarcity means that if contract *A* is accepted, contract *B* must be rejected and *vice-versa.* Such interdependencies are recognized under the opportunity cost approach either explicitly by the inclusion of a cost representing the contribution foregone elsewhere or implicitly by comparing the contributions from competing opportunities. Where, as is often the case, the need to forego other opportunities is caused by the existence of scarce resources, the choice between alternatives may be made by applying linear, and other mathematical, programming techniques which reflect the cost of displaced alternatives in the dual or shadow prices (see, e.g., Arnold, 1973a). Dual prices are particularly helpful in assessing the desirability of marginal changes in plans; their application to the evaluation of new opportunities indicates whether a change in (scarce) resource allocation is worthwhile. If it is not, there is no need to incur the cost involved in re-solving the mathematical programming problem in order to determine the changes required to plans. Using conventional accounting practice, only the amount paid for a resource is treated as a cost; changes in benefits and costs elsewhere in the organization are not usually included, even though they are a direct consequence of the decision being taken.

In the example, the opportunity cost approach shows that either contract would add to the company's resources, and that contract *A* would add £8000 more than contract *B*. The differences outlined above may lead to conventionally prepared statements giving substantially different indications of whether or not an opportunity is worthwhile and how it compares with competing alternatives.

The evolution of the concept of relevant costs for decisions owes much to the contributions of British economists and accountants, and these are traced in the remainder of this section.

Historical Development (late 19th and early 20th centuries)

Outlined above are the three main respects in which the application of conventional accounting practice to costing for decisions is deficient: namely, the use of historical costs; the allocation of fixed costs; and the lack of explicit recognition of foregone alternatives. By the beginning of the 20th century these deficiencies had been recognized by a number of accountants and economists, although it was not until later that a comprehensive attempt was made to integrate the views of the two disciplines. Some of the important early contributions to the development of opportunity cost, particularly during the latter part of the 19th century were reviewed by Solomons (1968b), who also traced the historical developments of other aspects of costing. A paper more directly concerned with costing for decisions is Parker (1968) (see also Parker, 1969, particularly chapter 2). The discussion in this paper will be restricted to an attempt to highlight the major British contributions to the development of the main opportunity cost concepts.

One of the first writers to recognize explicitly the irrelevance of sunk costs for decisions was Jevons, who in 1871 wrote (Jevons, 1871, p. 159): 'In commerce, bygones are for ever bygones; and we are always starting clear at each moment, judging the values of things with a view to future utility'. Since then, the irrelevance of historical costs for decisions (except in so far as they are helpful in predicting future costs) has been widely recognized and accepted by economists, although not always by accountants.

The allocation of fixed costs has been a permanent and controversial feature of the literature of accounting, economics and engineering since the industrial revolution. Much of what has been written in accounting is concerned with how fixed (overhead) costs should be allocated, rather than with whether they should be allocated at all (see, e.g., Solomons, 1968b). From an opportunity cost perspective, it is the second question that is of interest. Robert Hamilton seems to have been ahead of his time in recognizing implicitly the futility of allocating fixed costs (Hamilton, 1788, p. 408): 'When we import a cargo of different kinds of goods which could not well be separated . . . it is proper to join them in one accompt, and complete the profit and loss account on the whole together. . . . Perhaps there might be gain on the one and loss on the other; but as we are obliged to import both together, it is the success of the whole that we should enquire into'.

Lardner, an Irish mathematician and economist, was amongst the first writers to recognize the importance of distinguishing between fixed and variable costs, although he did not oppose the common practice of allocating fixed costs (Lardner, 1850).

Major contributions on the problem of fixed overheads came from Garcke and Fells (1887). They went a substantial way towards recognizing the dangers of allocating fixed costs (Garcke and Fells, 1887, p. 74): 'The establishment expense (salaries of clerks, office rent, stationery) and interest on capital should not, however, in any case form part of the cost of production. There is no advantage in distributing these items over the various transactions or articles produced. They do not vary proportionately with the volume of business'. The passage quoted would be even more powerful had the authors addressed their remarks to all fixed costs and not just establishment expenses. In a later edition of their book, Garcke and Fells responded to criticism of their views on establishment expenses by arguing that costs which are relevant for some purposes may not be so for others (Garcke and Fells, 1922, p. 119). This argument was to become a most important component of subsequent works on opportunity cost. Garcke and Fells were an engineer and an accountant, respectively. In the economics literature, Marshall (1890) was perhaps the most influential writer to demonstrate the importance of the distinction between fixed and variable costs.

By the start of the 20th century, the more perceptive British writers (and, indeed, their counterparts overseas) were able to enunciate clearly the irrelevance of fixed cost allocation and the need to consider contribution margins in making decisions. In 1910, W. R. Hamilton wrote: 'What, for instance, is the use of splitting up a manager's salary between departments? If a department be shut up, can a portion of the manager be dispensed with?' Judd, writing in 1914, provided a numerical example demonstrating that the distinction between fixed and fluctuating (avoidable) costs is more important than that between direct (identifiable) and indirect costs, and that contribution is a more important measure of the desirability of a particular course of action than is 'full cost profit'.

The developments outlined above were concerned primarily with the irrelevance of sunk costs and of fixed cost allocations. Developments were taking place concurrently, in the economics literature, in the third of our problem areas, the relevance and role of foregone alternatives. A summary of the most important contributions to this debate is given in Parker (1968). This aspect of opportunity cost was developed initially by political economists for political economists and was not explicitly intended as a prescription for business behaviour. The concept of opportunity cost was first formulated by an Austrian, Friedrich von Wieser, in 1876 and was first published in English by D. I. Green in 1894 and by H. J. Davenport in the same year (see Parker, 1968, p. 622 for references to these works). Both Green and Davenport were American economists.

The first major British writer to recognize the importance of foregone alternatives in measuring cost was Wicksteed (1910). He defined relevant cost (1910, p. 380): 'in the sense of alternatives still open which must now be relinquished in order to produce this specific article'. Wicksteed has been recognized as a major influence on the opportunity cost school that subsequently developed at the London School of Economics.[1] He thus provides a bridge between the opportunity cost developments of the late 19th and early 20th centuries and those which took place during the second quarter of the 20th century.

Historical Development (from the early 20th century)

Prior to 1930, cost concepts had been developed more or less independently by accountants and economists. Accountants (and engineers) had been concerned primarily with the problems involved in allocating overheads and economists with the irrelevance of historical costs and the need to take account of foregone alternatives. During the 1930s, a breed of writers emerged who brought together and developed the cost ideas previously discussed separately in the literature of economics and accounting. These writers were trained in both economics and accounting, and most of them spent at least part of their careers at the LSE.

In terms of the development of opportunity cost as a relevant concept for business decisions, the most important early writings came from Edwards, Coase and Baxter.[2] Collectively, they made three main contributions. The first was to recognize the fundamental importance of defining cost in terms of the choice to be made; they recognized that the appropriate measure of cost depends upon the purpose to which it is to be put, and, consequently,

1 See Buchanan (1969, p. 17), Buchanan's book contains an interesting account of the development of the 'London Tradition'.

2 Buchanan's account of the development of opportunity cost at the LSE recognizes the contribution of other members of the Economics Department, for example Lionel Robbins, F. A. Hayek and Arnold Plant, see Buchanan (1969, Chapter 2).

a cost which is relevant for one decision might not be relevant for another. This line of thought led to the further conclusion that if a decision-maker is influenced by non-financial or subjective factors then relevant costs might also be subjective.

The second contribution was to adopt a 'common sense' approach to costing for decisions, based on providing relevant information for decision models. They did not feel constrained by the decades that had been spent on refining systems of allocating fixed overhead costs, for example. Their approach contrasted with the 'technical' line adopted by many previous (and subsequent) authors on cost accounting and concentrated on questioning the foundations of much cost accounting practice, rather than on suggesting minor modifications to extant procedures.

Their third contribution was to apply the cost concepts they developed to real world business problems. They addressed themselves to what are now recognized by many academic accountants as the major weaknesses of conventional accounting procedures for costing for decisions; the inclusion of historical costs, the arbitrary and irrelevant allocation of fixed costs, the failure to take account of foregone alternatives and the calculation of average rather than marginal costs and revenues.

During 1937, Edwards made a number of contributions which highlighted, in particular, the need for marginal analysis in making decisions (Edwards, 1937a, 1937b, 1937c). For example (1937a, p. 90): . . . the most important thing about costs is the extent to which they change with output.'; (1937a, pp. 90–91): '. . . to be worthwhile, the unit costed must generally add to the turnover of the firm at least the amount of this additional cost'. 'The Rationale of Cost Accounting' (1937a) includes a clear exposition of what the terms marginal cost and marginal revenue mean to the businessman. Edwards also recognized the irrelevance of historical costs (1937a, p. 94):

> 'Textbooks are prone to emphasise the fact that cost accounting analyses *past* costs not future estimates, but they often do not make clear the fact that this data is useful only in so far as it is a guide to future costs. . . .'

In addition, he enumerated the relevant alternative measures of cost (1937a, p. 95):

> '. . . what we have to decide is the additional cost which the use of the material imposes on the business. This additional cost is the replacement price of the materials if they have to be replaced; but if it is not intended to replace them, then scrap value would be more appropriate.'

In one paragraph, Edwards managed to emphasize the dangers of allocating fixed costs, the importance of distinguishing between fixed and variable costs and the need to consider the purposes of the cost calculation in deciding what is relevant cost information (1937a, p. 91):

'Many other expenses are similarly unavoidable. If we call the additional expense incurred by producing the unit to be costed "variable cost" and other expense "fixed cost", then we shall have a useful distinction, as the production is worthwhile if it covers the variable cost and contributes something, however little, to the fixed cost. There is nothing absolute about the term "variable cost"; the items composing it will differ with the change in the unit.'

In a series of articles in 1938, Coase (unlike Edwards) made explicit use of opportunity cost. His study covered all the major aspects of opportunity cost and it says much for its quality that it is not easy today to find better writings for students studying the area. Like Edwards, Coase recognized the irrelevance of fixed costs and the importance of marginal analysis (1938, p. 106):

'Whatever the character of the decision, one has to inquire into the variations in costs and receipts which will follow. Costs and receipts which will remain unchanged, whatever decision is taken, can be ignored.'

He also, like Edwards, acknowledged the irrelevance of historical costs, *per se*, for decision-making (1938, p. 108):

'. . . accounting records merely disclose figures relating to past operations. Business decisions depend on estimates of the future. Accounting records cannot therefore be used as a guide for future action without considering how far the conditions which have existed in the past will continue in the future.'

In an illustration (1938) Coase also argued that contractually committed costs should be treated in the same way as sunk costs. Coase's explanations of the ephemeral nature of relevant costs were clearer than those of Edwards. For example (1938, p. 141): 'One can discuss the meaning of the term "avoidable cost" but what costs *are* avoidable and their actual measurement can only be determined with reference to a particular decision'; (1938, p. 142): 'This linking of cost analysis to particular decisions makes any mechanical classification of costs almost impossible. The costs whose variations are of significance for one decision will be of no significance for others'.

Perhaps Coase's most important contribution was to recognize explicitly that decisions are concerned with choices between alternatives, and that this fact must be reflected in decision analysis (1938, p. 123):

'In this article, the notion of costs which will be used is that of "opportunity" or "alternative" cost. The cost of doing anything consists of the (highest alternative) receipts which could have been obtained if that particular decision had not been taken. . . . This particular concept of costs would seem to be the only one which is of use in the solution of business problems, since it concentrates attention on the alternative courses of action which are open to the businessman.'

In an article also published in 1938, Baxter discussed the irrelevance of allocating fixed overheads. (Although Baxter was not at the LSE when the article was written, he was clearly influenced by the LSE 'philosophy' as is evidenced by his references in the article to Edwards.) In addition, Baxter offered a novel interpretation of allocated overhead costs as approximate measures of opportunity cost (1938, p. 273):

> 'When overhead expenses are allocated between departments or jobs in what seems a defiance of logic, may the resultant charge not in some cases correspond closely to the neglected burden of opportunity cost? . . . Needless to say, however, accountants ought not to rely on this possibility, but should try to estimate the opportunity costs when working out the possible results of changes in policy.'

Baxter returned to this theme in 1961, in an article on cost-plus pricing written with A. R. Oxenfeldt. Discussing the margin added to direct cost to arrive at price, they say (1961, p. 302): 'Our interpretation thus implies that a costing margin should be regarded as a tacit allowance for opportunity cost . . .'.

The British authors of the 1930s should be credited with having popularized opportunity cost as a fundamental concept in determining relevant costs for decisions, at least amongst academics. They wrote with a clarity and insight that endowed their work with durability and interest. In particular, they stressed the apparently obvious, but often neglected, point that decisions are concerned with choices between alternatives and, consequently, any method of determining costs and revenues for decisions which attempts to deal with opportunities in isolation is unlikely to provide a complete analysis.

It is perhaps not surprising, in view of the rapid developments made during the 1930s, that subsequent progress in Britain was less dramatic. At the LSE, substantial contributions were made by Thirlby (1946a, 1946b, 1952, 1960) and Wiseman (1953, 1957) who refined and attempted to apply the opportunity cost concepts developed by their predecessors. Overseas writers (particularly in North America) have turned their attention to many of the problems involved in determining opportunity cost in the real world. Of particular importance has been the determination of the opportunity cost of scarce resources, made possible by developments in mathematical programming techniques. Some of these developments are considered below.

Some Applications of Opportunity Cost Theory

Many of the applications of opportunity cost theory have been developed by overseas writers, but there have been some British contributions. This section identifies three areas of the literature where the concept of opportunity cost has been applied. The first area is the use of opportunity costs derived from mathematical programming techniques. The second is the application of dual prices to the problem of determining transfer prices in divisionalized organizations. The final area is not obviously concerned with opportunity costs. However, the concept of opportunity cost lies at the heart of the problem and it is a peculiarly British debate. It concerns the role of residual income in measuring performance in divisionalized organizations.

Dual Prices as Opportunity Costs

During the 1960s British writers such as Samuels (1965a), Amey (1965 and 1969a), and Carsberg (1969) explored the role of mathematical programming in accounting and some attempts were made at building financial planning models, for instance see Deam *et al.* (1975). It was noted by Carsberg that various overseas writers, especially in North America, had shown that dual prices could be used to identify opportunity costs (Carsberg, 1969). He suggested a number of uses for such opportunity cost measures (1969):

(1) To approximate the optimal product mix in a situation where full estimates for all products available during a planning period have not been prepared, but where it is possible to calculate, at least approximately, the dual prices for all inputs used by the firm.

(2) To compute transfer prices for the resources used in a divisionalized organization.

(3) To evaluate the effect of small deviations from the optimal plan.

The first of the above uses may be criticized on the grounds that appropriate dual prices cannot be obtained until all the alternatives are enumerated, see Gould (1974 and 1977). Accordingly, managers would have no way of ascertaining whether they were close to, or very far away from, the optimal plan. Carsberg recognized this criticism, but argued that at least managers would be given an approximate indication of areas where the greatest effort should be expended in the search for new sources of resource inputs.

The second use of dual prices will be discussed in greater detail later. Arnold (1973b) applied the third use to another type of pricing decision, interim pricing—i.e. pricing decisions made other than at a regular (annual) planning point. He suggested that as computer time is not free, it may prove expensive to re-evaluate the entire mathematical programming problem each time a new opportunity is identified. Dual prices may be used to screen new products, i.e. to determine for new products the minimum price at which opportunity costs are just covered.

An additional use of dual prices relates to the evaluation of budget variances. Samuels (1965b) noted that much work had been done in developing techniques of mathematical programming for financial planning, for instance, Charnes *et al.* (1963); Charnes *et al.* (1959); and Ijiri *et al.* (1963), and also for transfer pricing (discussed below), Dopuch and Drake (1964); Shubik (1964); and Whinston (1964), but that little work had appeared which linked programming techniques with the accounting tools for planning and control.

The crux of Samuels' argument was (1965b, p. 183):

> 'If the firm achieves its optimal plan, the returns will be greater than from any other plan. But if it fails to reach its optimal plan, then these opportunities have been missed. These must be regarded as costs. . . . The shadow prices resulting from the solution of the dual of a programming problem provide the means for calculating these opportunity costs.'

The important contribution made by Samuels was his suggestion that these costs should be charged as variances to the departments responsible for them. Demski (1967) subsequently adopted a similar argument in making a case for variances based on *ex post* budgets. The case for opportunity cost variances was also argued by Bromwich (1969), but not in the context of mathematical programming.

Although certain methodological aspects of Samuels' calculations were questioned (Bernhard, 1968), his work was an important contribution to a literature which developed primarily in North America. This literature provided the basis for the extensive developments which have taken place recently (again mostly in North America) in the area of transfer pricing.

Transfer Pricing

The early analysis of the problem of setting transfer prices was undertaken by economists. Some significant developments took place in North America, principally through the work of Hirshleifer (1956, 1957, 1964). A British contribution was made by Gould (1964). Hirshleifer analysed transfer pricing both with and without a market for the 'intermediate product' (i.e. the product being transferred). Gould extended the analysis to the case where the buying and selling prices for the intermediate product are different.

A major problem of the Hirshleifer analysis is that it fails to generate a transfer pricing rule which has sufficient generality to be used in all divisionalized companies. Furthermore, the approach is not very useful for assessing the contribution which each division makes towards total corporate profit, Tomkins (1973, Chapter 3). These problems are overcome to some extent by the proposals of Ronen and McKinney (1970) who suggest a procedure for passing information between divisions which includes centrally administered taxes and subsidies on interdivisional transfers—but see also Abdel-Khalik and Lusk (1974); Ronen (1975); and Abdel-Khalik and Lusk (1975). Although the economists' approach does provide a number of insights into the transfer pricing problem, it fails to deal adequately with the existence of resource constraints, and alternative approaches have been suggested.

As indicated earlier, writers in North America proposed the use of dual prices in pricing interdivisional transfers. Amey (1969a) supported the use of dual prices derived from a company-wide mathematical programming model such as suggested by Dopuch and Drake (1964). Amey (1969a, p. 133) argued that: 'The "transfer price problem" is a problem in the adaption of price mechanisms to the internal environment of the firm. When optimally fixed, the transfer price should measure the opportunity cost of the product or service transferred *to the firm as a whole*'. Dual prices could be used to ascertain these opportunity costs. Transfer prices would be set at the variable cost plus any relevant dual prices. Accordingly, if the dual price was zero, then the transfer price would be set at the variable cost. Unfortunately, this may not encourage the supplying division to make transfers, as the contribution to its overheads and profits would be zero. Furthermore, there would be no indication of the optimal quantity of transfers.

Samuels (1969b) suggested a method for overcoming these problems. Instead of using dual prices to set the transfer prices, some central authority would supply each division with a schedule of transfer prices, indicating the quantities to be transferred at each transfer price. The divisional managers would then select the price-quantity relationship which would maximize divisional profit. The price schedule would be set in such a way (Samuels suggests using parametric programming) that the divisional selection will also maximize the profit of the whole company.

This suggestion does not overcome a further problem of the dual price approach—namely, the need for centralized control over the decision problem. The information must be available centrally and the central authority must compute the optimal plans for each division. Solomons (1965, p. 193) asked: 'But why, in these circumstances, bother about transfer prices at all? If divisions are not left free to regulate their relations with each other by means of freely negotiated prices, then why not directly dictate the types and volumes of products to be transferred instead of dictating the prices at which transfers are to pass between them?' His solution to the transfer pricing problem involved a two-part charge—a variable cost per unit transferred and an annual lump-sum payment for handling transfers (Solomons, 1965).

The need to decentralize both the data and control of the decision-making process has led to recent developments of the linear decomposition method, Baumol and Fabian (1964), Jennergen (1972), Hass (1968), and Godfrey (1971).

The Residual Income Debate

The nature of opportunity costs has been important in discussions of residual income. This section reviews the residual income literature (in a little more depth than the discussion of previous sections as it is almost entirely British) and examines the role of opportunity costs in the debate.

In the 1950s divisionalized structures were used increasingly by large companies, both in the U.K. and the U.S.A. This prompted a number of academics to study the control of divisionalized operations. At that time, the generally accepted view was that divisions should be evaluated according to their return on capital employed. Solomons demonstrated that such a measure of performance would not necessarily encourage managers to take optimal investment decisions, Solomons (1965). He favoured residual income (i.e. 'the excess of net earnings over the cost of capital') and argued as follows:

> '. . . the question . . . (which divisional management) is the more successful cannot be answered correctly without taking account of the cost of capital . . . unwise rules of divisional profit measurement (reflect) a failure to make a division bear the true cost of using capital. . . . The cost of capital, in the sense that we are now using it, is its opportunity cost.' Solomons (1965), as quoted by Amey (1969b).

This argument implies that divisions should be charged with the opportunity cost of the resources used in their operations, including the opportunity cost of capital. Amey argued, however, that (1969b, p. 5): 'The introduction of interest in evaluating past performance is . . . unnecessary or positively misleading, depending on the divisional objective'. He believes that once investment decisions are taken, they represent bygone costs which must be irrelevant for the assessment of operating decisions (Amey, 1969a).

Samuels suggested that the disagreement between Solomons and Amey reflected a disagreement about the extent and importance of divisional autonomy, particularly with respect to investment decisions (Samuels, 1969a). But Amey (1975) rejected this and argued that it would be incorrect in all cases to include an interest charge on the fixed (i.e. ordinary) share capital used within the division, although a charge could be made for any fixed-interest capital raised especially to finance divisional operations. Tomkins (1975, pp. 39–40) argued that:

> 'The manager of a profit centre is given certain capital assets which he has to use profitably. It is assumed that he has no discretion as regards the volume and value of *fixed assets* at his disposal. This does not mean, however, that he has no control over the *total* investment in his division

because he does decide at what level of output he should produce, and working capital requirements are a function of the level of output.'

This line of reasoning suggests that interest on *working capital* is an opportunity cost which should be charged against the productive activities of divisions in order to assess their profitability.

Tomkins supported residual income for the assessment of operating performance, but rejected the concept for investment decisions and suggested that it is simpler to rely on the NPV criterion for that purpose. Other writers have attempted to relate measures of operating performance directly to the NPV criterion. For instance, Lawson (1971) argued that performance should be monitored on a cash flow basis which is consistent with the use of net present value analysis in *ex ante* planning. A somewhat similar proposal was made by Henderson and Dearden (1966).

Flower (1971) compared the relationship between the period-by-period return on a project and its net present value. He suggested a profit report incorporating an interest charge on divisional capital assets and a depreciation method that produces irregular annual charges. Bromwich doubted the practical and theoretical relevance of such a depreciation method for decision-making, but he did not completely reject the concept of residual income. He observed (1973, p. 129): 'The real role of residual income seems to be to give some signal as to the ability of divisional management to select worthwhile investment projects'.

Both Amey and Bromwich appear concerned that a simple interest charge computed in terms of the historical cost (or even, market value) of capital employed may not adequately measure the opportunity cost to the company of using capital assets within a division. Scapens (1979) demonstrated that optimal production decisions at the divisional level require a capital asset base, on which interest is charged, computed at the marginal cost in the *optimal* investment plan (i.e. dual price from the capital investment problem).

Emmanuel and Otley (1976) found a general agreement in the literature that when a division's capital base is fixed outside the division, then the interest element is irrelevant. Scapens (1979) goes further, and suggests that in such cases all fixed costs associated with capital assets are irrelevant and, thus, divisional managers should be encouraged to maximize contribution, i.e. sales revenue less variable costs.

Amey (1975) has argued that divisions should not have the power to determine their own capital investment. Empirical evidence appears to indicate that investment decisions are frequently centralized; for a review see Gee (1977). Divisions normally require the approval of corporate management for all but the most minor capital expenditures. Nevertheless, in many cases it is the divisional management's responsibility to search for new projects and to put forward proposals for capital expenditure. In such cases, it could be argued that divisions have autonomy over their capital asset base, within the constraints imposed by the system of corporate approval, and that there is a potential role for a residual income measure, provided it reflects the opportunity cost of using capital assets.

Directions for the Future

The extent to which the opportunity cost approach is used in practice is unclear at the present time. It is generally supposed that the techniques are not widely adopted, but there is a shortage of empirical data. The collection of comprehensive empirical evidence on the use of opportunity costs in practice would provide a sound basis for further research. The case for an opportunity cost approach has been argued by a number of, mainly British, writers and opportunity costs appear to be superior to the more conventional historical costs for decision-making. Accordingly, it is appropriate to raise the question: why are opportunity costs apparently not used more in practice?

Dillon and Nash (1978) examined the role of 'relevant costs' in a world of uncertainty. They argued that when utility analysis is introduced the incremental approach may not be appropriate and 'irrelevant' items may become relevant as the decision-maker moves along his preference function. Accordingly, an evaluation of the total outcomes of the available alternatives may be necessary. The arguments advanced by Dillon and Nash 'lead to the conclusion that the conventional incremental approach to decision-making . . . needs to be used with caution under particular conditions, especially when large dollar amounts are involved and the decision involves uncertainty' (Dillon and Nash, 1978, p. 16).

The introduction of uncertainty into the analysis suggests a limitation of one aspect of the opportunity cost approach. An examination of the role of the entire opportunity cost approach in an uncertain world is potentially an interesting and necessary piece of further research.

The role of overhead allocation is another issue which is currently receiving some attention from academic writers in the U.S.A. Zimmerman (1979) presented cases to illustrate that overhead allocations can act as (a) a lump-sum tax which reduces the manager's consumption of perquisites and (b) a proxy variable for difficult-to-observe opportunity costs. The second of the two reasons for overhead allocation is reminiscent of the suggestion made by Baxter in 1938. Baxter suggested that accountants should not rely on this proxy measure. However, as overheads are frequently allocated in practice, it might be reasonable to infer that the costs of obtaining more accurate measures of the difficult-to-observe opportunity costs are likely to exceed the loss caused by using overhead allocations as a proxy measure—but empirical evidence is required.

New insights into the role of overhead allocation (and the use of opportunity costs generally) could be obtained by ascertaining empirically the magnitude of the various costs and benefits of using proxy measures for the difficult-to-observe costs. A study of the effects of alternative costing approaches on the allocation of resources within firms may also be worthwhile. Such a study might use simulation and/or empirical data and consider various decision situations. A prior survey of existing practice, as suggested earlier, would be helpful in designing such a study. The results of this research should give some indication of the effects of not using an opportunity cost approach in practice.

Further research might also examine the possibility that accounting methods other than those based on historical costs may provide a better measure of opportunity costs. For instance, would the introduction of methods of current cost accounting into the costing system lead to improved resource allocation? The empirical/simulation study suggested above could also explore this question. Furthermore, it might be possible to investigate the circumstances in which current costs (for instance) would provide an adequate measure of opportunity costs.

Thus, the nature, role and usefulness of opportunity cost techniques still require research, despite the general acceptance of the techniques (at least by academics). The research areas suggested above can be summarized by the following questions to which answers are still required:

(1) What is the nature and role of opportunity cost under conditions of uncertainty?

(2) Is opportunity cost widely used in practice? If not, why not?

(3) What is the effect on resource allocation of not using opportunity costs?

(4) To what extent and in what circumstances do current costs approximate opportunity costs?

Inevitably, the above list is not exhaustive. Nevertheless, it does provide a starting point for further research in an area in which British writers have traditionally played a major role.

References

Abdel-Khalik, A., Rashad, and Lusk, E. J., 'Transfer Pricing—A Synthesis', *The Accounting Review* (January 1974).

Abdel-Khalik, A., Rashad, and Lusk, E. J., 'Transfer Pricing—A Synthesis: A Reply', *The Accounting Review* (April 1975).

Amey, L. R., 'Mathematical Programming in Accounting—A Comment', *The Accountant* (5 June 1965).

Amey, L. R., *The Efficiency of Business Enterprises*. George Allen and Unwin (1969a).

Amey, L. R., 'Divisional Performance Measurement and Interest on Capital', *Journal of Business Finance* (Spring 1969b).

Amey, L. R., 'Tomkins on "Residual Income"', *Journal of Business Finance and Accounting* (Spring 1975).

Arnold, J. A., *Pricing and Output Decisions*. Haymarket (1973a).

Arnold, J. A., 'On the Problem of Interim Pricing Decisions', *Accounting and Business Research* (Spring 1973b).

Baumol, W. J. and Fabian, T., 'Decomposition, Pricing for Decentralization and External Economies', *Management Science* (September 1964).

Baxter, W. T., 'A Note on the Allocation of Oncosts Between Departments', *The Accountant* (5 November 1938), reprinted in Solomons (1952). The page reference in the text is to the reprint in Solomons.

Baxter, W. T. and Oxenfeldt, A. R., 'Costing and Pricing: The Cost Accountant *versus* the Economist', *Business Horizons* (Winter 1961), reprinted in Solomons (1968). The page reference in the text is to the reprint in Solomons.

Baxter, W. T., and Davidson, S. (eds.), *Studies in Accounting*. ICAEW (1977).

Bernhard, R. H., 'Some Problems in Applying Mathematical Programming to Opportunity Costing', *Journal of Accounting Research* (Spring 1968).

Bonini, C. P., Jaedicke, R. K. and Wagner, H. M. (eds.), *Management Controls: New Directions in Basic Research*. McGraw Hill (1964).

Bromwich, M., 'Standard Costing for Planning and Control', *The Accountant* (19 April, 26 April, 3 May 1969).

Bromwich, M., 'Measurement of Divisional Performance: A Comment and an Extension', *Accounting and Business Research* (Spring 1973).

Buchanan, J. M., *Cost and Choice: An Inquiry in Economic Theory*. Markham (1969).

Buchanan, J. M. and Thirlby, G. F. (eds.), *LSE Essays on Cost*. London School of Economics and Political Science and Weidenfeld and Nicolson (1973).

Carsberg, B. V., *An Introduction to Mathematical Programming for Accountants*. George Allen and Unwin (1969).

Charnes, A., Cooper, W. W. and Miller, M., 'Application of Linear Programming to Financial Budgeting and the Costing of Funds', *Journal of Business* (January 1959).

Charnes, A., Cooper, W. W. and Ijiri, Y., 'Break-Even Budgeting and Programming to Goals', *Journal of Accounting Research* (Spring 1963).

Coase, R. H., 'Business Organisation and the Accountant', *The Accountant* (1 October—17 December 1938), reprinted in Solomons (1952). Page references in the text refer to this reprint.

Cooper, W. W., Leavitt, H. J. and Shelly, M. W. (eds.), *New Perspectives in Organization Research*. John Wiley (1964).

Deam, R. J., Bennet, J. W. and Leather, J., 'Firm: A Computer Model for Financial Planning', *Research Committee Occasional Paper No. 5*. ICAEW (1975).

Demski, J. S., 'An Accounting System Structured on a Linear Programming Model', *The Accounting Review* (October 1967).

Dillon, R. D. and Nash, J. F., 'The True Relevance of Relevant Costs', *The Accounting Review* (January 1978).

Dopuch, N. and Drake, D., 'Accounting Implications of a Mathematical Programming Approach to the Transfer Price Problem', *Journal of Accounting Research* (Spring 1964).

Edey, H. C. and Yamey, B. S. (eds.), *Debits, Credits, Finance and Profits.* Sweet and Maxwell (1974).

Edwards, R. S., 'The Rationale of Cost Accounting', a lecture delivered at the London School of Economics on 8 February 1937a, reprinted in Solomons (1952).

Edwards, R. S., 'Cost Accounting and Joint Production', *The Practising Accountant and Secretary* (7 May 1937b), reprinted in Solomons (1952).

Edwards, R. S., 'The Approach to Budgetary Control', *The Practising Accountant and Secretary* (23 July and 6 August 1937c), reprinted in Solomons (1952).

Emmanuel, C. R. and Otley, D. T., 'The Usefulness of Residual Income', *Journal of Business Finance and Accounting* (Winter 1976).

Flower, J. F., 'Measurement of Divisional Performance', *Accounting and Business Research* (Summer 1971).

Garcke, E. and Fells, J. M., *Factory Accounts* (1st edn.). Crosby Lockwood (1887).

Garcke, E. and Fells, J. M., *Factory Accounts* (7th edn. 1922).

Gee, K. P., *Management Planning and Control in Inflation.* Macmillan (1977).

Godfrey, J. T., 'Short-Run Planning in a Decentralised Firm', *The Accounting Review* (April 1971).

Gould, J. R., 'Internal Pricing in Firms where there are Costs of Using an Outside Market', *Journal of Business* (January 1964).

Gould, J. R., 'Opportunity Cost: The London Tradition', in Edey and Yamey (1974).

Gould, J. R., 'The Economist's Cost Concept and Business Problems', in Baxter and Davidson (1977).

Hamilton, R., *Introduction to Merchandise.* Edinburgh (1788).

Hamilton, W. R., 'Some Economic Considerations Bearing on Costing', *The Accountant* (5 February 1910).

Hass, J. H., 'Transfer Pricing in a Decentralised Firm', *Management Science* (February 1968).

Henderson, B. D. and Dearden, J., 'New System for Divisional Control', *Harvard Business Review* (September–October 1966).

Hirshleifer, J., 'On the Economics of Transfer Pricing', *Journal of Business* (July 1956).

Hirshleifer, J., 'Economics of the Divisionalised Firm', *Journal of Business* (April 1957).

Hirshleifer, J., 'Internal Pricing and Decentralised Decisions', in Bonini, Jaedicke and Wagner (1964).

Ijiri, Y., Levy, F. R. and Lyon, R. C., 'A Programming Model for Budgeting and Financial Planning', *Journal of Accounting Research* (Autumn 1963).

Jennergen, P., 'Decentralisation on the Basis of Price Schedules in Linear Decomposable Resource-Allocation Problems', *Journal of Financial and Quantitative Analysis* (January 1972).

Jevons, W. S., *The Theory of Political Economy* (1st edn.) Macmillan (1871).

Judd, H. C., 'Fixed and Fluctuating Oncost', *Accountants' Magazine* (March 1914).

Lardner, D., *Railway Economy.* Taylor, Walton and Maberly (1850).

Lawson, G. H., 'Measuring Divisional Performance', *Management Accounting* (U.K.) (May 1971).

Marshall, A., *Principles of Economics.* Macmillan (1890).

Parker, R. H., 'Early History of Cost Concepts for Decision-Making', *Accountancy* (September 1968).

Parker, R. H., *Management Accounting: an Historical Perspective*. Macmillan (1969).

Ronen, J. and McKinney, G., III, 'Transfer Pricing for Divisional Autonomy', *Journal of Accounting Research* (Spring 1970).

Ronen, J. and McKinney, G., III, 'Transfer Pricing—A Synthesis: A Comment', *The Accounting Review* (April 1975).

Samuels, J. M., 'Mathematical Programming in Accounting', *The Accountant* (27 February 1965a).

Samuels, J. M., 'Opportunity Costing: An Application of Mathematical Programming', *Journal of Accounting Research* (Autumn 1965b).

Samuels, J. M., 'Divisional Performance Measurement and Interest on Capital: A Contributed Note', *Journal of Business Finance* (Autumn 1969a).

Samuels, J. M., 'Penalties and Subsidies in Internal Pricing Policies', *Journal of Business Finance* (Autumn 1969b).

Scapens, R. W., 'Profit Measurement in Divisionalised Companies', *Journal of Business Finance and Accounting* (Autumn 1979).

Shubik, M., 'Incentives, Decentralized Control, the Assignment of Joint Costs and Internal Pricing', in Bonini, Jaedicke and Wagner (1964).

Solomons, D. (ed.), *Studies in Costing* (1st edn.) Sweet and Maxwell (1952).

Solomons, D., *Divisional Performance: Measurement and Control*. Irwin (1965).

Solomons, D. (ed.), *Studies in Cost Analysis* (2nd edn.) Sweet and Maxwell (1968a).

Solomons, D., 'The Historical Development of Costing', (1968b) in Solomons (1968a).

Thirlby, G. F., 'The Subjective Theory of Value and Accounting "Cost"', *Economica* (February 1946a), reprinted in Buchanan and Thirlby (1973).

Thirlby, G. F., 'The Ruler', *South African Journal of Economics* (December 1946b), reprinted in Buchanan and Thirlby (1973).

Thirlby, G. F., 'The Economist's Description of Business Behaviour', *Economica* (May 1952), reprinted in Buchanan and Thirlby (1973).

Thirlby, G. F., 'Economists' Cost Rules and Equilibrium Theory', *Economica* (May 1960), reprinted in Buchanan and Thirlby (1973).

Tomkins, C. R., *Financial Planning and Divisionalised Companies*. Haymarket (1973).

Tomkins, C. R., 'Another Look at Residual Income', *Journal of Business Finance and Accounting* (Spring 1975).

Whinston, A., 'Price Guides in Decentralized Operations', in Cooper, Leavitt and Shelley (1964).

Wicksteed, P. H., *The Common Sense of Political Economy*. Macmillan (1910).

Wiseman, J., 'Uncertainty, Costs and Collectivist Economic Planning', *Economica* (May 1953), reprinted in Buchanan and Thirlby (1973).

Wiseman, J., 'The Theory of Public Utility Price—an empty Box', in *Oxford Economic Papers* (1957) reprinted in Buchanan and Thirlby (1973).

Zimmerman, J. L., 'The Costs and Benefits of Cost Allocations', *The Accounting Review* (July 1979).

Commentary on 'The British contribution to opportunity cost theory'

J B Coates
Senior Lecturer in Finance and Accounting, University of Aston in Birmingham

This paper is based on three main themes: the gaining of an historical perspective of developments toward a theory of costing; establishing the concept of opportunity costing as the correct basis for such a theory in contrast to traditional cost accounting, and, finally, a discussion of possible future research areas.

I am in broad agreement with the authors' analysis throughout, but would wish to emphasize some points and take a somewhat different view of others.

The paper clearly brings out the distinction between theory and practice in costing. 'Traditional' costing implies absorption costing based on sometimes complex schemes of allocation and apportionment of indirect expense. This obscures the kind of cost information necessary for decision-making (it is implicit in the paper that the authors' interpretation of the term costing theory is a costing for decisions theory) and to the extent that it is based on historical cost data is almost useless for this purpose. Yet costing departments continue to produce such information, though it is an improvement if it is in the context of variance accounting and incorporates well-defined fixed-variable cost classifications; even so, however, it remains too rigid a structure for decision-making. Academic writings have long since pointed out the serious shortcomings of traditional costing systems but they continue to be much in evidence in practice today. An obvious question to ask is why, but without a much fuller understanding of practice it is doubtful if it can be properly answered at the moment.

It is interesting to note also that Solomons (1952) in his well-known article on the Historical Development of Costing did not include any reference to the incorporation of opportunity costing into the philosophy and practice of costing, despite the lengthy history of debate on opportunity costing and acceptance of the ideas by others by then. Observation of practice at least suggests that little progress has been made since the Solomons article first appeared in formally introducing the concept of opportunity costing into the framework of costing for decision-making.

One could be forgiven for wondering whether management accountants have split personalities on this point: on the one hand, many of them, before entering the profession, are trained as economists, and those who are trained within the profession have considerable exposure to the ideas of economics, in which the opportunity cost concept occupies a position of fundamental significance. Once established within companies, however, it would appear that they operate in a manner predominantly consistent with 'traditional' costing, with little reference to opportunity costing, except maybe with a nod in that direction through limited application of marginal analysis.

It is difficult to find a rational explanation for this so it seems sensible to enquire whether the truth of the situation could be being obscured by certain factors.

Buchanan (1969) certainly provides a framework for thinking about costs, which leads to the thought that opportunity costing may be present in the process of decision-making, though often a good deal less than explicitly. The book summarizes contributions from economists and accountants to ideas on cost and choice from many sources, but, especially with a chapter devoted to 'The Origins and Development of a London Tradition', the view of the authors of this paper being reviewed that the British contribution to costing theory is substantial and important obtains great support. Detailed exposition of the work of Thirlby, Coase, Wicksteed and other British writers is included in the book.

Buchanan is summarizing these various contributions, including the British, when he distinguishes in Chapter 3, three perspectives of cost:

(a) the subjective cost of predictive theory;
(b) choice-influencing cost;
(c) choice-influenced cost;

(b) is essentially opportunity cost in the present context, though as he says (p. 45) . . . 'any one of the three . . . may be meaningfully treated in opportunity cost terms'.

Buchanan further identifies six features of cost relevant to (b):

(i) cost must be borne exclusively by the decision-maker; it is not possible for cost to be shifted or imposed on others;

(ii) cost is subjective; it exists in the mind of the decision-maker and nowhere else;

(iii) cost is based on anticipations; it is necessarily a forward-looking or *ex ante* concept;

(iv) cost can never be realized because of the fact of choice itself; that which is given up cannot be enjoyed;

(v) cost cannot be measured by someone other than the decision-maker, because there is no way that subjective experience can be directly observed;

(vi) finally, cost can be dated at the moment of decision or choice.

This view of choice influencing cost, which stresses the forward-looking and subjective nature of cost used in the decision-making context, is a far cry from what might be termed the average perception of cost. Indeed, the practical businessman's reaction to confrontation with these ideas could still be to demand to know what the actual costs (and cost consequences) of making a particular decision are.

However, is the problem really so intractable? It seems that a good deal of the controversy could lie in failure to specify clearly what aspects of cost are under discussion. Most companies of a size sufficient to include a management accounting section are unlikely to be basing their operating policies on historical costs: forward-looking cost estimation and variance accounting will be the essential basis of the management accounting system.

The point to be borne clearly in mind is the distinction between choice-influencing and choice-influenced cost, even if the latter can also be linked back to the opportunity cost concept. Essentially, choice-influenced cost is the result of the decisions that have been made with respect to sales volumes, and so on. Once the latter have been made, costing, on a forward-looking basis, swings into action in the traditional sense, providing product and department costs, average, variable and fixed costs etc; this data is related to the programme to be achieved and actual progress toward its achievement, though no doubt some would argue what the point of all this information is, besides satisfying a management demand for it.

What is unclear is how the programme is determined in the first place and possibly, also, how progress over time is assessed with a view to taking up opportunities which have arisen subsequent to the determination of the initial programme. It is in this area that the major role of opportunity cost may lie, although its potential applicability to a wide range of management accounting problems is noted in the paper. The main vehicle serving to bring opportunity costing formally into the decision-making process is seen by the authors to be mathematical programming, which, in theory, could be used in both a long-term (capital budgeting) and short-term decision-making context. Yet, despite the outward attractions of this group of techniques which, apparently, could be used to quantify opportunity costs, the authors are uncertain of the extent of its current application to practice, perhaps implying they do not think it extensive. This is certainly the experience of the present writer so far as the engineering industry is concerned. In the context of cost control, no examples of specific employment of an opportunity cost based approach have been seen in operation.

This, naturally, leads to the final point of the paper: research. Neither the authors nor myself can claim an overview of costing or management accounting practice sufficient to know how widely an opportunity costing approach to decision-making is used in practice in any of the potential applications outlined in the paper. Further, if it were discovered that—as is suspected—the approach is not extensively employed, then there is the question of why not? There would be a considerable gap between an apparently attractive theoretical approach and actual practice, not the first time that such a division has arisen, of course, but, nonetheless, one well-deserving further investigation.

I certainly welcome and support the view of the authors that further substantial research in this area is needed. Intuitively, one would agree with them that there will be problems in establishing general costing systems which reflect opportunity costs, even if the conditions for initial acceptance of the system could be satisfactorily determined and specified. The attraction of the Zimmerman suggestion of the adaptation of the traditional costing approach to an opportunity cost based scheme is evident, but is also apparently untried and untested in an empirical situation; it also has something of the 'if you can't beat them, join them' element about it.

References

Buchanan, J. M., *Cost and Choice: An Inquiry in Economic Theory*. Markham (1969).

Solomons, D., *Studies in Cost Analysis*. Sweet and Maxwell (1968). The article referred to is the 'Historical Development of Costing' first published in 1952.

8 A social and organizational view of management accounting

David Cooper
Senior Lecturer in Accounting, University of East Anglia

I would like to thank David Hayes, Anthony Hopwood, Tony Lowe and Tony Tinker (in alphabetical order) for their support and discussions over the last few years. I acknowledge the helpful comments of the editors, Trevor Hopper and David Otley, on an earlier draft of this paper.

> 'Daughter: Daddy, why do things get in a muddle?
> Father: What do you mean? Things? Muddle?
> Daughter: Well, people spend a lot of time tidying things, but they never seem to spend time muddling them. Things just seem to get in a muddle by themselves. And then people have to tidy them up again.' (*Bateson*, 1972, p. 3.)

The above interaction outlines the themes of this paper. How do organizations resolve the tension between the need for order and the tendency towards disorder? In particular, what are the roles of accounting systems in maintaining order and responding to disorder?

I think there are some more profound and challenging implications in Bateson's (1972) interchange. He raises questions about the meaning of 'things' and of 'muddle'. What 'things' in an organizational context get 'muddled' and which are the important 'things' that then have to be unmuddled? What role do accounting systems play in the identification of 'things' and in the tidying process? Is it appropriate to treat all organizational participants as 'things'? Indeed, in what sense is it useful, rational or intelligent to spend time tidying up rather than muddling things up?

This paper is not a survey of the field. Rather it is concerned with the issues of accounting information system design focusing on the organizational and social context of accounting. Ultimately, I view accounting—as any science—as a means to achieve tidiness (order or control) in organizations and society. The paper has two major sections. In the section that follows—'accounting to order'—I argue that contingency theory has seemed to provide a useful guide for the design of accounting systems. Contingency theory offers prescriptions about the ways in which organizational control[1] may be achieved, and thereby provides managers with a means by which they can define their situations in order to choose, for

1 'Organizational control' refers to managing a system so that it best achieves its objectives.

example, the most appropriate accounting system. Contingency theory has seemed to provide a recipe to achieve organizational order or control.

Following Child (1977), Hopwood (1978), Otley (1979) and Wood (1979), it would appear that there are major problems with contingency theory and its use in management accounting. In the section—'order to order'—I indicate some of these concerns. The source of my concern relates to a tendency to equate control (managing a system so that it achieves its objectives) with a specific notion of order. I argue that order is regrettably frequently related to the idea of maintaining the domination and authority of a minority over the majority in an organization (and indeed, in society). But I do not think that order has to be equated with domination. Order can take on the same meaning as control (Buckley, 1968) and I do not, ultimately, reject contingency theory but suggest that contingency theory has, typically, failed to deal with several fundamental issues which relate to the nature of management (and accounting) science and its relationship with organizational effectiveness and whose interests science may serve. Contingency theory is, in short, rather 'muddled' and it may be useful at the present time for accounting researchers not only to develop a better theory for the design of accounting systems but also to investigate the nature and uses of management accounting as a preliminary to the development of theory which may form the basis of information system design.

Tidiness: Accounting to Order?

Management accounting seems to have developed, at least in part, to facilitate co-ordination of activities in diverse and dispersed organizations, to monitor performance of organizational sub-units and to allocate funds to these sub-units (Chandler and Daems, 1979). In short, accounting may, in part, have been developed to aid managers in making decisions about the most appropriate ways of achieving their (and the organization's) objectives. In the first half of the 20th century a variety of theories were developed and popularized that purported to indicate to managers how they might effectively carry out their tasks. The dominant perspective on the effective[2] management of organizations was that there was a universal model and associated set of universal prescriptions that could be followed which would lead to continued organizational survival and success. One set of universal prescriptions emerged from the scientific management approach to organizational control. This model continues to dominate management accounting. But alongside the development and prescriptions of the scientific management approach an alternative, apparently more

2 As I will argue in the next section, the concept of effectiveness is problematic and has rarely been addressed.

humanistic, set of prescriptions emerged that emphasized participation and individual commitment. In this section I will briefly outline both these sets of prescriptions and identify the prescribed role of accounting within each set. I will then indicate how contingency theory seemed to help managers choose between these two sets of prescriptions and thereby provide the appropriate 'accounting to order'.

Scientific Management

At its most basic, scientific management assumes that individual motivation and behaviour is based on economic rewards and penalties and that man is imaginative in maximizing his economic welfare. Control is achieved in scientific management through the manipulation of organizational rewards and sanctions and the directing of behaviour through a set of plans, rules and a hierarchy. This model of control is not only found in the work of Taylor (1947) and Weber (1947) but is also found in the economic theory of agency and organization (for example, Alchian and Demsetz, 1972; Demski and Feltham, 1978).

Most textbook pictures of management accounting fit into this model (Horngren, 1977). Accounting information is orientated towards score card and attention directing roles of information (Simon *et al.*, 1954). Formal systems of information recording—job costing and process costing systems—are based on the detailed rules for production and indeed represent a major part of the 'red tape' of bureaucracy. Accounting systems reflect the rules of how products are to be produced and the inter-relationships between production processes. Responsibility accounting systems and divisional reporting schemes reflect, reinforce, and thereby facilitate, the creation of the well-defined patterns of hierarchy, authority and responsibility that are found in bureaucracies. These accounting systems specify the actions to be reported, who has responsibility and authority to make decisions and on what criteria these decisions will be evaluated.

Most of the prescriptions offered by the applied economics branch of management accounting (e.g., Carsberg, 1975) reinforce bureaucratic rationality and act as a means of co-ordinating and directing individual activity. The development of optimal production plans, inventory policies, investment strategies, pricing policies and so on provide the specific rules of organizational activity that will facilitate the objectives of the owners of the firm. We may wish to question the optimality of such techniques under conditions of uncertainty and conflict over goals, yet there is little doubt that management science techniques seek to provide an optimal plan which limits individual discretion, defines individual activity and provides a means of integrating that activity.

Similarly, budgets and standard costing are typically viewed as techniques to achieve control through order. Budgets are seen as ways of imposing the goals of top managers on other organizational participants and as means of scheduling tasks and achieving organizational co-ordination (Livingstone, 1973). Not surprisingly, there has been some relatively careful work done on the optimal degree of difficulty of 'imposed' standards (Stedry, 1960; Stedry and Kay, 1966; Hofstede, 1968) and the 'best' way to use organizational reward systems in the evaluation of individual performance (Argyris, 1952; Hopwood, 1973; Cherrington and Cherrington, 1973; Otley, 1978). Yet whilst the results of each of these studies is interesting in its own right, a major conclusion has been that the conflicting results about the uses of budgetary control systems may be dependent on the state of the organization and its environment (Baumler, 1971; Otley, 1978).

Participative Model of Management

Industrial psychology in Britain (e.g. Myers, 1924), by challenging the simple-minded hedonism implicit in scientific management, opened the way for the human relations movement. Human relations—in its many forms—is based upon a psychological (and to a limited degree, a social) view of human motivation. Its appeal seems to have been based, at least in part, on a model of effective management that did not produce the alienative effects of scientific management. However, it is important to recognize that the concerns of industrial psychology and its American development, the human relations movement, were similar to those of scientific management: 'Taylorism and applied individual psychology—and later, human relations—were essentially concerned with problems of motivation and compliance' (Rose, 1978, p. 98).

The participative model of management is more than human relations. The participative approach also incorporates an alternative to bureaucracy as a means of co-ordination. Developing a technology of 'loose coupling' may be one mechanism for creating order without destroying individual responsibility (Glassman, 1973; Weick, 1976). The creation of decentralized organizational structures is a mechanism for de-coupling large organizations into smaller units. Sub-units may be somehow attached but each unit retains some separateness and the attachment may be infrequent, weak, unimportant and/or lack mutual response. Likert (1967) suggests an alternative means of co-ordination. He suggests the use of group structures in organizations which would provide support to each member of the group. These groups would be co-ordinated through a series of 'linking pins' or integrators. In general, within the participative approach, there has been a tendency to suggest organizational structures that are intended to widen individual and group autonomy and discretion. These structures have, on the one hand, involved apparent decentralization of decision-making (typically viewed as merely involving participation in discussing means to achieve given goals) and, on the other, co-ordination to achieve consistency through project teams, integrating units and committees as well as the mechanisms which are part of the repertoire of scientific management (e.g. rules, plans, etc.).

But whilst management accounting could have a role in aiding and sustaining new forms of work organization, that role has not been well explicated. Informal information systems (Galbraith, 1973; Clancy and Collins, 1979) would seem to play an important role in organizations emphasizing lateral communication. Formal management accounting systems that embrace the participative model of management are not well-developed. Management accounting systems such as responsibility accounting, standard costing and product cost accumulation systems tend to be hierarchical in nature. Management accounting systems that seem to be a part of decentralized structures (and indeed help to make such structures possible) appear, on close inspection, to revert to the scientific management model (Watson and Baumler, 1975). Even decentralized accounting systems based on decomposition programming methods which are intended to encourage divisional autonomy and independence, ultimately require centralized information flows and rigid rules that enforce central authority.

Although there have been one or two suggestions about lateral information systems (e.g. Lorsch, 1970) the participative approach has, I would suggest, influenced management accounting in only two significant ways. It has been used to facilitate the implementation of accounting techniques—'overcoming resistance to change'. There has been considerable activity in developing participative approaches to budgeting (Argyris, 1952; Hofstede, 1968; Milani, 1975; Swieringa and Moncur, 1975; DeCoster, 1976). Management accounting has also been affected by the informational requirements of a variety of participative management techniques—such as management by objectives and job enrichment programmes. One interpretation of human resource accounting (e.g. Likert, 1967) is that it is concerned with directing managerial attention towards the virtues of participation by collecting social and psychological measures of the 'human organization' (e.g. measures of employee turnover, absenteeism and attitudes). These measures, it is alleged, will demonstrate the 'long run benefit' (i.e. profitability) of participative management.

Contingency Model of Management

The development of contingency theory in the 1960s seemed to offer management a certain tidiness—a recipe for effective management of organizations. As we shall argue in the next section this tidiness is more muddled than is often recognized, although writers such as Woodward (1958, 1965), Burns and Stalker (1961), Emery and Trist (1965), Lawrence and Lorsch (1967) and Thompson (1967) provided important insights into organizational functioning. In particular, they helped reorientate organizational theory, and to a lesser degree accounting and management thought, towards the study and understanding of organizations rather than of individuals. To a degree, with their emphasis on organization rather than individuals, the contingency theorists developed from the Carnegie approach to organization and management (Simon, 1976; Simon *et al.*, 1954; March and Simon, 1958; Cyert and March, 1963; Bonini, 1963). This organizational level view also seems to reflect a more European and U.K. perspective on organizational functioning (Kassem, 1976). For example, the work of Lowe and Shaw (1968 and 1970) and Berry and Otley (1975) is concerned with forecasting and estimation in organizations (rather than forecasting by individuals). Similarly, Hofstede's (1968) research consistently emphasizes the organizational and cultural influences on budgeting. The difference in approach is well-demonstrated by comparing the content and viewpoints of two textbooks in the area. The British example (Hopwood, 1974) is orientated towards a social and organizational viewpoint; the American (Lawler and Rhode, 1976) is more individualistic. tic.

Contingency theorists argued that the appropriate model of the organization, the best way to manage the organization and the relevant role of information systems depends on a number of factors that affect the uncertainty faced by the firm. A fundamental conclusion is that 'the beginning of administrative wisdom is the awareness that there is no one optimum type of management system' (Burns and Stalker, 1961, p. 125). The uncertainty may be the result of a number of variables—the size of the organization, the nature and rate of change of the organization's environment, the technology of the organization or the degree of inter-relationship between units of the organization. In other words, the uncertainty relates to the variety that the organization's management system may need to handle in order to survive (Ashby, 1956; Beer, 1967).

When there is low variety or predictability in the environment of an organization—including its market situation, technical information and production technology—then control, it is suggested, is best achieved through the application of scientific management. For example, organizations producing standardized products by mass assembly production methods based on a well-defined technology to sell in a well-defined and unchanging market may be suited to this approach. Stability in the situation of the organization encourages the use of standard procedures, well-patterned lines of responsibility and authority and use of imposed standards. The performance of individuals—and the organization—can be assessed against well-defined and consistent standards (as set by the organization's controller).

In situations of high variety, when conditions are seen as unpredictable or novel, contingency theory would suggest that a fundamentally different kind of management system becomes appropriate. In conditions where the product market is rapidly changing, or the technological basis of the organization is changing or when production is faced with unforeseen requirements, then well-defined standards of performance are likely to produce inflexibility and an inability to deal with change. In unpredictable situations, no one is an expert and thus specialization of tasks become inappropriate. Instead, in these 'organic' systems individual tasks are constantly being redefined and responsibility is related to the solution of the inevitably novel problems of the organization rather than the execution of well-defined individual tasks. Creativity and commitment would appear to be at a premium. One of the alleged advantages of participative management is that the resultant management style may be more adaptable and flexible to changing situations. Research organizations and organizations producing to customer specifications with an uncertain technological base are examples of enterprises which contingency writers might suggest are more suited to the organic organization form. Moreover, despite the fact that organic systems require a great deal of commitment by individuals to both the organizational task and the values of the organization, organizations that effectively adapt to unpredictability tend to create anxiety for their members since the demands of the job are unspecified and ever changing. As a consequence participative controls can be used to provide just such commitment through the use of moral rather than remunerative encouragement.

However, contingency theory does not claim that organizational performance all depends on the environment of the organization. Rather, the argument is that the over-riding management task is to interpret the situation of the organization in terms of its predictability. For example, Lawrence and Lorsch (1967) suggest that management should identify the rate of change of environmental conditions over time, the certainty of information about conditions at any particular time and the speed of feedback on the results of decisions made. The greater the rate of change, the less certainty about conditions and the longer the feedback on results, the more an organization should be designed (or allowed to develop) to approximate to the organic type.

Contingency theory represents a move away from the universalism of scientific and participative models of management and a move towards an open systems approach to organization theory. These moves have led to an increased focus on design issues: how to create and change management systems so that they achieve organizational purposes (however defined). Recent work in accounting system design has reflected and utilized the contingency orientation—for example Bruns and Waterhouse (1975), Sathe (1975), Watson (1975), Gordon and Miller (1976), Lowe and Tinker (1976), Ansari (1977), Cooper (1977), Hayes (1977), Otley (1978) and Waterhouse and Tiessen (1978). The normative appeal (Legge, 1978) of contingency theory is that it provides a framework for choosing between theories of management and the design of information systems. But there is an associated tendency for contingency theory to be applied unthinkingly so that it ironically 'becomes itself a new panacea, the "situational approach to management"' (Wood, 1979, p. 336). In other words contingency theory provides a new form of tidiness in the choice of management models. Before considering the 'reality' of this tidiness, however, I wish to outline a more sophisticated version of contingency theory that begins to recognize some of the weaknesses of the 'new panacea' view of contingency theory, and to identify the crucial role of information in design alternatives. As such, Galbraith's contribution (1973 and 1977) provides a link between this section that emphasizes 'order' and the next that probably produces 'muddle'. Galbraith's work also has important implications for management accounting.

Galbraith argues that organizational performance is 'determined' by the difference between the uncertainty or variety it faces and the relevant information that the managers of the organization possess to handle that variety. Using Ashby's law of requisite variety, Lowe and Tinker (1976) make the same point. The contingency theorists identify a number of variables which affect the variety or uncertainty that the organization faces. Galbraith emphasizes that 'the amount of information to be processed in decision-making is a function of the division of labour, goal diversity and the level of goal performance required . . . The greater the uncertainty, the greater the amount of decision-making and information processing. It is hypothesized that organizations have limited capacities to process information and adopt different organizing modes to deal with task uncertainty. Therefore variations in organizing modes are actually variations in the capacity of organizations to process information and make decisions about events which cannot be anticipated in advance' (Galbraith, 1977, p. 39). The appropriate organizational model and the appropriate role of accounting systems will therefore depend on the variety of the organization and the variety required to respond (i.e. manage) to that variety.

What is particularly important is that we can rediscover through Galbraith (1973, 1977) and Lowe and Tinker (1976) the fundamental message of Simon *et al.* (1954) that has been avoided for the last twenty-five years. Accounting is an organizational artifact and its role will be dependent on the organization it is designed to serve, its structure, performance requirements and environment. Further, as Fig. 8.1 attempts to show, investment in information systems is only one of the ways an organization can match the complexity of its environment and thereby, it is hoped, improve its performance.

Virtually all organizations require some ability to handle exceptions. For Galbraith, managing exceptions is a fundamental managerial activity. Decision-making (in its widest sense) involves action and change. If there are no exceptions, there are no decision stimuli. Figure 8.1 suggests that all organizations have to develop strategies for managing exceptions. It is suggested that the scientific management model emphasizes those design

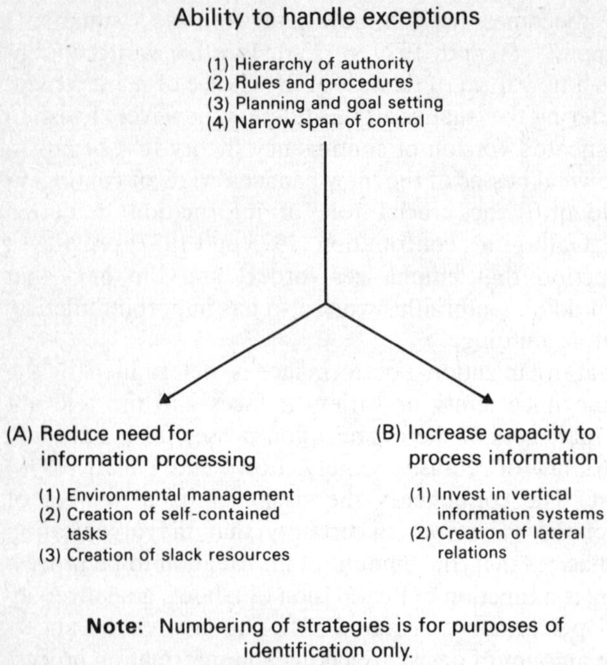

Fig. 8.1 Organization design strategies. (From Fig. 3.7 of Galbraith, 1977.)

strategies that handle exceptions. Management accounting systems provide rules and procedures for handling information and taking decisions. Rational prescriptive models in management accounting also provide plans and goals for the organization. Accounting systems also reflect and sustain organization hierarchy and structure. Yet as the uncertainty facing the organization increases, this technology to create order which is derived from scientific management is increasingly inadequate and organizational performance is likely to decline. This decline occurs because more and more exceptions to the plans and rules have to be handled by the organization and pathological forms of bureaucracy are likely to develop (Burns and Stalker, 1961).

Figure 8.1 identifies two broad strategies to cope with the increased uncertainty that the scientific management technology is unable to handle effectively. By recognizing alternative strategies, Galbraith is acknowledging the choice that managers face. Galbraith (1977) suggests that there are three ways of reducing the need for information processing. The organization can attempt to manage its environment: changing markets, technology or attempting to influence the munificence of the environment (Staw and Szwajkowski, 1975). We will return to this neglected theme in the next section. Secondly, the organization can create self-contained tasks in order to reduce the need to produce information for co-ordination or integrative purposes. Divisionalization, decentralization and semi-autonomous work groups are specific organizational forms whose purpose may, in part, be to reduce the flow of information within the organization. The third strategy to reduce information flows is to increase so called slack resources. This may mean the conscious investment in increased stocks of raw materials and finished goods or the reduction in quality control and other performance standards. Galbraith (1977) argues that organizations will inevitably but unconsciously increase slack resources or reduce performance standards if there is no conscious design strategy in the face of increasing complexity and environmental uncertainty.

Figure 8.1 also presents two strategies that increase the organization's ability to process information. Galbraith (1977, Chapters 8–11) seems to regard the possibility of designing organizations that encourage lateral relationships as particularly promising. Matrix structures (Davis and Lawrence, 1977), joint decision-making processes, and task forces are devices for increasing flows across levels in an organization. There has, as yet, been very little study of the roles of accounting and the design of accounting systems for these organizational forms. One assumption is that, at present, the accounting systems which exist in such organizations tend to be informal (Clancy and Collins, 1979).

The alternative strategy to cope with increased uncertainty is to invest in formal (and typically vertical or hierarchical) information systems. Galbraith (1977, Chapter 7) classifies information systems according to their frequency (periodic or continuous), scope (local or global), formalization (symbolic or verbal) and decision-making mechanisms (individual, group or automated). With increasing uncertainty and exceptions Galbraith argues that global-continuous systems will be more appropriate than the typical accounting systems which are often periodic and either global or local using individual decision-making mechanisms.

Galbraith does not consider in any detail the way in which the alternative strategies outlined in Fig. 8.1 will be chosen. He seems to assume that it will be based on a rational assessment of the costs and benefits of the alternatives. This may be the case. But the cost-benefit calculus tends to hide from view the constraints and pressures from within the organization and from its environment that may affect the choice. Further, I will argue in the next section that the traditional framework of rational (i.e. consistent) choice may be inappropriate in describing the manner in which choices (as an outcome) occur. For example, solutions that are available and decision-makers who have the time to make the decision may influence the 'choice' of design strategy (March and Olsen, 1976).

Galbraith provides a useful reminder that investing in accounting information systems is but one strategy to achieve organizational control. Whilst his model is within the tradition of contingency theory (i.e. it argues that the appropriate organizational form depends on its information-processing needs which in turn depends on the amount of exceptions the firm has to handle, which itself is dependent on the uncertainty it faces), Galbraith makes an attempt to deal with one or two of the problems of contingency theory. There is an element of managerial choice in the selection of organization and management systems, thereby addressing the criticism that contingency theory is overly deterministic (Child, 1972). There is a recognition of the possibility that an organization's environment may not be completely uncontrollable and an organization can develop strategies for changing environments (Pfeffer, 1978). However, I do not think either of these attempts to handle criticisms of contingency theory are altogether convincing and I think there are other problems that Galbraith, as well as other contingency theorists, have not yet resolved. These issues are discussed in the next section. There is false tidiness in the belief that contingency theory provides the solution to designers of accounting systems in their choice of accounting information system.

Muddle: Order to Order?

Contingency theory has become popular, I suggest, because it provides order to organization theory and, by implication, the design of management accounting systems within organizations. The theory suggests that designers of accounting systems should consider the unpredictability of the organization's situation, structure their organization accordingly and then modify or design their systems (or lack of them) consistent with the organization, its technology and environment. In this section I suggest that the 'order' typically created by the use of contingency theory will be the maintenance of the *status quo* (the existing order). Contingency theory as it has typically been understood in management accounting (Watson, 1975; Gordon and Miller, 1976; Cooper, 1977; Hayes, 1977; Waterhouse and Tiessen, 1978) has been used in an inherently conservative fashion. This conservatism has been reflected in three broad ways.

First, by accepting the fundamental validity of existing techniques of control, contingency theorists have typically failed to consider the meaning and nature of organizational control (Otley and Berry, 1980). We may question the assumption that control has to be equated with domination (Braverman, 1974; Nichols and Benyon, 1977; Cherns, 1978). Secondly, by focusing on choices of efficient organizations and information systems, contingency theory has ignored the question of whose interests organizations can or should serve. Questions of effectiveness are rarely considered (Churchman, 1968) and the problematic nature of concepts such as environment, uncertainty and organizations have not been sufficiently recognized when the design of information systems is being discussed (Ashby, 1956; Beer, 1975; Pfeffer, 1978). And thirdly, contingency theorists have taken an unduly restricted view of the varieties of control and their uses in organizations (Burchell *et al.*, 1980). By focusing on a simple-minded notion of science and rationality, there has been little consideration of organizations as social entities (Burns, 1966; Pondy and Mitroff, 1978; Boland, 1979) and thus little recognition of the more symbolic forms of organizational control such as culture (Pettigrew, 1979), myth (Jönsson and Lundin, 1977) and magic (Gambling, 1976). By using a relatively deterministic orientation to the study of organizational activity, many contingency theorists have tended to ignore issues of change and the ways organizations can learn, experiment and legitimate their activities in dynamic situations (Hedberg *et al.*, 1976; Amey, 1979; Weick, 1979).

These omissions and the problems in contingency theory are discussed in this section. Taken together I think they suggest that there is considerable 'muddle' in the theory. In particular, it suggests to me that control, rationality and order should be considered more carefully than hitherto so that a more 'liberated' view of accounting and management can be developed.

Control, Order and Domination

Contingency theory has both positive and normative elements. It describes how organizational structures and processes are influenced by contingencies in the environment. The normative element suggests the way in which organizations should be managed and designed; like much of science the normative element of the theory indicates how man can order or manage his external world. This is the control aspect of science—by furthering human understanding of reality, science may help to control (manage and change) that reality.

The first criticism of contingency theory (*inter alia*) comes almost exclusively from European sociologists. It is that the mode of managing that is implicit in contingency theory is one of domination (or repression). Contingency theory, like much of management thinking, is concerned with 'decision-making whose "rationality" is instrumental effectiveness and efficiency. Such mechanisms work against a broader mode of rationalization that would maximize the participation and individuality of affected people' (Schroyer, 1970, p. 211). In other words, the means of control that are available for managers are achieved through the power of one group over another group, despite any resistance that the latter may attempt.

Of course, the criticism that contingency theory identifies managerial choice over a set of essentially exploitative management methods is neither new nor limited to contingency theory. Both Weber (1947) and Etzioni (1961) place the concepts of power and authority at the centre of their theories of organization. Weick argues (1979) that the military metaphor dominates the business world. His explanation is partly that the metaphor is an attempt to conceal disorder and becomes a self-fulfilling prophecy (if business is assumed to be like waging war, then that presumption creates the very war predicted!). Part of Weick's explanation is that business organizations attract authoritarian people to powerful positions. These people 'adhere to conventional values and condemn those who don't; . . . they are preoccupied with dominance—submission, strong–weak, leader–follower in any relationship; they have an uncritical attitude . . .' (Weick, 1979, p. 50). Contingency thinking reinforces these attitudes and perspectives: providing an uncritical panacea (the situational approach) to management. As it is typically presented (e.g. Lawrence and Lorsch, 1967; Galbraith, 1977) contingency theory reflects the desire for domination, in that the choices of managing it offers are essentially alienative. For Cherns (1978) alienation is the product of social segmentation and stratification and organizations are the main vehicles for these processes. Contingency theory, like most management theory, because it is seen as a 'value free' science, reinforces the apparently self-evident necessity to conceive of people as 'things' in organizations: resources to be allocated, costs to be minimized. For example, Winkler (1974) found that the 'logic' of industrial society in the U.K. has led to 'the triumph in the boardroom of accountancy over economics and social psychology, not to mention more humanistic considerations. . . . For all the directors labour was simply a cost to be minimized'.

Habermas (1971) has referred to the tendency to regard techniques of control as 'givens' as the fusion of technology and domination—in this instance the technically necessary form of organization and its management and its relationship with the subordination, oppression and alienation of the mass of the people to their work. As has been pointed out previously (Rose, 1978) the shift from scientific management to participative management merely reflects a change from material to more psychological means of control. The purpose of the control is the maximization of output and profit. The logic of the system, it is suggested, dictates it. The crucial questions, which are easily overlooked, are who dictates the system and is it inviolate?

The implications of these 'abstractions' for contingency theory and management are profound and entirely practical. Contingency theory has provided for management accounting a 'science' that enables managers to control an organization. But to use Vickers' terminology, the controls that are identified are those of rule, purpose and norm. What is missing is the control by self-determination—'a process both individual and social which depends essentially on ethical debate and reflection about changing norms and values and on the policy-making which both expresses and generates that debate' (Vickers, 1973, p. 182). Cherns (1978) makes the same point: is it possible to design organizations that reject domination, stratification and segmentation as the technology of organization? Although he is confident about the possibilities (Cherns, 1977), he is concerned that accounting, with its mania for measurement, reinforces alienation. By focusing on existing technologies, contingency theory is offering the choice of existing technologies of control and deflecting attention away from any ethical debate about changing norms and values in society and organizations. In these senses, management accounting and contingency theory, as examples of management science in general, are essentially conservative.

The Conceptualization of Performance

There have been several criticisms made of contingency theory (Child, 1977) and its accounting variants (Otley, 1979) that relate to the preceding argument. These criticisms focus on the problematic nature of organizational effectiveness, its poor conceptualization and inadequate measurement. Although crude financial measures have been used (e.g. Child, 1974 and 1975; Woodward, 1965; Lawrence and Lorsch, 1967) other researchers have used reputational measures of performance (Woodward, 1965; Hayes, 1977) or failed to deal with performance altogether. Indeed, there is some confusion as to whether matching organizations with their environments actually improves financial performance (Pennings, 1975).

But just what is good organizational performance and do financial variables such as profit and loss reflect it? Concepts such as survival, adaptability and stability have been suggested as conceptions of performance. Ultimately, I would argue, these conceptions must be linked to a notion of social welfare: the organization providing net benefits to the society in which it operates. But what does 'net benefit' incorporate? This question cannot be answered by science: it is one of the 'ethical questions' that Vickers (1973) refers to in his discussion of control by self-determination.

It is certainly worth questioning whether the measurement of performance by financial measures is entirely warranted. Profit, productivity and output may not be related to the satisfaction of human needs. For example, conventional economic theory suggests that only under very limited and unrealistic conditions (including agreement on the equity of the existing distribution of resources in society) can profit be equated with social welfare (e.g. de Graaff, 1957; Little, 1957; Sen, 1973). Managing in the interests of managers or shareholders is unlikely to correspond to the interests of other organizational participants.

Contingency theory has not typically considered the issue of in whose interests management is working or should work. Indeed, by taking for granted the existing priorities of management, it is supporting the *status quo*: providing order for the existing order. Of course, management and management theory need not take such a passive stance. For example, Vanek (1975) has indicated how order can serve the interests of worker self-management and Carlssön *et al.* (1978) suggest how accounting can be utilized for the benefit of trade unions and the democratization of working life. Management accounting has a role to play in this order, but contingency theory says nothing about such a role (for some emerging perspectives see Rothschild-Whitt, 1979 and Swidler, 1979).

Environment and Order

A major development in Galbraith's work (compare his 1973 and 1977 books) is the recognition that environment, frequently the independent variable in contingency formulations, is not completely uncontrollable. There has been a tendency in contingency theory not only for the environment to be regarded as uncontrollable but also to confuse subjective from objective environment and to fail to consider any explanations for the creation of uncertainty, hostility or dynamism in environments.

Virtually all organizations—irrespective of their size—are capable of doing more than adjusting their internal structures and management systems to their environment. Indeed, part of the logic behind Lowe's paper in this collection is that organizations can develop information systems to monitor their environment and thence begin to manage it. Galbraith (1977) refers to two broad management strategies: independent, where the organization acts on its own, and co-operative, where it works in concert with other organizations. Recognition of the pervasiveness of such activity is beginning to inform organization theory (Benson, 1975; Hirsch, 1975; Pfeffer, 1978; Aldrich, 1979). Of course, the earlier work of Selznick (1957) and Burns and Stalker (1961) had emphasized the importance of leadership in steering organizations into desirable environments and negotiating, controlling and dominating their environments. Whilst virtually all organizations may be able to manage their own activities to respond to an environment or move into a new environment, relatively large or powerful ones may also have the ability to change the nature of their environment. Mergers and takeovers are one means to change the environment; influencing administrative and political bodies may be another. In a similar fashion, Ackoff (1974) has talked about organizations not only reacting to their environment but also pre-acting it. Studies in political science suggest that organizations can also pre-empt their environment (Crenson, 1971). Contingency theory, by ignoring the possibility of environmental management, has tended to limit the range of management possibilities and roles for management accounting.

The preceding discussion has treated the term environment in a non-problematic manner. Contingency theory has recognized the possibility of multiple environments and the associated possibility that differing parts of an organization may develop differing structures and management systems. But some critiques of specific contingency theories have pointed out the confusion between 'objective' and 'perceived' environments (Tosi *et al.*, 1973; Downey *et al.*, 1975). There is still considerable muddle concerning this issue: whilst organizational members can only act in accordance with their perceptions, it is probably the case that objective conditions of an environment can operate on an organization. Ways in which accounting systems might affect perceptions and ways in which accounting may be used in the process of learning are still poorly understood (Michael, 1973; Argyris, 1977). Further, Weick (1977a) has suggested that environments can be created by organizations; by acting as if an environment has certain characteristics, then it may indeed develop such characteristics. This suggestion leads to the possibility that the causality of contingency theory may be entirely mis-specified. If organizations may be able to affect or create their own environment, then it is possible to conceive that organizations exist in a dialectical rather than a causal relationship with their environments. Viewing the organization–environment relationship as dialectical provides fundamental challenges to managers and management accounting that contingency theory just does not consider. This view implies continual change in organization, its management and its information systems and suggests that organizations might wish to consider the possibility of accounting for, and obtaining an account of, their accounting systems.

Rationality and Organizations as Social Systems

Burns (1966) in his explanation of why organizations seem to develop 'pathological' responses to change emphasized the multiple rationalities in organizations. Many organizations are more than a work situation—they provide the potential, if not the opportunities, for career and personal development, for social interaction and for political behaviour. Contingency theory has tended to take a mechanistic view of organizations and management: in the language of Boulding's classification (1956), they have been regarded as 'clockworks' or simple closed loop control systems. Such systems tend to display simple rationality and single feedback loops: they focus attention on maintenance of internal structures in the face of disturbance (self-stabilization).

By focusing on self-stabilization and adaptation, contingency theory has tended to ignore two issues that may be important for an understanding of organizations and the role of management accounting within them. The first issue is that cognition, culture and symbols may be important elements of organizational life. Secondly, organizations may develop complex rationalities and rationalizations for their actions, especially when they are inter-acting with rapidly changing environments.

Language and Culture

Organizations are, in Boulding terms (1956), social systems. They are collections of 'individuals' who create a sense of social order, shared culture, a history, a future, and a value system. Organizations have a sense of consciousness, an image of themselves. To create and sustain that image, they develop a coding scheme or language (Daft and Wiginton,

1979). This view of organizations does not focus on the existence of communication in organizations but rather on the existence and continuity of shared definitions of organizational reality and the organization's situation (Berger and Luckman, 1967). The suggestion is that order may be achieved in organizations not so much by formal rules but by an elaborate system of shared meanings: an organizational culture. To understand (and, ultimately, manage) organizations, it may thus be useful to analyse organizational cultures (the symbols and systems of beliefs) and the way in which they are created, kept alive, modified, used and destroyed. Culture provides an interpretation for organizational participants of their own situation and impels them to action. And in the process of organizing their activities, organizational participants represent, enact and thereby create their situation and purposes. These representation of reality provide a set of beliefs about the way an organization works, its effectiveness, its goals, the use and distribution of power and the appropriate means of managing the system (Pettigrew, 1979).

Culture and symbols in organizations are created and will inevitably have favourable consequences for some groups and unfavourable consequences for others. Following from our earlier discussion about order and domination, it may be useful to analyse organizations as political systems (March, 1962; Lukes, 1975; Clegg, 1979) and attempt to identify the interests that are served by alternative organizational cultures.

Ritual, magic and myths are some of the infrequently considered means by which organizational cultures are sustained. Ritual may provide a sense of identity and reinforce what is valued. Myth helps to label what is acceptable and unacceptable by anchoring actions to the past and to explanations of past events. By explaining and reconciling 'contradictions between values and actual behaviour and legitimate established leadership systems faced with environmental threats' (Pettigrew, 1979, p. 576), myths justify and sustain specific values in organizations.

Whilst much of accounting has ignored these issues, there have been several attempts to indicate how information systems may be both important rituals and significant myths in organizations and society (Gambling, 1977; Jönsson and Lundin, 1977; Jablonsky and Dirsmith, 1978; Hayes *et al.*, 1979; Burchell *et al.*, 1980; Cooper, 1980). These attempts have typically not examined the relationship between culture, accounting information and power in organizations or society. As yet, normative issues about the relationship between myths and rituals and organizational performance have not been well-explicated. Yet these studies begin to adopt a perspective that may ultimately aid in the design of accounting systems by indicating how and in whose interests accounting systems operate.

Because of the novelty of these views, I will illustrate them further. Applying the perspectives of Silverman (1975), March and Olsen (1976) and Weick (1979), Hayes *et al.* (1979) argue that internal accounting systems may provide an important means by which a system of shared meanings is sustained, developed and modified. Cost accumulation systems and internal reporting systems provide vehicles to record what 'really' happened. Producing an organizational history may be important for creating a shared sense of values, to maintain continuity and to provide a common view of the world so that co-ordinated actions may take place. Further, these management accounting systems may help organizations to make retrospective sense of actions previously taken. Accounting systems may be important in rationalizing past action; providing the confidence to take action in the future by enabling organizations to create models of what has happened.

Rationalization of action would seem a fundamental role of accounting systems in situations of apparent disorder. The budget process, in particular, and management accounting, in general, may provide a means for justifying past actions and making them appear sensible to both the actor and others. Bower (1970), for example, discovered that the major use of capital budgeting procedures is to justify investment decisions already made, rather than simply providing information prior to the taking of a particular decision.

Further, the ritual of accounting practices—budgeting, variance analysis, cost accumulation—may help an organization to discover its goals, understand what has happened in the past and attach meaning to previous actions. The process of accounting may be more important than the outcome. Accounting may also facilitate the formulation of myths and shared realities by providing the various actors with a common language and framework for such negotiations. Accounting reports provide an 'explanation' of events. The boundaries of negotiation, the language in which it is discussed, and the set of phenomena to be incorporated into negotiation are all influenced by the existence of accounting and budgetary systems in organizations. Further, flexibility in interpretation is enhanced by the ambiguities of accounting methods, so providing grounds for agreement and disagreement within the negotiating process. By not being precise, the language enables multiple interpretation and broader bases for the negotiation of a common set of beliefs.

I am not suggesting that accounting systems are neutral in the negotiation process. By defining what is measured, how it is measured, and to whom reports are communicated, management accounting systems can effectively delimit the kind of issues addressed and the ways in which they are addressed. They reflect the *status quo*, the appropriate and acceptable ways of doing things and talking about issues.

Evidence on budgets and accounting systems as reflections of power, and as tools in internal dispute is widespread. Pfeffer and Salancik (1974), for example, indicate that for the universities they studied, budget allocations could be understood in terms of the relative power of departments (such power deriving from research reputations and ability to generate external funds). Wildavsky (1974) cites numerous examples of the political aspects of budgeting at the governmental level, many of which have ready parallels within both public and business organizations. Similarly, Cohen and March (1974) argue that planning is a pretext under which a number of activities which may be valuable to powerful interests take place. They suggest that plans are symbols, in that by announcing a plan to do something, actual circumstances may be disguised and paid less heed to. Further, they suggest plans are advertisements, which show an organization at its best. Planning is also viewed as a game, a way of testing commitments of people to programmes they espouse. Finally, they argue that planning provides an excuse for interaction among diverse groups, which may have positive benefits concerning current activities.

Complex Rationalities

Contingency theory has suggested that accounting and information systems may be organizational mechanisms to respond to increasing uncertainty. Information may be one way of identifying and thereby providing for a decision-maker sufficient alternatives (or variety) to match the exceptions (variety) that he faces. An alternative means of achieving this managerial variety is to make the decision-maker more adaptable and experimental.

One way of achieving adaptability is by designing information systems that are ambiguous or encourage experimentation. Hedberg and Jönsson (1978), for example, suggest that information systems should do more to sensitize managers to instability and change. Accounting systems tend to filter away conflict, uncertainty, inconsistency and ambiguity, thereby reducing potential signals for change. Hedberg and Jönsson (1978) therefore suggest the design of semi-confusing information systems using a model of scientific endeavour to indicate how information systems might create 'hypotheses' and be used to test them. Dialectical information systems would seem to offer the same promise of providing creativity and stability.

An alternative way of achieving adaptability is to encourage managers to be more experimental and 'playful'. March (1976) suggests a 'technology of foolishness' for decision-making in conditions of ambiguity and change. Together with Hedberg *et al.* (1976) and Weick (1977b), March develops a series of prescriptions about decision-making in ambiguous conditions: treat goals as hypotheses, treat intuition as real, treat hypocrisy as transitory, treat memory as an enemy and treat experience as theory. These prescriptions are intended to maximize learning, experimentation and discovery through the imitation of the learning patterns of young children.

The prescriptions for seemingly anarchic, chaotic and 'muddled' information systems and decision-makers is meant to lead to order and rationality. This point needs to be made explicit. These prescriptions are strategies for decision-making in conditions of extreme uncertainty, assuming that organizational survival (and other measures of performance) is linked to adaptability:

> 'An organization can reconcile the need for flexibility with the need for stability in several ways: by some form of compromise response (a solution which is tried too often with much too disastrous results), by alternation between stability and flexibility, or by simultaneous expression of the two necessities in different parts of the system. As will be argued later, only in the second two latter cases is continued existence possible. A compromise response accomplishes neither stability nor flexibility.' (Weick, 1969, p. 39.)

Muddle may be the means through which tidiness and order can be achieved!

Conclusion

The need—and guiding metaphor—for this paper has been the 'need' for order (tidiness) and the tendency to disorder (or muddle). In particular I have indicated some of the roles of management accounting in helping to achieve order in organizations.[3] My approach is essentially prescriptive: seeking ways in which accounting can aid in the achievement of organizational control. My view of science is that at least part of its purpose is to enable man to manage or control his activities in relation to his environment. Without active management all systems have a tendency to disorder. This tendency has been referred to as entropy (e.g. Ashby, 1956) and science as well as control is an attempt to reduce tendencies towards disorder.

In the first section of this paper 'accounting to order', I suggest that contingency theory has been seen as a means of reducing the tendency to muddle. It has provided for managers and designers of information systems a 'science' to guide their activities. Contingency theory provides not only a guide but a legitimation for choice—the whole process is regarded as rational. The argument in the section 'order to order' is that contingency theory is, in fact, not very good science and its prescriptive role is little more than an ideology to support existing controls and modes of domination in organizations.

Theories not only direct attention to some phenomena and issues, they also direct attention away from others. In a sense, widely espoused theories tend to be conservative: by focusing attention on issues and problems the model says are important, scientists tend to lose their sensitivity to other problems. In the case of contingency theory the issues that tend to be the focus are essentially those of the choice of means to

3 For an alternative, but I think quite consistent view, see Earl and Hopwood (1979).

achieve given ends. My concern, which is reflected in the criticisms of contingency theory is to address issues of ends as well as means. The concern for 'ends' might involve consideration of the alternative possible roles of accounting in different economic and social systems. Who benefits from accounting? This is an ethical concern: to bring issues of ethics to the centre of management accounting. The concern for means might involve consideration of alternative strategies of control—the critique of contingency theory suggests that environmental management, the creation of cultures and the encouragement of intelligent rather than consistent experimentation might be neglected forms of control. Perhaps most important, management accountants might recognize that the concern for means may be considered in the light of ends. It is about time that 'good' controls were distinguished from 'bad' controls.

There are several strategies for research in management accounting that are suggested by the preceding argument. One strategy might be to continue to focus on the prescriptive elements of management accounting and to modify contingency theory to incorporate some of the criticisms levelled against it. For example, consideration could be given to desirable accounting symbols and rituals and prescriptions for the creation of cultures that are appropriate to specific types of organization.

Another strategy may be to improve our understanding of the way management accounting systems operates in reality. Our knowledge of how accounting systems are used in organizations is incomplete. The rationalization, rationalistic and symbolic uses of accounting are not well-understood or documented. And only through a well-grounded understanding of how systems operate can we prescribe how accounting systems should be changed.

The third strategy for research focuses on the partiality of much of management accounting, and indeed management science, in general. The failure to question the ends of organizational activity and the ultimate purpose of management has led to the questioning of the scientific status of management science (Hales, 1974; Wood and Kelly, 1978). It is tempting to assert that the development of management accounting has merely reflected the changing problem of control (as defined by the powerful) as economic and social conditions have changed. Yet it is naive to portray management accounting and accountants as a whole as mere servants of power (Baritz, 1960), tamely fabricating manipulative techniques and pseudo-scientific managerial propaganda. Gouldner's (1970) arguments would seem more appropriate.

Gouldner maintains that most social scientists fail to recognize how managers will use their theories as apologia for the *status quo*. Indeed, by failing to emphasize its assumptions about ends, contingency theory implies that organizational problems are soluble by organizational engineering (Rose, 1978; Wood, 1979). Any challenge to change may then be interpreted as irrational rather than as representing a dispute about the goals that underlie the change. Thus unaware of the prejudices acquired during their social training and re-inforced by the perspective of the accounting profession, both academics and practising managers and management accountants produce theories and models which are distorted by sub-conscious bias. Profit (or contribution) is assumed to be the maxim and the ends will ultimately justify most means of achieving them.

Of course, some of the most influential and well-respected management scientists (e.g. Churchman, 1970) have recognized the essentially value-laden nature of management and their science. The question then would seem to be in whose interests do we (should we), as scientists, operate. Is a liberated accounting science possible? Marx insisted that the only liberation of science from capitalism would be through the abolition of capitalist relations of production. Social institutions, knowledge and relationships, he suggested, support or reflect the exploitative relationship between owners of wealth and the workers who create it. I have previously argued that order is maintained by domination: perhaps that form of order is inevitable in capitalist societies. Further, whether that order is maintained by bureaucratic rules, standard procedures, participative schemes or through a shared value structure, the order so created is in the interests of capital, and may not be in the interests of other segments of society (Cooper, 1980). But I believe that order can serve alternative ends: Hales (1974) and Vanek (1975) suggest worker self-management. Management accounting might have a role to play in, for example, self-management systems. To encourage the embracing of the inevitable 'muddle', that results from new forms of scientific investigation, let me end with the following:

> 'The unique function of man is to live in close, creative touch with chaos, and thereby experience the birth of order.' (Hans Hoffman, quoted in Leavitt and Pondy, 1964, p. 58.)

References

Ackoff, R., *Redesigning the Future: A Systems Approach to Societal Problems*. Wiley (1974).

Alchian, A. A. and Demsetz, H., 'Production, Information Costs and Economic Organization', *American Economic Review* (December 1972).

Aldrich, H. E., *Organizations and Environments*. Prentice-Hall (1979).

Amey, L., 'Towards a New Perspective on Accounting Control', *Accounting, Organizations and Society* (1979).

Ansari, S., 'An Integrated Approach to Control System Design', *Accounting, Organizations and Society* (1977).

Argyris, C., *The Impact of Budgets on People*. Controllership Foundation (1952).

Argyris, C., 'Organizational Learning and Management Information Systems', *Accounting, Organizations and Society* (1977).

Ashby, W. R., *Introduction to Cybernetics*. Wiley (1956).

Baritz, L., *The Servants of Power: A History of the Use of Social Science In American Industry*. Wesleyan University Press (1960).

Bateson, G., *Steps to an Ecology of Mind*. Ballantine (1972).

Baumler, J. V., 'Defined Criteria of Performance in Organizational Control', *Administrative Science Quarterly* (September 1971).

Beer, S., *Cybernetics and Management*. Unibooks (1967).

Beer, S., *Platform for Change*. Wiley (1975).

Berger, P. and Luckman, T., *The Social Construction of Reality*. Allen Lane (1967).

Benson, K., 'The Interorganizational Network as a Political Economy', *Administrative Science Quarterly* (June 1975).

Berry, A. T. and Otley, D. T., 'The Aggregation of Estimates in Hierarchical Organizations', *Journal of Management Studies* (May 1975).

Boland, R., 'Control, Causality and Information System Requirements', *Accounting, Organizations and Society* (1979).

Boulding, K. E., 'General Systems Theory—The Skeleton of Science', *Management Science* (April 1956).

Bower, J., *Managing the Resource Allocation Process*. Irwin (1970).

Bonini, C. P., *Simulation of the Information and Decisions Systems in the Firm*. Prentice-Hall (1963).

Braverman, H., *Labour and Monopoly Capital*. Monthly Review Press (1974).

Bruns, W. S. and Waterhouse, J. H., 'Budgetary Control and Organization Structure', *Journal of Accounting Research* (1975).

Burchell, S., Clubb, C., Hopwood, A., Hughes, J. and Nahapiet, J., 'The Role of Accounting in Organizations and Society', *Accounting, Organizations and Society* (1980).

Buckley, W., 'Society as a Complex Adaptive System', in Buckley, W. (ed.), *Modern Systems Research for the Behavioural Scientist*. Aldine (1968).

Burns, T. and Stalker, G., *The Management of Innovation*. Tavistock (1961).

Burns, T., 'On the Plurality of Social Systems', in Lawrence, J. R. (ed.), *Operations Research and the Social Sciences*. Tavistock (1966).

Carlsson, J., Ehn, P., Erlander, B., Perby, M. L. and Sandberg, A., 'Planning and Control from the Perspective of Labour', *Accounting, Organizations and Society* (1978).

Carsberg, B., *Economics of Business Decisions*. Penguin (1975).

Chandler, A. and Daems, H., 'Administrative Co-ordination, Allocation and Monitoring: A Comparative Analysis of the Emergence of Accounting and Organization in the USA and Europe', *Accounting, Organizations and Society* (1979).

Cherns, A. B., 'Can Behavioural Science Help Design Organizations?', *Organizational Dynamics* (1977).

Cherns, A. B., 'Alienation and Accountancy', *Accounting, Organizations and Society* (1978).

Cherrington, D. J. and Cherrington, J. O., 'Appropriate Reinforcement Contingencies in the Budgeting Process', *Empirical Research in Accounting*, supplement to *Journal of Accounting Research* (1973).

Child, J., 'Organizational Structure, Environment and Performance—The Role of Strategic Choice', *Sociology* (1972).

Child, J., 'Management and Organizational Factors Associated with Company Performance—Part I', *Journal of Management Studies* (1974).

Child, J., 'Managerial and Organizational Factors Associated with Company Performance—Part II', *Journal of Management Studies* (1975).

Child, J., *Organization: A Guide to Problems and Practice.* Harper and Row (1977).

Churchman, C. W., *The Systems Approach.* Dell Publishing (1968).

Churchman, C. W., 'Operations Research as a Profession', *Management Science* (October 1970).

Clancy, D. and Collins, F., 'Informal Accounting Information Systems: Some Tentative Findings', *Accounting, Organizations and Society* (1979).

Clegg, S., *The Theory of Power and Organization.* Routledge and Kegan Paul (1979).

Cohen, M. D. and March, J. G., *Leadership and Ambiguity.* New York, McGraw-Hill (1974).

Cooper, D., 'Organizational Aspects of Budgetary Control', in Lewis, J. E. and Dickinson, G. (eds.), *Handbook of Financial Management.* Kluwer-Harrap (1977).

Cooper, D., 'Observations on a Political Economy of Accounting', *Accounting, Organizations and Society* (1980).

Crenson, M. A., *The Un-politics of Air Pollution: A Study of Non-decision Making in the Cities.* John Hopkins Press (1971).

Cyert, R. M. and March, J. G., *A Behavioural Theory of the Firm.* Prentice-Hall (1963).

Daft, R. L. and Wigington, J., 'Language and Organization', *Academy of Management Review* (1979).

Davis, S. M. and Lawrence, P., *Matrix.* Addison Wesley (1977).

De Coster, D. T., 'An Intuitive Framework for Empirical Research in Participative Budgeting', in Previts, G. J. (ed.), *Accounting Research Convocation.* University of Alabama (1976).

De Graaff, J., *Theoretical Welfare Economics.* Cambridge University Press (1957).

Demski, J. and Feltham, G., 'Economic Incentives in Budgetary Control Systems', *Accounting Review* (April 1978).

Downey, H. K., Hellriegel, D. and Slocum, J., 'Environmental Uncertainty: The Construct and its Application', *Administrative Science Quarterly* (December 1975).

Earl, M. and Hopwood, A., 'From Management Information to Information Management', paper presented at IFIP TC 8–WG 8.2, Working Conference on the Information Systems Environment, Bonn 1979.

Emery, F. E. and Trist, E. L., 'The Causal Texture of Organizational Environments', *Human Relations* (1965).

Etzoni, A., *A Comparative Analysis of Complex Organizations.* Free Press (1961).

Galbraith, J., *Designing Complex Organizations.* Addison-Wesley (1973).

Galbraith, J., *Organization Design.* Addison-Wesley (1977).

Gambling, T., 'Magic Accounting and Morale', *Accounting, Organizations and Society* (1977).

Glassman, R. B., 'Persistence and Loose Coupling in Living Systems', *Behavioural Science* (1973).

Goodman, P. S. and Pennings, J. M. (eds.), *New Perspectives in Organizational Effectiveness*. Jossey Bass (1977).

Gordon, L. A. and Miller, D., 'A Contingency Framework for the Design of Accounting Information Systems', *Accounting, Organizations and Society* (1976).

Gouldner, A. W., *The Coming Crisis of Western Sociology*. Heinemann (1970).

Habermas, J., *Toward a Rational Society*. Heinemann Educational Books (1971).

Hales, M., 'Management Science and the "Second Industrial Revolution"', *Radical Science Journal* (January 1974).

Hayes, D., 'The Contingency Theory of Management Accounting', *Accounting Review* (1977).

Hayes, D. C., Wolf, F. M. and Cooper, D. J., 'Accounting in Organized Anarchies: An Explanation of the Budgetary Process' (unpublished, University of Manchester, 1979).

Hedberg, B. L. T., Nystrom, P. and Starbuck, W., 'Camping on Seesaws: Prescriptions for a Self Designing Organization', *Administrative Science Quarterly* (March 1976).

Hedberg, B. and Jönsson, S., 'Designing Semi Confusing Information Systems for Organizations in Changing Environments', *Accounting, Organizations and Society* (1978).

Hirsch, P., 'Organizational Effectiveness and the Institutional Environment', *Administrative Science Quarterly* (September 1975).

Hofstede, G. H., *The Game of Budget Control*. Van Gorcum (1968).

Hopwood, A. G., *An Accounting System and Managerial Behaviour*. Saxon House (1973).

Hopwood, A. G., *Accounting and Human Behaviour*. Accountancy Age (1974).

Hopwood, A. G., 'Towards an Organizational Perspective for the Study of Accounting and Information Systems', *Accounting, Organizations and Society* (1978).

Horngren, C. T., *Cost Accounting: A Managerial Emphasis*. Prentice-Hall (1977).

Jablonsky, S. and Dirsmith, M., 'The Pattern of PPB Rejection: Something About Organizations, Something About PPB', *Accounting, Organizations and Society* (1978).

Jönsson, S. A. and Lundin, R., 'Myths and Wishful Thinking as Management Tools', in Nystrom, P. C. and Starbuck, W. (eds.), *op cit.*, 1977.

Kassem, M. S., 'Introduction: European Versus American Organization Theories', in Hofstede, G. and Kassem, M. S. (eds.), *European Contributions to Organization Theory*. Van Gorcum (1976).

Lawler, E. E. and Rhode, J. G., *Information and Control in Organizations*. Goodyear Publications (1976).

Lawrence, P. R. and Lorsch, J., *Organization and Environment*. Division of Research, Harvard Business School (1967).

Leavitt, H. J. and Pondy, L. R. (eds.), *Readings in Managerial Psychology*. University of Chicago Press (1964).

Legge, K., *Power, Innovation and Problem Solving in Personnel Management*. McGraw Hill (1978).

Likert, R., *The Human Organization*. McGraw Hill (1967).

Little, I. M. D., *A Critique of Welfare Economics*. Oxford University Press (1957).

Livingstone, J. L., 'Managerial Accounting and Organizational Co-ordination', in Stone, W. E. (ed.), *The Accountant in a Changing Business Environment.* University of Florida Press (1973).

Livingstone, J. L. (ed.), *Managerial Accounting: The Behavioural Foundations.* Grid Inc. (1975).

Lorsch, J., 'A Critique', in Burns, T. J. (ed.), *The Behavioural Aspects of Accounting Data for Performance Evaluation.* Ohio State University (1970).

Lowe, E. A. and Shaw, R. W., 'An Analysis of Managerial Biasing: Evidence from a Company's Budgeting Process', *Journal of Management Studies* (1968).

Lowe, E. A. and Shaw, R. W., 'The Accuracy of Short Term Business Forecasting: An Analysis of a Firm's Sales Budgeting', *Journal of Industrial Economics* (1970).

Lowe, E. A. and Tinker, A. M., 'The Architecture of Requisite Variety', Parts 1 and 2, *Kybernetes* (1976).

Lowe, E. A. and Tinker, A. M., 'Sighting the Accounting Problematic: Towards an Intellectual Emancipation of Accounting', *Journal of Business Finance and Accounting* (1977).

Lukes, S., *Power: A Radical View.* Macmillan (1974).

March, J. G., 'The Technology of Foolishness' in March, J. G. and Olsen, J. P., *op cit.*, 1976.

March, J. G., 'The Business Firm as a Political Coalition', *Journal of Politics* (1962).

March, J. G. and Olsen, J. P., *Ambiguity and Choice in Organizations.* Universitetsforlaget (1976).

March, J. G. and Simon, H. A., *Organizations.* Wiley (1958).

Michael, D., *On Learning to Plan and Planning to Learn.* Jossey Bass (1973).

Milani, K., 'The Relationship of Participation in Budget Setting to Industrial Supervisor Performance and Attitudes: A Field Study', *Accounting Review* (1975).

Myers, C. S., *Industrial Psychology in Great Britain.* Cape (1924).

Nichols, T. and Benyon, H., *Living with Capitalism.* Routledge and Kegan Paul (1977).

Nystrom, P. C. and Starbuck, W. (eds.), *Prescriptive Models of Organization.* North Holland (1977).

Otley, D. T., 'Budget Use and Managerial Performance', *Journal of Accounting Research* (Spring 1978).

Otley, D. T., 'Towards a Contingency Theory of Management Accounting: a Critical Assessment' (unpublished, 1979).

Otley, D. T. and Berry, A. J., 'Control, Organisation and Accounting', *Accounting, Organizations and Society* (1980).

Pennings, J., 'The Relevance of the Structural-Contingency Model for Organizational Effectiveness', *Administrative Science Quarterly* (September 1975).

Pettigrew, A., 'On Studying Organizational Cultures', *Administrative Science Quarterly* (December 1979).

Pfeffer, J. and Salancik, G. R., 'Organizational Decision Making as a Political Process: The Case of a University Budget', *Administrative Science Quarterly* (June 1974).

Pfeffer, J., *Organizational Design.* A.H.M. Publishing (1978).

Pondy, L. and Mitroff, I., 'Beyond Open Systems Models of Organization', in

Staw, B. M. and Cummings, L. L. (eds.), *Research in Organizational Behaviour*. JAI Press (1978).

Rose, M., *Industrial Behaviour: Theoretical Developments since Taylor*. Penguin (1978).

Rothschild-Whitt, J., 'The Collectivist Organization: an Alternative to Rational Bureaucratic Models', *American Sociological Review* (August 1979).

Sathe, V., 'Contingency Theory of Organizational Structure', in Livingstone, J. L. (ed.), *op cit.*, 1975.

Schroyer, T., 'Toward a Critical Theory for Advanced Industrial Society', in Dreizel, H. P. (ed.), *Recent Sociology No. 2*. Macmillan (1970).

Selznick, P., *Leadership in Administration*. Row Peterson (1957).

Sen, A., *On Economic Inequality*. Oxford University Press (1973).

Silverman, D., 'Accounts of Organizations—Organizational "Structures" and the Accounting Process', in McKinley, J. B. (ed.), *Processing People: Cases in Organizational Behaviour*. Holt Rinehart and Winston (1975).

Simon, H. A., Kozmetsky, G., Guetzkow, H. and Tyndall, G., *Centralization v. Decentralization in Organizing the Controller's Department*. The Controllership Foundation (1954).

Simon, H. A., *Administrative Behaviour*. Macmillan (1976).

Staw, B. M. and Salancik, G. R. (eds.), *New Directions in Organizational Behaviour*. St Clair Press (1977).

Staw, B. and Szawajkowski, E., 'The Scarcity–Munificence Component of Organizational Environments and the Commission of Illegal Acts', *Administrative Science Quarterly* (September 1975).

Stedry, A. C., *Budget Control and Cost Behaviour*. Prentice-Hall (1960).

Stedry, A. C. and Kay, E., 'The Effects of Goal Difficulty on Performance', *Behavioural Science* (1966).

Swindler, A., *Organization Without Authority: Dilemas of Social Control in Free Schools*. Harvard University Press (1979).

Swieringa, R. J. and Moncur, R. H., *Some Effects of Participative Budgets on Managerial Behaviour*. N.A.A. (1975).

Taylor, F. W., *The Principles of Scientific Management*. Harper and Row (1947).

Thompson, J. D., *Organizations in Action*. McGraw-Hill (1967).

Tosi, H., Aldag, R. and Storey, R., 'On the Measurement of the Environment: an Assessment of the Lawrence and Lorsch Environmental Subscale', *Administrative Science Quarterly* (March 1973).

Vanek, J. (ed.), *Self Management: Economic Liberation of Man*. Penguin (1975).

Vickers, G., *Making Institutions Work*. Associated Business Programmes (1973).

Waterhouse, J. and Tiessen, P., 'A Contingency Framework for Management Accounting Systems Research', *Accounting, Organizations and Society* (1978).

Watson, D., 'Contingency Formulations of Organizational Structure: Implications for Managerial Accounting', in Livingstone, J. L. (ed.), *op cit.*, 1975.

Watson, D. and Baumler, J., 'Transfer Pricing: A Behavioural Context', *Accounting Review* (October 1975).

Weber, M., *The Theory of Social and Economic Organization* (translated by Henderson, A. M. and Parsons, T.). The Free Press (1947).

Weick, K. E., *The Social Psychology of Organizing* (1st ed.). Addison-Wesley. (1969).

Weick, K. E., 'Educational Organizations as Loosely Coupled Systems', *Administrative Science Quarterly* (March 1976).
Weick, K. E., 'Enactment Processes in Organizations', in Staw, B. and Salancik, G. (eds.), *op cit.*, 1977(a).
Weick, K. E., 'Repunctuating the Problem', in Goodman, P. S. and Pennings, J. M. (eds.), *op cit.*, 1977(b).
Weick, K. E., *The Social Psychology of Organizing* (2nd ed.). Addison-Wesley (1979).
Winkler, J., 'The Ghost at the Bargaining Table: Directors and Industrial Relations', *British Journal of Industrial Relations* (July 1974).
Wildavsky, A., *The Politics of the Budgetary Process*. Little Brown (1974).
Wood, S. and Kelly, J., 'Towards a Critical Management Science', *Journal of Management Studies* (February 1978).
Wood, S., 'A Reappraisal of the Contingency Approach to Organization', *Journal of Management Studies* (October 1979).
Woodward, J., *Management and Technology*. HMSO (1958).
Woodward, J., *Industrial Organization: Theory and Practice*. Oxford University Press (1965).

Commentary on
'A social and organizational view of management accounting'

David T Otley
Lecturer in Accounting, Department of Accounting and Finance, University of Lancaster

The Role of Management Accounting in Organizational Control

There has been much progress in the past ten years. In 1970, what would then have been described as 'behavioural accounting' was considered to be an esoteric art and discussion of it was confined to a few research papers of a mainly speculative nature. If behavioural factors were mentioned in a management accounting text, which was often not the case, they tended to be confined in a brief appendix. 'Behaviour' was seen as a gloss which was to be added after a solid technical foundation had been established.

The title of David Cooper's paper is indicative of some of the changes that have occurred since 1970. Management accounting is being increasingly seen as explicable only in its social and organizational context. The definition of what constitutes a good accounting information system is seen to depend upon a variety of organizational and environmental factors, and this recognition has led to the development of contingency approaches.

Enough work is being carried out for a new journal, *Accounting, Organizations and Society*, to have become established, and its contents include much of relevance to the design of management accounting systems. Thus an entirely new perspective on the role of accounting information systems is being developed and, as has been pointed out, it has a specifically European rather than an American flavour.

The central thesis of this new perspective is that accounting information systems are an aid to achieving order in organizations and are concerned with the attainment of overall organizational control, defined as the optimal achievement of objectives. It is argued that there is a need to match the accounting information system with the circumstances in which the organization finds itself, most notably with the degree of flexibility that it needs to maintain in order successfully to adapt to a dynamic environment, and that a contingency theory rather than a universal theory is appropriate. Although in the development of this contingency theory various restrictive assumptions have been made that equate control with the preservation of the *status quo*, it is here argued that such assumptions are not essential. It is possible to conceive of an improved contingency theory that meets many of the criticisms advanced against its cruder forebears. The research task presented is that of giving substance to this more sophisticated framework for studying the role of accounting in organizational control.

So far, so good. There is much in this argument with which it is possible to agree. The control framework gives a sharpened focus to the choice of contingent variables; a contingency approach can direct attention towards unstated assumptions; organizations can be usefully observed as interacting with their wider environment in culturally rich manners; intensive research methods that provide deeper insights into organizational functioning are to be encouraged. Nevertheless, there is implicit within this framework a view of the organization and, indeed, of society, and a view of the nature of scientific activity that must be explicated. This view is that the organization is the servant of the wider society in which it is set and that science is a tool of societal control; or put more generally, that the whole is more important than its parts.

Such a point of view is most apparent in the discussion of organizational effectiveness. As is rightly pointed out this is an under-developed area conceptually, and ill-defined 'weasel' words abound in the literature: effectiveness, efficiency, performance, success, survival, management, control, needs and requirements. We have to ask for what and for whom is an organization deemed to be effective? Is the integrity of the whole an objective to be optimized or a constraint that might have to be satisfied? Is the purpose, or role of the organization to be taken as more important than the purposes, and roles of the people who comprise it? Indeed, what is the organization, where are its boundaries and what and whom are to be included or excluded?

Despite the appeal of systems approaches to the study of complex organizations, where it is argued that the part cannot be properly understood in isolation, but only by giving due attention to its context and its inter-relationships with other parts, they are nevertheless fundamentally holistic and functionalist in nature. That is, the behaviour of a part is explained in terms of its purpose or function for a wider whole. Thus, the accounting system is explained in terms of its role in aiding organizational control and the organization is explained in terms of social welfare and of its function in a wider society. But here the chain of logic is inevitably broken for there is no higher order system to refer to, and by which the role of society is to be explained. Systems explanations are thus recursive, and require an ever larger over-arching system to contain them.

To be concerned about the recursive nature of holistic explanations does not imply that one must adopt a reductionist approach, for it is equally evident that the explanation of individual human behaviour must take into account its wider social context and cannot be reduced to purely individual characteristics. There is a dialectical tension between holistic and reductionist approaches which, if it is accepted that both have insights to offer, can be used to generate a variety of possible research approaches. It is, therefore, quite proper for contingency theories to concern themselves with the appropriate means for attaining particular ends; the only danger is that only a limited set of possible ends will be considered fitting topics for research. The prevailing research paradigms in accounting have tended to encourage a narrow approach and to cause a concentration on financial measures of organizational effectiveness; an important facet of Cooper's paper is that it suggests a wider variety of approaches.

This pluralistic approach suggests a range of possible research approaches, even within a managerial perspective. These could range from studies of the ways in which information can be used to help individual managers become more effective through studies of the role of accounting information in decision-support systems (as against decision-making systems) and the design of information systems appropriate to different styles of management, to studies of the role of accounting information in the overall management control of the organization. Such a pluralistic approach is not only possible but also appears to be highly desirable in encouraging a wider variety of work aimed at serving different purposes.

By way of conclusion, it appears that the contingency approach is capable of providing a fruitful framework for research in management accounting. However, it carries within it a range of problems, some inherent and some accidental, of which prospective researchers need to be aware. These include the following:

(a) The contingency approach assumes the existence of an objective for the system being studied, although this is often not explicitly stated. A good contingency theory will specify the end it seeks to attain, whether this is in the nature of an overall organizational objective or the satisfaction of a particular interest group.

(b) Much contingency theory in management accounting has derived from that developed in organization theory. It is important to recognize the deficiencies of some of these theories and also to appreciate that organizational design is just one of a range of controls used as a means of managerial control.

(c) An accounting information system is only one part of a much wider package of organizational controls that are highly inter-dependent. It cannot, therefore, be studied in isolation.

(d) The control perspective is likely to be valuable in defining appropriate contingent variables, but it inevitably focuses attention upon the welfare of the higher-order system and tends to minimize the attention given to the values held in its parts, these latter tending to be treated as constraints rather than objectives.

(e) Although particular contingent variables may be found to have a well-defined impact on an accounting information system, it is likely in any practical situation that the values taken by the complete set of contingent variables will generate conflicting recommendations. The generation of contingency theories does not therefore remove the element of choice and balance faced by those involved in designing an accounting system.

(f) As useful contingency theories in management accounting draw upon a variety of disciplinary inputs, there is a temptation to incorporate (often obsolete) theories intact from other disciplines with which the accounting researcher is relatively unfamiliar. In the present state of knowledge, it would seem unwise to place too great a reliance on theories developed in other contexts and for other purposes. The pressing need is for the generation of appropriate theories and the more intensive research methodologies would appear to offer more insight than 'arm's length' methods.

The issues raised in this paper are encouraging not only for the way in which they reflect the broader perspective now being taken by accounting researchers, but also for the role the study of accounting systems can have in studies of organizational functioning. The study of the role of accounting in organizational control represents an important link between two hitherto separate fields. At this initial stage of development it is, perhaps, more useful to encourage the 'muddle' of disparate approaches than to impose an inappropriate 'tidiness'.

9 The management of purposive environmental enquiry: suggestions for the development of MIS thinking

E A Lowe
Professor of Accounting and Financial Management, University of Sheffield

(The author is much indebted to his immediate colleagues Mr A G Puxty and Mr T Hopper for their valuable comments. But, clearly, they are not responsible for any remaining deficiencies in the paper.)

The purpose of this paper is to argue for a definite change in the direction and thrust of academic thought on the design of management information systems (MIS). First, brief consideration is given to the present, general state of the MIS literature relating to the various approaches to MIS design. The following section considers the defects of the present literature whilst recognizing its strengths. Thereafter, the subsequent sections present the author's argument for a definite change in the main direction of academic research on MIS design.

A Categorization of Approaches to the Design of Management Information Systems

For the purpose of providing some brief, relevant (although, necessarily, incomplete) account of the recent history of MIS ideas in the western literature it is helpful to quote from the recent work of this author and a colleague:

> 'The genesis of management control is difficult to trace—perhaps because, in the manner of Humpty-Dumpty, different writers use the term to mean what they want it to mean. Giglioni and Bedeian (1972) see the earliest writings in the area being those of Emerson, Church and Diemer, who were writing in 1912, 1914 and 1915, respectively. Already at that date, the link between accounting and the control of the enterprise was being forged: they emphasized the importance of adequate records, of comparison with standards, and with the adequacy of those standards. Giglioni and Bedeian quote Church as follows:
>
> > (The comparison function is based on) three elements:
> > (a) recognition of what facts are truly significant;
> > (b) accurate record and convenient presentation of these facts;
> > (c) judicious action based on study of the facts'.

The modern development of management control as a subject within the field of accounting must, however, be credited to Robert Anthony and his colleagues at the Harvard Business School. Management Control was seen as a broadening out of the more technical kinds of accounting which were then taught—the mechanics of costing and book-keeping methods. This broadening out was also to be seen in other areas at the same time: see, in particular, the emergence of "business policy" as a subject. Through this, it was felt, one of the essential functions of accounting could be applied in its context, and at the same time be enriched by the findings of other management researchers where they impinged on accounting. The sole link between accounting and other disciplines had until then been economics, and the development of income theory had already reached a considerable degree of sophistication. Law, of course, has also been seen as important throughout accounting's history because of the significance accorded to accounting information in corporate legislation—although this has tended to affect the thinking of practitioners rather than academics.

But by the early 1960s it was becoming evident that other disciplines could throw light on the relevance of accounting to the firm: and chief among these was social psychology.

The link between accounting and social psychology can probably be traced at its earliest to the pioneering work of Chris Argyris (1952) who researched the effects budgeting systems had on middle management and supervisory grades. Development of the link, of the evident enrichment which could come from the insights social psychology could add to the accounting process, were at first slow. But they gained momentum throughout the decade, and by the 1960s academics could base their research on a growing body of knowledge at the level of the individual: in particular, the effects of budget systems on motivation.

This body of knowledge was, of course, known at Harvard: but they were also able to add insights from the rapidly-growing area of organization theory. This had been fragmented, the interest of a minority of sociologists and industrial psychologists: but perhaps the turning point may be traced to publication of March and Simon's classic book *Organizations* (1958). This is not to suggest that this work was a sudden efflorescence: its roots may be seen in the earlier work by Simon *et al.* (1954). Here, perhaps for the first time, the particular characteristics of the organization were being looked at within a coherent framework of their own. No longer did the reader have to turn to the (fragmented) translations of Max Weber (whose orientation was in any case very different from his own, interested as Weber was essentially in the interrelation between organization type and societal development) or the mechanical prognostications of Frederick Taylor, or the equally mechanical if broader writings of practical businessmen such as Fayol,

Urwick and Brech. A basis now existed for a theoretical and rigorous approach to the analysis of organizations.

With these as sources, then, a body of knowledge known as "management control" could be tentatively developed. It can be seen from the first edition of Anthony, Dearden and Vancil's *Management Control Systems* (1965) just how tentative they were at the time.' (Lowe and Puxty, 1979)

'The approach taken by these writers (Anthony, Dearden and Vancil) . . . might still be said to be the ruling paradigm of management control, both in the eyes of management teachers and in the eyes of practical businessmen. Yet the insights available from the disciplines marshalled—principally, as we have said, social psychology—are limited in their applicability. Other disciplines can add much (such as general systems theory, sociology and cybernetics). . . . In taking these authors as our touchstone, we hope it is therefore quite clear that we are not questioning the value of the orientation which they have given accounting, in helping it more from a technical perspective to a more useful organizational perspective. Indeed, Anthony recognized early on the role of a preliminary framework:

. . . development of a framework or a conceptual scheme often has led to progress, *even though the framework turns out to be wrong* (his emphasis, Anthony, 1965).

. . . rather we are choosing . . . Anthony and Dearden's work as a subject for critique precisely because of its authority.' (Lowe and Puxty, 1979)

Another important writer in the recent development of MIS thinking, R. L. Ackoff, supports Anthony's general use of the term MCS (rather than MIS) when he writes:

> 'to overcome these assumptions and the deficiencies which result from them a management information system should be imbedded in a management control system'. (R. L. Ackoff, 1967)

But, quite clearly, in the light of his full conception of MIS and MCS, Ackoff does so for quite different reasons, as will be taken up further in a subsequent section of the paper. However, it is also of significance to note that in much of their detailed writings, Anthony and his Harvard colleagues tend to prefer to use the term 'Planning and Control Systems'.

The above references to the use of terms such as MIS, MCS and Planning and Control Systems serve to provide some indication of the existing richness and variety in the conceptualization of the subject of MIS. In a paper describing their recent, interesting research, Ein-Dor and Segev (1978b) present a useful categorization of:

> 'the role assigned a particular information system' (p. 1635).

as follows:

(a) 'a decision and planning tool';
(b) 'an analogue or model of the organization';
(c) 'an information bank';
(d) 'a problem finding and solving aid'.

In support of this analysis and categorization they refer to a large number of more recent (although almost exclusively North American) research studies which apparently fall within those (overlapping) categories. These categories collectively serve a very useful purpose in organizing that literature in terms of the various plausible conceptualizations of the purposes of MIS. And indeed such an analysis would, one surmises, meet with the widespread agreement of the academic, professional and management communities. The intent of the various contributors to the present status of MIS are quite different and this is very evident from the analysis of the literature by Ein-Dor and Segev—in all they cite 103 references. For categories (a) and (d), above, are attempts to identify MIS with the process of rational managing, namely planning, decision-making and problem analysis; category (b) implies a view of MIS as being closely related to organizational theory in all its aspects—organizational design, analysis and behaviour—and therefore also to social psychology; category (c) is representative of those approaches to MIS design which emphasize the collection and analysis of data either presumed to be useful to managers and to the managing activity or indeed, in some information theoretic sense, shown to be so relevant.

Introvert, Bureaucratic, and Empiricist Conceptions of MIS

The recent research already referred to (Ein-Dor and Segev, 1976, 1978a, 1978b) is a most helpful contribution to the literature in that it represents a thorough attempt to present the essentials of the work of (predominantly American) management scientists over the preceding decade or more in the MIS/MCS area. Also, their work is itself representative of the prevailing empiricist nature of much of that literature. For instance their definition of an MIS is:

> 'A management information system is a system for collecting, sorting, retrieving and processing information which is used, or desired, by one or more managers, in the performance of their duties'. (Ein-Dor and Segev, 1978b)

This definition may be profitably compared and contrasted with Anthony's well-known definition of management control:

> 'Management Control is the process by which managers assure that

> resources are obtained and used effectively and efficiently in the accomplishment of the organization's goals'. (Anthony and Dearden, 1976, p. 8)

The Ein-Dor and Segev definition is hopelessly procedural, introverted and bureaucratic. Indeed, it resembles the worst definitions of accounting processes and systems and says little more than that: the book-keeper shall write his double-entries; or more in terms of modern computerized data processing, which dominates some present approaches to MIS design: the MIS computer expert will feed in his program. Whilst Anthony's definition is broader in terms of its clear reference to the underlying managerial process, both seem to invest MIS/MCS as a subject with a predominantly introverted and bureaucratic flavour.

Both these definitions may thus be criticized in the following terms:

> 'It is generally recognized in much recent literature that the environment of an organization has a critical role in the determination of the organization's success. The organization exists because there is a need for it within the environment, whether a need for employment, a need for products or whatever. Much research (for example, Rhenman, 1975, Lawrence and Lorsch, 1967, Duncan, 1972, Terreberry, 1972, Aldrich, 1979, Karpik, 1978) has analysed the environment and its crucial significance for the organization. The most basic message of cybernetics and general systems theory is that control of an organization is dependent on its being able to control its relationship with its environment (Lowe, 1971; Lowe and McInnes, 1971). Yet, in the whole of the approach advocated by Anthony's paradigm, we find no central acknowledgement of the environment. Instead of relating control to the environment it is defined as
>
> > "(1) *planning* what the organization should do, (2) *co-ordinating* the activities of the several parts of the organization, (3) *communicating* information, (4) *evaluating* information and deciding what, if any, action should be taken, (5) *influencing* people to change their behaviour, and (6) *processing information* that is used in the other functions." (p. 6)
>
> The emphasis of this is evidently on internal processes: on actions to be taken within the organization. It is, of course, true that these actions will affect the relationship of the organization to its environment, but this relation is not made explicit and the specific ways in which it should be governed discussed. The result is an inward-looking philosophy of control which, by concentrating on a small part of the control process, ignores the most important part.' (Lowe and Puxty, 1979)

Interestingly, Ein-Dor and Segev (1978a) quote, with evident approval, the work of Mason and Mitroff (1973) concerned with defining:

'the key variables comprising a Management Information System'. (Mason and Mitroff, 1973)

But in their definition Ein-Dor and Segev (1978a) miss the greater refinements and breadth of the Mason and Mitroff definition, which is:

'an information system consists of at least one PERSON of a certain PSYCHOLOGICAL TYPE who faces a PROBLEM within some ORGANIZATIONAL CONTEXT for which he needs some EVIDENCE to arrive at a solution and that the evidence is made available to him through some MODE OF PRESENTATION.' (the emphasis being by the authors) (Mason and Mitroff, 1973)

Although Ein-Dor and Segev consider the 'organizational context', emphasized by Mason and Mitroff in their definition, they omit the further (inseparable) aspects of 'Problem' and 'Evidence', again emphasized by Mason and Mitroff. All three of those terms, in turn, must inevitably relate to the relationship between the organization and its environment. Organizations which are more aware of that relationship may be defined as 'extrovert organizations' in contrast to 'introvert organizations'. Rhenman (1973) has produced an important contribution to the literature of MIS/MCS in emphasizing such a contrast and has used some interesting kinds of analogies for this purpose. The fundamental problem may be characterized as follows:

$$O = f(S_i, E_j)$$

That is to say O, organizational performance, is a function of S, the structure of the organization, including its MCS; and E, the state of the environment as it (causally) affects the organization. From such a model values for the design of the organization, $S_{(1, \ldots, m)}$, are found which optimize measures of the system's performance, O, for each particular value of the (predicted) environmental state. (For simplicity, the problem has been stated in vector form but given that S and E are analysed into their respective systemic elements a more complex matrix formulation becomes necessary.) In this important sense the variable, $E_{(1, \ldots, n)}$, *cannot* be deemed to be uncontrollable. Controllability in this context is achieved by explanation and prediction of the environmental variables affecting the prosperity and welfare of the organization (Lowe and Tinker, 1977a, 1977b; Rhenman, 1973). Thus it is important to observe in the light of the above characterization that the MCS design problem is essentially an 'ill-structured' or 'wicked' problem and to understand the consequences of that fact for MIS/MCS design (Churchman, 1967; Rittel, 1971; Lowe, 1970).

The Ein-Dov and Segev research also seems to be guilty of the worst empiricist excesses of the literature to which they refer and upon which they rely most extensively. Their essence for MIS design and use may be gleaned from the following:

> 'A survey of the scientific, managerial professional and trade literature which has accumulated over the past decade on the construction and use of MIS. . . . Our tendency, therefore is to glean relevant knowledge wherever we find it in the entire field of computer and management science application. Since new variables stopped turning up well before the end of the search, we are confident that the list obtained is quite complete. The final list contains about 120 variables which have been presented in a previous paper'. (Ein-Dor and Segev, 1978a)

It seems quite incredible that they should take such an 'incremental, additive' approach to their scientific work of literature discovery! In this respect, particular emphasis should be given to their reference in the above quotation to the fact that:

> 'Since new variables stopped turning up well before the end of the search, we are confident that the list obtained is quite complete'.

Apparently, one can take an assorted set of MIS/MCS literature and it will all fit together into one large MIS model despite all of the large discrepancies that must inevitably be present between them as to approach and methodology and, indeed, their more general, differing epistemological positions! Ein-Dor and Segev themselves evidently do not need to take some prior, coherent epistemological position before 'diving into' the literature in the manner they have! Indeed it would appear that the authors see themselves as delving into a gold-mine of research endeavours! The researches of all those contributors to the literature seemingly can be added to it in some simple mathematical manner, none (apparently) need be subtracted from it, and the literature surveyed indeed was seen as being neither no more nor no less than the whole of the literature on MIS! Can all this really be so?

This author cannot suggest too strongly that it is absolutely essential for the would-be designer of MCS/MIS to take up a clear, prior epistemological position before going into empirical observation, if he wishes to construct such a system that will be *effective in practice*. The following two sections are addressed to this matter.

Purposive Enquiry

Feyerabend (1968) uses a most telling quotation from Wilkie Collins' Moonstone in his attack on the orthodox scientific attitude:

> '"Facts?" he repeated. "Take a drop more grog, Mr. Franklin, and you'll get over the weakness of believing in facts! Foul play, Sir!"'

An appreciation and understanding of the significance of that quotation is crucial to human endeavours generally (and no less to the design of MCS). Mitroff (1971) in effect strongly argues very much the same point:

> '. . . against the widely held and naive distinction between "fact" and "theory" (and) . . . for a new way of treating statistical data, in a sense for a "new" theory of statistics'.

Mason (1969), within the more immediate context of management planning, makes a very closely related assertion also:

> 'Man lives by his imagination. This is as true of the modern organization as it is for an individual. The particular set of beliefs or assumptions about the world that an organization adopts guides its activity and dictates its success or failure. This is especially true of an organization's strategic plan' (B-403, *op. cit*).

and

> 'To date the main thrust of the research effort in management science has been directed towards the task of finding "optimal solutions" to planning type problems *once they have been formulated and defined.* In these approaches, the underlying assumptions delimit the solution "phase space" in terms of already specified predictions, values and alternative means.'

It is, of course, no coincidence that Mason and Mitroff are students of West Churchman, who is himself a student of E. A. Singer. Singer attempted to 'synthesize within one frame of reference the poles of human thought that are so often at odds with one another' (Mitroff, 1971). In that same general spirit and concern, Churchman (1971) has devoted considerable energy, learning and wisdom to 'The Design of Inquiring Systems'. In principle, Churchman attempts to show that, on the one hand, knowledge cannot be separated from theory and the modelling of problems and that, on the other hand, information and what (we think) we know cannot be separated from how we have obtained that information and the knowledge system (or epistemology) from which it derives. In this manner, communication and our particular system of enquiry are closely related to the idea of an information system. In relation to the application of these general philosophic ideas to MIS, Churchman has argued that MIS designers and managers take too passive a viewpoint concerning the users of MIS information and do not sufficiently question in such terms as:

— why is the information required?
— what is the purpose in requesting information?
— what is the related underlying problem for which the information is desired?

This argument and questioning is in the Hegelian spirit that there is no such thing as 'raw data' and that 'raw data' as such is meaningless when separated from the implicit hypothesis or 'world view' from which that data has been in the first instance derived. Turner (1968), as quoted by Mitroff (1971), writes:

> '. . . The student who is new to his science is blind to the facts put before him. He has to learn to see what is in the microscope, has had to learn to detect the significant patterns in an oscilloscope. . . . One does not just open his eyes and see, he brings with him perceptual hypotheses. Otherwise, he remains blind to the facts' (pp. 11–12, *op. cit.*)

That is, the so-called 'facts'. Essentially, there are no such 'objective' facts. Similarly, it can be argued that presented with the 'raw data' of, say, national income and economic activity, the new student of economics cannot see the 'facts' before him. And, equally, we can argue that the 'old students' (e.g. the professors) will put entirely different constructions from one another on those same 'raw data' according to whether they are 'monetarists' or 'Keynesians'. Similar kinds of examples in the subject matter of financial management can soon be brought to mind which tend to show that 'raw data' is never neutral, but that it implies one or more corresponding, related theories by which a particular piece of data acquires its particular character, quality, description and, indeed, name: thus facts, so-called, are a property of the observer and his experience rather than of a universe independent of the observer.

The concern expressed here for a dose of 'purposive enquiry' to be injected into the ideas of MCS/MIS may seem like a cry in the wilderness of ignorance. For the question: 'What kind of purposive enquiry?' has still to be asked and then settled. This is a difficult (if not impossible) question to settle at least in simple terms of information, for the commodity 'information' cannot be disentangled from the enquiry system of which it is an integral part, as is further discussed in the next section. In the case of some enquiring system, information may be the resulting output of that system, obtained from a structure of (almost) pure logic. In other cases, the enquiry system is (purposely) structured with bits of information. Churchman (1971) identifies a number of kinds of enquiring systems derived from some recent notable western philosophers and argues for these as providing candidate bases for an enquiring system upon which to base an MCS/MIS. Such bases are thus, clearly, limited in their overall scope according to the narrowness of the base, in historical time, geographical location, and the cultural and value context from which they are chosen.

Epistemological Candidates for a System of Enquiring Knowledge

The central concern of epistemology is the nature and derivation of knowledge:

— how is knowledge acquired?;
— what precisely is meant by a claim to know something?;
— what is the reliability of such a claim?

These are not issues that have been or, indeed, perhaps can, in any final sense, be settled. But are these issues which need concern workers in MIS/MCS and accounting? Are propositions in these subjects free of, or independent of, such concerns? The argument in the previous section suggests it is impossible to be uninvolved whilst our concern is with information (or knowledge) related to problems and decisions. An information system is surely a 'machine' for acquiring knowledge and information through processes of enquiry. The matter cannot simply be shrugged off or assumed away. There appear to be two principal, proponent schools of thought in epistemology: first, the rationalists, who argue that the source of knowledge must be the ideas and reasoning intrinsic to the mind and obtained by logical deduction (Plato, Descartes, Spinoza, and, perhaps, above all, Leibnitz, are principal proponents of that school); secondly, empiricists, who argue that sense experience, through inductive processes, is the primary source of ideas, and knowledge (and who include Locke, Hume and Berkeley). Kant successfully attempted a synthesis of these opposing schools of thought by proposing an integrated learning and enquiring system with both formal (rational) and sensing (empirical) aspects of human thought and experience, and thus overcame some of the weaknesses of both Leibnitzian and Lockean traditions. He argued that it is necessary to make certain *a priori* assumptions or possess particular theoretical notions in order to observe, but that both (i.e. understanding and sensibility) are necessary for knowledge, and thus for an information system.

This led Kant to suggest that there may be two or more possible alternative explanations of a particular phenomenon or resolution of a problem. For each such alternative there are likely to be different sets of supporting data or observations. Such analyses seem particularly appropriate to social science phenomena or problem situations which may have a multitude of aspects, characterizations and attributes; and which are, therefore, of a multi-disciplinary nature. Hegel built on the work of Kant both in his argument that the mind is in an active relationship to its objects, and in his development of dialectical argument; that is that argument, knowledge, understanding and information proceeds in trials: first a thesis, or initial proposition; secondly, the antithesis, which is generated by the inadequacy of its opposite; and thirdly, the synthesis, which maintains what is rational but counters the irrational elements of both thesis and antithesis. Mitroff (1971) has formulated a communication model of such an Hegelian-based dialectical inquiring system as an information system for strategic planning. Elsewhere, Mitroff (1973) supports such proposals for management control:

> 'These opposing representations constitute the contrary underlying assumptions regarding the theoretical nature of the problem. Both of these Leibnitzian representations are then applied to the same Lockean data set in order to demonstrate the crucial nature of the underlying theoretical assumptions, i.e. the point that the *same* data set can be used to support *either* theoretical model. The point is that data are not information; information is that which results from the interpretation of data. It is hoped that out of a dialectical confrontation between opposing interpretations (e.g. the opposing 'expert' views of a situation), the underlying assumptions of both Leibnitzian models (or opposing policy experts) will be brought up to the surface for conscious examination by the decision-maker who is dependent upon his experts for advice . . . the decision-maker will be in a better position to form his own view . . . that is a creative synthesis'.

Singer (1959), and his student, Churchman (1971), have further extended the idea of an inter-disciplinary synthesis for an inquiring system. Whilst most philosophers of science had been concerned to elucidate the basic design of science 'by removing all the rubble' to reveal the mathematical analysis of proof in terms of one discipline only, logic, and thus discovered merely the 'tactics' of the mathematics for problem-solving activity, Singer discovered its 'strategy', by recognizing that the design task required a whole inter-disciplinary effort, reflecting the whole variety of models of thought: scientific, ethical, aesthetic, etc., for any attempt to integrate all kinds of knowledge and thought. Moreover, unlike the other founders of enquiring systems referred to above, who tended to regard their systems as reality itself, *Singer regarded the reality of his system as crucially depending upon the ability to convince sufficient others* (e.g. decision-makers) of its status as a reality; for it could be no more than a representation of reality and, indeed, of no consequence unless, and until, it showed a capacity for actually influencing and changing human behaviour.

In this section an outline sketch has been provided of several candidate-bases, in the history of the philosophy of science, for inquiring systems which may serve as a way of developing MCS as instruments of 'purposive behaviour' in organizations. However, it is again necessary to emphasize that this line of thought depends, critically, upon the notion that we are dealing with a 'wicked', 'ill-structured problem' for which mechanistic, operational-level, information systems are quite unsuited except for limited, assumption-ridden purposes. As such this section constitutes a suggestion of the manner in which we should proceed down a path of inquiry, already trodden by philosophers of science and some management scientists, most notably Churchman, Mitroff and Mason.

With regard to empirical research which might tend to support such 'dialectical inquiry' as effective MIS/MCS the slight evidence so far obtained is mixed: Mitroff, Barabba and Kilmann (1977) report supportively, whilst Cosier *et al.* (1978) note that:

> 'even though the conflict component of DIS [Dialectical Inquiry System] was perceived as more useful in one instance, in general the DIS did not lead to significantly better objective performance when compared to alternative planning approaches'.

Clearly, much further research is required in this area to clarify its usefulness in MCS/MIS design.

Control through Extroversion

An examination of Ashby's work (1964) has provided important models for understanding the nature of control problems. However, they are, of course, not adequate for addressing all problems of management control because of the complexity of human social systems in terms of inter-relatedness and inter-dependence (rather than of sheer, physical size) which in turn determines the amount of 'variety' in the system's universe. That complexity leads to uncertainty, and to problems of explanation and prediction which cannot be adequately addressed by traditional statistical theory and techniques (as mathematical statisticians readily recognized) but can, at least, be more satisfactorily confronted (that is to say characterized, as a problem) by general system theory (Von Bertalanffy, 1968; Klir, 1969; Van Gigch, 1978) and cybernetic regulation (Ashby, 1964) because of their capability for handling more complex ideas of cause and effect. But, clearly, a more sophisticated statistical theory than is presently available is also required to enable the development of a more adequate statistical measure of available 'system fit' (Bonini, 1963, especially Chapters 7, 8 and 11). Often the control must, of necessity, be more or less 'imperfect' rather than 'perfect' in the cybernetic sense (Ashby, 1964, Chapter 13). 'Requisite variety' cannot be achieved, and control, in the sense of desired, purposive behaviour of the whole system, is not accomplished. In this context, controls as specific measurements and information by which it is expected that *control* can be achieved, can, by definition, only have functional meaning when so related to each other such that control can be achieved. This proposition is clearly developed in Ashby's idea of 'Regulation by Veto' (Ashby, 1964, Chapter 13). In the context of human situations, controls must, therefore, be so devised as to be motivators which lead to control, i.e. desired, purposive behaviour of the system, as a whole entity. It is quite understandable, however, that organizational life may lead us to focus too readily on internal enterprise controls, concerns and procedures and thereby away from their end purpose: the effectiveness of the whole enterprise, and what makes it succeed, or survive as an entity at a given, desired level of prosperity. Success must be defined both in terms of the entity's own criteria as well as those of *the values, beliefs, norms and culture of its environment* in order to resolve the problems of inter-personal and inter-organizational conflict.

In these terms organizations are only successful in so far as they are permeated by the values and norms of their environment. And management control consists partly of the creation of an organization which is purposeful in terms of environmental norms and partly of a mapping in terms of information and enquiry between the 'substantial' environment and the organizational structure. Organizational problems in this context, are defined as sanctions emanating from the environment through enterprise misperceptions of the needs of the environment and of the structural changes in it. Problem-solving may then be considered as re-design of the enterprise wholly or partially, but only so as to better fit the environment. Thus 'morbid' organizational diagnosis and too much introverted concern for the 'right' organizational design and behaviour may be said to be looking entirely in the wrong direction. The concept of 'equifinality' (Von Bertalanffy, 1968) becomes important in this context for often there is a tendency to make unhelpful analogies between human individuals as living systems and human enterprise system. Rhenman (1973), in arguing similarly, produces a helpful listing of the 'Limitations of Analogies between Organisms and Organizations'.

It is important to bear in mind that disorder and illness in living organizations suggests a disequilibrium in vital structural processes and elements whereas organizations do not have to develop rigid structure, subject to incurable disorder and illness. Organizations merely require to re-orientate themselves in terms of the needs of the environment. Rhenman's argument leads him to formulate the following kinds of important, perceptive propositions:

Proposition 1

Organizations with stable environments have no real problems. Thus organizational problems are the results of change processes in its environment.

and its corollary is:

Organizations with stable environments have virtually no problems, or only the most trivial ones.

Proposition 2

Organizations are in fact subject to social control and are judged and rewarded and punished accordingly by society.

Proposition 3

Cyclical changes and disturbances can be met by measures based on the principle of 'negative feedback'. This is not so for structural environmental changes. To deal with these it is necessary to recognize as early as possible that the changes are structural and require an adjustment of the whole structure of the firm.

Thus the whole rationale of this approach to problem-solving is that problems which *seem* to be intra-organizational are, in reality, inter-organizational and environmental. Thus it is traditional in management analysis to state a set of problems and analyse them in terms of the organizational function to which they may be assigned, whereas, in fact, they are problems emanating from the environment and should be treated, for their solution, extrovertly in terms of the organizational-environmental relationship. Hence an assignment according to the structural change in the environment affecting the organization is much more relevant in problem-solving terms since, it is argued, it represents an attempt to identify the end cause and effect aspects of the problem which, more superficially, often manifest themselves as of an intra-organizational kind.

Conclusion

The argument of this paper is that the literature of management information and control systems is far too introverted in two important respects:

First, in terms of the disciplines which are thought to be relevant both to fundamental enquiry and to realistic, empirical propositions upon which MCS/MIS should be designed;

Secondly, in terms of the analysis of the organizational systems to which the theory relates.

The subject of MCS/MIS should be much more widely informed by reference to social science, the philosophy and theory of knowledge (epistemology), general system theory and cybernetics, in order to attempt to cope with what is a 'wicked', 'ill-structured' problem.

References

Ackoff, R. L., 'Management Misinformation Systems', *Management Science* (December 1967).

Aldrich, H. E., *Organizations and Environments*. Prentice-Hall (1979).

Anthony, R. N., *Planning and Control Systems*. Harvard University Press (1965).

Anthony, R. N., Dearden, J. and Vancil, R. F., *Management Control Systems*. Irwin (1965).

Argyris, C., *The Impact of Budgets on People*. Controllership Foundation (1952).

Ashby, R. W., *An Introduction to Cybernetics*. Methuen (1964).

Betz, F., 'On the Management of Inquiry', *Management Science* (December 1971).

Bonini, C. P., *Simulation of Information and Decision Systems in the Firm*. Prentice-Hall (1963).

Churchman, C. W., *The Design of Inquiring Systems*. Basic Books (1971).

Churchman, C. W., *Singerian Inquiring Systems*, Internal Working Paper 122, University of California, Berkeley (October 1970).

Churchman, C. W., 'Letter to the Editor', *Management Science* (December 1967).

Cosier, R. A., Ruble, T. L. and Aplin, J. C., 'An Evaluation of the Effectiveness of Dialectical Inquiry Systems', *Management Science* (October 1976).

Duncan, R. B., 'Characteristics of Organizational Environments and Preceived Environmental Uncertainty', *Administrative Science Quarterly* (September 1972).

Ein-Dor, P. and Segev, E., 'A Paradigm for MIS', Faculty of Management, Working Paper 256 (Tel-Aviv University, May 1976).

Ein-Dor, P. and Segev, E., 'Organizational Context and the Success of Management Information Systems', *Management Sciences* (June 1978a).

Ein-Dor, P. and Segev, E., 'Strategic Planning for Management Information Systems', *Management Science* (November 1978b).

Feyerabend, P. K., 'How to be a good empiricist—a plea for tolerance in matters epistemological', Nidditch, P. H. (ed.), *The Philosophy of Science.* Oxford University Press (1968).

Giglioni, G. B. and Bedeian, A. G., 'A Conspectus of Management Control Theory: 1900–1972', *Academy of Management Journal* (June 1974).

Hoos, I. R., 'Information Systems and Public Planning', *Management Science* (June 1971).

Karpik, L., *Organization and Environment.* Sage (1978).

Klir, J. G., *An Approach to General Systems Theory.* Van Nostrand, Rheinhold (1969).

Lawrence, P. R. and Lorsch, J. W., *Organization and Environment.* Harvard University Press (1967).

Lowe, E. A., 'The Information Content of Financial Statements, Financial Planning, and Management Control: towards an integration', *Journal of Business Finance* (Summer 1970).

Lowe, E. A., 'On the Idea of a Management Control System', *Journal of Management Studies* (February 1971).

Lowe, E. A. and McInnes, J. M., 'Control in Socio-Economic Organizations: A Rationale for the Design of Management Control Systems', *Journal of Management Studies* (May 1971).

Lowe, E. A. and Puxty, A. G., 'The Problems of a Paradigm: A Critique of the Prevailing Orthodoxy in management control'. A paper presented to the EIASM Workshop on Information and Control Systems (Brussels, December 1979).

Lowe, E. A. and Tinker, A. M., 'New Directions in Management Accounting', *Omega* (1977a).

Lowe, E. A. and Tinker, A. M., 'The Architecture of Requisite Variety', *Kybernetes* (1976b) pp. 145–154 (July) and pp. 197–207 (October).

March, J. G. and Simon, H. A., *Organizations.* Wiley (1958).

Mason, R. O., 'A Dialectical Approach to Strategic Planning', *Management Science* (April 1969).

Mason, R. O. and Mitroff, I. I., 'A Program for Research on Management Information Systems', *Management Science* (January 1973).

Mitroff, I. I., 'A Communication Model of Dialectical Inquiring Systems—A Strategy for Strategic Planning', *Management Science* (June 1971).

Mitroff, I. I., 'Systems, Inquiry, and the Meanings of Falsification', *Philosophy of Science* (June 1973).

Mitroff, I. I., Barabba, V. P. and Kilmann, R. H., 'The Application of

Behavioural and Philosophical Technologies to Strategic Planning: A Case Study of a Large Federal Agency', *Management Science* (September 1977).
Rhenman, E., *Organization Theory for Long-Range Planning*. Wiley (1973).
Rittel, H., 'Some Principles for the Design of an Educational System of Design', *Journal of Architectural Education* (Winter-Spring, 1971).
Singer, E. A., *Experience and Reflection*. University of Pennsylvania Press (1959).
Terreberry, S., 'The Evolution of Organizational Environments', reprinted in Thomas, J. M. and Bennis, W. G. (eds.), *Management of Change and Conflict*. Penguin (1972).
Van Gigch, J. P., *Applied General Systems Theory* (2nd edn.). Harper and Row (1978).
Von Bertalanffy, L., *General System Theory*. Penguin (1968).

Commentary on **'The management of purposive environmental enquiry: suggestions for the development of MIS thinking'**

J C Higgins
Director and Professor of Management Sciences, Management Centre, University of Bradford

Professor Lowe's overall thesis might be translated as a plea for interdisciplinarity in our understanding of management information and control systems. I would support this thesis and also agree that the literature does suffer from both a lack of 'careful definition of purpose' and a relative 'unwillingness to recognize the ill-structured nature of the MISC problem'.

This first weakness leads on to questions of definitions, and many of the definitions in the literature are misleading. One cited is not only 'procedural, introverted and bureaucratic' but also tends to focus attention on computer methods. Professor Lowe's incorporation of the word *control* has the merit of underlining the basic purpose of a management information system. An alternative definition is the following: a system which provides each manager in the organization with the information he needs in order to take decisions, plan and control within his particular area of responsibility (Higgins, 1980, p. 80). Linked to this definition, I would also highlight that not only the planning and control requirements but also individual managers' needs, management style, the external environment, and organizational structure are important determinants of the MIS.

Professor Lowe rightly argues that the organizational context is underemphasized in the literature and, I would add, in MIS practice. There is a major problem of the adaptiveness of the organization to its environment and, more specifically, the problem that organizations are often very poorly organized with respect to the external components of their MIS's. Whereas the internal parts of the MIS are often based on existing and successful management accounting systems, there is frequently no substantial or effective external monitoring and forecasting system on which to base that part of the MIS.

I would agree that the overall MISC problem is 'ill-structured' and 'wicked'. However, to proceed from the general assertion one now needs to discuss the level in the organization and the type of decision if one is to make progress either in systems design or in research. This takes me to a general question. How does the paper help (a) a researcher, (b) a systems designer, (c) a manager? I will leave Professor Lowe to answer the first and make some comments as to how I think one proceeds to help the second and third category of individual.

To this end, I introduce a number of diagrams to illustrate my own

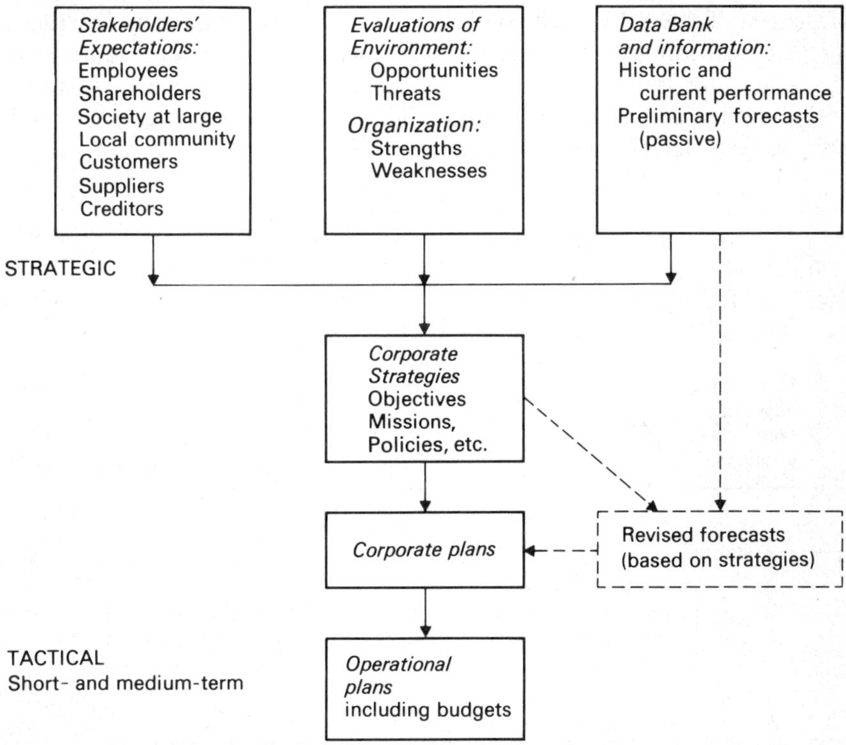

Fig. 9.1

Table 9.1.

Level	*Nature of decisions*	*Examples of information*
Strategic	Long-term, high risk and uncertainty, poorly-structured, often one-off	External: macro-economic trends Internal: long-term trends in, for example, productivity and ROI
Managerial	More medium-term, low-medium risk, more recurrent, resource allocation	Performance against budgets/plans
Operations	Short-term, repetitive, low or zero risk (deterministic), programmable	Sales dispatch and invoicing Personal tax records for wage calculations Production inventory levels and WIP

perspective. Figure 9.1 summarizes the nature of strategic and operational planning and relates the data bank and information system to these processes. Table 9.1 is based on R. N. Anthony's (Anthony and Dearden, 1976) classification and shows the relationship between level, nature of decisions and information. Such an analysis has a number of major implications for this design. Finally, Figure 9.2 highlights the system and sub-system interrelationships for an effective MIS.

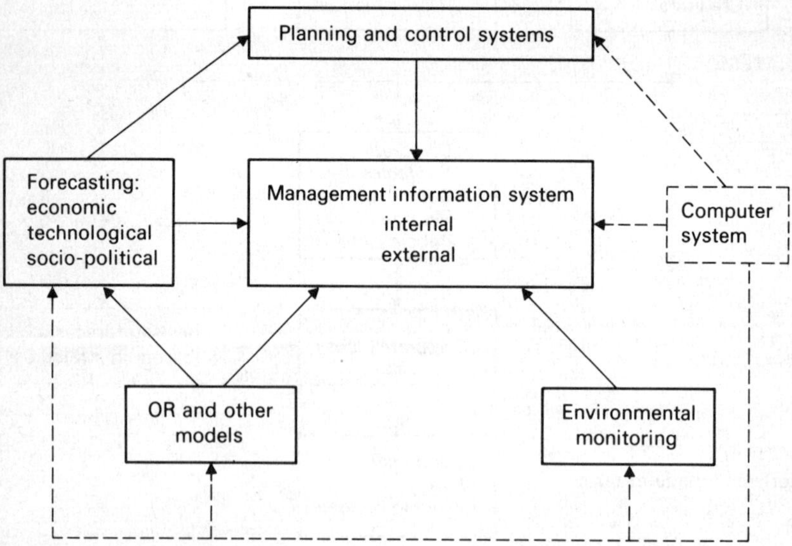

Fig. 9.2

Thus, although one endorses the holistic philosophy of systems design, to make practical progress we must analyse the systems along the lines summarized by the three figures and proceed to some degree piecemeal whilst recognizing that our ultimate objective is to produce an overall well-integrated MIS. In practice, for example, the second level, namely the managerial, is often relatively neglected in terms of computer applications. Also, the external components for marketing and for R & D may show very poor linkage and so again one must, whilst allowing that they may develop relatively independently, constantly bear in mind the need for integration.

It is worth noting that the higher forms of systems design contemplated by Ackoff (1974) would posit a highly adaptivizing system, or 'pre-active' system, which would not need forecasts or planning in the context I have implied or, better still, one designed by an *interactivist*, someone who wants 'to design a desirable future and invent ways of bringing it about'. Ackoff also stresses that the MIS must be part of the total management system.

Several comments on the use of terms are in order:

(a) I believe Professor Lowe is using 'management control' in a broader sense than I am using it (detection and analysis of the difference between plan and performance and action taken to reduce that difference or improve future plans). His definition presumably subsumes planning.

(b) His usage of the word 'structure' seems to subsume much of what is called process as well—in other words, not only the organizational structure itself *and* the product market posture of the organization but also processes such as those involved in communication, allocation of resources etc.

(c) The references to vectors and matrices can be sharpened by the example of a Markov process in the prediction of market shares namely:

S_{t+1}	$=$	(a_{ij})	S_t
State vector at time $t + 1$ giving the market shares		brand-switching matrix of transition probabilities	State vector at time t

Conclusion

The paper usefully extends the systems perspective, underlines the complexity of systems design problems, stresses that information is in the eye of the beholder and illustrates the value of the dialectic, perhaps not as formulated in Mitroff's terms, as quoted, but nevertheless at the strategic and managerial levels; this is what systems design should be all about.

References

Ackoff, R. L., *Redesigning the Future*. Wiley (1974).
Anthony, R. N. and Dearden, J., *Management Control Systems*. Irwin (1976).
Higgins, J. C., *Strategic and Operational Planning Systems: Principles and Practice*. Prentice-Hall (1980).

10 Quantitative aspects of management accounting

K N Bhaskar
Professor of Accountancy and Finance, University of East Anglia

The problem of establishing a generally accepted definition of management accounting is still the subject of considerable debate. For convenience, management accounting will be defined in this review as accounting information to aid the organization in planning and control (for alternative definitions and discussion see Amey and Egginton, 1973, p. 1). Similar problems of definition apply to the term 'quantitative aspects' and this too will be abstracted from. A special problem for this article is that relevant ideas are found in a number of disciplines. In general, this review will focus on accounting and finance journals in the belief that few major pieces of research concerning quantitative techniques relevant to accounting, have failed to filter through to these journals. This review is generally limited to the literature of the 1970s. It is drawn from an extensive examination of six major accounting and finance journals published in the U.K. and U.S.A.[1]

Two observations can be made. Certain topics are more popular than others; and some journals specialize in certain areas. Management accounting topics which seem to have fairly broad coverage in all journals include: risk and uncertainty, forecasting, short-run cash planning, financial modelling, and mathematical programming. Topics which are the most popular include: overhead allocation, risk and uncertainty, cost-volume-profit analysis, forecasting, mathematical programming, DCF problems, cost control and variance investigation, capital structure, financial information systems, and portfolio analysis.

Unfortunately, time and space limitations do not allow a complete survey of every topic, but a number of major topics of relevance to management accounting are discussed in some detail. The paper starts by considering an easily definable area, that of cost-volume-profit analysis. Other major topics covered are: cost allocation; cost control and variance

1 These journals were:
U.K.:
Accounting and Business Research
Journal of Business Finance and Accounting
U.S.:
Accounting Review
Journal of Accounting Research
Journal of Finance
Journal of Financial and Quantitative Analysis

investigation; and mathematical programming. Financial information systems and the determination of cost relationships are covered briefly. The remaining topics are not further considered.

Cost-Volume-Profit Analysis

Cost-volume-profit (CVP) analysis of the traditional sort is a subject that is central to management accounting. Recent extensions made to CVP analysis have earned this subject a place within the set labelled quantitative research. Much of the research in this area is concerned with whether analytical solutions are preferable to probabilistic simulation. Whatever the academic merits of the two solutions, one must ask which technique, if either, is preferable to the practitioner? Mathematical analysis can easily involve generally unavailable mathematical skills, and probabilistic simulation may be an expensive process which may crucially depend upon the state of development of computer systems and the sophistication of their users.

Traditional CVP analysis is a well-known technique in management accounting which is used both for a decision-making and control. The standard model is:

$$Y = Q(P - V) - F \tag{1}$$

where

Y = aggregate profits
Q = sales volume in units
P = unit selling price
V = unit variable cost
F = aggregate fixed cost

One of the limitations of simple CVP analysis is that it makes no allowance for uncertainty.

Jaedicke and Robichek (1964) in a seminal paper derived a model which enabled the computation of the expected value and the standard deviation of profit for a single product. Suppose that only Q (the sales volume) is a random variable. Then the expected value of profits is:

$$E(Y) = E(Q)(P - V) - F \tag{2}$$

but the variance of expected profits is more difficult to calculate. Representing the standard deviation by σ and assuming that Q is normally distributed then,

$$\sigma_Y = \sigma_Q(P - V) \tag{3}$$

and the probability distribution of Y will also be normally distributed.

The determination of the expected value and standard deviation of profit enables a decision-maker to estimate the probability of achieving the break-even point, and also the probability of achieving any other level of profit or loss.

Jaedicke and Robichek correctly defined expected profit for situations where several variables in the model were normally distributed random variables as,

$$E(Y) = E(Q)[E(P) - E(V)] - E(F) \tag{4}$$

However, their derivation of profit in these circumstances overlooked the problem that the product of two or more independent and normally distributed random variables is not necessarily a normally distributed random variable.

Ferrara *et al.* (1972) addressed this problem and showed that the multiplication of two normal variables only yielded a normal variable under restrictive conditions. Strictly speaking, the product of two normally distributed and statistically independent random variables approximates the normal when the sum of coefficients of variation (defined as the standard deviation divided by the expected value), approaches zero. Their conclusion was that the hypothesis of normalcy could be accepted if the sum of the coefficient of variation associated with volume (Q) and the unit profit contribution ($P - V$) was less than or equal to 12 per cent.

The next problem for CVP analysis under uncertainty was how a general analytical solution could be developed which would yield meaningful probabilistic statements when the volume (Q) and the unit profit contribution ($P - V$) were non-normal variables. Buzby (1974) argued that the problem could be solved by the use of Tchebycheff inequalities.

An alternative approach to non-normalcy of the profit distribution was initiated by Hilliard and Leitch (1975). They suggested a solution to the problem which assumed that sales, Q, and contribution to profit, $P - V$, were lognormally distributed. They, in practice, argued that it would be surprising if variables were perfectly symmetric around their means. Lognormal distributions which are skewed to the right, seemed to them more likely to be representative of the data. Buzby was severely criticized for his use of Tchebycheff type inequalities. Liao (1975) argued that these inequalities were too restrictive for the problem, in the sense that the probability statements they gave rise to were too conservative and too restrictive.

Ferrara *et al.* (1975) provided a fuller critique of Buzby and extended the work of Hilliard and Leitch (1975). They argued that the use of Tchebycheff inequalities in probabilistic models was expedient only when the chi-square goodness-of-fit test was available for use (for which it was necessary to have something in the order of 100 or more observations), but with current knowledge, more sophisticated techniques were available (such as the Kolmogorov–Smirnov and Cramer–von Mises tests).

Buzby (1975) strongly objected to the suggestion by Ferrara *et al.* (1975)

that the Tchebycheff type inequalities were obsolete. He argued, seemingly correctly, that as a substantial number of companies do not utilize sophisticated methods of analysis in their decision-making, Tchebycheff inequalities were, indeed, a useful tool.

Kottas *et al.* (1978) pointed out that to reduce the mathematical analysis to a manageable level, previous analytical attempts in CVP analysis had made the simplifying assumption that the random variables in the problem belong to standard distributions, most of which they found to have defects. Even the lognormal distribution was shown to have some shortcomings by Lau–Lau (1976). The advance made by the Kottas *et al.* (1978) paper was to use mathematical statistical analysis by assuming independence of those primary variables which determined the value of the objective variable (profit). This procedure is to estimate the first four moments of the probability distributions of these primary variables and then to derive the four moments of the objective variable (profit) according to certain rules. When the four moments of the profit distribution can be calculated, two possible avenues for further progress appear. The first is the classical procedure of fitting the first four moments of a random variable to a Pearson's curve and has been fully treated by Liao (1975). Secondly, a practitioner may use a simpler technique; for the availability of a set of tables (Johnson *et al.*, 1963), has greatly reduced the computations required for this operation.

The Kottas *et al.* approach (1978) still leaves the decision-maker with a problem if the primary variables are inter-dependent. They suggested the use of probabilistic simulation to aid in solving this problem. The arguments normally used to cast doubt on what some would regard as a less academically respectable technique include the following points.

First, probabilistic simulation yields estimations which are subject to sampling errors. Secondly, the required computer resources may be excessive. Thirdly, a company using CVP analysis may not have the necessary software or personnel to conduct the simulations. Kottas *et al.* (1978) recognized these reservations; it was therefore surprising that Kottas and Lau (1978) came down on the side of direct simulation.

Kottas and Lau concluded that 'in practice, simulation is perhaps the most obvious and straightforward approach'. They paid scant regard to their previous paper (Kottas *et al.*, 1978), and argued forcefully for simulation as the ideal in all situations—whether the primary variables are independent or dependent. Kottas and Lau (1978) analysed the strengths and weaknesses of simulation relative to model sampling—see also Liao (1975). Model sampling involves running a small simulation to provide an estimated standard deviation, which is then used in a larger simulation (in which a sample size is estimated to provide a predetermined degree of accuracy). The results of the larger simulation run can be used to provide estimates of the first four moments of the profit distribution. A Pearson's curve can be fitted using the four moments. Numerical integration of the fitted curve provides probability statements. Kottas and Lau (1978) argued that simulation had the following relative advantages: power of accurate modelling; simplicity of technique; low cost of implementation; and accuracy of solution. Kottas and Lau conclude that direct probabilistic simulation is a very powerful, simple, inexpensive and accurate approach to stochastic CVP analysis. They say (p. 705) 'that, given the current state-of-art and the increasing accessibility of computers, direct simulation should be used for the majority of SCVPA (stochastic CVP analysis) and similar stochastic management problems. For the SCVPA researcher, this study has established direct simulation as the "benchmark" with which further "improved SCVPA approaches" should be compared.'

Other CPV Analysis

Most of the foregoing discussion was published in the *Accounting Review*. No other journal has dealt with stochastic CVP analysis and techniques for deriving solutions. A number of U.S. journals (including the *Accounting Review*) have, however, dealt with related questions in stochastic CVP analysis. Johnson and Simik (1971) started a smaller debate over stochastic multi-product CVP analysis in the *Journal of Accounting Research*. This work addressed a problem which was not tackled by Jaedicke and Robichek, that of the interdependency of demand in a multi-product firm.

A subsequent article by Johnson and Simik (1974) extended their multi-product analysis to situations in which the probability density functions of the primary variable (now a vector) is not known. By using Tchebycheff type inequalities, certain probabilistic statements can be made; they, however, suffer from the same criticisms as Buzby's (1974) analysis.

Dickinson (1974) took Johnson and Simik (1971) to task in a subsequent issue of the *Journal of Accounting Research*, for not addressing the problem of the derivation of values for the expectations, variances, and co-variances of the probability distributions of future sales demands. Dickinson dismissed subjective estimates as a means of valuing the parameters of these probability distributions, and suggested the use of historic data to derive the estimated expected value and variance of profits.

Dickinson's suggestions raise the whole question of how to obtain valid estimates of the probability distributions of the variables in CVP models. Past data may give one approximation but the sample size will be relatively small. As yet no approach exists, though Bayesian analysis has been suggested in the literature and this is one avenue open to the researcher.

CVP and Portfolio Analysis

Another research area for CVP analysts is the intersection of their research with that of portfolio analysis/capital market theory. This gap was plugged by Magee (1975). Magee summarized the content of Johnson and Simik (1974) as suggesting that a decision-maker in firm j might use the expected profit $E(\pi_j)$, the standard deviation of profit (σ_π) and a measure of the firm's risk/return trade off (δ_j) to maximize the expression below in order to make decisions:

$$\text{Max } [E(\pi_j) - \delta_j \sigma_{\pi_j}] \tag{5}$$

Using the usual capital asset pricing model assumptions, Magee derives an alternative model: stockholders of firm j will unanimously approve of changes in a decision variable (Z_j) if the decision-maker attempts to maximize the following expression:

$$\text{Maximize } \{E[\pi_j(Z_j)] - P \,.\, C[\pi_j(Z_j), r_m]\} \tag{6}$$

where

$\pi_j(Z_j)$ = the increased profits from firm j resulting from an increase in Z; where Z_j represents a managerial decision variable

r_m = the market return which is assumed to be unaffected by any actions of the decision-maker

P = the market price of risk, i.e. the rate of substitution between expected return and variance

$E[\ ]$, $C[\ ]$ = the expectation and co-variance operators respectively

In the above model, the manager's short-run behaviour is a function of the expected value of profit and the co-variance of profit with the return on the market portfolio. Not surprisingly, this model yields different optimal decisions compared with the earlier models based on the expected value of profit and the variance of the expected profit.

The two models are drawn from essentially different paradigms and therefore should yield different optimal decisions and require the management accountant to supply different sets of information in order to aid the decision-maker in dealing with uncertainty in short-run planning situations. As Magee succinctly puts it (1975, p. 246):

> 'Rather than the variance of a product's sales (Jaedicke and Robichek) or the co-variance of a product's sales with the sales of the firm's other products (Johnson and Simik) the decision-maker might desire a measure of the co-variance of the product's sales with the return on his shareholders' alternative investment opportunities. In addition, an estimate of the market's risk-return trade off parameter, P, may be desired.'

Cost – Volume – Profit and Utility Analysis

Meanwhile back at the *Accounting Review* another interesting development was taking place. Adar *et al.* (1977) combined stochastic CVP analysis with the risk preferences of decision-makers and opened a new area of analysis—that of cost–volume–utility analysis, utility is defined within a standard Tobin–Markowitz–Lintner 'mean–standard deviation' framework. Adar *et al.* restricted their problem to include only one random element. Fixed costs (F) and unit variable costs (V) are not stochastic. Decision-makers are assumed to rank alternative pairs of expected profits ($E(Y) = \bar{Y}$) and the standard deviation of profits (σ_Y) by a risk averse utility function.

The only random element in the system is assumed to be the unit selling price (P) which is defined by:

$$P = E(P) + u \tag{7}$$

where the expected value of u is zero with a finite variance (σ_u). Optimal utility maximizing behaviour is derived by maximizing utility with respect to output subject to risk return opportunities. Hence:

$$\text{Maximize} \quad U(\bar{Y}, \sigma_Y) \tag{8}$$

$$\text{Subject to} \quad \bar{Y} - b\sigma_Y + F = 0 \tag{9}$$

The solution to this problem is where the slope of the indifference curve is tangential to the slope of the constraint line of feasible possibilities which is a straight line since,

$$b = \frac{\bar{P} - V}{\sigma_u} \tag{10}$$

where σ_u (the standard deviation of price) is finite and invariant and $\bar{P}$ is the expected value of the unit selling price. The second order condition simply specifies that the indifference curves must be convex. Following the Adar *et al.* (1977) analysis optimal production decisions depend on decision-makers' attitudes, as well as on fixed costs, F, and the price of risk, defined in terms of the expected contribution margin ($\bar{P} - V$), per unit of standard deviation of price, σ_u. This model is interesting because of its conclusion that the desirability of alternative plans involves not only variable costs but also fixed costs. Under certainty, fixed costs are irrelevant to short run decision-making but with uncertainty, fixed costs interact with the decision-maker's attitude to risk and therefore may change his optimal behaviour.

Appraisal of the CVP Debate

This concludes the review of the CVP debate. Papers such as Dopuch (1963) and Groves *et al.* (1970) which deal with mathematical programming and CVP analysis are discussed later; other papers in the CVP area include that of Ijiri and Itami (1970) which dealt with the timing of demand information within a quadratic CVP relationship. It is interesting to note that the sole British contributions which followed the central debate were Dickinson (1974) and Groves *et al.* (1970).

The answer to the question of what, if any, has been the contribution of the debate, must reflect a uniquely personal opinion. In stochastic CVP analysis, it was evident that many of the papers reviewed attempted to display the author's mathematical and statistical ability without always extending the frontiers of knowledge. The extent to which authors tried to avoid using probabilistic simulation, or, alternatively, argued that the world should be constrained to fall within certain standard probability distributions, is remarkable. Despite these contortions, probabilistic simulation has won through as the most acceptable solution and it is at this point that the debate seems to have ended. Although the theory is ahead of practice, at least the practitioner has a technique which can be implemented.

Some academic researchers seem to assume that the existing knowledge of the practitioner is either irrelevant to academic articles or that though the practitioner's knowledge of computing is small, his or her knowledge of calculus, algebra, and mathematical statistics is high. This might explain the absurd preference for numerical integration and curve fitting in some of the papers reviewed.

One final observation can be made on the debate: it seems that no matter what the topic is being discussed, sooner or later someone will try to relate that topic to the portfolio theory/capital asset pricing model. Evidence of this was seen in Adar *et al.* (1977) and Magee (1975). Magee implicitly assumed that Johnson and Simik (1974) were incorrect in not using this approach, whereas a more objective appraisal would point out that they were following the bulk of the received literature in CVP analysis in attempting to derive probabilistic statements about expected profit. A more cynical comment might be that unless the relationship between the topic under discussion and the capital asset pricing model is made explicitly clear, the author is leaving himself open for attack.

Directions for Future Research in the CVP Debate

It is surprising that during the CVP debate, although the most sophisticated tools have been used to handle the stochastic element, little has been done, fundamentally, to question the CVP relationship in its deterministic form. Essentially, equation (1) and all that follows, assumes the following micro-economic climate; perfect competition with a straight line demand curve, and constant short-run marginal costs. A second avenue for future research is to examine multi-product and multi-period CVP analysis with respect to *dependent* random variables.

It would also seem desirable fundamentally to reappraise the role of CVP analysis. Deterministic CVP analysis is a simple rule-of-thumb aid to calculating profits, given alternative output levels. In being a simple rule-of-thumb technique, many simplifying assumptions are made. Stochastic CVP analysis applied sophisticated statistical analysis to this simple model. The idea being that in the appraisal of, say, two new products with identical expected sales volumes, prices and costs may not be viewed equally desirable by a decision-maker: the riskiness of the two products must also be assessed.

A more rational approach would be to build a more complex deterministic model with revenue and cost relationships of the two products more accurately reflecting the real world. Once this had been completed, and if further information were still required by the practitioner, a logical approach would be to transform this more complex deterministic model into a probabilistic simulation model. The more complex deterministic CVP model is often termed a 'financial model' or a 'financial simulation model'. This area is now examined in a little more detail.

Financial Simulation Models

Financial simulation models are defined as deterministic simulation models where a number of endogenous variables are converted (by means of linear and non-linear functions, together with step and other discontinuous functions) into a set of exogenous variables. This set of output variables normally includes all those necessary to produce a projected balance sheet and profit and loss account. The simulation process involves starting from a set of initial exogenous variables and simulating the system's results sequentially through time; the initial assumptions are augmented by subsequent values of the exogenous variables. Apart from Carleton *et al.* (1973), the U.S. journals are entirely devoid of papers in this area. This is a great pity, since financial simulation models are often the most useful quantitative technique of all those available to the practitioner.

The gap in the research literature is more than compensated by a great number of books in this area. Recent publications include: Naylor (1971, 1979a, 1979b), and Meier *et al.* (1969). The British contribution includes some books by Bhaskar (1978b and 1979a), Flower (1973), Deam *et al.* (1975) and Grinyer and Wooller (1978). Research publications include: Precious and Wood (1975), Chambers *et al.* (1971), Courtis (1978), and Wood (1972).

The practitioner has certainly wielded this tool in a much more ready fashion than any other discussed in this article. Why? The technique does not involve any complex statistical or optimizing techniques. The inputs and outputs of the model are under the control of the practitioner and he or she can readily understand the relationships embodied in the model. Put simply, the financial simulation model is an extension of the practitioner's desk calculator.

Cost Allocation

One area of management accounting research which has resulted in a large number of papers is that of cost allocation. The problem can be presented in many forms but usually involves the allocation of a fixed cost such as depreciation over time, or the allocation of a service division's costs among a number of operating divisions. Papers which are predominantly concerned with motivational factors, despite a heavy quantitative bias (such as Zimmerman, 1976, and Bodnar and Lusk, 1977), will not be considered. There are three main categories of papers to be reviewed: those concerned with mathematical programming; those using input–output analysis; and those drawing upon game theory.

Before reviewing these approaches, some authors such as Thomas (1969, 1974, and 1978) would question why so many people have banged their heads against a 'seemingly' brick wall? Thomas' thesis is that financial cost allocations, in general, and depreciation allocations, in particular, are arbitrary and incorrigible (i.e. incapable of verification or refutation by reference to external real world phenomena), whenever the firm's revenues are generated by interacting assets. This salutary thought should be kept in mind, throughout the following review.

Mathematical Programming and Cost Allocation

The application of mathematical techniques to cost allocation and the related area of asset valuation has a distinguished pedigree. It was built on the use of LP technique in the latter area (see Samuels, 1965, Wright, 1968 and 1969, Carsberg, 1969, and Colantoni *et al.*, 1969).

Kaplan and Thompson (1971) seem to have sown the seed for the more recent research. Their objective was to devise a way of allocating overheads so that identical decisions would be made before and after the allocation of overheads. That is, they sought allocation schemes which were neutral with regard to decision-making. Kaplan and Thompson concluded that the allocation of common overheads should be in proportion to the total imputed value of the scarce resources employed in the production of each good.

Kaplan and Thompson concluded that two types of overhead charges could be identified. The first charge is associated with costs directly traceable to scarce resources, and the allocation of these overheads should be in proportion to the total inputed value of the scarce resources employed in the production of each good (i.e. costs allocated to their use of each capacity resource). The second type of overhead charge is not directly traceable to any scarce resource, these residual costs are placed in a common overhead pool and allocated to products proportionately to their profitability.

A different procedure would have to be used for problems involving escapable overheads and fixed product costs, and resource set up costs. The former situation is one in which with each possible product, j, there is an associated fixed cost, F_j (≥ 0), which is incurred if project j is produced in any positive amount, and avoided if j is not produced. In the latter case, with each scarce resource i, there is a fixed cost G_i (≥ 0), which is incurred if the facility is used at all (and avoided if the resource is not used). Mathematically, both situations can be modelled using zero-one integer programming techniques and then solving for the duals of an ordinary LP. Groves *et al.* (1970) also reached the same conclusion.

Using linear programming techniques, Hartley (1971) addressed the problem of deciding whether to process joint products beyond their split-off point. Jensen (1973) criticized Hartley's assumption of linear demand curves and suggested using non-linear programming models. Hartley (1973) replied arguing that although Jensen's quadratic programming technique was theoretically more elegant, ultimate users might be more familiar with LP. He constructed a multi-stage technique which used LP in some stages and parametric programming in others in order to obtain the same optimal solution as given by the quadratic programming model using LP techniques.

Kaplan and Welam (1974) sought to extend the analysis of Kaplan and Thompson (1971). This earlier work was subject to certain limitations: Kaplan and Welam's contribution was to obtain similar results under more general conditions. Curvilinear demand and cost curves, and complementary and substitute products could all be incorporated into the analysis by using non-linear techniques.

Other Approaches

Dhaliwal (1979) showed that an alternative to mathematical programming is the use of graph and network theory: the two techniques differ only in their pedagogical approach to the problem. Bailey (1973) used dynamic programming to examine differing costing methods for overheads.

Cost Allocations and Input–Output Analysis

The use of input–output analysis to aid the cost allocation problem has a distinguished history which includes: Manes (1965), Livingstone (1968) and (1969), Feltham (1970), Gambling and Nour (1970) and many others. A clear exposition of the use to which input–output analysis could be put in accounting (including the question of cost allocations) was provided by Butterworth and Sigloch (1971). Their conclusions were not, however, clear cut. Corcoran and Leininger (1973) showed how in-process inventories could be incorporated into Feltham's (1970) multi-product, input–output system. Feltham (1973) strongly defended his original position. Bentz (1973) demonstrated that a version of the matrix cost allocation model (various versions of the matrix cost allocation model are given in Minch and Petri (1972)) is identical to the input–output model; this is to be contrasted with Livingstone's (1969) conclusion that the matrix cost allocation model is a special case of the more general input–output model.

The matrix cost allocation model is built up by using an $n \times r$ matrix D (the matrix of reciprocal cost allocation proportions) where d_{ij} is the proportion of the jth service department's cost to be allocated to the ith service department. Another matrix, $B(m \times n)$, represents the cost allocation proportions for clearing the service department costs to the operating department; b_{ij} is the proportion of the jth service department's cost to be charged to the ith operating department. The pre-allocated departmental costs are contained in vectors b_1 and b_2 for the service and operating departments respectively. The vectors of gross departmental costs are x_1 and x_2 for the service and operating departments, respectively. The system of cost equations are therefore:

$$x_1 - Dx_1 = b_1 \tag{11}$$

or $(I - D)x_1 = b_1$

where I is the identity matrix.

Let $A = I - D$ (12)

then $x_1 = A^{-1}b_1$ (13)

which defines the vector of service department costs. The vector of operating department costs is the sum of the pre-allocation costs of the operating departments plus the costs charged to the operating departments by the service departments; that is

$$\begin{aligned} x_2 &= b_2 + Bx_1 \\ &= b_2 + BA^{-1}b_1. \end{aligned} \tag{14}$$

Livingstone (1973) and Bentz (1973) produced equivalent results from a different set of structural equations.

Corcoran and Leininger (1973) attempted to combine stochastic analysis and the input–output cost allocation technique. This was achieved by means of an absorbing Markov chain, but the suggested framework is far from general.

Cost Allocation and Game Theory

Martin Shubick recently said[2] that in 1962 (Shubick, 1962) he had introduced many novel concepts into the overhead allocation problem which were only just being rediscovered—he was correct. Hamlen *et al.* (1977) resurrected the use of the core concept borrowed from game theory to solve a particularly difficult problem. Joint cost allocation may lead to

2 In a personal communication.

suboptimal decisions in a divisionalized organization, whenever the marginal cost function for the allocated cost is decreasing, and the joint cost allocation scheme results in a charge to a division which exceeds the charge which that division would incur when acting independently.

Core theory originated from a consideration of the set of Pareto optimal points within an Edgeworth Box. An example may help to illustrate the concept. The function $V(S)$ describes the total benefit available to coalition S when the members in S co-operate among themselves rather than act independently. Assume that there are three members (1, 2, 3) and these members may form coalitions (S) of between 1 to 3 members; the 'grand' coalition is designated by $N = \{1, 2, 3\}$. The function $V(S)$ is called the characteristic function. The assumed values of the characteristic values for these coalitions are:

	Coalitions	*Assumed values of characteristic function in %*
The empty set	φ	$V(\varphi) = 0$
Coalitions of one	$\{1\}$, $\{2\}$, or $\{3\}$	$V(1) = V(2) = V(3) = 0$
Coalitions of two	$\{1,2\}$, $\{1,3\}$, or $\{2,3\}$	$V(12) = V(13) = V(23) = 1$
The grand coalition	$= \{1,2,3\}$	$V(123) = 1.5$

(15)

Acting alone, a member benefits to the value of zero; a coalition of two benefits to the tune of 1; and the value available to a grand coalition is 1.5.

The core conditions can now be examined. For any rational member to remain in the grand coalition, the payoff X_i must be at least as great as the value the member can obtain alone in a coalition of one, i.e.

$$X_i \geq V(i),\ i = 1, 2, 3 \qquad (16)$$

Rationality requires that the proceeds of the grand coalition should be entirely allocated to the individual members, that is:

$$X_1 + X_2 + X_3 = V(N) \qquad (17)$$

The core concept arguably carries rationality one step further, requiring that every possible coalition behave rationally, that is:

$$\begin{aligned} X_1 + X_2 &\geq V(12) \\ X_1 + X_3 &\geq V(13) \\ X_2 + X_3 &\geq V(23) \end{aligned} \qquad (18)$$

With a $V(N)$ of 1.5, the core is unique and is given by $X_1 = X_2 = X_3 = .5$, since this is the only payoff set which satisfies all three criteria. For $V(N)$ values greater than 1.5, there will be an infinite number of solutions. If $V(N) \leq 1.5$, then no core exists, for any payoff will leave at least one member dissatisfied.

Hamlen *et al.* (1977) compared four joint cost allocation schemes with respect to their core conditions, these were: the activity level method (where the charge is in direct proportion to the division's activity level), two contributions from the game theoretic literature and a fourth scheme proposed by Moriarity (1975). The two game theoretic schemes tended to divide the total value of co-operation evenly among the divisions. This result may be viewed as unfair by a large division which has contributed a proportionately larger part of the joint benefits (i.e. the spoils to be bargained for). An allocation scheme based on activity level would appear to favour smaller divisions, whilst the Moriarity scheme favoured the larger division to such an extent that the payoff was not in the core. Jensen (1977) also analysed the utility of the Shapley approach for allocating the cost of a shared facility under different cost function specifications.

Callen (1978) attempted to refute a body of literature which included Thomas (1969, 1974, and 1978) and Eckel (1976) by using core theory and, in particular, Shapley values. Thomas's thesis is that financial cost allocations are arbitrary and incorrigible whenever the firm's revenues are generated by interacting assets. Callen concluded that Shapley values represent a defensible and corrigible cost allocation mechanism. Intuitively, Shapley values allocate the benefits of the coalition to each member in the following way: as a grand coalition is formed by the sequential addition of the weighted average of each division's benefit; each division is allocated as a share of the joint costs, an amount equal to the expected marginal benefit gained by the coalition it enters. For example, the Shapley value allocation for division 1 in a grand coalition of three divisions is:

$$\begin{aligned} &\tfrac{1}{3}V(1) + \tfrac{1}{6}[V(12) - V(2)] \\ &\quad + \tfrac{1}{6}[V(13) - V(3)] \\ &\quad + \tfrac{1}{3}[V(123) - V(23)] \end{aligned} \tag{19}$$

where $V(1)$ is the benefit from division 1 acting alone; $[V(12) - V(2)]$ is the extra benefit of division 1 entering into a coalition with division 2 less the minimum benefit division 2 would have received had it acted alone; and $[V(123) - V(23)]$ is the extra benefit from division 1 entering into a coalition with divisions 2 and 3 less the minimum benefit divisions 2 and 3 would have received had they formed their own coalition to the exclusion of division 1. Using the numerical values given earlier, expression (19) becomes:

$$\tfrac{1}{3}(0) + \tfrac{1}{6}[1 - 0] + \tfrac{1}{6}[1 - 0] + \tfrac{1}{3}[1.5 - 1] = .5 \tag{20}$$

Thus the Shapley value allocation for division 1 in a grand coalition of three divisions is £.5, given the information contained in (15).

Jensen (1977) fundamentally reappraised the allocation problem. By defining mutually satisfactory allocations as agreements among users of a common facility to share the facility's cost, Jensen was able to point out that a role for the accountant was to contribute two types of knowledge which may lead to those allocations: accountants may either provide characterizations of alternative allocation methods, or they may recommend an allocation method that exhibits certain properties desired by the collaborators. Loehman and Whinston (1971 and 1974) had suggested a list of properties which Jensen was able to manipulate so that a similar allocation to a Shapley function could be made but from a different set of properties. The allocation averages the incremental cost determined by each possible allocation scheme.

Jensen's (1977) major contribution was essentially to refocus the research on to the contribution of the accountant rather than explore various allocation and bargaining mechanisms. Jensen did not suggest that the Shapley allocation function should or would accompany collaboration. He argued that the Shapley allocation function and the Loehman–Whinston approach to it exemplify the knowledge an accountant might contribute to the negotiation of a mutually satisfactory allocation.

Appraisal of the Cost Allocation Debate

This topic seems to have produced a number of, supposedly, definitive approaches on the subject, including: mathematical programming techniques, input–output analysis and the identical matrix allocation methods. It was the papers which tried to use core theory to provide an efficient allocation in the economic sense, which provoked Jensen (1977) into attempting to put the research work into focus. The allocation process is essentially a bargaining situation of sub-coalitions within an economic unit. Unless there is a degree of centralization the accountant can only help advise and provide information. If there is total centralization, then the central authority can make all the decisions and the question of individual divisions negotiating for a share of the benefits of co-operation is meaningless. If total centralization does not exist, then there is, indeed, a true bargaining situation in which organizational theory, as well as behavioural accounting, are important. The use of mathematical programming models that produce cost allocations based on optimal decisions may be defensible, but begs the control question. Allocations are not completely defensible because, given the model of maximizing behaviour for the firm, it is not clear what benefit the firm derives from allocating joint costs, acquisition costs and overhead costs to products or time periods. The only justification for allocations, based on centrally determined decisions, is the motivational impact on notionally decentralized decision-making. One of the implications of this branch of management accounting is that decision-makers should continue to be urged not to base their decisions on the basis of figures derived by allocating common costs. However, a formal allocation model may be recommended if decision-makers persist in allocation practices against the accountant's advice.

Dopuch (1977) considers this problem why firms continue to allocate common costs and apparently base decisions on such allocations. His suggestion is that the technique is a way of coping with uncertainty;

individuals and managers in decentralized organizations may strive to make optimal capacity decisions under uncertainty by taking decisions based on the arbitrary allocation of overheads.

The British contribution to the cost allocation debate was significant with contributions by Carsberg (1969), Groves *et al.* (1970) and Samuels (1965) who directed their research efforts to the use of mathematical programming, whilst Gambling and Nour (1970) used the related input–output technique. However, there have been no recent British contributions.

Future Directions for Research

Two suggestions have been made to explain why the sub-optimal policy of making decisions based on cost allocations persists. The suggestions are that there are motivational requirements and behavioural reactions to decide on the validity of these suggestions. It may, of course, be found that there is no rational explanation for this sub-optimal behaviour, in which case imperfections in the educational process associated with management accounting may be blamed.

Cost Control and Variance Investigations

Although Samuels (1965) was probably the first to recognize the possibility of incorporating the control system within a formal decision model of linear programming, Dopuch *et al.* (1967) first identified three broad classifications of variance. The first variance is due to normal random variation when the process is in statistical control. The second and third types of variance relate to situations when costs are no longer in statistical control. The second type of variance is controllable; that is, if detected, the process can be reset to its previous level of performance. The third type is a permanent change in cost structures, that is, if detected, the variance cannot be corrected. The whole area of cost control is interesting; a type 2 variance is worth investigating, since the costs can be brought back into statistical control. However, a type 3 variance is also worth discovering; once it is known that there is a permanent change in a cost structure or relationship, then decisions should be made on the basis of the changed, and now correct, cost data. Cost variance investigation is one branch of cost control.

Cost Variance Investigation

Any control system should generate a set of variances each period. Although the management accounting literature has spent much time in analysing how to report the variances, relatively little work has been carried out on the mechanics of, for example, standard costing control systems. Nor has the isolation of the most significant variances and their subsequent investigation received sufficient attention. The seminal work in this area was a review paper by Kaplan (1975a). A necessary assumption is that corrective action will follow the report of some variances and the location of their sources—e.g. a type 2 variance.

Kaplan's (1975a) survey paper identified four types of models to aid in deciding whether to investigate cost variances, and his taxonomic framework will be followed here. First, two types of models are dealt with in which there are assumed to be no costs of investigation and no likelihood of misclassification—these types of models are categorized according to their ability to deal with single or multiple observations (e.g. time series). Such a taxonomy ignores important work, such as Lev (1969) which deals with the problem of isolating the most important variances from a large set; Demski (1970) which considers the actual investigation process; and Ronen (1974) which discusses methods for aggregating variances to enhance the reporting and investigation process.

Decision Models Based on Single Observation and No Costs of Investigation or Likelihood of Misclassification of Variances

The simplest control formulation usually establishes a target mean and an estimated standard deviation for the process when it is in control. Typically, control limits are set so that the probability of an in-control process with normally distributed outcomes producing a signal beyond these limits (Type 1 error) are small. Such information can be graphically displayed by means of a Shewhart chart and much of the literature, where the null hypothesis assumes that the process is in control, is a variation of this chart. Papers which fall in this category include those of Buzby (1974), Juers (1967), Koehler (1968), Luh (1968), Probst (1971) and Zannetos (1964). This is the simplest type of control technique: investigation is determined by reference to a targeted mean and an acceptable deviation—both argued on subjective or *a priori* grounds. The investigator could, for example, assume that all variables behaved as if they were normally distributed, and in this instance a control chart approach would signal an investigation if, say, the most recent cost report is more than two standard deviations (at the 95 per cent confidence level) from the expected value. Hence the model is based on a *single* observation with costs and benefits from the investigation decision not being considered.

Decision Models Based on Multiple Observations and No Costs of Investigation or Likelihood of Misclassification

This category of model is distinguished from the former type by the attempt that is made to combine previous observations with the current observation of the variable of concern to reach a statistical conclusion as to whether the process is currently in control. These procedures make use of a systematic examination of trends. Kaplan (1975a) considered the cusum chart technique (see Page, 1954) and the more formal process of identifying non-stationery processes, included in the latter are papers by Barnard (1959), Hinich and Farley (1966), and Farley and Hinich (1970). However, Kaplan (1975a) did not review papers which used multiple-regressive techniques to estimate (and explain) cost variances. Notably, Comiskey (1966) and Jensen (1967) have used these techniques. Their work is discussed later.

Decision Models Based on Single Observation, with Cost of Investigation and the Likelihood of Misclassification

Bierman *et al.* (1961) provide an example of a single observation model modified to take into account investigation with costs. With an investigation cost of C and a potential benefit from correcting an out-of-control situation of L, an investigation is signalled if,

$$C < (1 - P)L \tag{21}$$

where P is the probability that this observation comes from the null (in-control) distribution and L is the present value of costs that will be incurred in the future if an investigation is not made now.

Ozan and Dyckman (1971) and others have criticized this approach on the basis that since the investigation decision is made on the most recent observation, it ignores prior information—either sample information from previous periods or subjectively determined priors. This class of models simply adds an investigation cost to the previous single observation type of model.

Decision Models and Multiple Observations; Cost of Investigation and Likelihood of Misclassification Included

There are two types of models within this classification; discrete state and continuous state models. Discrete state models are dealt with first. They assume that the number of states which govern whether a process is in control or out of control in the current period *and* whether the process will be in control or out of control in future periods is finite—usually four states are assumed. This type of model uses the past history of observations and incorporates a cost benefit analysis of the variance investigation decision.

Cusum charts have been adopted to minimize long run average costs (see Taylor, 1968, and Goel and Wu, 1973), but control charts tend to be non-Bayesian in that no prior information about in- or out-of-control probabilities are combined with sample evidence. This weakness was overcome by Dyckman (1969) and modified by Kaplan (1969) to include a multi-period cost structure. Kaplan (1975a) has advocated the superiority of the Kaplan (1969) model to that of Dyckman (1969) and the Kaplan model is now further discussed.

Kaplan used dynamic programming to compute the optimal cost/

investigation decisions which minimized future discounted costs. A two-state Markov model is used to summarize all the relevant information from prior observations as a simple state variable (the probability that the system is currently in-control). This variable is updated after each observation to incorporate information from the most recent observation. Thus q, the probability of being in control, would be updated in a Bayesian revision (the operator τ_x) after receiving the observation x gained in the last investigation and using the prior probability of being in control, q.

Thus the new updated probability would be:

$$\tau_x q = g\{1 + \left(\frac{f_2(x)}{f_1(x)}\right)\left(\frac{(1-q)}{q}\right)\}^{-1} \tag{22}$$

where

$\frac{f_2(x)}{f_1(x)}$ = is likelihood ratio of the out-of-control distribution to the in-control distribution

g = probability that in period t the system will remain in control.

The two-state Markov process ($i = 1$ = in-control; $i = 2$ = out-of-control) with a transition matrix,

$$G = \begin{pmatrix} g & 1-g \\ o & 1 \end{pmatrix} \tag{23}$$

can be interpreted as the probabilities of the following states:

in-control this period, given that the process was in-control in the last period, probability $= g$	out-of-control this period, given that the process was in-control in the last period, probability $(= 1 - g)$
in-control this period, given that the process was out-of-control last period, probability $= 0$	out-of-control this period, given that the process was out-of-control last period, probability $= 1$

(24)

The state of the system at the end of a cost period is defined as the probability of being in control next period. The objective function to be minimized is the expected discounted total cost. This is for each period:

Minimum of
- (a) current and expected future costs when an investigation is made; this includes the expected investigation cost and the effect of permanently resetting the process to its desired mean;
- (b) expected costs when no investigation is made; i.e. the expected costs of operating for one period at the current level with no investigation and the same discounted costs one period in the future.

This class of models revises the probability estimates of the process being out of control each period as a new cost report is received. An investigation is signalled when the discounted future expected benefits from an investigation exceed the costs. The investigation decision is optimized to a finite horizon by the use of a multi-period dynamic programming model.

Unfortunately, there are a number of criticisms on the Kaplan model as Kaplan (1975a) has indicated. First, there is a problem of choosing a planning horizon. The second concerns the simplification of the process to a two-state system, in- and out-of-control, with a sudden transition between the two states. Thirdly, the model assumes that the process can always be returned to the in-control state (i.e. that the variance is a type 2 variance). The possibility of a fundamental shift in the process which may not be reversible is not considered (i.e. type 3 variances are ignored).

A fourth criticism was levelled by Hughes (1975 and 1977): namely that the cost report contained one observation for every period whereas there may be many other sampling bases—such as obtaining cost reports determined at times calculated by an optimizing function.

A second type of model within the multiple observation and explicit investigation costs classification is the continuous state model. With the discrete state model, the transition matrix G defined the entire set of possibilities. The continuous state model, however, adopts a more flexible approach: a state is described by a single continuous variable which represents the performance level of the process. The continuous state model, therefore, has a transition matrix with an infinite number of elements. As with the discrete model, a dynamic programming model is set up and solved to find the set of optimal policies.

Duvall (1967) suggested that any deviation from a standard should be divided into controllable and uncontrollable components both of which are assumed to be normally distributed. Kaplan (1975a) showed that Duvall's technique was non-operational and resurrected a technique suggested by Bather (1963).

It is interesting to note that there has been no major advance of the continuous state model since Kaplan (1975a). The remaining papers to be discussed revert to the simpler two state discrete model.

Magee's Contribution

After Kaplan the most influential writer in the field is Magee. In his 1976 paper, he explored the relative effectiveness of the various cost investigation models by means of simulation. Magee (1976) found that the simpler techniques were sometimes almost as cost effective as the more sophisticated. He suggested that a control policy using a fixed cost control limit could capture much (but not all) of the benefits obtained from Kaplan's more complex model. (Magee was later to substitute Kaplan's model for an even more complex model.) Magee also tackled a problem that has been highlighted before; namely the problem of the large (some would say excessive) amount of information required by these analytical techniques.

Magee (1977a), using a dynamic programming investigation model recognized that users of such techniques, did not have perfect knowledge of the model parameters. He calculated the expected loss arising from mis-estimating the parameters by means of both numerical analysis and probabilistic simulation. He then introduced a scheme whereby actual costs were used to make inferences about the parameters—parameter information thus becomes a by-product of the investigation decision. A manager may use an investigation to learn both about the cost structure of the process under investigation and to correct an out-of-control situation.

Magee's (1977b) third contribution addressed the problem of investigating variances arising from different cost processes affected by common factors. Magee was concerned to provide information for the choice between those 'simplified' investigation models already surveyed. His approach is based on comparing the results of models for investigating individual cost variances with those which jointly consider all multiple-cost variances. Magee concluded that the 'complete' or multi-variance model has lower expected operational costs and greater organizational benefits. These latter accrue from a more equitable distribution of the bonuses assumed to be paid to those managers who keep their cost processes under control.

The complexity of the dynamic programming models considered above made Dittman and Prakash's (1978) contribution particularly welcome. They present a technique which offers the practising accountant a method for determining an investigation policy for cost control which neither requires dynamic programming nor the Bayesian updating of probabilities after each cost report. Their technique requires the matching of a reported cost variance against a fixed critical limit. The richness of the model was found to compare favourably with the more sophisticated cost control model of Kaplan (1969).

The same two state Markovian transition matrix, as above, is assumed but the functioning of the process generates a cost, $\bar{x}$, in each period which is a random variable with its probability distribution function, F_i, depending on the operating condition, i, of the process. Thus:

$$\left.\begin{array}{l} Pr\{\bar{x} \leqslant x \mid i\} = F_i(x) \\ E\{\bar{x} \mid i\} = \mu_i \end{array}\right\} \quad i = 1,2 \tag{25}$$

and $\Delta\mu = (\mu_2 - \mu_1)$ (26)

Cost reports provide information about the current status of the process.

The manager bases his decision to investigate on whether the actual cost $\bar{x}$ exceeds some constant critical value x. The conditional probabilities of committing Type I and Type II errors are constant and are, respectively:

$$\begin{aligned} Pr\{\text{Investigate} \mid \text{in-control}\} &= Pr\{\bar{x} > x \mid (i = 1)\} \\ &= I - F_1(x) \end{aligned} \tag{27}$$

$$Pr\{\text{Don't investigate} \mid \text{out-of-control}\} = Pr\{\bar{x} \leqslant x \mid (i=2)\} = F_2(x) \quad (28)$$

where

I = fixed discretionary cost
x = cost in a period which behaves as a random variable
$F_i(x)$ = probability density function of the random variable x for process i such that $Pr\{\bar{x} \leqslant x \mid i\} = F_i(x)$ for $i = 1,2$.

Using the 2×2 transition matrix and a control matrix, Dittman and Prakash (1978) define a number of decision rules. The decision never to investigate is made, if the expected value of the investigation costs plus the correction cost for resetting a process found to be out-of-control, is less than the expected value of the increased costs arising as a result of the process continuing to be out-of-control. An investigation is always called for when the investigation costs are outweighed by benefits elsewhere in the system.

It is worthwhile to defer investigation provided that there is at least one cost level for which the probability of the process performing as well or better in the in-control condition is 'sufficiently' large compared with the probability of its doing so in the out-of-control condition. This may restrict the range of critical cost values in which the process needs to be researched. If the cost value lies within this critical range then the investigation should not be deferred.

Jensen and McKeown (1977) attempted to extend further the single observation with cost of information model in the tradition of Bierman *et al.* (1961). Their analysis is subject to all the limitations of single-period analysis. Jensen and McKeown suggest an interesting procedure to uncover sources of cost variance by means of a multiple-step investigation process which minimizes both the expected cost of the sequence of investigative steps and the future expected losses as a result of not finding the out-of-control condition. The authors also suggest a novel sensitivity analysis to assess the effect of errors in probability estimates on the choice of an investigative sequence.

The contribution by Capettini and Collins (1978) would have been that much greater if they had used the Kaplan (1969) model. Instead, they examined situations where the two states have unequal variances within the context of a Dyckman (1969) model in which a sequential multi-period decision problem is represented within a simplified single-period model. Capettini and Collins defended their model on the basis of their interpretation of Magee's (1976) simulation results. The authors were able to devise similar decision rules to Dittman and Prakash (1978). For example:

$$\text{Investigate if} \quad \sigma(x \mid s_1) > \sigma(x \mid s_2) \quad (29)$$

$$\text{Do not investigate if} \quad \sigma(x \mid s_1) < \sigma(x \mid s_2) \quad (30)$$

There is also a 'grey' area in which no clear-cut answer can be given to the manager with regard to the worthwhileness of investigation but the decision will be more complex. A criticism of the Capettini and Collins work concerns the calculation of the standard deviation—which can only be made by *a priori* means or by gathering a sufficiently large sample over time.

Multiple Observations and Acceptable Cost Behaviour

Multiple regression and time series forecasting techniques provide useful aids in management accounting. First, these statistical techniques can be used to estimate cost relationships such as the fixed and variable elements of a total cost function. Secondly, the statistical technique can be made to produce statistical probability intervals (e.g. standard errors, T statistics). A signal that the process under consideration is out-of-control would be provided by any statistically significant deviation from the forecast/budgeted value. Benston (1966) and Jensen (1967) discussed the problems and pitfalls of using regression analysis, and this topic is reconsidered later.

Kaplan (1975b) showed how the statistical probability intervals obtained using a regression equation could be used as an input to a control chart model for cost variance investigation. Specifically regression analysis can provide standard errors of estimates which are useful in cost variance investigation models. However, this view is probably too simplistic. Errors in a predicted cost relationship can be broken up into two discrete components: first, there is the change in the structure of the cost relationships (due perhaps to a change in technology). Secondly, there is the genuine random element operating normally within the system. The genuine random element may be difficult to isolate from changes in the cost structure.

Appraisal of Cost Control and Variance Investigation Debate

The practitioner is almost bound to dismiss most of the literature as far too complex with excessively high information demands. In a similar manner to stochastic CVP analysis, much of the research into cost control and investigation seems to be an exercise showing the ability of academics to use sophisticated mathematical analysis. The use of dynamic programming and the Bayesian revision of probabilities after each cost report meant that the research efforts of Dittman and Prakash (1978), concerning 'rules of thumb', were particularly welcome, though practitioners may find their 'rules' far too complicated to be of operational use.

Kaplan (1977) agrees that the models appear to be far ahead of current practice. This raises the question of guidance for future research and the task of discovering the remaining crucial issues, if any. Kaplan (1977, p. 46) sums up the problem:

> 'We have no evidence on the stochastic process which tends to shift the mean of generated cost data away from standard cost levels and no studies on the magnitude of costs associated with wasted investigations or opportunity losses incurred for not investigating variances soon enough. It is not clear that there is much fertile ground left for developing more elaborate models in this area without a data base on the type and magnitude of problem we are dealing with here'.

Dopuch's (1977) critique of the variance investigation model is concerned with the difficulty of establishing the types of conditions under which a formal approach to the problem would produce greater benefits than a less formal heuristic approach—e.g. investigate all variances over 10 per cent. There are, moreover, other criticisms which are equally important. It is not clear that the cost of investigation is anything other than a fixed cost, since in most organizations it would represent a body of accountants who would be retained on the staff of a company, irrespective of whether they investigated a variance or not.

For the practitioner the most appealing of the techniques listed above is control charts and some of the simpler decision rules emanating from the above research. As input into the control chart, more use could be made of econometric and time-series forecasting.

Variance investigation could be conducted in a similar manner to auditing. Certain variances which exceed their control limit would be investigated individually. Other variances could be randomly investigated, whilst a whole batch of variances might be systematically investigated. As well as negative variances being investigated, some effort could be made to investigate favourable variances, on the grounds that for a given amount of investigation time the rewards in costs saved might be greater.

Another way of minimizing cost investigations is to provide breakdowns of variances where these are readily available. An unfavourable variance of £80,000 on administrative costs may be far easier to explain if £75,000 of that variance proves, on disaggregation, to be finance charges. Similarly, splitting raw material variance into price and efficiency variances may clarify which variances justify further investigation.

Mathematical Programming

In management accounting, it is rarc to find a paper purely on the technique of mathematical programming. Most papers apply a mathematical programming technique to a particular application or problem area. Viewed in this context, the number of recent publications in mathematical programming is large and some have already been discussed in previous sections, but there are many more papers addressing a variety of applications. Unlike the previous sections, the British contribution in this broad area is the greatest of all sectors and has, in my view, been significant. One particular technique that has featured prominently is that of linear programming (LP). An advantage of LP is that computer packages are readily available and processing time is relatively small. A disadvantage is the inheritance of linear relationships and fractional solutions. For certain applications fractional solutions can cause problems. Hughes and Lewellen (1974) criticized the divisibility assumptions of LP and concluded that mathematical programming solutions of capital rationing problems conferred insufficient benefits to justify their cost. If divisibility is a problem then integer programming techniques can be used. Examples of papers which use integer programming include: Rappaport (1969), Jensen (1968), Currin and Spivey (1972), Glover (1969 and 1972) and Pettway (1973). However, there is a more compelling reply to the divisibility question.

To use a sophisticated technique such as LP in an application where the basic assumptions do not apply (e.g. no limiting resources) creates a real problem. However, violation of the divisibility assumption may be less serious and may even provide additional information. For example, consider the possibility of accepting or rejecting two mutually exclusive contracts: the classic example concerns building either a wooden or a steel bridge. The LP solution may reveal that the optimal strategy is to build half a wooden and half a steel bridge; a ludicrous result at first glance—but is it really? Surely the LP solution is informing the accountant that, given the financial resources available (which incidentally *are* infinitely divisible), a durable steel bridge may be too expensive whilst a temporary wooden bridge may not be cost effective. The obvious solution is to *search* for new alternatives; this could take the form of a narrower bridge or one that is constructed of a material more durable than wood but cheaper than steel—reinforced concrete perhaps?

Decision-making and planning in their broadest context can be divided into seven stages:

(1) Perception of a problem
(2) Formulation of objectives
(3) Search for solutions to a problem
(4) Evaluation of these alternatives
(5) Choice of alternatives
(6) Implementation of plan
(7) Control to ensure adherence to the plan.

Techniques such as mathematical programming need not be instrumental only in stage (5); the running of a LP can highlight new problems, give rise to new objectives, help in the search for new solutions, and provide a mechanism for integrating the control system with the 'choice' stage of the decision-making process.

Mathematical programming models are now widely spread in the accounting literature. For this reason, the review of the literature has been analysed by subject area. To begin with the control stage of the above decision-making format is discussed.

Control

Attempting to place *ad hoc* boundaries on a continuous spectrum is always fraught with difficulties and this section is close to that of cost control and variance investigation. Mention has already been made of the contribution by Samuels (1965) in mixing formal decision models and the control function. This represents something of a first for British academics but it was left to the Americans to follow through. Demski's (1967) seminal paper on the isolation of *planning* and operational variances using LP techniques to calculate the *ex ante* and *ex post* optimal plans is renowned. This, in effect, achieves one of the objectives recommended in the previous section; the variance is broken down into a number of components which may shed more light on the reason for the 'out-of-control' situation. The variance can be decomposed into a forecasting variance (planned outcome minus the *ex post* optimum) and an opportunity loss variance (*ex post* optimum minus the actual outcome). Ronen (1970) and Wolk and Hillman (1972) also developed ways of decomposing or evaluating variances. Demski (1969, 1970 and 1971) and a host of others have become involved in the investigation process itself and the behavioural effects of control systems.

Short Run Decisions

Apart from the papers already mentioned in earlier sections, there are a variety of papers dealing with short run planning problems and the British contribution in this field is substantial. Of the American publications, those of Godfrey (1971) and Grinnell (1977) are the most significant. There is an enormous range of British publications: Godfrey (1971) and Barron (1972) tackle the decomposition and decentralization problems; Wilkes and Harrison (1975) examined pricing rules within the context of programming models; Arnold (1977) dealt with general non-linear pricing analysis; and Grinnell (1977) used LP techniques to compare direct and absorption costing. A number of American publications have applied mathematical programming to working capital management. (Examples include Robichek *et al.* (1965), Pogue and Bussard (1972), Merville and Tavis (1973a), and Sartoris and Spruill (1974).)

Long Run Planning

From the British viewpoint, management accounting often encompasses both short run and long run planning. The American tradition is to segregate long run decisions and planning and place them into the subject area of finance. Thus using a British approach and pleading boundary problems, the incorporation of a brief review of mathematical programming and capital budgeting models into this paper can be argued as justifiable, if only to set the context for subjects reviewed in more depth. However, the use of mathematical programming in capital budgeting is not relevant for all situations; its justification arises because of the constraints introduced to capital budgeting models by such imperfections as capital rationing, imperfect capital markets, and organizational and administrative constraints. The British contribution includes works by Amey (a sometime British professor), Ashton, Bhaskar and Wilkes. The set of articles dealing with capital rationing and mathematical programming techniques within capital budgeting is large. The list of publications include: Bernhard (1969), Elton (1970), Carleton (1970), Myers (1972), Ma and Tydeman (1972), Merville and Tavis (1973b), Myers (1974), Hughes and Lewellen (1974), Bhaskar (1974, 1976, 1978a), Wilkes (1977), Weingartner (1977), and Ashton (1978). Sub-debates among the authors have developed; such as the Amey and Whitmore (1973) critique of the capital budgeting formulation proposed by Lusztig and Schwab (1968 and 1970). In my opinion, many of the earlier conclusions have been superseded by the more recent publications.

Myers and Pogue (1974) represents an attempt to define a general purpose integer programming model of financial management, incorporating debt and equity as financing alternatives. They incorporate financial risk by utilizing a concept known as 'probability of trouble' in an ingenious way. The problem with their model for some researchers is that it is heavily dependent on MM's views both on the cost of capital and the irrelevance of dividends (Modigliani and Miller, 1958 and 1961). Bhaskar's (1978a) solution to the problem of obtaining a general model involves an iterative LP solution. He chose dividends as the appropriate endogenous variable to use as a maximand. In general, the cost of equity will vary with leverage and the future discounted dividend stream, which is the maximand of the model, will vary with a change in the cost of equity. A more elegant solution would be to use a non-linear formulation; in time these techniques will be developed to deal with complex functions efficiently—until then the iterative LP technique is the next best solution.

Transfer Pricing

Apart from some relevant papers already discussed in earlier sections dealing with, for example, short run decisions, further references on transfer pricing can be found in the literature. Two are from the *Accounting Review*: Abdel-Khalik and Lusk (1974) and Merville and Petty (1978); three from the *Journal of Business Finance and Accounting*: Amey (1969), Samuels (1969) and Stewart (1977). In addition Tomkins (1973) produced an authoritative book on the subject. The British contribution was once again significant and included Amey, Samuels, Gambling and Tomkins. Kaplan (1977) doubted whether programming approaches would have much influence on the transfer pricing problem. His reaction was based on the difficulty of obtaining reliable information from subordinates as an input to the model, when the same subordinates might know that this information would then be used as a basis to evaluate their performance.

Multiple Objectives and Mathematical Programming

One of the limiting factors of mathematical programming is the assumption of a single objective in the maximand of the model. This begs the question of whether firms and organizations are motivated by a single objective. Assuming that they are, the practitioner often finds that a single overriding objective is too vague and amorphous to be used as a direct tool of evaluation and control. It is often easier to adopt a number of surrogates which may take the form of several practically-oriented targets or goals. Of course, firms may be motivated by true multiple objectives (as opposed to surrogates of a single primary objective). In either case, the ability to incorporate multiple objectives or targets within a mathematical programming model is an important consideration.

Although the main debate concerning multiple objectives and mathematical programming has occurred outside the accounting literature, there is now a respectable list of publications with Killough and Souders (1973), Kornbluth (1974), Chateau (1975), Sealey Jr. (1978), Kumar *et al.* (1978) and Bhaskar (1979b). Contained in the above papers are a number of different techniques for incorporating multiple objectives into mathematical programming models. My preference is for goal-programming which seems to provide the most versatile modelling technique (Bhaskar, 1979b), though Chateau (1975) prefers multiple criteria programming techniques.

One of the most interesting research studies is that of Lin (1978). He examined the effects of alternative planning models taken in combination with various accounting control systems. By means of simulation he analysed a product-mix problem with an uncertain demand using first a satisfying goal programming model and second an optimizing multiple objective LP model. The two alternative accounting control systems used with these two planning models were traditional variance analysis and *ex post* optimum variance analysis. The joint effect of planning methods and variance analysis techniques were considered together. The simulation exercise revealed that the highest profits were generated using a multiple objective LP with *ex post* variance analysis. Since this now takes us into the realm of control and behavioural studies mentioned earlier, the conclusions of other research in this area will be abstracted from. One direction for future research is to rework some of the results based on single objective formulations by using multiple objective mathematical programming models.

The British Contribution

Of the total set of papers reviewed in the area of mathematical programming (excluding cost allocation), one third have been published in U.K. journals. It is believed that these publications are neither trivial nor peripheral, but have contributed significantly to the research effort in this area (e.g. Samuels, 1965). The usefulness of the mathematical programming research is seen in the steady expansion of knowledge gained along a number of different fronts.

Appraisal of the Contribution by Mathematical Programming

There seems to be an overwhelming number of articles based on LP techniques and the consequent result is that the restrictive assumption of linearity has caused authors to produce many agonized attempts to remove the problems thereby created. Yet the use of non-linear programming techniques is placing this branch of management accounting even further from the practitioner's reach; whereas LP packages are readily available, non-linear programming packages are few and far between. The operations research literature attests to the continuing search for an efficient means of solving the general non-linear programming problem. The other criticism of research concerning mathematical programming is that it does not satisfactorily deal with risk and uncertainty. However, chance-constrained programming provides a limited way of incorporating probability (see, for example, Gonedes, 1970, and Merville and Tavis, 1973a). Perhaps, the solution to this problem in mathematical programming is to combine probabilistic simulation with mathematical programming. In this situation each run of the mathematical programming problem would sample a set of parameters from a probability distribution of each parameter: in this way a probability distribution of primal and dual solutions could be constructed. This would be expensive in terms of computer resources, but could become a possibility as the price of computers continues to fall and their power increases.

Financial Information Systems

The management accounting literature has, by and large, ignored the mechanics of how computerized accounting systems work. The design of hardware and software constrain the ability of the accounting system to provide information. Since management accounting concerns the provision of information for decision-making, research in accounting might pay more attention to the choice of hardware, systems software and the design of the accounting and costing systems embedded in the applications software.

There are two basic avenues along which to proceed: examine existing hardware and software configurations and their effect on accounting systems, or discuss an ideal accounting system. What little literature there is seems to have concentrated on the latter.

The research into an ideal accounting system has originated in the *events* and *entity* view of accounting. Sorter (1969) argued for an events approach to accounting; namely the storing information about economic events. The traditional value approach summarizes information by value. This can be criticized on the ground that it places subjective weights on the basic events affecting a business. Johnson (1970) examined some of the implications and requirements of Sorter's events approach. Johnson (1970) was able to extend and refine the meaning of an event. He argued that forecasting is logically prior to deciding on management action; that is accuracy in forecasting is a necessary criterion for data inputs to action decisions. But accounting data are useful for decisions and current thinking argues that decision models should determine the design and content of accounting communication systems (i.e. financial statements). Johnson's counterposition, and one that I fully endorse, is that since forecasting is prior to decision-making, forecast accuracy should determine the accounting system. Mock (1971) extended this analysis, but the most authoritative work in the area is Libby (1975).

Godfrey and Prince (1971) discussed the way in which an accounting system could be adapted to meet the requirements of a formal information system. This paper extended and widened an earlier paper by Crandell (1969); Mock (1971) later built upon Godfrey and Prince's work. Other authoritative papers in this area include Mock and Driver (1975), Prakash and Rappaport (1975), Lucas (1975), and Savich (1977). Colantoni *et al.* (1971) took up the theme of an ideal accounting system based on the events approach (Sorter, 1969) but at the same time used as much of a conventional accounting system as possible. Their solution was to store events in a multi-dimensional accounting system by means of a sophisticated file organization. Their database was founded on a tree structure. Imagine a tree with the data items being contained in the leaves. To access a particular piece of information (data), you need to find the relevant branch and continue down the correct branches until you came to the relevant data item. Butterworth (1972) presented the accounting system as a functional relationship between observable events and descriptions of them by an accounting system. By developing a model of information value, the relative value of an information system was shown to depend on its 'fineness' or 'coarseness' due to varying levels of aggregation.

Building upon Colantoni *et al.* (1971), Lieberman and Whinston (1975) laid the foundations for an implementation of the events-oriented accounting system, having three parts.

(a) A mass of data contained in a data base.

(b) User-defined structures for use both by the applications programmers and accounting users (sometimes called sub-schemas).

(c) User-defined functions—a query language for the retrieval of data.

However, the structure of their accounting system was once again a tree network which severely limits the type of information which can be extracted. Haseman and Whinston (1976) extended this analysis by providing a theoretical model for designing data structures for multi-dimensional accounting systems—they too used a tree-like structure. A tree-like structure permits new data to be added to a database only in well-defined and predetermined ways; the possibility of answering any *ad hoc* enquiry is therefore not available unless the consequential data access paths were built-in when the database was created.

Databases can be divided into two broad classifications—formatted and relational. In formatted data bases (e.g. CODASYL), a variety of data structures are used to represent relationships. The formatted approach whilst being a significant advance on conventional files, allows only a limited number of pre-defined access paths. Relational data bases overcome the limitations of formatted databases by providing universal access. Access is provided to each data item directly by value through algebraic operations on relations. In relational databases all data structures are reduced to two-dimensional tables of a specified relation. In essence a relational model should be able to answer all possible enquiries at all possible times. A relational database, therefore, provides maximum independence between programs and data whilst providing the maximum flexibility for adding new data or changing the way in which the data may be associated (via relations). A relational database therefore allows versatility in representing relationships between data items as well as allowing the speedy handling of spontaneous information requests. In other words, a relational database renders redundant the concept of a rigid information system. Information systems can be infinitely flexible with the capability of supplying various types and aggregations of information at little or no extra cost.

It was, therefore, logical that Everest and Weber (1977) should have moved away from the limitations of a formatted database type structure to one in which there was greater freedom. Hence, they suggested the use of a relational database for an events-oriented accounting system.

Everest and Weber provided two accounting examples of how a relational system might work. These examples were illustrative and could not be classified as providing a comprehensive relational model of accounting. McCarthy (1979) attempted to remedy this deficiency by promoting an entity view of a relational accounting system. Whilst being an elegant theoretical piece of work, the practicalities remain to be unravelled. Moore (a Ph.D. student at the University of East Anglia) is currently researching into this area.

The only other British contribution to this debate has been Mace (1977) who dealt with the more general methodological problem of choice of accounting method within a financial reporting context.

Cost Relationships

Assuming that research into ideal accounting systems continues, what other apparatus do we need in order to make better decisions? Financial simulation models with the appropriate cost relationships can predict the consequences of alternative actions—or can they? The question mark centres around the word appropriate. The causal relationships determining costs are indeed not always well-known and not always easy to estimate. There are a number of distinct ways in which cost behaviour may be estimated by:

(1) Subjective estimates of relationships.
(2) Calculation of costs from first principles and through detailed technical information.
(3) Time-series analysis of costs.
(4) Econometric analysis of costs.

The first two are non-scientific in that it would be difficult for new personnel to reproduce the results (see Bhaskar, 1978b for (2) above).

Time-series analysis simply uses the information contained in the past values of a variable, whilst econometric analysis builds up a set of causal relationships (in reduced form) which may be represented as a single equation (or a set of simultaneous equations if more than one endogenous variable is employed).

The main focus of the research seems to be the analysis of past data (rather than forecasting) and the examination of whether there is evidence of systematic patterns in the time series behaviour of annual and quarterly accounting data. Using autoregressive techniques, for example, Box-Jenkins (which is an autoregressive integrated moving average (ARIMA) technique) the properties of accounting time series have been examined by, for example: Beaver (1970), Ball and Watts (1972), Kinney (1971), Foster (1977 and 1978), Mabert and Radcliffe (1974), Day (1972), Collins (1976), Brooks and Buckmaster (1976), Lookabill (1976), Griffin (1977), Albrecht, Lookabill and McKeown (1977), Watts and Leftwich (1977), and Ruland (1979).

In providing research on the subject of the technique itself, notable papers include: Kinney (1978) which compared the performance of ARIMA and regression within the context of analytical review; Lloyd (1975) and Smith (1976) discussed the use of two-stage least square models in financial modelling, whilst Elliott and Uphoff (1972) discussed the feasibility of using econometric (as opposed to time-series) models. Earlier studies include Benston (1966), Comiskey (1966), and Jensen (1967). A more promising piece of research is a British contribution by Barnes and Parkinson (1978). Demski and Feltham (1972) and Brandon and Jarrett (1976) cover the difficult question of evaluating forecasts.

Kaplan (1977) went so far as to point to two British studies on estimating short-run marginal costs: Oliver (1962) and Mansfield and Wein (1958), although he excluded Johnston (1960). Kaplan (1974 and 1975b) also conducted some detailed work on cost estimation in hospitals. There is still a long way to go. The use of autoregressive techniques and full-information-maximum-likelihood models have not filtered through into management accounting as academically standard techniques. This area has been sadly neglected and offers a wealth of future research possibilities. Cost behaviour is important as an input to CVP analysis, financial simulation models, cost control, and cost variance investigation.

Conclusion

Faced with what is a difficult, if not impossible task, this paper has attempted to provide a comprehensive survey of the literature in a number of areas within the general subject of 'quantitative aspects of management accounting'. The most important conclusion is that the area is an artificially defined one which cannot be justified on logical or theoretical grounds. All aspects of management accounting have their quantitative side or branch, whether it be the development of a theoretical model of management and a system behaviour or the appraisal of various courses of action.

In carrying out research, there are two fundamental attitudes. One attitude can be described as broadening the frontiers of knowledge. This would include the exploration of 'empty boxes' so that future researches know that such areas are barren. The alternative attitude would adopt a more pragmatic point of view; research should be of benefit to the practitioner. Proponents of the first approach would argue that all research may ultimately benefit the practitioner in the same way as penicillin; which was discovered by accident. The ultimate benefit of pure research can never be quantified in terms of short-run benefits. The frontiers of knowledge are being chipped away slowly and progress is slowly but surely being made.

The practitioner will not always be able to identify what progress has been made. Sometimes, one paper will trigger a series of papers which may ultimately lead to something that a practitioner may classify as 'progress'. Research efforts, however, must be placed in perspective. Broadly, one can identify three categories of research paper: each with very differing characteristics and value to the practitioner and academic.

First, there are those papers which attempt to produce operational 'rules of thumb' for the practitioner. Very often the rules of thumb so produced are still too complicated to be applied in everyday situations. Dittman and Prakash's (1978) research produced some rules which were simple compared with the alternative dynamic programming with the Bayesian updating of probabilities. From the academic point of view, such papers seem to receive only modest praise.

A second category of papers use models and techniques which may be classified as relatively sophisticated and theoretically elegant. Many of the papers using dynamic or some other mathematical programming technique fall into this category. Although I have been fortunate enough to apply such techniques in the real world, the practitioner would probably not be able to identify a problem which could be solved by these techniques. Even if he (or she) did, it is likely that specialists (in the form of consultants) would be brought in to administer these techniques. The correct identification of a situation in which a specialist may be brought in is the best that can be hoped for in the short-run. However, this two tier type 'medical' solution is still a long way off. A specialist may be brought in for 'special' situations; such as a major capital investment project or the setting up of cost centres or a costing system. However, it is less likely that a specialist would be called in for a routine cost variance investigation decision. Yet many of the problems discussed in this review deal with mundane, everyday problems. Progress in this category of theoretical models must be written primarily for the academic market, where high praise is given for the most elegant solution to a (usually well-defined) problem.

It is this category of paper which is most responsible for the widening gap between the practitioner and the academic. This gap can be explained on behavioural grounds. The academic accountant is part of a wider academic community in which accounting is a relatively new academic discipline, often seen to be vocationally and practically oriented. Spurred on by his colleagues in other more 'pure' disciplines, the academic accountant turns to those disciplines and adopts a pseudo-scientific approach in order to gain academic respectability.

The third type of paper concerns the use of sophisticated models and techniques which are used to further research often by testing the value of some of the theoretical models derived in the second category of paper. An example of this was Magee's (1976) work in which he found that a cost investigation policy of using a fixed cost control limit performed nearly as well as the more complex dynamic programming model. The use of simulation to prove that simple techniques can be almost as cost effective as the more sophisticated is well-established, though of less interest to an academic audience bent on achieving the best solution.

A parallel occurs in the risk and uncertainty literature. The example concerns the theoretically elegant time-state preference model which places enormous information demands on an organization prior to implementation. These demands rule such a technique out of court in so far as the practitioner is concerned. Sundem (1974), however, used this technique as a research tool to test the effectiveness of some simple decision rules. His simulation study yielded results that were useful to the practitioner: by splitting projects into two or three different risk classes and discounting at different interest rates, decisions could be made which were nearly as good as the most sophisticated model. Although the practitioner would not be able to understand how Sundem reached his conclusion, the conclusion is simple enough to be of practical use.

Of the papers surveyed in this review, the majority fall into the second category: the theoretical and sometimes elegant model. Why is the practitioner so eager to reject such a model? Complexity may be a significant problem but there is another more compelling reason—the information requirements of the model. To the practitioner desperately struggling alone to derive a point estimate, leave alone a variance/co-variance matrix or probability distribution, some of the theoretically elegant papers seem unreal and remote.

The information requirements of techniques and models is important. Accounting systems can only record historical events and monitor their progress against current plans. The connection between information about the past and decision-making is indirect: it must be by way of whatever forecasts the user makes with the information at his disposal and his preferred forecasting technique.

Directions for Future Research

One of the arguments for favouring 'rules of thumb' over more sophisticated solutions, is that such rules are simpler to calculate. The silicon chip now means that the tediousness of long calculations can be removed. What may have been dismissed by the practitioner as being too complex can be fully utilized by today's practitioner. The chip, however, will not aid the information requirements of such techniques and the problem of understanding how they work.

On 'public relations' grounds, I would like to see a greater number of papers either developing 'rules of thumb' or following Magee (1976) and Sundem (1974) in using sophisticated techniques to derive simple decision rules. Both approaches yield simpler rules for the practitioner.

The implication of the above view is that research into the more theoretical models must also continue. Simpler techniques can only arise through performance comparisons against the more sophisticated models. In this paper, some detailed suggestions were provided in a number of areas. One area in which the practitioner may see little benefit from future research is the question of overhead allocation. From the behavioural point of view, the existence of overhead allocations can be as a reaction to uncertainty (one of the conclusions of the Adar *et al.* (1977) paper). If uncertainty cannot be removed, then decision-makers may be acting rationally in basing decisions on fixed costs. Research into the explanation of the phenomena may ultimately yield a method of persuading the real world to make better decisions.

The area of planning has been covered by the organizational/behavioural area, the corporate planning and financial simulation model area. The latter should fall within the province of quantitative techniques in management accounting, but has largely been shunned as not academically respectable. Yet, the increasing use of computers will probably mean that financial modelling will become widespread among practitioners. This is a time when the practitioner, in dealing with a new technique, may look to the academic for help. However, the academic has either moved on to new pastures or detoured this area.

In decision-making and control, most of the literature proposes techniques, the demands of which for information may be deemed excessive by practitioners. Using Mack's (1971) terminology, one needs to have a better understanding of the relationships between actions and outcomes. Given certain events that have been monitored, decision-making and control could be improved by a greater knowledge of the action-payoff matrix.

In order to achieve this, the practitioner may not require the ultra-sophisticated model: his (or her) need may be for better information. My own view is that better information flowing from improved financial information systems might be able to:

(1) enable the accounting user to recognize an event sooner and with greater clarity;

(2) enable the accounting user better to understand the relationships within the organization—including the consequences of certain actions;

(3) provide feedback on the results of any changes in actions. This in turn will help to provide information which will facilitate the cost investigation/cost control areas;

(4) provide a limited amount of information which can be used to derive probabilistic information.

This is not to say that the various quantitative techniques are not useful—I believe that they are—it is just that it seems as if the cart has been put before the horse: all these techniques have large information appetites. Surely, research should concentrate a little more on the quality and quantity of information provided to users? In the absence of better information, simpler methods may be preferred to the more complex and sophisticated techniques.

I believe that more research is required into financial information systems, with the long run objective of partially restoring the balance between the information currently available in accounting systems and that which may be indirectly required by some of the techniques reviewed above.

With this end in mind, the one other area which is sadly deficient in accounting research is the range of techniques for accurately predicting future consequences of actions. More research needs to be conducted into the problems, pitfalls and limitations of using time-series and econometric techniques and financial simulation models to forecast the outcomes of 'actions' given a set of historical 'events'.

References

Abdel-Khalik, A. R. and Lusk, E. J., 'Transfer Pricing—A Synthesis', *Accounting Review* (January 1974).

Adar, A. Barnea and Lev, B., 'A Comprehensive Cost-Volume. Profit Analysis under Uncertainty', *Accounting Review* (January 1977).

Albrecht, W. A., Lookabill, L. L. and McKeown, J. C., 'The Time Series Properties of Annual Earnings', *Journal of Accounting Research* (Autumn 1977).

Amey, L. R., 'Divisional Performance Measurement and Interest on Capital. Divisional Performance Measurement A Postscript and Contributed Note', *Journal of Business Finance and Accounting* (Spring/Autumn 1969).

Amey, L. A. and Egginton, D. A., *A Conceptual Approach*. Longmans (1973).

Amey, L. A. and Whitmore, G. A., 'Capital Budgeting under Rationing: Comments on the Lusztig and Schwab Procedure', *Journal of Financial and Quantitative Analysis* (January 1973).

Arnold, J., 'An Approach to Pricing and Output Decisions when Prices are Changing', *Journal of Business Finance and Accounting* (Winter 1977).

Ashton, D. J., 'The Reasons for Leasing—A Mathematical Programming Framework', *Journal of Business Finance and Accounting* (Autumn 1978).

Ball, R. and Watts, R., 'Some Time Series Properties of Accounting Income', *Journal of Finance* (June 1972).

Bailey, Jr., A. D., 'A Dynamic Programming Approach to the Analysis of Different Costing Methods in Accounting for Inventories', *Accounting Review* (July 1973).

Barnard, G. A., 'Control Charts and Stochastic Processes', *Journal of the Royal Statistical Society* (Series B [XXI], 1959).

Barnes, P. and Parkinson, J., 'Measuring the Financial Performance of an Individual Building Society: An Explanatory Study and a Suggestion', *AUTA Review* (Autumn 1978).

Barron, M. J., 'The Application of Linear Programming Dual Prices in Management Accounting', *Journal of Business Finance* (Spring 1972).

Bather, G. A., 'Control Charts and the Minimisation of Costs', *Journal of the Royal Statistical Society* (Series B [XXI] 1963).

Beaver, W. H., 'The Time Series Behaviour of Earnings', *Empirical Research in Accounting Selected Studies 1970. Journal of Accounting Research* (1970).

Benston, George J., 'Multiple Regression Analysis of Cost Behaviour', *Accounting Review* (October 1966).

Bentz, W. F., 'Input–Output Analysis for Cost Accounting, Planning and Control', *Accounting Review* (April 1973).

Bernhard, R. H., 'Mathematical Programming Models for Capital Budgeting—A Survey Generalisation and Critique', *Journal of Financial and Quantitative Analysis* (June 1969).

Bhaskar, K. N., 'Borrowing and Lending in a Mathematical Programming Model of Capital Budgeting', *Journal of Business Finance and Accounting* (Summer 1974).

Bhaskar, K. N., 'Linear Programming and Capital Budgeting: A Reappraisal', *Journal of Business Finance and Accounting* (Autumn 1976).

Bhaskar, K. N., 'Linear Programming and Capital Budgeting: The Financing Problem', *Journal of Business Finance and Accounting* (Summer 1978a).

Bhaskar, K. N., *Building Financial Models: A Simulation Approach*. Associated Business Press (1978b).

Bhaskar, K. N., *Manual to Building Financial Models*. Associated Business Press (1979a).

Bhaskar, K. N., 'Multiple Objectives in Capital Budgeting', *Accounting and Business Research* (1979b).

Bierman, H., Fouraker, L. E. and Jaedicke, R. K., 'A Use of Probability and Statistics in Performance Evaluation', *Accounting Review* (July 1961).

Bodnar, G. and Lusk, E. J., 'Motivational Considerations in Cost Allocation Systems: A Conditioning Theory Approach', *Accounting Review* (October 1977).

Brandon, C. H. and Jarrett, J. E., 'Evaluating Accounting Forecasts', *Journal of Business Finance and Accounting* (Autumn 1976).

Brooks, L. D. and Buckmaster, D. A., 'Further Evidence of the Time Series Properties of Accounting Income', *Journal of Finance* (December 1976).

Butterworth, J. E., 'An Accounting System as an Information Function', *Journal of Accounting Research* (Spring 1972).

Butterworth, J. E. and Sigloch, B. A., 'A Generalised Multi-Stage Input–Output Model and some Revived Equivalent Systems', *Accounting Review* (October 1971).

Buzby, S. L., 'Extending the Applicability of Probabilistic Planning and Control Models', *Accounting Review* (January 1974).

Buzby, S. L., 'Extending the Applicability of Probabilistic Management Planning and Control Models: A Reply', *Accounting Review* (October 1975).

Callen, J. L., 'Financial Cost Allocations: A Game-Theoretic Approach', *Accounting Review* (April 1978).

Capettini, R. and Collins, D., 'The Investigation of Deviations from Standard Costs in the Presence of Unequal State Variances', *Journal of Business Finance and Accounting* (Winter 1978).

Carleton, W., 'An Analytical Model for Long-Range Financial Planning', *Journal of Finance* (May 1970).

Carleton, W. T., Dick, Jr., C. L. and Downes, D. H., 'Financial Policy Models: Theory and Practice', *Journal of Financial and Quantitative Analysis* (December 1973).

Carsberg, B. V., 'On the Linear Programming Approach to Asset Valuation', *Journal of Accounting Research* (Autumn 1969).

Chambers, D. J., Singhal, H. S., Taylor, B. D. and Wright, D. L., 'Developing Dividend and Financing Policies with a Computer Terminal', *Accounting and Business Research* (Autumn 1971).

Chateau, J. P. D., 'The Capital Budgeting Problem Under Conflicting Financial Policies', *Journal of Business Finance and Accounting* (Spring 1975).

Colantoni, C. S., Manes, R. P. and Whinston, A., 'Programming Profit Rates and Pricing Decisions', *Accounting Review* (July 1969).

Colantoni, C. S., Manes, R. P. and Whinston, A., 'A Unified Approach to the Theory of Accounting and Information Systems', *Accounting Review* (January 1971).

Collins, D. W., 'Predicting Earnings with Sub-Entity Data: Some Further Evidence', *Journal of Accounting Research* (Spring 1976).

Comisky, E. E., 'Cost Control by Regression Analysis', *Accounting Review* (April 1966).

Courtis, J. K., 'Modelling a Financial Ratios Categoric Framework', *Journal of Business Finance and Accounting* (Winter 1978).

Crandell, R. H., 'Information Economics and Accounting Theory', *Accounting Review* (July 1969).

Currin, D. L. and Spivey, W. A., 'A Note on "Management Decision and Integer Programming"', *Accounting Review* (January 1972).

Day, C. L., 'Forecasting Industry Profits', *Journal of Business Finance and Accounting* (Winter 1972).

Deam, R. J., Bennett, J. W. and Leather, J., *Firm: A Computer Model for Financial Planning*. Institute of Chartered Accountants in England and Wales (1975).

Demski, J., 'An Accounting System Structured on an LP Model', *Accounting Review* (October 1967).

Demski, J. S., 'Predictive Ability of Alternative Performance Measurement Models', *Journal of Accounting Research* (Spring 1969).

Demski, J., 'Optimising the Search for Cost Deviation Sources', *Management Science* (April 1970).

Demski, J., 'Implementation Effects of Alternative Performance Measurement Models in a Multivariate Context', *Accounting Review* (April 1971).

Demski, J. and Feltham, G. A., 'Forecast Evaluation', *Accounting Review* (July 1972).

Dickinson, J. P., 'Cost-Volume-Profit Analysis Under Uncertainty', *Journal of Accounting Research* (Spring 1974).

Dittman, D. A. and Prakash, P., 'Cost Variance Investigation: Markovian Control of Markov Processes', *Journal of Accounting Research* (Spring 1978).

Dhaliwal, D. S., 'Cost Allocation and Resource Requirement Planning: An Alternative Approach', *Accounting and Business Research* (Spring 1979).

Dopuch, N., 'Mathematical Programming and Accounting Approaches to Incremental Cost Analysis', *Accounting Review* (October 1963).

Dopuch, N. J., 'Discussion of Applications in Quantitative Models in Managerial Accounting', *Management Accounting—State of the Art*. Robert Beyer Lecture Series: University of Wisconsin-Madison (1977).

Dopuch, N., Birnberg, J. and Demski, J., *Cost Accounting*. New York, Harcourt Brace Jovanovich (1974).

Duvall, R. M., 'Rules for Investigating Lost Variances', *Management Science* (June 1967).

Dyckman, J. R., 'The Investigation of Cost Variances', *Journal of Accounting Research* (Autumn 1969).

Eckel, L. G., 'Arbitrary and Incorrigible Allocations', *Accounting Review* (October 1976).

Elliott, J. W. and Uphoff, H. L., 'Predicting the Near Term Profit and Loss Statement with an Econometric Model: A Feasibility Study', *Journal of Accounting Research* (Autumn 1972).

Elton, E. J., 'Capital Rationing and External Discount Rates, *Journal of Finance* (June 1970).

Everest, G. C. and Weber, R., 'A Relational Approach to Accountancy Models', *Accounting Review* (April 1977).

Farley, J. and Hinich, M., 'Detecting Small Mean Shifts in Time Series', *Management Science* (November 1970).

Feltham, G. A., 'Some Quantitative Approaches to Planning for Multiproduction Systems', *Accounting Review* (January 1970).

Feltham, G. A., 'In-process Inventories and Multiproduct Production Systems: A Comment', *Accounting Review* (April 1973).

Ferrara, N. L., Hayya, J. C. and Nachman, D. A., 'Normalcy of Profit in the Jaedicke-Robichek Model', *Accounting Review* (April 1972).

Flower, J. F., *Computer Models for Accountants*. Haymarket (1973).

Foster, G., 'Quarterly Accounting Data: Time Series Properties and Predictive Ability Results', *Accounting Review* (January 1977).

Foster, G., *Financial statement Analysis*. Prentice-Hall 1978).

Gambling, T. E. and Nour, A., 'A Note on Input–Output Analysis: its Uses in Macro-Economics and Micro-Economics', *Accounting Review* (January 1970).

Glover, F., 'Management Decision and Integer Programming', *Accounting Review* (April 1969).

Glover, F., 'Comment on a Note by Currin and Spirey', *Accounting Review* (January 1972).

Godfrey, S. T., 'Short Run Planning in a Decentralized Firm', *Accounting Review* (April 1971).

Godfrey, J. T. and Prince, T. R., 'The Accounting Model from an Information Systems Perspective', *Accounting Review* (January 1971).

Goel, A. L. and Wu, S. M., 'Economically Optimum Design of Cusum Charts', *Management Science* (July 1973).

Gonedes, N. J., 'Accounting for Managerial Control: An Application of Chance-Constrained Programming', *Journal of Accounting Research* (Spring 1970).

Gonedes, N. J., 'Corporate Signalling, External Accounting, and Capital Marketing Equilibrium: Evidence on Dividends, Income and Extraordinary Items', *Journal of Accounting Research* (Spring 1978).

Griffin, P. A., 'The Time Series Behaviour of Quarterly Earnings: Preliminary Evidence', *Journal of Accounting Research* (Spring 1977).

Grinnell, D. J., 'Using LP to Compare Direct and Absorption Costing', *Accounting Review* (April 1977).

Grinyer, P. H. and Wooller, J., *Corporate Models Today* (2nd edn.). ICAEW (1978).

Groves, R., Manes, R. and Sorensen, R., 'The Application of the Hirsh-Dantzig "fixed change" Algorithm to Profit Planning: A formal Statement of Product Profitability Analysis', *Accounting Review* (July 1970).

Hamlen, S. S., Hamlen, W. A., Jr. and Schirhart, T. T., 'The Use of Core Theory in Evaluating Joint Cost Allocation Schemes', *Accounting Review* (July 1977).

Hartley, R. V., 'Decision Making when Joint Products are Involved', *Accounting Review* (October 1971).

Hartley, R. V., 'A Note on Quadratic Programming in a Case of Joint Production: A Reply', *Accounting Review* (October 1973).

Haseman, W. D. and Whinston, A. B., 'Design of a Multidimensional Accounting System', *Accounting Review* (January 1976).

Hayya, J. C., Ferrara, W. L. and Saniga, E., 'Extending the Applicability of Probabilistic Management Planning and Control Models: A Comment', *Accounting Review* (October 1975).

Hilliard, J. W. and Leitch, R. A., 'Cost-volume Profit Analysis Under Uncertainty: A Log Normal Approach', *Accounting Review* (January 1975).

Hinich, M. and Farley, T., 'Theory and Application of an Estimation Model for Time Series with Nonstationary Means', *Management Science* (May 1966).

Hughes, J. S., 'Optimal Timing of Cost Information', *Journal of Accounting Research* (Autumn 1975).

Hughes, J. S., 'Optimal Timing of Cost Information—Author's Correction', *Journal of Accounting Research* (Autumn 1977).

Hughes, J. A. and Lewellen, W. G., 'Programming Solutions to Capital Rationing Problems', *Journal of Business Finance and Accounting* (Spring 1974).

Ijiri, Y. and Itami, H., 'Quadratic Cost-Volume Relationship and Timing of Demand Information', *Accounting Review* (October 1973).

Jaedicke, R. K. and Robichek, A. A., 'Cost-Volume-Profit Analysis Under Conditions of Uncertainty', *Accounting Review* (October 1964).

Jensen, D. L., 'Hartley's Demand—Price Analysis in a Case of Joint Production', *Accounting Review* (October 1973).

Jensen, D. L., 'A Class of Mutually Satisfactory Allocations', *Accounting Review* (October 1977).

Jensen, D. L. and McKeown, J. C., 'Multiple-step Investigations of Standard Cost Variances', *Journal of Business Finance and Accounting* (Summer 1977).

Jensen, R. E., 'A Multiple Regression Model for Cost Control—Assumptions and Limitations', *Accounting Review* (April 1967).

Jensen, R. E., 'Sensitivity Analysis and Integer Linear Programming', *Accounting Review* (July 1968).

Johnson, O., 'Towards an "Events" Theory of Accounting', *Accounting Review* (October 1970).

Johnson, N. L., Nixon, E., Amos, D. E. and Pearson, E. S., 'Table of Percentage Points of Pearson Curves', *Biometrika* (vol. 50) (1963).

Johnson, G. L. and Simik, S. S., 'Multiproduct C-V-P Analysis under Uncertainty', *Journal of Accounting Research* (Autumn 1971).

Johnson, G. L. and Simik, S. S., 'The Use of Probability Inequalities in Multiproduct C-V-P Analysis under Uncertainty', *Journal of Accounting Research* (Spring 1974).

Johnson, J., *Statistical Cost Curves*. McGraw-Hill (1960).

Juers, D. A., 'Statistical Significance of Accounting Variances', *Management Accounting* (October 1967).

Kaplan, R. S., 'Optimal Investigation Strategies with Imperfect Information', *Journal of Accounting Research* (Spring 1969).

Kaplan, R. S. and Thompson, G. L., 'Overhead Allocation via Mathematical Programming Models', *Accounting Review* (April 1971).

Kaplan, R. S. and Welham, U. P., 'Overhead Allocation with Imperfect Markets and Nonlinear Technology', *Accounting Review* (July 1974).

Kaplan, R. S., 'Management Accounting in Hospitals: A Case Study', in J. L. Livingstone and S. Gunn, *Accounting for Social Goals: Budgeting and Analysis of Non-Market Projects*. Harper and Row (1974).

Kaplan, R. S., 'The Significance and Investigation of Cost Variances: Survey and Extensions', *Journal of Accounting Research* (Autumn 1975a).

Kaplan, R. S., 'Analysis and Control of Nursing Staffing', *Health Service Research* (Autumn 1975b).

Kaplan, R. S., 'Application of Quantitative Models in Managerial Accounting: A

State of the Art Survey', *Management Accounting—State of the Art*. Robert Beyer Lecture Series: University of Wisconsin-Madison (1977).

Killough, L. N. and Souders, T. L., 'A Goal Programming Model for Public Accounting Firms', *Accounting Review* (April 1973).

Kinney, W. R., 'Predicting Earnings: Entity versus Subentity Data', *Journal of Accounting Research* (Spring 1971).

Kinney, W. R., Jr., 'ARIMA and Regression in Analytical Review: An Empirical Test', *Accounting Review* (January 1978).

Koehler, R. W., 'The Relevance of Probability Statistics to Accounting Variance Control', *Management Accounting* (October 1968).

Kornbluth, J. S. H., 'Accounting in Multiple Objective Linear Programming', *Accounting Review* (April 1974).

Kottas, J. K., Lau, A. and Lau, H. S., 'A General Approach to Stochastic Management Planning Models: An Overview', *Accounting Review* (April 1978).

Kottas, J. F. and Lau, H. S., 'Direct Simulation in Stochastic CVP Analysis', *Accounting Review* (July 1978).

Kumar, P. C., Philippatos, G. C. and Ezzell, J. R., 'Goal Programming and the Selection of Portfolios by Dual Purpose Funds', *Journal of Finance* (March 1978).

Lau, A. and Lau, H. S., 'CVP Analysis Under Uncertainty—A Log Normal Approach—A Comment', *Acçounting Review* (January 1976).

Lev, B., 'An Information Theory Analysis of Budget Variances', *Accounting Review* (October 1969).

Lloyd, W. P., 'A Note on the Use of the Two-Stage Least Squares Estimator in Financial Models', *Journal of Finance and Quantitative Analysis* (March 1975).

Libby, R., 'Accounting Ratios and the Prediction of Failure: Some Behavioural Evidence', *Journal of Accounting Research* (Spring 1975).

Liao, M., 'Model Sampling: A Stochastic Cost-Volume-Profit Analysis', *Accounting Review* (October 1975).

Lieberman, A. Z. and Whinston, A. B., 'A Structuring of an Events-Accounting Information System', *Accounting Review* (April 1975).

Lin, W. T., 'Multiple Objective Budgeting Models: A Simulation', *Accounting Review* (January 1978).

Livingstone, J. L., 'Matrix Algebra and Cost Allocation', *Accounting Review* (July 1968).

Livingstone, J. L., 'Input–Output Analysis for Cost Accounting, Planning and Control', *Accounting Review* (January 1969).

Livingstone, J. L., 'Input–Output Analysis for Cost Accounting, Planning and Control: A Reply', *Accounting Review* (April 1973).

Leohman, E. and Whinston, A., 'A New Theory of Pricing and Decision-Making for Public Investment', *Bell Journal* (Autumn 1971).

Leohman, E. and Whinston, A., 'An Axiomatic Approach to Cost Allocation for Public Investment', *Public Finance Quarterly* (April 1974).

Lookabill, L., 'Some Additional Evidence on the Time Series Properties of Accounting Earnings', *Accounting Review* (October 1976).

Lucas, H. C., 'The Use of an Accounting Information System, Action and Organisational Performance', *Accounting Review* (October 1975).

Luh, F., 'Controlled Costs: An Operational Concept and Statistical Approach to Standing Costing', *Accounting Review* (January 1968).

Lusztig, P. and Schwab, B., 'A Note of the Application of Linear Programming to Capital Budgeting', *Journal of Financial and Quantitative Analysis* (December 1968).

Lusztig, P. and Schwab, B., 'The Discount Rate Problem in Capital Rationing Situations', *Journal of Financial and Quantitative Analysis* (September 1970).

Ma, R. and Tydenman, J., 'Project Selection Criteria Wealth Maximisation and Capital Rationing', *Journal of Business Finance and Accounting* (Winter 1972).

Mabert, V. A. and Radcliffe, R. C., 'A Forecasting Methodology as Applied to Financial Time Series', *Accounting Review* (Spring 1974).

Mace, J. R., 'A Systems Approach to the Analysis of Financial Reporting', *Accounting and Business Research* (Autumn 1977).

Magee, R. P., 'Cost-Volume-Profit Analysis, Uncertainty and Capital Market Equilibrium', *Journal of Accounting Research* (Autumn 1975).

Magee, R. P., 'A Simulation Analysis of Alternative Cost Variance Investigation Models', *Accounting Review* (July 1976).

Magee, R. P., 'Cost Control with Imperfect Parameter Knowledge', *Accounting Review* (January 1977a).

Magee, R. P., 'The Usefulness of Commonality Information in Cost Control Decisions', *Accounting Review* (October 1977b).

Manes, R. P., 'Comment on Matrix Theory and Cost Allocation', *Accounting Review* (July 1965).

Mansfield, E. and Wein, H. H., 'A Regression Control Chart for Costs', *Applied Statistics* Vol. 7 (March 1958).

McCarthy, W. E., 'An Entity Relationship View of Accounting Models', *Accounting Review* (October 1979).

Meier, R. C., Newell, W. T. and Pazer, H. L., *Simulation in Business and Economics*. Prentice-Hall (1969).

Merville, L. J. and Petty, J. W., 'Transfer Pricing for the Multinational Firm', *Accounting Review* (October 1978).

Merville, L. J. and Tavis, L. A., 'Optimal Working Capital Policies: A Chance Constrained Programming Approach', *Journal of Financial and Quantitative Analysis* (January 1973a).

Merville, L. J. and Tavis, C. A., 'A Generalised Model for Capital Investment', *Journal of Finance* (March 1973b).

Minch, R. and Petri, F., 'Matrix Models of Reciprocal Service Cost Allocation', *Accounting Review* (July 1972).

Mock, T. J., 'Concepts of Information Value and Accounting', *Accounting Review* (October 1971).

Mock, M. J. and Driver, T. J., 'Human Information Processing, Decision Style Theory and Accounting Information Systems', *Accounting Review* (July 1975).

Modigliani, F. and Miller, M. H., 'The Cost of Capital, Corporation Finance and the Theory of Investment', *American Economic Review* (June 1958).

Modigliani, F. and Miller, M. H., 'Dividend Policy, Growth and the Valuation of Shares', *Journal of Business of the University of Chicago* (October 1961).

Moriarity, S., 'Another Approach to Allocating Joint Costs', *Accounting Review* (October 1975).

Myers, S. C., 'A Note on Linear Programming and Capital Budgeting', *Journal of Finance* (March 1972).

Myers, S. C., 'Interactions of Corporate Financing and Investment Decisions—Implications for Capital Budgeting', *Journal of Finance* (March 1974).

Myers, S. C. and Pogue, G. A., 'A Programming Approach to Corporate Financial Management', *Journal of Finance* (May 1974).

Naylor, T. H., *Computer Simulation Experiments with Models of Economic Systems*. John Wiley (1971).

Naylor, T. H., *Simulation Models in Corporate Planning*. Praeger (1979a).

Naylor, T. H., *Corporate Planning Models*. Addison-Wesley (1979b).

Oliver, F. R., 'A Cross-section Study of Marginal Cost', *Applied Statistics* Vol. 11 (June 1962).

Ozan, T. and Dyckman, T. R., 'A Normative Model for Investigation Decision Involving Multi-Origin Cost Variances', *Journal of Accounting Research* (Spring 1971).

Page, E. S., *Continuous Inspection Schemes*. Biometrika (1954, XLI).

Pettway, R. H., 'Integer Programming in Capital Budgeting: A Note on Computational Experience', *Journal of Financial and Quantitative Analysis* (September 1973).

Pogue, G. A. and Bussard, R. N., 'An LP Model for Short-Term Financial Planning under Uncertainty', *Sloan Management Review* (Spring 1972).

Prakash, P. and Rappaport, A., 'Informational Interdependencies: System Structure Induced by Accounting Information', *Accounting Review* (October 1975).

Precious, J. R. and Wood, D. R., 'Corporate Modelling: When Success can be a Long-Term Forecast', *Accounting and Business Research* (Autumn 1975).

Probst, F. R., 'Probabilistic Cost Controls: A Behavioural Dimension', *Accounting Review* (January 1971).

Rappaport, A., 'Integer Programming and Managerial Analysis', *Accounting Review* (April 1969).

Robichek, A. A., Teichrdew, D. and Jones, J. M., 'Optimal Short-Term Financing Decisions', *Management Science* (September 1965).

Ronen, J., 'Capacity and Operating Variances: An Ex Post Approach', *Journal of Accounting Research* (Autumn 1965).

Ronen, J., 'Nonaggregation versus Disaggregation of Variances', *Accounting Review* (January 1974).

Ruland, W., 'The Time Series of Earnings for Forecast Reporting and Non-reporting Firms', *Journal of Business Finance and Accounting* (Summer 1979).

Samuels, J. M., 'Opportunity Costing: An Application of Mathematical Programming', *Journal of Accounting Research* (Autumn 1965).

Samuels, J. M., 'Penalties and Subsidies in Internal Pricing Policies', *Journal of Business Finance and Accounting* (Autumn 1969).

Sartoris, W. L. and Spruill, M. L., 'Goal Programming and Working Capital Management', *Financial Management* (Spring 1974).

Savich, R. S., 'The Use of Accounting Information in Decision Making', *Accounting Review* (July 1977).

Sealey, Jr., C. W., 'Utility Maximization and Programming Models for Capital Budgeting', *Journal of Business Finance and Accounting* (Autumn 1978).

Shubik, M., 'Incentives, Decentralized Control, the Assignment of Joint Costs and Internal Pricing', *Management Science* (April 1962).

Smith, V. K., 'On the Use of Two-Stage Least Squares in Financial Models: A Comment', *Journal of Financial and Quantitative Analysis* (June 1974).

Sorter, G., 'An "Events" Approach to Basic Accounting Theory', *Accounting Review* (January 1969).

Stewart, J. C., 'Multinational Companies and Transfer Pricing', *Journal of Business Finance and Accounting* (Autumn 1977).

Sundem, G. L., 'Evaluating Simplified Capital Budgeting Models Using a Time-State Preference Metric', *Accounting Review* (April 1974).

Taylor, H. M., 'The Economic Design of Cumulative Sum Control Charts for Variables', *Technometrics* (August 1968).

Tomkins, C., *Financial Planning in Divisionalised Companies*. Haymarket (1973).

Thomas, A. L., 'The Allocation Problem in Financial Accounting Theory', *Studies in Accounting Research No. 3, American Accounting Association* (1969).

Thomas, A. L., 'The Allocation Problem: Part Two', *Studies in Accounting Research No. 9, American Accounting Association* (1974).

Thomas, A. L., 'Arbitrary and Incorrigible Allocations: A Comment', *Accounting Review* (January 1978).

Watts, R. L. and Leftwich, R. W., 'The Time Series of Annual Accounting Earnings', *Journal of Accounting Research* (Autumn 1977).

Weingartner, H. M., 'Capital Rationing: Authors in Search of a Plot', *Journal of Finance* (December 1977).

Wilkes, F. M., 'Dividend Policy and Investment Appraisal in Imperfect Capital Markets', *Journal of Business Finance and Accounting* (Summer 1977).

Wilkes, F. M. and Harrison, R., 'Classified Pricing Rules, Cost Plus Pricing and the Capacity Constrained Firm', *Journal of Business Finance and Accounting* (Spring 1975).

Wolk, H. I. and Hillman, D., 'Materials Mix and Yield Variances: A Suggested Improvement', *Accounting Review* (July 1972).

Wood, D., 'A Decision System Approach to Financial Strategy', *Journal of Business Finance and Accounting* (Spring 1972).

Wright, F. K., 'Measuring Asset Services: Linear Programming Approach', *Journal of Accounting Research* (Autumn 1968).

Wright, F. K., 'On the Linear Programming Approach to Asset Valuation: Reply', *Journal of Accounting Research* (Autumn 1969).

Zannetos, Z. A., 'Standard Cost as a First Step to Probabilistic Control: A Theoretical Justification, An Extension and Implications', *Accounting Review* (July 1964).

Zimmerman, J. L., 'Budget Uncertainty and the Allocation Decision in a Non-profit Organisation', *Journal of Accounting Research* (Autumn 1976).

Commentary on 'Quantitative aspects of management accounting'

Robert W Scapens
Senior Lecturer and Research Co-ordinator in Accounting and Business Finance, University of Manchester

In the introduction to his paper, Bhaskar indicated the diversity of articles on quantitative aspects of management accounting which appeared in the last decade in four American and two British journals. It would have been an impossible task to provide a comprehensive survey. The selection of particular topics for detailed discussion could be described as arbitrary, but this must be inevitable in any survey of such an extensive area of the literature. Bhaskar is to be congratulated on the paper he has presented; in particular, on the way he has reviewed and explained some very complex articles.

In this discussion, individual topics will not be examined in detail, rather attention will be given to the role of quantitative methods in management accounting. While I am in broad agreement with the conclusions reached in the paper, there are some further implications which I would like to explore.

The general impression to be gained from a review of the quantitative aspects of management accounting is that theory is far ahead of practice. This can be seen in an extreme form in the CVP literature, where theory is so far ahead that it is quite out of sight. This is a frequent criticism raised by practitioners, and it should not be dismissed lightly.

It seems to be a generally accepted assumption (Watts and Zimmerman notwithstanding) that practice will lag behind theory. It is argued that time is required for new techniques to be accepted and implemented by managers and accountants. However, the time lag seems excessively long and only relatively simple techniques are adopted. If new techniques have the power their advocates suggest, then one would expect managers in a competitive world to hire suitably qualified specialists to explain and implement them. Firms that did not do so would be placed at a competitive disadvantage. Nevertheless, many of the quantitative techniques developed 5–10 years ago are, even now, not widely adopted, either in the U.K. or the U.S.[1] It is very convenient to blame this on practitioners' lack of knowledge. But are there any more fundamental reasons? The large

1 For a review of quantitative models in management accounting with a U.S. perspective see Kaplan (1977).

companies in the U.S. are increasingly employing accountants with substantial academic training. Recently, I discussed methods of divisional performance measurement with senior accountants at a large steel company in the U.S. The individual who explained the reasons for adopting what could be described as a simple approach has a Ph.D. in accounting and he was clearly not unfamiliar with the more complex quantitative models—models which were considered inappropriate for his company.

In his appraisal of the CVP debate, Bhaskar implies that analytical development may be solely for academic respectability, and not to enhance the usefulness of the techniques. Simple techniques may be the most appropriate in practice. For instance, Magee (1976) demonstrated in a simulation study that when estimation and implementation costs were considered, simple variance investigation models would be preferred by rational managers. Sundem (1974) came to a similar conclusion in his study of investment appraisal techniques. Does this imply that complex models should be avoided? To investigate this question consider the role of models in management accounting.

It is possible to distinguish two separate roles for such models. First, models may be used by managers and accountants, in practice, *on a day to day basis*. These models assist the decision-maker in arriving at particular decisions; for instance, NPV rules for investment appraisal, models for variance investigation and CVP models. For the present discussion, these models will be called decision models, although they might be termed simply decision rules, or decision aids. Secondly, models are used by academics and consultants to analyse decision situations and to prescribe decision models. These models, which may be described as analytical models, include valuation models used to derive criteria for investment appraisal, allocation models used to derive performance measures and criteria for decision-making.

In distinguishing these two roles for models in management accounting two separate groups have been identified. The first encompasses managers and accountants in practice, who may be called *practitioners* and the second, academics and consultants who may be called *researchers*.

The classification of models as either decision models or analytical models implies that decision situations can be quantitatively modelled. This is unlikely to be true of all decision situations. Simon (1966, pp. 5–6) suggested a dichotomy in which decisions are either programmable or non-programmable. Programmable decisions are well-structured with a clear link between actions and outcomes, and, in particular, it is possible to enumerate the alternative actions and outcomes. Such decisions are generally inconsequential, but highly repetitive. Non-programmable decisions, however, are usually unique and consequential, and more importantly, unstructured. It may be impossible to recognize all the available alternatives and to evaluate, or even identify, the possible outcomes.

Combining the two categories of management accounting user and

Table 10.1

Types of Decisions	*Management Accounting*	
	Practitioner	*Researcher*
Programmable	Quantitative decision models (or aids)	Quantitative analytical models
Non-programmable	Data bases	Organizational and behavioural analysis

researcher, with the decision dichotomy gives the matrix shown in Table 10.1. The role of simple and complex models can be investigated by examining the cells in this matrix. The quantitative models which are the primary concern of Bhaskar's paper are only applicable for programmable decisions. A non-programmable decision cannot, by definition, be modelled. Nevertheless, it will be appropriate to make some comments later about the use of quantitative data for non-programmable decisions. Furthermore, the distinction between programmable and non-programmable decisions is not static, as new techniques become available it may be possible to model particular decisions which were previously non-programmable.

Now consider the researchers' use of models of programmable decisions. These quantitative analytical models may be very complex. As they are used to prescribe particular decision models (or aids), they should include the costs and benefits of implementation. It may be that complexity will add to the academic respectability of analytical models; but simplicity should be regarded as a desirable characteristic of their prescriptions.

A strong case can probably be made for more complexity in analytical models, especially in the treatment of risk and uncertainty. Many of the techniques of management accounting, conventionally supported by academics, were developed without explicit consideration of risk.[2] A reassessment of such techniques using the recently developed methods of dealing with risk would be a useful piece of further research which might indicate some of the reasons why particular methods are adopted in practice. Some steps have already been taken in this direction. Adar *et al.* (1977) looked at CVP in this way, Dillon and Nash (1978) at relevant costs and Zimmerman (1979) at cost allocations.

A further extension of analytical models should incorporate the costs and benefits of using the associated decision models in practice. Such research will indicate whether the information costs associated with the complex decision models are justified by the benefits obtained. More

2 For a discussion of the development of opportunity cost theory see Arnold and Scapens in this volume.

research is required to identify the estimation and implementation problems and costs associated with the proposed decision models.

At this point, a word of caution is necessary. When building analytical models, interpreting their results and prescribing decision models it is important not to over-estimate the role of accounting information. Frequently, non-quantifiable variables enter into business decisions and, accordingly, quantitative models are unlikely to be complete.

The analytical evidence which is available, such as Magee (1976) and Sundem (1974), suggests that simple decision models are often the most appropriate. The empirical evidence of firms not adopting complex models, in practice, provides further support for simple models. I believe that the introduction of further complexities into analytical models, will probably lead to simpler decision models for practical application.

In the latter part of the paper, Bhaskar discussed extended data base approaches—i.e. providing the decision-maker with as much data as possible. As can be seen from Table 10.1, my view is that such an approach is most appropriate for non-programmable decisions. In such circumstances decision models cannot be used and the role of management accounting should be to provide data which the decision-maker can access. But if the decisions are programmable management accounting research should attempt to develop appropriate decision models. However, I accept the author's point that the information required to implement the models must be made available.

Non-programmable decisions lack structure and cannot be quantitatively modelled. Attempts to apply quantitative techniques to such decisions will have no practical relevance. Accounting researchers can serve a more useful role in this area by providing organizational and behavioural analysis which will assist in the design of data bases.

Finally, let me emphasize that it is important to recognize the limitations of quantitative techniques. Quantitative decision models can be extremely useful for programmable decisions—but of little use for non-programmable decisions. The researcher who does not recognize this may produce very elegant, but totally useless, models.

References

Adar, Z., Barnea, A. and Lev, B., 'A Comprehensive Cost-Volume-Profit Analysis under Uncertainty', *The Accounting Review* (January 1977).

Dillon, R. D. and Nash, J. F., 'The True Relevance of Relevant Costs', *The Accounting Review* (January 1978).

Kaplan, R. S., 'Application of Quantitative Models in Managerial Accounting: A State of the Art Survey', in *Management Accounting—State of the Art*. Robert Beyer Lecture Series: University of Wisconsin-Madison (1977).

Magee, R. P., 'A Simulation Analysis of Alternative Cost Variance Investigation Models', *The Accounting Review* (July 1976).

Simon, H. A., *The New Science of Management Decision*. Harper and Row: New York (1966).

Sundem, G. L., 'Evaluating Simplified Capital Budgeting Models Using a Time-State Preference Metric', *The Accounting Review* (April 1974).

Zimmerman, J. L., 'The Costs and Benefits of Cost Allocations', *The Accounting Review* (July 1979).

11 The study of accounting history

R H Parker
Professor of Accountancy, University of Exeter

The study of accounting history is beginning to flourish. Following the success of the first world congress of accounting historians held in Brussels in 1970, the newly founded (American) Academy of Accounting Historians organized, in 1976, a second international congress in Atlanta, Georgia and, in 1977, launched *The Accounting Historians' Journal*. The Arno Press of New York is reprinting accounting classics and producing numerous useful anthologies. In the U.K. the Accounting History Society organized the third international congress held at the London Business School in August 1980. Fifty papers from 14 countries were delivered. The Scottish Committee on Accounting History has published several useful books, e.g. Pryce-Jones and Parker (1976); Stewart (1977). The editors of such influential academic journals as *The Accounting Review, Abacus* and *Accounting and Business Research* number accounting history among their major research interests.

Accounting history, like accounting itself, is an international activity, but Britain has produced some notable accounting historians. Since this chapter is not a comprehensive survey of the field, not all of them receive here the attention they deserve, but mention must be especially made of the pioneering contribution of Brown (1905) and, more recently, Yamey (1978). A number of younger writers are making important contributions throughout the accounting history area. It is difficult to discern a specifically British approach, but in recent years there has been a natural tendency to concentrate on those periods when Britain was not only the leading industrial and commercial nation, but also the leading accounting nation. Both the industrial revolution and modern professional accountancy occurred in Britain first.

Why Study Accounting History?

Charles Waldo Haskins gave a brief answer in 1900: 'The better to understand our present and to forecast or control our future' (1904, p. 141). A detailed answer was attempted in 1970 by the Committee on Accounting History of the American Accounting Association:

> Accounting history is the study of the evolution in accounting thought, practices, and institutions in response to changes in the environment and societal needs. It also considers the effect that this evolution has worked on the environment.
>
> The ends of accounting history are both intellectual and utilitarian: *Intellectual*, for it illuminates the process by which accounting thought, practices, and institutions develop, identifying the factors in the environment that induce change and revealing how this change actually occurs. It also seeks to determine the effect on the environment of changes in accounting thought, practices, and institutions. Finally, it contributes to a better understanding of economic and business history. *Utilitarian*, for history throws light on the origins of concepts, practices, and institutions in use today, yielding insight for the solution of modern accounting problems. Given an understanding of the past interaction of the environment and changes in accounting practices and institutions, it may become somewhat easier to predict the consequences of currently proposed solutions. (1970, p. 52.)

A rather different view has been put forward by Goldberg:

> To sum up, the study of accounting history will help us to understand the past (in whatever sense we use the word 'understand'), it will give us appreciation of how our current practices and problems came into being and will help to put them into some sort of perspective. It should act as a caution against attempting to predict the future but it should help us to appreciate the complexity of the circumstances from which the future will unfold. It will give intellectual exercise and it should provide tools of thought for solving problems, not only by showing us how our predecessors solved or failed to solve some of their problems but also through its requirement for painstaking, meticulous accuracy in the examination of material. (1974, p. 410.)

It is an important function of the accounting historian to ask how well accounting and accounts satisfied the needs of *contemporary* users. If they failed to do so, what factors were responsible for the failure? One should not lightly assume, for example, that English medieval accounts would have been better kept by double entry than by charge and discharge (Jack, 1966). Vlaemminck (1956, p. 211) has asked, for example:

> Why in 3rd century Alexandrian Egypt did Zenon keep accounting records for salaries and entertainment expenses, and neglect the value of tools, seeds, transport costs and taxes, so numerous at that time? Quite simply, because, in the state of knowledge relative to the entity to be managed, it only appeared useful *to him* to record the former costs. Why, in early medieval commercial accounting, does one find only accounts of creditors and debtors? Once again, because they were the only facts which they believed useful to record.

This lesson from history is not, however, acceptable to Chambers (1966a, pp. 345–6):

> The development of accounting practice, the adoption and abandonment of principles or rules, merely on the basis of what was useful or justifiable at some time results in private usefulness (for concealment or other tactical effects) being accepted as equally good grounds with general informativeness. Communicative and uncommunicative practices alike may thus be justified.

Thus, although Littleton and Zimmerman (1962, p. 254) could find in accounting a discernible pattern of continuity in the midst of change, a tendency for the ideas that persist to be the useful ones, and a demonstrated capacity for accounting to make substantial contributions to society, Chambers sees only a tendency towards the diffuseness of ideas and diversity of practices (1966a, p. 359) and a series of disconnected episodes rather than a history of development (1966b, p. 38). Littleton's views have been characterized as 'accounting Darwinism': accounting is continually in evolution, and the elements that have withstood the succession of challenges have, at least thus far, earned a place in current practice (American Accounting Association, 1977, p. 9).

Watts and Zimmerman (1979), on the other hand, argue against such a public interest explanation. Their hypothesis is that much of accounting theory is the product of government intervention and that accounting theory satisfies a 'demand for excuses'.

The Committee on Accounting History accepts without argument that accounting theory, practice and institutions have *evolved*. Is there a case for saying that there has been revolution rather than evolution? No accounting historian has discerned revolutions in accounting practice (if the invention of double entry was a revolution it was a very long drawn out one) but Wells (1976) has suggested that financial accounting *thought* is undergoing a revolution.

To what extent have accounting historians achieved the objectives set out above? I shall attempt to answer this question by looking at four areas which have attracted their attention:

(i) double entry;
(ii) corporate financial reporting;
(iii) accounting institutions;
(iv) accounting history in relation to economic history and business history.

These four areas are illustrative only. There is no space, for example, to look at the important area of cost and management accounting (on which see Garner (1954); Solomons (1968); Parker (1969); Pollard (1965); Wells (1978)).

Double Entry

The reasons for studying the history of double entry (which not so long ago would have been regarded as forming the bulk, if not the entirety, of accounting history) are intellectual rather than utilitarian. The study of the double entry of the past has not led to any improvements in the present practice of double entry. It *could* have done, by demonstrating, for example, that such frills as 'To' and 'By' were only the vestiges of an historical development but it did not, in fact, do so. The dropping of 'To' and 'By' was, in fact, brought about mainly by the mechanization of book-keeping. On the other hand, researchers have tackled with some success the intellectual tasks of explaining where, why and how double entry originated, developed and spread and what influence, if any, double entry had on its environment.

The best account in English of the origins of double entry is still that by Raymond de Roover (1956). It needs to be supplemented by G. A. Lee (1973 and 1977). According to de Roover, double entry developed in Italy in response to the needs of nascent capitalism. Italian business organization was already so complex by the 14th century that merchants could not get along without an efficient system of book-keeping. The three factors which contributed most to its development were partnership (which led to the recognition of the firm as an entity distinct from its owners), credit and agency. Accounting, as actually practised, was far ahead of the rather simple system described in the early treatises from 1494 onwards. Until about 1500 double entry was a business technique known only to Italian merchants. Double entry did not penetrate the rest of Europe until the invention of printing aided its diffusion. The 14th and 15th centuries were perhaps the most brilliant and progressive period in the history of accounting. There followed a long period of stagnation until the 19th century.

Double entry was thus one of the products of capitalism. Can it be argued with the same force that capitalism could not have developed without the help of double entry? This view, associated with Sombart (1921, vol. 2.1, pp. 118–25) and others has been summarized by Yamey (who does not share it) as follows:

> . . . systematic or scientific accounting, identified with the double-entry system, played an important part in releasing, activating, stimulating or accentuating the 'rationalistic pursuit of unlimited profits', an essential element in the capitalistic spirit . . . by transforming assets into abstract values and by expressing quantitatively the results of business activities, double-entry book-keeping clarified the aims of acquisitive business; moreover, it provided the rational basis on which the capitalist could choose the directions in which to employ his capital to best advantage; and finally, it made possible the separation of the business firm from its

owners and hence the growth of large joint-stock businesses. (Yamey, 1962.)

Sombart's propositions have led to much fruitful discussion among accounting historians, notably by Yamey (1949, 1962, 1975), Most (1972) and Winjum (1972). Winjum attempted to test the hypothesis by assessing the role of accounting in the economic development of England from 1500 to 1750, a period in which economic development and the growth of accounting knowledge occurred simultaneously. He concluded that although double entry had the potential to accomplish what was attributed to it by Sombart it did not, in fact, do so. Its great practical contribution was instead that of a comprehensive record of past activities and present assets and liabilities.

Accounting history is a history of thought as well as practice and much effort has been devoted to a study of early books on double entry, beginning with Luca Pacioli's *Summa* of 1494. Researchers have interested themselves, especially, in the extent to which the early writers borrowed, almost always without acknowledgement, from each other. The writings of Jan Ympyn of Antwerp provide an example. The extent of Ympyn's debt to Pacioli is disputed; his book was the first text on double entry in both Dutch and French and the earliest to survive in English. The title of the English edition, which has been reproduced and discussed by Kojima and Yamey (1975), illustrates how 'the Italian method' spread throughout Europe:

> A Notable and very excellente woorke, expressyng and declarying the maner and forme how to kepe a boke of accomptes or reconynges . . . Translated with greate Diligence out of the Italian toung into Dutche, and out of Dutche, into French, and now out of Frenche into Englishe.

Double entry was still being diffused in the 19th century, e.g. into Japan after the Meiji restoration (Nishikawa, 1956).

A great deal of work has been done by historians and economists on the diffusion of techniques (Rogers, 1971). Accounting historians have discussed diffusion (Tritschler, 1970; Parker, 1977a) but no-one has yet looked at double entry in this context.

Corporate Financial Reporting: Predictions and Perspectives

Accounting historians have so far shown less interest in the development of corporate financial reporting than in double entry (Lee and Parker, 1979). Financial reporting is an area in which utilitarian ends can be argued to be as important as intellectual ones. Can one hope, as the AAA Committee 1970 suggests, that 'Given an understanding of the past interaction of the environment and changes in accounting practices and institutions it may become somewhat easier to predict the consequences of currently proposed solutions'? Goldberg (1974) has his doubts:

> For prediction in this sense implies a basically mechanistic view of the universe and all that happens in it—a view that was widely accepted a hundred years or so ago among scientists and many others but which, I believe, has been largely discarded by the thinkers of the century in which we happen to find ourselves living. A mechanistic view is appropriate to mechanical systems, of course, but not to everything in the universe, and, I suggest, certainly not to much that relates to human behaviour.

It is, in fact, difficult to find overtly predictive papers in the accounting history literature. Mumford (1979) is an exception. He discerns eight stages in two British inflation accounting cycles and finds the steps so predictable that they could be described as 'a blueprint for the next surge of inflation'. He believes the cycle could only be broken by a programme of research.

Moonitz (1974) has argued from historical evidence that a professional accounting body, acting by itself, cannot agree upon a set of accounting standards, much less enforce it in practice. Chatov (1975) has used the historical record to question why standards of corporate financial reporting, power over which was granted by the U.S. federal government to the Securities and Exchange Commission, are partly controlled by a private accounting group.

Other writers have placed more stress on the possibility of gaining perspective on current problems. Lee (1979) argues that:

> The upheaval of recent events in financial accounting may have persuaded many accountants that these are uniquely critical times for their profession. However, to do so would be to view the present too narrowly and without a relevant context. The problems of accounting must be placed within a wider perspective, otherwise they may appear to be more troublesome than they deserve. The most relevant context appears to be the historical one, in which the problems of today can be seen also to have been the problems of yesterday. In other words they are long-lasting problems, and may not lend themselves to permanent solutions.

Inflation accounting, for example, regarded by so many as a 'new' problem, has been discussed many times within the last sixty years (Zeff, 1976). Is any real progress being made, or is accounting thought merely moving in circles, rediscovering what was known a generation ago? Whittington (1980) concludes that progress has been made, even if the pace leaves something to be desired. He suggests that one should read earlier writers not in the hope of rediscovering ancient truths but 'to gain a perspective of how present-day ideas have evolved and, perhaps, by reading the original statements of important ideas, to see them more vividly and understand them more clearly'.

Accounting Institutions

Accounting institutions and their members attracted historical attention as early as the 1890s in Worthington's pioneer work *Professional Accountants: an Historical Sketch* (1895). Brown's *History of Accounting and Accountants* (1905), written to celebrate the first fifty years of chartered accountancy in Scotland, devotes much attention to this subject and is still well worth reading.

Worthington states in his preface that he 'whether to his disadvantage or otherwise, is in no way connected with any Association of Accountants'. Brown, on the other hand, was Secretary and President of the Edinburgh Society and very much an insider and most of the histories of the professional bodies (e.g. Garrett, 1961; Institute of Chartered Accountants of Scotland, 1954; Institute of Chartered Accountants in England and Wales, 1966; Carey, 1969 and 1970) and of particular firms (e.g. Cooper Brothers and Co., 1954; Winsbury, 1977) have been written, often not very critically, from the inside. A rather less loving account by a semi-outsider is Stacey's *English Accountancy: A Study in Social and Economic History, 1800–1954* (1954).

Table 11.1 shows how mightily accountants have grown in numbers in the British Isles not only since the granting of a charter to the Society of Accountants in Edinburgh in 1854, but also since Brown's fiftieth anniversary celebrations of that event. At the same time the larger firms have grown in size not only in absolute terms, but also relative to the size of the smaller (Briston, 1979). Professional accountancy has become international and has become dominated by such multinationals as Peat, Marwick, Mitchell & Co.; Price Waterhouse & Co.; Deloitte Haskins and Sells; Coopers & Lybrand and the rest—all familiar in our mouths as household words.

The questions to ask seem obvious. Why did a new profession grow up in the 19th century? Why has it been so successful? Who were the men who

Table 11.1

	1904	*1957*	*1977–79*	
Scottish chartered accountants	906	6,187	9,812	(8/9/78)
English chartered accountants	3,177	20,124	68,010	(5/6/79)
Irish chartered accountants	62	1,044	3,257	(31/7/77)
Incorporated accountants	2,068	11,335	—	
	6,213	38,690	81,079	

Sources: R. Brown (ed.), *History of Accounting and Accountants* (Edinburgh: Jack, 1905); A. A. Garrett, *History of the Society of Incorporated Accountants 1885–1957* (Oxford 1961); Lists of Members.

founded the new profession? Who was Peat? Who was Price? Were they typical? Why have their firms grown into multinationals?

According to Johnson (1972, p. 52):

> The conditions for professionalism developed in Britain in the second half of the nineteenth century in association with the rise to power of an urban middle class, which provided an expanding market for various services based largely on individual needs, whether private or entrepreneurial.

He sees the profession as at first subservient to business interests and as a 'prop of capitalism', subject to 'corporate patronage', but later also an instrument of the State in its role of mediating between producers and consumers. In such a situation, writes Johnson, 'The accountants could not lose' (Johnson, pp. 73–4). As their corporate patrons expanded multinationally so did the accounting firms.

Johnson, perhaps, treats accountants as more passive than they are and were. The British profession has shown a notable ability to adapt its skills to the changing needs of the consumers (users) of its services—at first creditors, later shareholders, managers, taxpayers and others (Parker, 1977b). The British legal profession, it could be argued, has shown less ability to adapt.

Johnson goes on to argue that the emerging urban middle class of 19th century Britain not only created an expanding demand for professional services, but also provided recruits for the growing ranks of professionals. 'Middle-class power provided the basis from which the expanding "professions" created their own autonomous organizations' (Johnson, 1972, p. 52). Insufficient detailed work has been done on the 'recruits' to the accountancy profession. In making a modest attempt at such work (Parker, forthcoming) I found it surprisingly difficult to obtain information about some of the early leaders (Price, for example).

Pixley (1852–1933), a self-proclaimed father of the accountancy profession (Kitchen and Parker, 1980), claimed in 1894 that:

> Those who have been articled to our members since the date of the charter (1880) come from the same class as do those who are now at Woolwich, Sandhurst, and the Inns of Court. They have been educated at the same class of schools . . . (Pixley, 1897, p. 128).

Such statements can only be checked by the compilation and analysis of collective biographies. Short, individual biographies of Scottish chartered accountants from 1854 to 1879 are already available (Stewart, 1977) and Kedslie of the University of Dundee is preparing a collective biography for the period 1854–1904 which shows that 60 per cent of Scottish chartered accountants went to fee-paying schools. Much larger numbers and the scattered nature of the sources make a collective biography of English chartered accountants much more difficult and none has been attempted.

Johnson (1972, Ch. 5) has used his corporate patronage model to explain the accountancy profession's approach to theory. He argues that a major criterion of theory in such a situation will be its applicability to the needs of the patron. Knowledge tends to be particularistic in content and local in orientation. Professional associations will be apathetic to the development of basic knowledge through research, since such knowledge appears to be less important than knowledge which is applicable to the current practical needs of the patron. Johnson's approach may be contrasted with that of Watts and Zimmerman (1979) already described. These 'theories about theories' can only be tested by looking at the historical evidence.

A study of the development of accounting institutions serves both intellectual and utilitarian ends. It emphasizes their changing rôle and the way in which accountants have responded to, or been moulded by, their environment. There is nothing inevitable in present institutional arrangements or accounting theories. Both have changed and are changing. To understand how and why is both a stimulating intellectual exercise and a guide to policy-makers.

Accounting History and Economic and Business History

How valid is the claim that a study of accounting history can contribute to a better understanding of economic and business history? For the economic or business historian, accounting is mainly a tool, a means to an end. Advice on how the historian can make use of accounting techniques is available from Yamey (1960). It is given to few to be equally renowned as economic historians and accounting historians. The shining exception is de Roover, as illustrated, for example, by his 'The Story of the Alberti Company of Florence 1302–48, as revealed in its Account Books' (1958). De Roover, it has been aptly said, studied mercantile capitalism through 'a close and hard examination of the merchant in his counting-house, an understanding of what he counted, how he counted and how he directed his complex affairs' (Herlihy, 1972).

Baxter's *House of Hancock* (1945) is a business history of 18th century Boston which could only have been written by an accountant. Looking at a very different period of American history, Johnson (1975a) has argued that accounting historians can contribute significantly to the understanding of the development of big business. He has illustrated this in his studies of E. I. du Pont de Nemours Powder Company, 1903–12 (1975b) and of General Motors in the 1920s (1978).

Sometimes, indeed, it is the mainstream historian not the accounting historian who is master of the necessary accounting skills. A recent example is Dom Hockey's edition of *The Account-Book of Beaulieu Abbey* (1975), a 13th century account-book described by Harvey (Hockey, 1974) as:

perhaps the most extraordinary monument to survive of the early history of accounting in England: a volume containing a specimen annual account not only for each of the abbeys, manors and granges, but also for every other officer or servant who had funds entrusted to his care, some fifty different accounts in all, interspersed with rules and tables for checking the accuracy of the accounts and the honesty of the officials.

No *accountant* historian is likely to acquire a deeper knowledge of the accounting methods of the medieval English Exchequer and the use of pipe rolls than is displayed by Charles Johnson in his edition (1950) of the *Dialogus de Scaccario*, or in his introduction to Stenton's edition (1925) of *The Great Roll of the Pipe for the Second Year of the Reign of King Richard the First*. What he can do, however, is to ask whether any lessons can be learned from these methods. Accounting historians trained in modern accounting techniques have too often uncritically assumed that the double entry, balance sheets and profit and loss accounts which they are so used to are necessarily 'better' than other forms of accounting.

Historians writing accounting history have had less narrow viewpoints. Jack, in 'An Historical Defence of Single-Entry Book-keeping' argues that:

> Medieval accounts . . . were public accounts, kept because it was necessary to settle affairs between one man and another whether the two were King and subject, man and servant, fellow servants or independent individuals.
>
> As such the method of auditing and the ethics and morality which developed around them in some ways more nearly anticipate mid-nineteenth century developments than do the practices associated with the mercantile book-keeping on which accountants have concentrated so much attention (Jack, 1966, p. 158).

Similarly, Ramsey has written of Tudor accounting that:

> . . . the distinction between business and private affairs would have seemed meaningless to a sixteenth-century merchant, who was not accountable to anyone but himself. The absence of the modern profit and loss account and balance sheet, in fact, mattered little before the advent of the modern shareholder and tax-collector. The experienced Tudor merchant undoubtedly had a perfectly clear idea of the progress of his affairs whatever the technical deficiencies of his book-keeping (Ramsey, 1956, p. 201).

And Clanchy (1979, p. 96) writes of the tallies used by the English Exchequer that they:

> were not a primitive survival from the preliterate past, but a sophisticated and practical record of numbers. They were more convenient to

> keep and store than parchments, less complex to make, and no easier to forge . . . the earliest records of the Exchequer were deliberately destroyed because they were in a medium, wood, which was too uncouth for scholars to appreciate.

These historical reflections should help us appreciate better the increasing modern dissatisfaction with the balance sheet and the profit or loss account as the only, or even the main, financial statements. The profit and loss account, in particular, embodies an important assumption about the dominant role of the shareholder.

Accounting records of little interest to those concerned with developments in accounting thought or practice can be of immense use even to the literary historian: for example, the life of Lord Byron has recently been illuminated through his accounts (Moore, 1974). Conversely, literary historians have found themselves researching the lives of accountants: for example, James Peele, the author of two of the earliest (1553 and 1569) English works on book-keeping and the father of the Elizabethan dramatist George Peele (Horne, 1952).

The benefits of collaboration between accounting and other historians are clearly reciprocal. Surprisingly, the marked trend towards a more quantitative approach to economic history has evoked little response from accounting historians. It is difficult to think of examples in the accounting literature other than Deakin's study (1976) of the effect of enforced increases in disclosure in the 1930s on the behaviour of securities returns. (There are related articles by Stigler (1964) and Benston (1973) in the economic literature.) The compilation and analysis of collective biographies will, of course, involve some statistics and a fair amount of computer time.

Encouraging Research into Accounting History

It is hoped that this paper has demonstrated that accounting history is a worthwhile activity. Most accountants, however, for reasons for which accounting history helps to provide an explanation, are not educated and trained in an environment which encourages them towards research. Also, the very success of the profession has meant that academic accounting has little financial appeal—and anyone suited to accountancy is unlikely to be completely indifferent to monetary reward.

What then should be done? It is suggested that in accounting history more co-operation between accountants and historians willing to work in fields of interest to accountants should be encouraged. There have, in fact, been several recent collaborations of this nature (e.g. Edwards and Baber, 1979).

What topics, in particular, should British accounting historians be encouraged to research? The following criteria (which take account of shortages of both money and manpower) may help us to make a choice:

(a) the research data should be available in the U.K.;
(b) the research should preferably have both intellectual and utilitarian objectives;
(c) any research assistants necessary need not be qualified accountants;
(d) the research results should be of interest to a wider audience than accounting historians alone, e.g. to accountants who are not historians or to historians who are not accountants;
(e) some moderate use of quantitative techniques.

Three topics in 19th and 20th century British accounting history which meet these criteria, and in the first two of which I must disclose a personal interest, are:

(a) the development of company financial reporting;
(b) a collective biography of English chartered accountants; and
(c) the development of cost and management techniques in relation to the development of large enterprises.

A research programme on these lines would prove of great value to accountants and historians alike.

References

American Accounting Association, Committee on Accounting History, *Accounting Review*, Supplement to vol. XLV (1970).

American Accounting Association, Committee on Concepts and Standards for External Financial Reports, *Statement on Accounting Theory and Theory Acceptance*. American Accounting Association (1977).

Baxter, W. T., *House of Hancock*. Harvard University Press (1945); reprinted Russell and Russell (1965).

Benston, G. J., 'Required Disclosure and the Stock Market: An Evaluation of the Securities Exchange Act of 1945', *American Economic Review* (March 1973).

Briston, R. J., 'The UK Accountancy Profession—the Move towards Monopoly Power', *Accountant's Magazine* (November 1979).

Brown, R. (ed.), *History of Accounting and Accountants* (Jack, 1905; reprinted Franklin, 1966).

Carey, J. L., *The Rise of the Accounting Profession* (American Institute of Certified Public Accountants, 2 vols. 1969 and 1970).

Chambers, R. J., 'A Theory of the Development of Accounting Practices', pp. 341–363 of his *Accounting Evaluation and Economic Behavior*. Prentice-Hall (1966a).

Chambers, R. J., 'The Development of Accounting Theory', pp. 18–35 of Chambers, R. J., Goldberg, L. and Mathews, R. L. (eds.), *The Accounting Frontier*. F. W. Cheshire (1966b).

Chatov, R., *Corporate Financial Reporting—Public or Private Control*. The Free Press (1975).

Clanchy, M. T., *From Memory to Written Record. England 1066–1307*. Edward Arnold (1979).

Cooper Brothers & Co., *A History of Cooper Brothers & Co. 1854 to 1954*. Privately published by B. T. Batsford (1954).

Deakin, E. B., 'Accounting Reports, Policy Interventions and the Behavior of Securities Returns', *The Accounting Review* (July 1976).

De Roover, R., 'The Development of Accounting Prior to Luca Pacioli according to the Account-Books of Medieval Merchants', pp. 114–174 of Littleton and Yamey (1956).

De Roover, R., 'The Story of the Alberti Company of Florence, 1302–1348, as Revealed in its Account Books', *Business History Review* (Spring 1958) 14–59; reprinted in his *Business, Banking and Economic Thought in Late Medieval and Early Modern Europe*. University of Chicago Press (1974).

Edwards, J. R. and Baber, C., 'Dowlais Iron Company: Accounting Policies and Procedures for Profit Measurement and Reporting Purposes', *Accounting and Business Research* (Spring 1979).

Garner, S. P., *Evolution of Cost Accounting to 1925*. University of Alabama Press (1954).

Garrett, A. A., *History of the Society of Incorporated Accountants 1885–1957*. Oxford University Press (1961).

Goldberg, L., 'The Future of the Past in Accounting', *Accountant's Magazine* (October 1974).

Haskins, C. W., *Business Education and Accountancy*. Harper (1904); reprinted Arno Press (1978).

Herlihy, D., 'Raymond de Roover, Historian of Mercantile Capitalism', *Journal of European Economic History* (Winter 1972).

Hockey, S. F. (ed.), *The Beaulieu Cartulary*. Southampton University Press, Southampton Records Series, v. 17 (1974).

Hockey, S. F. (ed.), *The Account-Book of Beaulieu Abbey*. Royal Historical Society, Camden Fourth Series, v. 16 (1975).

Horne, D. H., *The Life and Minor Works of George Peele*. Yale University Press (1952).

ICAEW, *The History of the Institute of Chartered Accountants in England and Wales 1880–1965 and of its founder accountancy bodies 1870–1880*. Heinemann (1966).

ICAS, *A History of the Chartered Accountants of Scotland from the Earliest Times to 1954*. ICAS (1954).

Jack, S. M., 'An Historical Defence of Single Entry Book-keeping', *Abacus* (December 1966).

Johnson, C. (trans. and ed.), *Dialogues de Scaccario*. Nelson (1950).

Johnson, H. T., 'Management Accountancy in an Early Integrated Industrial: E. I. du Pont de Nemours Powder Company, 1903–1912', *Business History Review* (Summer 1975b).

Johnson, H. T., 'The Role of Accounting History in the Study of Modern Business Enterprise', *The Accounting Review* (July 1975a).

Johnson, H. T., 'Management Accounting in an Early Multidivision Organization: General Motors in the 1920s', *Business History Review* (Winter 1978).

Johnson, T. J., *Professions and Power*. Macmillan (1972).
Kitchen, J. and Parker, R. H., *Accounting Thought and Education: Six English Pioneers*. ICAEW (1980).
Kojima, O. and Yamey, B. S. (eds.), *A notable and very excellente woorke*. Daigakudo Shoten (1975).
Lee, G. A., 'The Development of Italian Bookkeeping 1211–1300', *Abacus* (December 1973).
Lee, G. A., 'The Coming of Age of Double Entry: The Giovanni Farolfi Ledger of 1299–1300', *Accounting Historians Journal* (Fall 1977).
Lee, T. A., 'The Evolution and Revolution of Financial Accounting: a Review Article', *Accounting and Business Research* (Autumn 1979).
Lee, T. A. and Parker, R. H., *The Evolution of Corporate Financial Reporting*. Nelson (1979).
Littleton, A. C. and Yamey, B. S., *Studies in the History of Accounting*. Sweet and Maxwell (1956); reprinted Arno Press (1978).
Littleton, A. C. and Zimmerman, V. K., *Accounting Theory: Continuity and Change*. Prentice-Hall (1962).
Moonitz, M., *Obtaining Agreement on Standards in the Accounting Profession*. American Accounting Association, Studies in Accounting Research, No. 8 (1974).
Moore, D. L., *Lord Byron Accounts Rendered*. David Murray (1974).
Most, K. S., 'Sombart's Propositions Revisited', *The Accounting Review* (October 1972).
Mumford, M., 'The End of a Familiar Inflation Accounting Cycle', *Accounting and Business Research* (Spring 1979).
Nishikawa, K., 'The Early History of Double-Entry Book-keeping in Japan', pp. 380–387 of Littleton and Yamey (1956).
Parker, R. H., *Management Accounting: An Historical Perspective*. Macmillan (1969).
Parker, R. H., 'Explaining National Differences in Consolidated Accounts', *Accounting and Business Research* (Summer 1977a).
Parker, R. H., *Men of Account* (University of Exeter, 1977b) reprinted as 'British Men of Account', *Abacus* (June 1978).
Parker, R. H., *British Accountants: A Biographical Sourcebook*. Arno Press (forthcoming).
Pixley, F. W., *The Profession of a Chartered Accountant*. Henry Good and Son (1897); reprinted Arno Press (1978).
Pollard, S., *The Genesis of Modern Management*. Edward Arnold (1965).
Pryce-Jones, J. and Parker, R. H., *Accounting in Scotland. A Historical Bibliography* (2nd edn.), ICAS (1976).
Ramsey, P., 'Some Tudor Merchants' Accounts', pp. 185–201 of Littleton and Yamey (1956).
Rogers, E. M. with Shoemaker, F. F., *Communication of Innovations* (2nd edn.). Free Press of Glencoe (1971).
Solomons, D., 'The Historical Development of Costing' in his *Studies in Cost Analysis*. Sweet and Maxwell (1968).
Sombart, W., *Der Moderne Kapitalismus* (4th edn.). Duncker & Humblot (1921).
Stacey, N. A. H., *English Accountancy: A Study in Social and Economic History, 1800–1954*. Gee (1954).

Stenton, D. M. (ed.), *The Great Roll of the Pipe for the Second Year of the Reign of King Richard the First*. Publications of the Pipe Roll Society, vol. 39, N.S., vol. 1 (1925).

Stewart, J. C., *Pioneers of a Profession*. ICAS (1977).

Stigler, G. J., 'Public Regulation of the Securities Markets', *Journal of Business* (April 1964).

Tritschler, C. A., 'A Sociological Perspective on Accounting Innovation', *International Journal of Accounting* (Spring 1970).

Vlaemminck, J. H., *Histoire et Doctrines de la Comptabilité*. Editions du Treurenberg (1956); reprinted Editions Pragnos (1979).

Watts, Ross L. and Zimmerman, Jerold L., 'The Demand for and Supply of Accounting Theories: The Market for Excuses', *The Accounting Review* (April 1979).

Wells, M. C., 'A Revolution in Accounting Thought?', *The Accounting Review* (July 1976).

Wells, M. C., *Accounting for Common Costs*. International Center for Education and Research in Accounting (1978).

Whittington, G., 'Pioneers of Income Measurement and Price-Level Accounting: a Review Article', *Accounting and Business Research* (Spring 1980).

Winjum, J. O., *The Role of Accounting in the Economic Development of England: 1500–1750*. Center for International Education and Research in Accounting (1972).

Winsbury, R., *Thomson McLintock & Co.—The First Hundred Years*. Thomson McLintock (1977).

Worthington, B., *Professional Accountants*. Gee (1895); reprinted Arno Press (1978).

Yamey, B. S., 'Scientific Bookkeeping and the Rise of Capitalism', *Economic History Review* (June 1949).

Yamey, B. S., 'Business Accounts', pp. 30–36 of Barker, T. C., Campbell, R. H. and Mathias, R., *Business History*. The Historical Association (1960).

Yamey, B. S., 'Notes on Double-Entry Bookkeeping and Economic Progress', *Journal of European Economic History* (Winter 1975).

Yamey, B. S., 'Accounting and the Rise of Capitalism: Further Notes on a Theme by Sombart', pp. 833–57 of *Studi in Onore di Amintore Fanfani* (Dott. A. Giuffre, 1962), reprinted in *Journal of Accounting Research* (Autumn 1964) and in Tucker, K. A., *Business History. Selected Readings*. Frank Cass (1977).

Yamey, B. S., *Essays on the History of Accounting*. Arno Press (1978).

Zeff, S. A. (ed.), *Asset Appreciation, Business Income and Price-Level Accounting: 1918–1935*. Arno Press (1976).

Commentary on 'The study of accounting history'

Anthony G Hopwood
Institute of Chartered Accountants; Professor of Accounting and Financial Reporting, London Graduate School of Business Studies

Parker is correct to start his paper by emphasizing the enormous increase in interest in accounting history. Compared with many other areas of accounting inquiry, it has shown a tremendous vitality in recent years, attracting younger scholars, many of whom, earlier, had demonstrated rather ahistorical concerns, and spawned an impressive investment in research groups, seminars and conferences, networks for the distribution of working papers and even a fully-fledged specialist journal.

Just why should this have been so? Of course, in part, at least, present interests undoubtedly reflect the efforts of those pioneers, much of whose work is reviewed by Parker. By slowly continuing with their investigations and concerns they have been able to demonstrate to a wider community the potential of their endeavours. Moreover, the impressive investments which accounting historians have made in an institutional infrastructure of networks, groups and symposia, no doubt, also has facilitated the growth of scholarship and research in the area—a factor which should not be ignored by those with other interests. However, important as these two factors might have been, I think that at least one other consideration has contributed to a more widespread acknowledgement of the rôle of historical inquiry. For the last few years have witnessed an increasing number of changes in the accounting domain: new institutions for accounting regulation have been established in many countries; fundamental debates have been initiated into accounting concepts and practices; and, practices themselves have been seen to be emergent in the realms of both financial reporting and management accounting. In such a context, it is hardly surprising that more emphasis has been placed on the dynamic features of accounting development and change. With the accounting present being seen as ever more problematic, more scholars have started to inquire into the processes through which it has come to be and through which it continues to change. In part, at least, such a combination of intellectual and utilitarian concerns, to use the phrases noted by Parker, have stimulated a more active and widespread concern with the historical development of the accounting craft.

Hardly surprisingly, many of the recent interests in accounting history differ from those that sustained inquiry in the days when the area only appealed to the few. With only intellectual curiosity influencing the paths of inquiry, emphasis was placed, as Parker notes, on the early development of accounting practice, particularly on the emergence of double entry book-keeping. As a result of such emphasis, however, we still have minimal insights into the development of forms of corporate reporting and of management accounting and control systems, the emergence of interests such as that of the State in the accounting domain, and the growing professionalization of the craft—paradoxically, the very subjects which have stimulated more recent interest in the historical area. Moreover, the more recent inquiries also have differed from at least some of those undertaken in the past in so far as they have articulated more explicitly a wider rationale for their concern with accounting history. For increasingly the development of technical practice is no longer seen as being of such interest in and of itself. Whilst an interest in accounting change undoubtedly remains, it is fair to say that today there is a much more active concern with understanding the processes underlying that change, the broader social, economic and institutional factors that both facilitate and constrain it, and the consequences which it has for organizational and social functioning.

What factors, some researchers are now asking, have facilitated the development of management accounting and control systems? What rôles did they play in the emergence of the modern organization? And what consequences have they had for its functioning and impacts? Similarly, others are starting to inquire into what factors might be behind the growing concern with the standardization of accounting practice. What might such an emphasis on the achievement of calculative order say about the changing structures of the societies in which we live, the growing power of the state and the rôles which accounting might play in the establishment of relationships of power and control?

In retrospect, it is a pity that Parker did not give more consideration to the rôle which historical inquiry can play, and, indeed, is playing, in the investigation of such substantive issues. For whilst he provides a useful and honest overview of much of the historical research undertaken to date, he does little to question, let alone criticize, the forms which it has and has not taken. Yet in view of the work that now has been done and that which is starting to be done, I think that such a critical survey of the area could provide a useful stimulus for further inquiry and debate.

Just why has so much of the research into accounting history emphasized the documentation of the technical to the detriment of any broader concern with the processes and consequences of accounting change? Also why has accounting history adopted until so very recently such an atheoretical stance? And why has it tended to remain so isolated from those patterns of intellectual development which have done so much to reconstitute historical inquiry into so many other significant economic and social institutions and practices in recent years? Indeed, why has it done so little to promote a consciousness of the problems of historical inquiry and reconstruction?

Although Parker has not provided answers to such questions, he has most certainly provided a survey which points to their significance.

12 Accounting research in the public sector

John R Perrin
Director of the Centre for Industrial, Economic and Business Research, University of Warwick

Accounting academics in Britain have been very slow to accept that the public sector offers distinctive accounting problems that may be amenable to useful and interesting research. Less than one per cent of the papers published in the two British academic accounting and finance journals during the decade of the 1970s were concerned specifically with accounting or finance in public-sector institutions. And yet the public sector accounts for well over one-third of all employment and gross domestic product in the U.K. Moreover, not only has public-sector accounting been neglected by the academics, but also it has not developed as a professional activity in many parts of the public sector to the same extent as in the private sector. Central government employs only a few hundred qualified accountants, and more in a consulting role than on accounting systems and reports, and their audit. The National Health Service employs four per cent of the total working population of the nation, but less than one per cent of the nation's qualified accountants. It appears that all aspects of accounting, and not least academic accounting research and publication, offer abundant scope for further development in the public sector.

A high proportion of the accounting problems met in dealing with current income and expenditure, and with the budgetary control of current operations, probably differ little between the private sector and the public sector (even including the non-trading part of the latter), except in two respects that may be important and also amenable to academic research. First, in the non-trading public sector the output very often consists of professional services (e.g. social service, teaching or clinical care). Furthermore, the professional person who acts as a line manager in directing the supply of these services may not himself hold budgetary responsibility (e.g. as with health-service clinicians), and even where he is a responsible budget-holder he may face, and have to adapt to, conflict between his roles as a professional person and as an operational manager. Secondly, even where the professional element of service provision is not so obvious or so personalized (e.g. in highway, sewage or electricity services), the profit-maximizing or cost-minimizing ethos of the private sector is muted, and may be in conflict with 'service' standards and other social and career value-systems to a much greater extent than in most institutions within the private sector.

The financing of, as distinct from accounting for, revenue does differ substantially among the different public-sector institutions, and this may offer scope for new research. Wider differences exist within the public sector in respect of the range of capital-asset financing and accounting practices, than in respect of revenue financing and accounting. Capital financing and accounting, and the derivative issues of capital amortization or depreciation that link capital to revenue funds and accounts, offer great research interest. Indeed, the problems involved in understanding and evaluating public-sector capital-asset accounting, amortization and depreciation, and the related issues of self-financing and capital maintenance, provide the main theme connecting the separate sections of this paper.

From a financial viewpoint the public sector can be considered in three parts. First, there is central government together with services under its immediate control, such as defence. Here the accounting systems in use are simple cash-accounting systems, allied to a financial information system based on central monitoring of progress to cash limits. Financing is from annual taxation and borrowing, and the financing of central government activities appears largely inseparable from the wider problems of national public finance, where the issues more directly affect the economics discipline than the accounting discipline. This paper will not consider central government accounting and finance further. Secondly, there are the nationalized industries together with certain lesser public corporations that 'trade' or at least raise their revenues by some system of fees for services, in a way independent of central-government allocation and regulation of public moneys. A number of topics of interest for accounting research in the nationalized industries will be discussed in the first main section of this paper. Thirdly, there are organizations that exist to provide public services, and that are funded wholly or largely by allocations of central-government tax revenues, or else by local rates (i.e. local property taxes). Prominent among these public-service organizations are health, water and local authorities: there are substantial and interesting differences in their respective financing and accounting systems, and these will be considered in the second main section of this paper. The paper will conclude with a section bringing together some topics of capital financing and accounting that are of general concern to both the nationalized industry and the public-service parts of the public sector.

Nationalized Industries

Central government has responsibility for three different forms of trading organizations. They are government 'trading funds', public companies in which the government holds all the shares or at the least a controlling interest, and the nationalized industries and other public corporations with trading activities. This section will concentrate upon the latter form, but brief explanation will be given of the first two.

The government has designated a few of its activities as 'trading funds' for the purpose of influencing management attitudes and operational performance, and it requires that these funds should maintain accounts and prepare accounting reports according to best commercial practice. The funds include operations such as the Royal Ordnance Factories and the Royal Mint, both of which have large sales to overseas customers and could be considered as suitable for nationalized industry status were it not for considerations of security and public policy which require closer control from government ministers than would be feasible under the normal arrangements for nationalized industries or other public corporations. Property Services Supply, which provides furnishings, design and other services and supplies primarily for non-industrial activities, is also organized as a trading fund—apparently, largely because its operations are directly comparable with private-enterprise operations outside government, and it is hoped that the use of commercial transfer prices encourages more rational spending decisions by user departments, in addition to stimulating commercial attitudes within the supply agency itself. The published accounts of the government trading funds are not so detailed, nor so well-supplemented by notes and additional information, as are the accounts of the main nationalized industries and private-sector companies of equivalent size. Nevertheless, some of the trading fund accounts are noteworthy for having adopted current cost accounting based on the Sandilands Report (1975) well in advance of public encouragement from government for the adoption of current cost accounting methods in the accounts of the nationalized industries and the private sector.

The second form of organization includes British Leyland, Rolls Royce and the companies taken over or formed by the National Enterprise Board, where the government is the dominant shareholder in companies operated under public company legislation, or where it is at least the major shareholder, as in British Petroleum. In these companies the accounting methods and reports follow the same general conventions as in private-enterprise firms, so that they offer nothing distinctive to discuss within the boundaries of this paper—although, of course, they pose a number of interesting economic and political questions.

The third main form of trading organization responsible to central government is the nationalized industry. Nationalized industries form a sub-set of 'public corporations' and it is not precisely clear what combination of criteria serve to justify the segregation of particular public corporations into the nationalized industry category, except, of course, in the case of the major undertakings that obviously comprise an entire industry or public utility on their own, and that have been nationalized out of private or local-authority ownership at some time in the past (e.g. British Rail or the electricity industry). For example, it is not immediately obvious why the British Broadcasting Corporation (which practises commercial accounting and is expected to be self-supporting within its revenue from fees and sales of programmes and publications, with subsidy only for overseas broadcasting services conducted as a matter of national policy) should be omitted from the category of nationalized industries, while British Rail (which receives massive social subsidies and in 1979/80 had the highest cash-limit allocation (i.e. deficit) of any organization with significant trading or fee-charging operations) is accepted within that category without question.

It is not essential to this paper to draw a sharp definitional boundary between nationalized industries and the remaining public corporations. On the contrary, the relevant point is to emphasize that any such boundary is arbitrary, however measured, on some composite weighting of factors such as monopoly power, public-service importance, or scale of subsidy received. Indeed, it may be more useful to view the public corporations as lying along a spectrum where the scale of the spectrum measures the degree of direct comparability to the commercial and financial organization and practices of private-sector trading enterprises.

To date, the nationalized industries, clustering towards one end of the spectrum, have attracted the greatest research interest. Presumably, this arises because the principal nationalized industries tend to be larger and to have a more visible daily impact upon everyday life, and to be more often in the news and in economic trouble, than is the case for most of the other public corporations. Economists have made the nationalized industries a major field for research, and for speculation on normative models for optimal scale, investment and pricing, etc. However, in contrast, accounting researchers have only just begun to study the nationalized industries seriously.

Likierman (1979) considered the reports and accounts of eighteen nationalized industries in his study. His list of eighteen includes all the larger industries but omits many of the smaller ones and kindred public corporations. Likierman's eighteen industries employ about seven per cent of the working population of the U.K. and account for almost 15 per cent of current new industrial and commercial capital formation. Most nationalized industries are considerably more capital-intensive than most private-sector enterprises. On an estimated current-cost valuation basis, British Gas in 1979 had about £75,000 of capital per worker, and the Electricity industry about £130,000, with probably a similar value in the telecommunications side of the Post Office. Whilst the most highly capital-intensive of the nationalized industries tend to be industries that have grown and been commercially successful in recent years, many even of the less successful nationalized industries have quite high capital intensity by private-sector standards. Indeed, it was inability to raise adequate capital in the light of their commercial records that brought about the virtual inevitability of nationalization for several of the industries. Moreover, aside from specialized problems of accountability and reporting that may arise generally from public ownership, it may be that the opportunities for distinctive accounting research in the nationalized industries relate particularly to the features associated with high capital-intensity—viz. asset specificity, long but problematic asset lives, uncertainty over appropriate valuation and depreciation methods, and also the problems derived from the scale of the interest burden on capital, exacerbated by high inflation.

Nationalized Industries' Accounts

The financial accounts and reports of the nationalized industries are prepared under government instructions to adhere to best commercial practice. The published accounts are audited under 'true and fair view' criteria by major professional firms. It might be inferred that nationalized industries offer no distinctive research interest in financial accounting and reporting, at least independent of the more general case of research concerned with all organizations (predominantly private sector) whose accounts and audits are conducted under the same precepts. However, it has been pointed out in a study commissioned by the Consumers' Association (CA, 1979) that there are quite a few audit qualifications to the recent published accounts of nationalized industries, and that it is, at present, not possible to compare the financial performance of the industries from their published accounts, nor to assess how they perform against the financial targets laid down for them by government. The authors of the study indicated also that they believed that the public is entitled to a greater degree of comparability between the accounts of nationalized industries than between the accounts of private-sector companies (CA, 1979, p. 23). The study reports on the difficulty of extracting information from the published accounts sufficient to enable them to be put into a comparable state by the external readers of the accounts, and it suggests that accounting policies appear to have been changed too frequently, and in ways that suggest that individual nationalized industries were influenced by the effect the changes would have upon their published profits (CA, 1979, pp. 21–3).

The cited report's conclusions may well be correct, but they are based upon a study of only eight nationalized industries. A fruitful possibility for further research would be the carrying out of a more detailed study, involving a larger number of nationalized industries and including also, for comparative purposes, an equal number of large private-sector companies. While such research, of itself, might not prove or disprove the hypothesis, it seems not implausible to suggest that, free of the degree of need existing in the private sector to validate the financial viability of an enterprise on behalf of individual shareholders and creditors, accountants and auditors in the nationalized industries may be less protected by their professional status to resist changes in accounting policies and methods, at least where these appear to be desired by the sponsoring government departments as well as by the management of particular nationalized industries.

Annual accounts and reports conventionally concentrate upon financial and other commercial information: traditionally, they have not sought to report upon wider social or economic performance in any regular, structured or quantified manner. The nationalized industries have been asked to determine and report upon selected key non-financial performance indicators, but when these are fully developed it seems likely that they will concentrate upon economic performance rather than upon wider social issues. Whilst nationalized industries already include more extensive supplementary information in their public reports than do many private-sector firms as regards health and safety at work, environmental impact, strategic planning and the implications and outcomes of particular initiatives, disclosure in these matters doubtless still offers much opportunity for experiment and improvement. The form of disclosure, and the underlying critical factors and methods for their objective measurement, are all matters offering research opportunities. Indeed, one team of researchers under Dr R. A. Bryer of Warwick University is currently working with steelworkers on an action-research project to study how workers' union representatives use accounting and related information in negotiations (e.g. concerning plant closures), what further information they need, and the implications for fuller disclosure by management.

Nationalized Industries' Capital Structure

The most obvious difference between the published accounts of nationalized industries and those of public companies is in the composition of the capital section of the balance sheet. Nationalized industries do not have equity share capital in the commercial sense, although four of the eighteen industries included in the Likierman study (1979, p. 10) had a proportion of their capital in what is termed 'public dividend capital', on which dividends are payable when trading profits and cash-limits performance permits. Whereas in private industry the amount of dividend declarations is in the hands of the company board alone, although with due regard for market pressures, in general it appears that government ministers may have at least as much say as do the industries' boards in determining the declaration of nationalized industry dividends, and their size.

Apart from British Steel, none of the financially weaker nationalized industries have any public dividend capital, nor, generally, do they have significant earned reserves from trading. Thus, nearly all their active capital is loan-financed and attracting interest charges regardless of trading success or failure, from year to year. This handicap to commercial flexibility, and to comparability with private-sector firms, was noted and criticized in a study published by the National Economic Development Office (NEDO, 1976). It is an especially severe handicap for those industries exposed to cyclical market fluctuations, or to direct market competition (e.g. British Steel). While for the public sector it has been traditional for research and policy advice on financial matters to be provided by economists rather than by accountants, there appears to be no reason why academic accountants should not extend their research remit for the public sector into the problems of determining optimal capital structure and financing for nationalized industries and other public corporations.

Likierman (1979, p. 13) notes the considerable difference in average interest rates paid on loan capital by different nationalized industries (dependent on the timing of their past needs of major capital for growth, modernization or refinancing), and he points out the argument for a uniform interest rate—essentially equity and comparability between the separate industries—while noting also the opportunity-cost argument that, if managements choose to borrow at times of high interest rates, this should be reflected in their accounts. To do otherwise would be to distort the working of the capital market as a rationing and balancing mechanism between the needs of the nationalized industries and other borrowers.

Nationalized Industries' Depreciation and Profitability

Turning to the asset side of the balance sheet, differences from typical private-sector firms are not so obvious. However, given that most nationalized industries are relatively capital-intensive, it is not surprising that the asset structure often contains relatively high proportions of fixed assets, and relatively low proportions of working capital. Where the bulk of the fixed assets have a long life, are very specific to one particular use and site, and are associated with wide bands of uncertainty regarding their future economic life and possible technical or market obsolescence, then enormous problems arise in the determination of depreciation charges, and in associated revaluations and write-offs. The problems associated with depreciation and revaluation become magnified once inflation and accounting for changing prices are taken into account. Indeed, the nationalized industries have attracted considerable criticism in Parliament, and in articles in the financial and professional press, because of popular suspicion that the treatments given in some cases to depreciation, deferred charges and revaluations, were chosen more particularly to justify desired levels of reported profits, or of prices, than because of any clear economic or accounting logic. The British Gas Corporation has been a particular target for criticism, being examined by Wright (1980), while more general discussions of the nationalized industries' problems of accounting for fixed assets during inflation also have been published (CA, 1979; Wright, 1979). Ample scope exists for further research on the nationalized industries' fixed-asset and depreciation accounting practices to date; their likely validity; their impact on prices, profits and cash flows available for investment; and the implications for them of the new accounting standard for inflation, SSAP 16 (ASC, 1980).

Although SSAP 16 will expect nationalized industries to give prominence in their income statements to profit after tax but before interest (which should aid comparability between industries), it will not require a capital gearing adjustment in respect of the proportion of loan-financed capital. This reflects the reality of a government decision, rather than any consensus that capital gearing adjustments are, beyond doubt, conceptually irrelevant to public-sector institutions. A research project might usefully estimate the size of the forgone capital gearing adjustments for the nationalized industries, and speculate on the likely effect of the gearing-adjustment exemption upon financial targets, financial results, and pricing policy.

Reference has already been made to the diverse levels of profitability among nationalized industries, to the differing levels of capital-intensity, to the variation in the average rates of interest paid, and to the variation in the proportions of real capital on which loan interest is paid. The variability in these factors, and certainly the variability in reported profits, is probably greater than among large private companies, and the average return lower (CA, pp. 1 and 13). Variability is reduced if profit is measured and compared before deduction of interest (or dividends, where they infrequently arise), but although this may make the returns more directly comparable in respect of matters under a high degree of control by management (which in the public sector, by and large, exclude financial structures and interest rates), such comparisons are misleading for purposes of economic evaluation of overall performance, investment decisions or the pricing of output dependent on new investment. All these issues have been of concern to economists, and to governmental and advisory bodies: for example, see Turvey (1969), HMSO (1961 and 1967), Tivey (1973), Webb (1973), NEDO (1976). However, this paper has no brief to explore such wider aspects of economic debate, and, indeed, little interest in these matters has been demonstrated by accountants in their academic research and publication.

Nationalized Industries' Investment and Financial Targets

Prior to 1978, guidance to nationalized industries and some other public bodies regarding their investment policies required a test discount rate (TDR) to be applied in discounted cash flow appraisals (HMSO, 1967). The TDR was set at eight per cent, and, for a time, at ten per cent. But a TDR to be applied *ex ante* in a net present value analysis of incremental investment projects provides no proper indication of acceptable rates of return measured *ex post* in terms of conventional accounting profitability—especially given rising inflation and the incompatibility between accounting depreciation and the annuity depreciation implicit in the DCF appraisal model (and distortion is the more pronounced in the case of long-life assets and lengthy investment projects). The need for guidance on financial and other objectives and measures of performance was amongst proposals in the report from the National Economic Development Office (NEDO, 1976). Subsequently, the government issued a White Paper, *The Nationalized Industries* (HMSO, 1978). The 1978 White Paper included provision for abandoning the use of the test discount rate and substituting a five per cent real rate of return to be applied over and above the rate of inflation on the appraisal of new investment programmes as a whole (**n.b.**, the alternative rate of seven per cent was suggested for use where appropriate in the non-market branches of the public sector). In addition, financial targets were to be agreed with each separate nationalized industry or other relevant institution. These targets would be related to current accounting and financial-performance information, would be negotiated and agreed separately for each institution, and would take account of market prospects, the scope for improved efficiency, the opportunity cost of capital, and other criteria specific to each industry or institution. Each financial target would be reviewed every few years.

The initial round of financial targets have been agreed with the major nationalized industries (for summaries see CA, 1979, p. 20; Likierman, 1979, p. 31). These financial targets range from 'break-even', which is, typically, the long-term financial objective already specified for nationalized industries in governing legislation (although it is not always clear that the full costs of capital and of inflation are required to be included in the break-even requirement), through positive net returns relative to historic costs, on to a positive net return after all costs including adjustments to depreciation for inflation. There are also two examples of targets based on profit related to turnover rather than to capital (i.e. assets employed): these are British Gas and the postal services, conventionally viewed as occupying almost the extreme opposite ends of the profitability league table amongst nationalized industries.

Likierman considers the relative merits of alternative types of financial targets (1979, pp. 16–21), and the Consumers' Association study concludes that the diversity of financial targets in use, and the variations in what is included in their measurement, makes it almost impossible to make useful comparisons of performance between separate industries. Part of the non-comparability problem can be explained by recent uncertainty over adoption of inflation-adjusted accounts, so within a few years the diversity may be reduced. For the present, however, the diversity offers opportunity for research into the validity of the differences in the targets in use, and into methods of reconciling the differences so as to generate performance figures more directly comparable between separate industries.

In addition to the financial objectives and targets, and the required rates of return criteria for investment planning—all of which may be viewed as prescribing a norm for performance which may be achieved, on average, over a period of years, but which may not necessarily be achieved or achievable in each separate year—there are certain financial regulations for the nationalized industries that may be described as constraints, not to be exceeded. These include predetermined levels of grant or subsidy for the supply of specified services, or agreed limits on overall operating losses. Generally, however, the definitive constraint is the 'cash-limit' system of public expenditure control. Whereas in the case of the non-market public-sector institutions, the cash limit defines total allowed-expenditure during each budget year, in the nationalized industries the cash limit excludes all expenditure directly financed by current trading revenue, but includes all other external cash-flow needs (e.g. capital expenditure, working capital increments, and operational losses, whether funded from governmental sources or from private financial markets). The function of the cash-limits system is to control public expenditure, and, thus, to facilitate control of public borrowing and growth in the money supply. It is the government's intention that cash limits should *not* be exceeded without strong justification, and without the knowledge and consent of relevant government departments.

A nationalized industry that requires no external funds, and, thus, can accept a zero cash limit, may be said to be in a state of 100 per cent self-financing. Alternatively, self-financing might conceal the arbitrary use of monopoly power in certain circumstances, whereby prices are set high to generate cash for the net expansion of capital resources.

It may be argued that the accrual accounting systems operated by the nationalized industries under the 'best commercial practice' requirement should signal any expansion of capital resources otherwise disguised within self-financing, but, given capital-intensive long-life assets whose real useful life is very much a matter of judgment, it is very difficult to be certain that depreciation charges (especially where augmented for inflation) do not overstate real economic depreciation and, thus, conceal the degree of real capital expansion occurring. The problem seems likely to be significant only where prices, fees or other revenues can be levied at managerially-determined cost-plus rates, without material constraint from market or regulatory forces. This problem poses concern for the regional water authorities even more than for the main nationalized industries. Resolving the problem needs consideration of whether or not public bodies are obliged to maintain a constant stock of capital resources, and, when the stock is enlarged or contracted, whether current consumers (or taxpayers or ratepayers) should pay the costs of service improvement or expansion, or only the later generations who will receive the benefit. These issues are of even greater social importance, possibly, in the non-market public services than in the nationalized industries, so further discussion will be left until the final section of the paper. Even for the nationalized industries, however, the problems of measurement and reporting of self-financing, of performance to cash limits and financial targets, and of associated difficulties in the measurement of depreciation and inflation effects, should provide interesting scope for new accounting research.

The Public Services

This section considers a few of the research interests that exist in the non-market part of the public sector—the public services. Apart from central government and centrally-controlled services such as defence, most public services are organized on a local or regional basis. These public services often operate limited trading activities that may be asked to account on a commercial basis (e.g. local authority direct-works undertakings, or university vacation conference and holiday-accommodation enterprises), but the latter are not of the essence. In addition, there are particular major services occupying an uncertain borderland between commercial status and public-service status; notable among these are public transport undertakings and regional water authorities.

Except for shorter articles, largely in professional journals (e.g. *Public Finance and Accountancy*), very little research has been published by academic accountants on financial and accounting problems in the public services. Thus, here, even more than in the section on nationalized industries, the discussion will focus mainly on interesting topics for future research, rather than on published work, and will be based largely on the personal research experience of the author and his colleagues. The discussion will concentrate upon the health services, water (and sewage) services and local authorities, which together comprise the majority of locally-determined or locally-administered public services. The accounting systems of these three major public services are very different, arising from divergent methods of funding and of political accountability for the use of funds, different organizational arrangements, and accidents of history. An interesting research question is whether or not the latter factors are sufficient to justify the great differences in accounting systems—which differences are such as to prevent any meaningful comparisons of resource use and effectiveness across the three services. Space limitations prevent exhaustive explanation and comment on all three systems; attention will focus on aspects that are distinctively different from commercial accounting and from the practices followed in the nationalized industries.

The National Health Service

The National Health Service (NHS) employs one million persons and disposes of almost six per cent of gross domestic product. It is a decentralized arm of central government and ultimately accountable to Parliament through the Secretary of State. It is organized (Levitt, 1980) with policy-making, planning, monitoring and financial control functions in the Department of Health and Social Security, in England, and in equivalent departments in Wales, Scotland and Northern Ireland. In England, the strategic management role is largely delegated to fourteen regional health authorities, whose particularly relevant power is the allocation and management of major capital expenditure within their regions. Operational management, and control of the larger part of revenue funds, is largely delegated to area health authorities and their constituent health districts. But the present operational management structure is considered over-elaborate, and it is intended to simplify it to a single tier of district health authorities (DHSS, 1979a).

The total funding allocated to the NHS, nationally, is a matter for political decision, taken at Cabinet level. These funds are derived from the national pool of taxation, and are allocated to regional health authorities under separate headings for revenue and capital. The bulk of the revenue and a small part of the capital are reallocated to the local-level health authorities. The shares of funding at each stage of allocation are determined by compromise between the historical trend of expenditure for each organizational unit involved, and a target future expenditure derived from a nationally-applied formula intended to share out resources to each locality according to need, where need is related primarily to the size of the local population (DHSS, 1976).

The accounts of individual health districts and authorities are maintained on an income and expenditure basis (i.e. essentially cash accounts with limited end-of-year adjustments for stocks, debtors and creditors). Annual financial reports are prepared on the same basis, according to criteria laid down by the sponsoring government department, but these reports are slow to be made public and do not appear to have great use, or importance, in respect of public accountability or control. Nearly all revenue is derived from allocations from higher tiers of the health service (small trust funds and local donations aside), so revenue accounting is not complex. Expenditure accounting is based upon 'functional budgets' that reflect the functional organization of the management structure. There are no balance sheets. Fixed assets are not capitalized, and no depreciation is charged to revenue account, or even calculated in detail on a memorandum basis. Plant and property registers, largely non-existent until recently, are now gradually being compiled. Capital, as well as revenue funds, are supplied by central government on a permanent basis, with no obligation for interest or capital repayments.

The importance of the income and expenditure accounts for financial control in the NHS has been eroded since the introduction, in 1976, of the same cash-limits system of money allocation, reporting and control as is applied to nearly all the non-trading activities of the public sector. There is an exception, however. Spending on family-practitioner services, inclusive of family doctors, dentists, and pharmaceutical and optician services, etc. is exempted from the cash limits because the independent-contractor status of the practitioners prevents fixed limits on expenditure. In practice, family practitioner expenditure is reasonably predictable and controllable except for the costs of prescriptions supplied by family doctors.

Health authorities are allowed limited facilities for virement of funds from revenue to capital, or vice versa. Whilst some carry-forward of unspent allocations is permitted at year-end, no advance drawing on the next year's allocation is permitted. Authorized funds are drawn from the government according to need; authorities operate bank accounts but are expected to maintain minimum working balances, and are not allowed to invest surplus funds (except funds held in relatively small trust funds). Although the degree of discretion described for the NHS in respect of accounting and financial arrangements may seem highly restrictive, the flexibility is somewhat greater than exists in most other organizations operating as parts of, or extensions of, central government services.

Budgetary Control in the Health Service

It was noted that expenditure accounting follows the structure of functional budgets. For example, the district nursing officer holds the budget for all nursing staff and training costs, and below him/her a sector nursing officer holds a delegated budget (typically, for a group of hospitals), while at unit (i.e. hospital) level the lowest-tier subdivision of the budget is administered. Similar budget arrangements are operated for the other functions such as ambulances, catering, works and engineering—and for paramedical services such as pathology and radiology. But the clinicians in charge of specialties (branches of medical or surgical treatment) do not hold any budgets, nor are any costs charged, allocated or apportioned to their activities—in spite of the fact that it is these clinicians who most directly determine and control the workload of patient mix and throughput, utilizing wards and operating theatres, and causing consequential demands for supporting services upon other functions. This situation has been a matter for comment in RCNHS (1978), Lapsley and Prowle (1978), Bevan *et al.* (1980), and it is a source of considerable concern to finance officers working in the NHS. The basic problem is that clinicians working in the health service have, traditionally, held that direct involvement in financial responsibility for budgets and costs would conflict with their clinical responsibility to seek the supply of all resources needed for the proper care of individual patients. A secondary problem has been that systems have not been perfected for tracing or otherwise linking functional costs to the clinician, ward, specialty or patient care-group (i.e. children, the elderly, etc.) causing particular resources to be consumed. In brief, the budget system has placed financial responsibility on the managers in charge of making resources and services available, rather than upon those who determine their rate of consumption.

The desirability of ascertaining accurate costs of treatment, and of involving clinicians in the review and control of costs and budgets, has been recognized by the Department of Health and Social Security as well as by NHS officers, and projects in specialty costing (Magee, 1978) and clinician involvement in consultations and decisions on resource use and budgets, have been commissioned (Jaques and Wickings, 1978; and Morgan *et al.*, 1979). There is scope for academic research linked to the existing projects, or working in parallel to them in other localities. Similarly, development projects have started on new computerized information systems (e.g. the Standard Accounting System being developed within the West Midlands Regional Health Authority) which may improve the speed and accuracy of financial information available for management control and decision-making, and there may be useful opportunities for academic research co-operation on some of these projects. In these various research initiatives the most valuable academic contribution may consist of behavioural accounting and systems involvement, given that the NHS is likely already to have available the purely technical accounting expertise required. The essential requirement for many of the possible improvements in the use of management information and control in the NHS (as in other organizations) is that both management and professional staff should be enabled to develop the motivation, mutual understanding, and mutual self-interest to make improved systems acceptable, and thus workable (Schatz, 1975).

Aside from the possible benefit to the NHS itself from the greater involvement of clinical staff in resource control and accountability, accounting research could relate usefully to a very general problem widespread in the public services. It is common in the public services that many of the 'managers' are also 'professionals' first and foremost, and that their role as professional persons (with obligations to clients, services, standards etc.) conflicts with the conventional role of the manager in accepting hierarchical discipline over such matters as restriction of services and economizing on resources. The differences between professional and managerial roles and ethics may be as great in the health services as in any other public service, so that if progress can be made in creating a more constructive fusing of the two roles within the health services, this may yield useful insights for other branches of the public service.

Capital in the National Health Service

Within the NHS, control of capital expenditure is recognized as important not only for the avoidance of waste of capital, but also because most capital acquisitions create a continuing demand and need for increased revenue expenditure in each succeeding year. To take one example, the use of small wards and certain other features in hospital design can substantially increase the numbers of nursing and ancillary staff needed to serve a given number of patients (Chapman, 1979, Chap. 21). To take a second example, the building of hospital facilities on a scale adequate to service specialties not already provided locally (e.g. open-heart surgery), or indeed the provision of revenue-funding through the application of a resource-allocation formula that increases funding in certain localities to compensate for past 'deprival' of locally-based facilities, may create a temptation to replicate relatively low-volume, high-cost specialties or supporting services already available for access in another not-too-distant health authority. This may be wasteful. The health departments exercise a restraint on this problem to the extent that they must approve the creation of each new consultant's post, which is the essential starting point for the creation or enlargement of a specialty in a particular hospital or health district. But no-one knows the best balance between local accessibility and economies of scale, and the better technical quality of care or cure that may be associated with larger-volume centres of specialized treatment. The data available from existing accounting systems in the NHS is not sufficient to resolve the kind of problem outlined here. This offers an interesting prospect for accounting research, although ultimate resolution of the problem depends on a form of cost-benefit assessment that involves economic concepts and social factors at least as much as accounting information and analysis.

There is a further aspect of the NHS capital expenditure problem that is more closely related to the accounting and finance discipline. The NHS is totally lacking in the conventional disciplines of the commercial and industrial world as they affect the use of capital. Capital is a 'free good' to health service authorities. No depreciation is charged, no interest is paid, no repayments are made, and no primarily economic or financial case has to be made to the satisfaction of outside parties (i.e. as in a financial market) before funds are awarded, although all larger capital commitments have to be approved by the Department of Health and Social Security. Capital appraisals employing discounted cash flows can be applied to potential cost-saving expenditure (e.g. a new boiler system or a new laundry), or to the cash-saving for alternative schemes to achieve the same service output, but the largest capital outlays are on new district hospitals, and, by and large, no effective appraisal techniques are employed on these decisions. Owen (1978), Perrin (1978) and Lapsley (1980) discuss the existing methods and problems, but there is scope for several research projects on the problems involved, and possible solutions.

In summary, the state of accounting and financial practice in the National Health Service is primitive, or at best, under-developed. Progress is handicapped both by shortages of experienced accounting staff (**n.b.** the finance function in the NHS has been subject to management cost and staffing cutbacks since 1975), and by the reluctance of many clinical and ancillary staff to welcome the introduction of managerial and financial information systems and controls that might become threats to traditional modes of working. But the state of under-development mirrors the potential for improvement to which academic research can make a wide variety of contributions.

Local Authorities' Distinctive Accounting Methods

Local authorities are organized in two tiers in England, 'district' and 'county' (or the equivalent in London and other major conurbations), and their differentiation is by type of function and service provided, rather than by hierarchical accountability. Internally, they are organized by reference to the service provided—e.g. education or highways—and budgetary allocation and control tends to be based upon these services, each of which has specialist officers and supervisory committees drawn from the elected council membership. Compared to the NHS, the range and diversity of activities carried out by local authorities is far greater, and their activities are far more influenced by political judgments and priorities related to the programmes of the national political parties. Local authorities obtain some 40 per cent of their revenue from locally-determined rates (i.e. property taxes) and fees for services, with the balance of 60 per cent being supplied in 'rate support grant' by central government.

While unlike the NHS the local authorities have a long history of the development and use of their own forms of financial accounting and financing, it is not surprising, given the high level of revenue-income support from central government, that there are many restrictions upon the freedom of action of local authorities in respect of their expenditure allocation and control. Nevertheless, the basic traditions of local authority accounting and reporting practices remain largely intact. Lengthy and very detailed annual accounts are supplied some months after the end of each financial year: these are called abstracts of accounts, and their organization gives prominence to the disclosure and accountability of expenditure for individual services, rather than to the performance of the authority as a whole.[1]

There is much scope for research on local authority accounting methods (e.g. the merits of 'fund accounting'); on the particular problems of achieving effective financial performance-measurement, reporting and accountability at the level of the individual specialist service; and on whether or not it is useful and practicable to measure and report the overall financial performance of local authorities viewed as entities, in a more effective and cohesive manner than has so far been achieved.

Local authorities obtain limited amounts of cash for capital expenditure from central-government grants, from donations, from revenue-account budgets directly, or by withdrawal from repairs and renewals funds that have received annual contributions from the revenue budgets of relevant services. The repairs and renewals funds are used to ensure availability of finance for the replacement of vehicles and certain classes of equipment

1 Space does not allow full explanation here of all the distinctive features of English local authority financial arrangements (but see Hepworth, 1979), and anyway some of the important arrangements are currently being reviewed for alteration and simplification by Parliament (House of Commons, 1980).

and plant that have a much shorter life than the major buildings or other installations with which they are used. It is interesting that the annual revenue charges transferred to these funds are quite often calculated by reference to replacement costs, or by index-linking prior-year allocations (Owen, 1980); this is possibly the only existing manifestation of inflation accounting in local authority accounts, although it seems likely that direct works and other trading undertakings owned by local authorities will be required to adopt current cost accounting, at least for their depreciation measurements, to encourage price quotations and out-turn performance comparable with the private firms with which they may be in competition.

The major part of local-authority capital funds is raised by long-term borrowing. Principal and interest are subsequently paid to the source of borrowing and the annualized amounts are termed 'loan charges'. The annual loan charges are debited to the individual services utilizing the assets funded by borrowing. No conventional measures of depreciation are calculated or charged either to the service accounts or to the overall accounts of the local authority (except for the depreciation implicit in the charges for contributions to the repairs and renewals fund). Thus, the annualized cost of financing fixed assets is charged to revenue account in place of the estimated depreciation cost that would be charged in conventional industrial accounts. As it happens, the loan charges applied will be equal to the total charge that would result from the use of annuity depreciation taken on historical cost and augmented by a cost-of-capital charge for interest on the unrecovered balance of the investment. Whereas industrial accountants would be unhappy about using annuity depreciation in respect of long-life assets, given uncertainty regarding obsolescence and market viability, this method of depreciation might not be so unreasonable in respect of local-authority assets which are primarily buildings and other structures with a long life and the prospect of continuing use (but consider the case of schools that may not easily be converted to other uses, and that may become redundant as the result of reduced birth rates). However, given significant inflation, the amount of the annual loan charge may fall significantly behind the total depreciation-plus-interest charge that might be argued to represent the true economic cost of resource use—where 'economic cost' is defined as the annualized current *replacement* cost of the assets in use. Whether or not this shortfall of current charge below the level of replacement-cost-depreciation plus interest constitutes a major defect in the methods of local authority accounting depends upon the answers to two questions. First, do local authorities have an obligation to maintain their stock of capital assets (overall, if not within individual services), and secondly, how far should the current costs of capital facilities be borne by the current generation of taxpayers and ratepayers, as opposed to later generations who may receive equal benefit from them, yet at a declining cost in real terms. This problem will be considered further in the final section of this paper.

Regional Water Authorities

Local government (as also the NHS) was reorganized in 1974. Previously the management of pure water, sewage and storm water drainage was in the hands of local authorities, or of private water companies (a few of which remain). Water catchment, river management and recreational water use were responsibilities that fell haphazardly on various organizations. Given that several of the above functions would be best co-ordinated on a geographical basis much larger than even the larger local authorities, the 1974 reorganization provided that England and Wales should be divided into ten regional water authorities, to take charge of all the above functions. Generally, each of the new regional water authorities is a separate public corporation, responsible to the Department of the Environment, although for certain purposes they may act or be dealt with collectively through the National Water Council.

The regional water authorities raise their revenue by a combination of rates levied on domestic users, plus water-meter charges levied on heavy users (mainly agricultural, industrial and commercial) and miscellaneous fees. Perhaps because of the latter sources of revenue, which imply a degree of 'market' involvement (even if as a monopolist), the 1974 reorganization required that the new water authorities should prepare and publish their accounts according to best commercial practice. In effect, their accounting is most directly comparable with the nationalized industries, although the requirements stop short of imposing a 'true and fair view' audit certificate. Capital funds are obtained from revenue-account cash flows to the extent that depreciation costs are taken into account in determining rate demands and water-meter charges, and any extra capital needed is obtained by long-term borrowing from the National Loans Fund (on a similar basis to much of the borrowing of the nationalized industries). A particular problem (shared with some of the nationalized industries) is the determination of realistic asset lives and depreciation rates, given that in the water industry the greatest proportion of asset value relates to underground water and sewerage systems, dams and water conservation works, and processing plants—types of assets where professional judgments may be highly approximate, subjective, and sometimes too conservative. Prior to reorganization detailed asset registers were seldom kept, although this is gradually being remedied. Given recent rates of inflation, and the apparent willingness of the government to allow replacement-cost depreciation to be taken into account by many public bodies in the setting of their charges, the task of assessing reliable and defensible levels of depreciation cost in the water industry has become a major concern—bearing in mind that the replacement cost of all assets in the water industry may approach £15,000m, a value that may be exceeded only by the electricity industry amongst British public utilities and other nationalized industries.

Table 12.1 *Differences in Capital Asset Financing and Accounting Among Health, Water and Local Authorities*

	Local Authorities	*Water Authorities*	*Health Authorities*
Type of financing used for capital assets.	Mainly borrowed, but some from revenue and donations. Repaid with interest.	Partly borrowed, partly from depreciation costed into revenue charges. Borrowings repaid.	Supplied as free good by central govt. No interest or repayment.
Type of accounting system in use.	Fund and loan-charge accounts. Annual abstract.	Full accruals and best commercial practice.	Income and expenditure accounts. No balance sheet.
Capital asset valuation.	At gross historic cost until scrapped.	At net historic cost until scrapped.	Not capitalized. No valuations published.
Depreciation method used.	None: loan charges to service accounts in lieu, plus use of contributions to repairs and renewals funds, and some replacements charged direct to revenue account.	Full commercial depreciation accounting is used. National norms for depreciable life are available.	Depreciation not calculated, charged or reported—some replacement fixed assets are charged direct to current revenue expenditure.
Accounting adjustments for inflation.	None to assets, but some repair and renewal contributions are calculated on replacement cost basis.	Full current cost accounting under consideration on basis similar to nationalized industries.	None presently, and none feasible under existing accounting methods.
Attitudes to self-financing.	Not considered relevant beyond repairs and renewals replacement of short-life assets used with long-life buildings and services.	Considered desirable except for financing major expansion of service capacity.	Desired in the sense of eliminating separate funding of capital and revenue, for greater autonomy in use and timing of capital spending.
Approach to capital maintenance.	As above *re*. self-financing—loan-charge accounting cannot measure capital maintenance during periods of inflation.	Methods and views similar to those in nationalized industries and commercial firms.	None—replacement subject to national political priorities and resource allocation formulae. Accounts cannot measure capital maintenance.

Capital Asset Financing and Accounting Compared

This section has noted some of the distinctive features of financing and accounting systems in three public services—health, water, and local authorities. Their accounting systems and published accounts and reports mirror their organizational differences and, especially, their financing differences. These differences are most pronounced in respect of capital finance, capital accounting, and the interaction between capital and revenue accounts. The major differences are summarized in Table 12.1.

The differences observed highlight a number of possible issues for research and debate. Considering each service individually, one may question whether or not its financing system, and, indeed, more particlarly, its accounting system, is appropriate to the management and control needs of services under decentralized local management and intended to be responsive to local views and needs. The accounting system used in health authorities appears to be particularly vulnerable to challenge (and research) as regards its appropriateness. Present NHS accounting requirements may meet the essential needs of central government for control over the amount and probity of health service expenditure, but they do not produce information and reports which appear sufficiently comprehensive or appropriately structured to meet the requirements of effective managerial planning, execution, monitoring and control at local and regional levels.

Capital Maintenance and Self-Financing

Capital maintenance is the process of renewing investment so as to maintain intact within an organization some prescribed quantum of resources, which are specified and measured in historic-cost, physical or real (economic) terms. Self-financing is the process of obtaining funds for capital (as well as operational) purposes from revenue sources, at least nominally under management control, with no formal need to negotiate borrowing or equity capital from external sources, and with no contractual commitment to pay interest or dividends. The concepts of capital maintenance and self-financing interact. If self-financing is inadequate, then capital maintenance cannot be achieved unless external capital is raised. But achieving a state of 100 per cent self-financing provides no proof that capital maintenance is being achieved, or indeed, that it is not being greatly exceeded. Self-financing can be measured and verified easily, since it is a concept based on cash-flow and funds-flow. Capital maintenance cannot be measured or verified easily, however, at least by persons outside the organization lacking full access to internal information regarding expectations of future operations and asset use. Various arguments in favour of capital maintenance depreciation accounting are considered by Perrin

(1978, 1979), whilst Likierman (1979) has discussed certain aspects of self-financing in the nationalized industries. The purpose of this section is to consider the possibility that financing may excessively influence depreciation measurements recorded in accounting systems incorporating capital maintenance.

Table 12.1 summarized the differences among three major public services in respect of the degree to which their financial and accounting arrangements take account of capital maintenance. The position of the water industry is not dissimilar to that of typical nationalized industries. Yet health and local authorities, although they differ between themselves greatly in the mechanics of their financing and accounting systems, have in common that they ignore theories of capital maintenance, or even the need to report (however approximately) the degree to which capital maintenance is being achieved. Nevertheless, by one means or another both health and local authorities arrange to charge much of their short-life fixed-asset replacements direct to revenue account. This implicitly recognizes the case for capital maintenance to the extent of keeping-up the stock of minor assets needed to keep the long-life buildings and other major installations in an operational state. But it leaves major-asset replacement as a matter for political will and choice, without requiring the attempt to measure and report depreciation even as memorandum information so that citizens can judge for themselves whether or not sufficient capital replacement is taking place to maintain the community's stock of real capital.

Accountants working in the health and local authorities have given thought to the possible advantages, and disadvantages, of introducing depreciation accounting. Personal contact with health-service finance officers suggests greater interest among them, than among local-authority finance officers. A case for depreciation accounting in the NHS is made by Lapsley (1980). In local authorities it can be argued that loan-charge accounting would be awkward to abandon quickly, gives results that may not be too different from depreciation accounting, and is less expensive to administer than depreciation accounting (with its reliance upon detailed registers and possible asset revaluations). In the NHS, having no alternative system, resistance to depreciation accounting might be less than in local authorities—especially if the notion of capital-maintenance accounting could be linked to the evolution, additionally, of a more stable, self-financing system of capital allocations. In a recent discussion document (DHSS, 1979b) there is evidence of the health departments developing more sophisticated approaches to strategic planning for capital, and to capital appraisals of alternative uses of capital (embodying both cost-benefit and net present value techniques). The document does not consider the accounting systems or measurement aspects of improved capital management, however, so it may be assumed there is no will or interest at the central-government pinnacle of the NHS for any radical substitution of a capital-maintenance approach to claims on capital, in place of the present machinery of political choice in determining annually the total scale of NHS capital funding, for allocation within the regions by negotiation and by priorities reflecting both central and local perceptions of need.

If capital-maintenance depreciation is employed at realistic current-cost rates applied to accurate estimates of commercially-useful asset lives, and if prices are set no lower or higher than necessary to achieve the level of self-financing that provides a cash flow for asset replacement equal to the current-cost depreciation (plus viable profit margins), then the financial situation would be in equilibrium, with current consumers paying 'fair' charges for the benefits that they receive in goods and services. If self-financing is at a lower level, then capital is not being maintained from current operations—although *if* money can be borrowed, then the capital stock may be maintained by transferring most of the cost burden of the maintenance from present consumers to future consumers, taxpayers or ratepayers. Alternatively, if the self-financing cash flow exceeds true current depreciation, then, presumptively, current consumers (or ratepayers or taxpayers, as the case may be) are paying for the expansion of real capital stock for the benefit of future generations of consumers. The latter growth through self-financing may be prudent from a managerial point of view, and it may be virtuous from society's collective point of view (at least if there is reasonable certainty that the particular industry or public-service activity concerned will be genuinely needed in future). But such growth should at least be measured and disclosed. Those who are currently paying for growth should have the opportunity to know that they are doing so.

The recent report commissioned by the Consumers' Association (CA, 1979) supports the view that nationalized industries have held down depreciation charges and other cost adjustments if their cash and profit flows were weak, and have followed the opposite tack if cash and profit flows were strong. This is only a variation on the theme of 'income smoothing' which may be presumed to flourish in private-sector accounting as well; but what happens in the private sector does not raise the same question of public policy as arises when nationalized industries or other public bodies subordinate the measurement of true costs to the exigencies of explaining or justifying a particular scale of cash flow and self-financing. In principle, decisions on cost measurement and reporting ought to be independent of the measurement and reporting of self-financing: until this is achieved it is perhaps fair to state that the accounting and audit functions are not themselves demonstrating the degree of independence that should be expected from major professions.

During periods of restraint of prices and incomes it seems probable that government influence held down nationalized industry prices (and self-financing) to a greater extent than occurred in the private sector, or than was managerially prudent. To that extent, nationalized industries' managers and accountants may be forgiven for seeking to use accounting information most favourable to their cause. Now, with government emphasis redirected from prices and incomes policy to control of the money supply and the reduction of the public-sector borrowing requirement, it appears that nationalized industries will be discouraged from borrowing public funds, and will be encouraged to rely, as fully as possible, on self-financing. It has been suggested (*Sunday Times*, 30 March 1980) that borrowing by the nationalized industries will be cut back by at least £1000m during the next few years, relative to the plans agreed under the previous government. Some of the cut-back in borrowing may result simply in less investment, but much of the borrowing may be replaced by self-financing cash flow generated by higher prices (where the 'market' permits). Current consumers will be asked to pay for scale expansion or quality enhancement (e.g. telephone, electricity and gas services, and perhaps water also) for which the benefits will be enjoyed by later 'generations' of consumers. It may be hoped that the scale of the increase in self-financing and in the shift of the payment burden will not be disguised by conservative depreciation-accounting methods that depart from the neutrality and objectivity that should be implicit in accounting for capital maintenance.

How far is the foregoing discussion transferable to the public services discussed earlier in the paper? The water industry, with its cost-plus fee-setting and its inclusion of depreciation accounting when establishing costs, would appear to have the same opportunity as the nationalized industries for distorting capital maintenance and raising its self-financing above a true capital-maintenance level. The NHS financing and accounting arrangements, of course, are not directly comparable, but it may be argued that the recent heavy increase in prescription charges was a political necessity to fend off a demand for cut-backs in NHS capital expenditure: that is, incremental prescription-fee income was levied to provide indirect self-financing for the NHS's planned capital-expenditure programme.

Turning to the local authorities, while their methods of financing and accounting do not allow for the explicit measurement of capital maintenance, it follows that they escape the risk of capital-maintenance accounting being misused to justify or partly conceal a level of self-financing that may be higher than revealed in published accounts. Local authorities borrow their major capital, although a substantial amount of revenue funding, additionally, is expended on the support of some capital schemes. The flexibility of using revenue to support capital may be modified, and the classification and disclosure of information may be improved, as the result of clauses in the Local Government, Planning and Land (No. 2) Bill now before Parliament (HMSO, 1980). It would be ironic if current government initiatives result in some reduction in the discretion of local authorities to practise a degree of self-financing (i.e. without formal borrowing) in capital schemes, at the same time as developments in other parts of the public sector appear to encourage increased self-financing. Nevertheless, although local-authority use of loan-charge accounting may introduce some distortion during times of inflation, the system offers objectivity in apportioning the cost of capital to individual years and individual services. It is certainly possible that loan-charge accounting may provide as useful information, and be less open to distortion for the justification of unnecessarily high rates and fees, than the capital-maintenance and best-commercial-practice system of accounting introduced into the regional water authorities. The only safe conclusion is that no-one yet knows what is the ideal system of accounting for general use in public-service organizations.

Conclusion

This paper has sought to create wider interest in academic research in public-sector accounting, by illustrating some research issues relevant to nationalized industries, and to three types of public-service authorities (i.e. health, water and local authorities) whose financing and accounting practices contain sharper differences than may be found in the private sector. Many research topics in management, social and behavioural accounting can be pursued as well in the public sector as in the private sector, and in some cases the contrast between the two sectors may be illuminating in itself. Perhaps the most interesting public-sector accounting research possibilities arise directly from the wide variety of financing arrangements applying to different branches of the public sector. Public-sector accounting methods appear to be shaped by the arrangements for financing and political control for each class of institution, rather than by the inherent nature of the operations carried on, or management's need for information on the operational use of resources. Moreover, in the public sector there may be greater doubt than in the private sector (with its market constraints) that management's natural interest in maximizing self-financing is compatible with the effective use and reporting of capital-maintenance performance information, or with the objective determination of 'fair prices, fees or rates'. These factors reflect an opportunity for research concerning the objectives of accounting measurement systems, and how to satisfy the distinctively different information and disclosure needs in the public sector.

References

Accounting Standards Committee, Standard Statement of Accounting Practice 16 (SSAP 16). ASC (1980).

Bevan, G., Copeman, H., Perrin, J. and Rosser, R., *Health Care: Priorities and Management*. Croom Helm (1980).

Chapman, L., *Your Disobedient Servant* (rev. edn.). Penguin (1979).

Consumers' Association, *Nationalised Industries' Accounting Policies*, report prepared by Phillips & Drew. CA (1979).

Department of Health and Social Security (DHSS), *Sharing Resources for Health in England*, Report of the Resource Allocation Working Party (the RAWP Report). HMSO (1976).

Department of Health and Social Security (DHSS), *Patients First*, a Consultative Paper. HMSO (1979a).

Department of Health and Social Security (DHSS), *Review of Health Capital*, a discussion document. DHSS (1979b).

HMSO, *The Financial and Economic Objectives of the Nationalised Industries*, Cmd 1337. HMSO (1961).

HMSO, *Nationalised Industries: a Review of Economic and Financial Objectives*, Cmd 3437. HMSO (1967).

HMSO, *The Nationalised Industries*, Cmd 7131. HMSO (1978).

Hepworth, N. P., *The Finance of Local Government* (5th edn.). Allen & Unwin (1979).

House of Commons, 'Local Government, Planning and Land (No. 2) Bill', Bill 128. HMSO (1980).

Jaques, E. and Wickings, I., 'Some Concepts for Planning, Budgeting, and Expenditure Control for Medical Activities', Discussion Doc. No. 2064. Brunel Institute of Organisation and Social Studies (1978).

Lapsley, I., 'The Use of Accounting Information in Consensus Management Teams', *Journal of Business Finance and Accounting* (Winter 1979).

Lapsley, I., 'The Case for Depreciation Accounting in U.K. Health Authorities', 3rd Annual Congress Paper. European Accounting Assn. (1980).

Lapsley, I. and Prowle, M., 'The Effectiveness of Functional Budgetary Control in the National Health Service: an Empirical Investigation', RCNHS technical paper. CIEBR, University of Warwick (1978).

Levitt, R., *The Reorganised National Health Service* (3rd edn.). Croom Helm (1980).

Likierman, A., *The Reports and Accounts of Nationalised Industries*, Civil Service College Handbook No. 20. HMSO (1979).

MacArthur, J. B., 'An Approach to Asset Valuation in the Financial Accounts of U.K. Nationalised Industries', *Journal of Business Finance and Accounting* (Spring 1980).

Magee, C. C. and Osmolski, R. J., 'A Comprehensive System of Management Information for Financial Planning, Decision Making and Control in the Hospital Service', RCNHS technical paper. CIEBR, University of Warwick (1978).

Morgan, K. D., Baskin, R. J. and Owen, J. W., *Towards Improved Health Care: Making Budgeting Work in a District*. St. Thomas' Health District (Teaching) (1979).

National Economic Development Office, *A Study of U.K. Nationalised Industries*. NEDO (1976).

Owen, A. J., 'Health Authority Capital Budgeting: the State of the Art in Theory and Practice', RCNHS technical paper. CIEBR, University of Warwick (1978).

Owen, A. J., 'Capital Financing and Accounting in Local Authorities', unpublished mimeo. CIEBR, University of Warwick (1980).

Perrin, J. R., 'Capital Maintenance and Allocation in the Health Service', RCNHS technical paper. CIEBR, University of Warwick (1978).

Perrin, J. R., 'Accounting for Depreciation in the Public Sector', Papers Presented at the 94th Annual Conference. Chartered Institute of Public Finance and Accountancy (1979).

Royal Commission on the National Health Service, *Management of Financial Resources in the National Health Service*, Research Paper No. 2, ed. Perrin, J. R. HMSO (1978).

Royal Commission on the National Health Service Report, Cmd 7615. HMSO (1979).

Sandilands, F., *Inflation Accounting*, Cmd 6225. HMSO (1975).

Schatz, M., 'Behavioural Considerations in Management', in Cyert, ed., *The Management of Nonprofit Organizations*. Lexington/D.C. Heath (1975).

Tivey, L., *The Nationalised Industries Since 1960*. Allen & Unwin (1973).

Turvey, R., 'Marginal Cost', *Economic Journal* (June 1969).

Webb, M. G., *The Economics of Nationalised Industries*. Nelson (1973).

Wright, D. M., 'Inflation Accounting in the Nationalised Industries: a Survey and Appraisal', *Accounting and Business Research* (Winter 1979).

Wright, D. M., 'Real Rates of Return on Capital: Some Estimates for British Gas', *Journal of Business Finance and Accounting* (Spring 1980).

13 Financial control in local authorities: potential research

Cyril Tomkins
Professor of Accounting and Finance, School of Management, University of Bath

Very few academics in the accounting area have been interested in studying the financial control processes of local government authorities. This paper aims to highlight some areas where empirical research would be both interesting and challenging. The focus will be on issues which practitioners in the area currently perceive to be important. Rather than aiming to provide a comprehensive coverage of all the literature on public sector and local authority financial control processes, emphasis is placed on the literature which is seen as being relevant to such issues of practical significance. In addition, many of the research suggestions draw upon a research study of the financial control processes of a large local authority in the west of England which the author and colleagues are currently undertaking. (Financial support from the SSRC is gratefully acknowledged.)

Recognizing that the principal mechanism for formalizing resource allocation in local authorities is the budgetary process, both short and long term, the paper has the following structure. Given the growing disillusionment with PPBS and other 'rational' resource allocation methods, local authority budget procedures are compared to national procedures and the relevance to local authorities of recent literature on national government budgeting is examined. Thereafter, the discussion is broadened to consider the whole question of attaining 'value for money' in local authorities. In this context, brief consideration is given to the roles that various internal local authority sections and external agencies seem to play. The paper concludes with some comments on the nature of the research processes that might help to further our understandings of these areas.

The Resource Allocation Process
(From PPBS to PESC and continuation budgets)

Most literature on public sector budgeting relates to the level of the State rather than the local authority, and at that level there is probably more accounting literature relating to planning, programming and budgeting systems (PPBS) than any other aspect. The 1960s saw many U.S. public sector organizations attempting to apply PPBS. However, numerous authors (Novick, 1973; Wildavsky, 1975; van Gunsteren, 1976; Jablonsky and Dirsmith, 1978), have pointed out that PPBS has had very limited success. Probably the most hard-biting comments come from Wildavsky who goes so far as to say that PPBS fails *everywhere*. More important, he says that, while many have observed the difficulties with PPBS, they have argued that the:

> 'problems lay in interests, recalcitrant politicians and hide bound bureaucrats . . . by lack of trained manpower, absence of crucial data and inadequacies in the state of the art.'

To Wildavsky, however, the real problem lies in the fact that PPBS, though, seemingly, a rational and highly natural approach, asks human beings to perform cognitive operations beyond their capabilities. In his opinion it is impossible for them to state social objectives precisely and then rank them, then specify alternative ways of achieving them, cost them all, and then select actions in order of merit.

The same criticisms can be applied to zero-based budgeting which is still strongly supported by some (e.g. Sarant, 1978). For as Wildavsky states:

> 'Whatever else they may be, budgets obviously are political documents . . . and participants in budgeting drastically simplify their task by concentrating on the relatively small proportion of the budget that it is politically feasible to change.' (1975, p. 278)

Wildavsky's analysis therefore suggests a prime area of research for local authorities. Numerous important questions come to mind. To what extent are local authority budgets incrementally established and what is the nature of the whole process? What roles do accountants, spending department and politicians play in these processes? To what extent is there an ongoing commitment, contractually or politically, to existing budget bases? What adjustment processes occur when the central government calls for a limit on expenditure with respect to previous year levels? Some preliminary thoughts on these questions may be derived from a description of budget processes at the national level, although even at the State level empirical work is not yet extensive.

After savagely criticizing PPBS and ZBB, Wildavsky (1975) praises the British Public Expenditure Survey Committee (PESC) system. The main thrust of the process leading to the PESC report is to agree the future cost of *existing* government policies if these remain unchanged over each of the next five years. Consequently, Wildavsky says that PESC has 'enshrined incrementalism with a vengeance' and that it works because it employs man and administrative machinery as they exist. It will be useful to investigate the PESC system further in order to provide research hypotheses relating to local authority budgeting.

The U.K. PESC system is now virtually two decades old and has undergone various modifications since its inception (see Wright, 1979).

The essence of the system is that the U.K. Treasury and government spending departments liaise, in the first instance, to agree upon the costs likely to be incurred in continuing existing policies for several years into the future. (Initially, the projections were five years ahead, the fifth year has now been dropped and the main emphasis is on years one and two.) It is only after agreement of this first stage that consideration is given to possible new policies and their costs. Procedurally, the derivation of a revised budget for existing policies follows straightforward stages as described by Wright (1979). Agreements have to be reached on cost increases in respect of changes in prices and wages, changes in policy commenced since the previous survey but now considered to be part of 'existing policy' and changes in *real* costs of existing policies due to changes in beneficial populations, etc. However, while, apparently, involving no major conceptual problems, the practical problems can be immense mainly because at the detailed operational level the definition of 'existing policy' can be highly subjective. Government policies are usually defined in broad terms and it is always open to debate whether amendments in activities, quality of service, etc. are within agreed policy or not. According to Wright (1979, p. 34), this causes the main dialogue between the Treasury and the spending department because it is only when the Treasury can establish that an activity is a new policy, or extension of an existing one, that its prior approval is seen to be required and it can exercise some restraint. The Treasury has considerable difficulty resisting plans for increasing expenditure for an activity which it is forced to agree is part of existing policy.

Because of the central importance of this debate in the U.K. government's budgeting procedures, and the difficulty of defining 'existing policies', it is interesting to note the process by which agreement is reached. Wright (1979, p. 35) is particularly revealing on this point. He says that the Treasury staff do not examine every item of expenditure but consider the merits of the case argued by the spending department on the few new items of expenditure. The onus of persuasion is squarely on the spending department. In this regard, it is important to remember that the Treasury official is not a specialist in the policy area. He:

> 'relies upon his knowledge of the department and of the judgement and reliability of his opposite numbers in the finance and policy divisions; knowledge acquired through the years as a result of day-to-day contact in a small community . . . it is unnecessary for the expenditure controller to know in great detail everything the department is doing, provided that he has established a good relationship based upon mutual confidence, trust and esteem' (Wright, 1979, p. 35).

Wildavsky (1975, p. 375) also stresses the creation of mutual understanding as the cornerstone of agreement between the Treasury and the spending department.

After early suspicions about the spectre of widening Treasury control, it is said that spending departments now have come to welcome the PESC for the continuity it provides and the safeguard against any unannounced loss of resources in future years. Hence, it does indeed appear to be 'incrementalism with a vengeance'. Indeed, this process is then reinforced by notions of ministerial prestige, which, it is often said, is equated with holding on to what the department has already as a minimum indicator of success.

However, PESC is not without weaknesses. Wildavsky (1975, p. 380) says that PESC certainly enables man to grapple with complex resource allocation problems, but it is weak in terms of asking fundamental questions about policy and significant changes in resource allocation. To help counter this he argues for a Programme Analysis and Review (PAR) for specific programmes on an individual basis trusting that PARs will create sufficient pressure for changing the balance of expenditure where needed. This procedure was indeed introduced by the Heath government, but it proved to be still too centralized and failed to gain the support of spending departments. The PAR system has now been abandoned by the new Thatcher government and it has not been superseded by any formal process other than the 'efficiency exercises' being conducted by Sir Derek Raynor. However, to date, these exercises do not seem to show the promise for achieving considerable savings.

The search for efficiency is being conducted essentially by asking staff *within spending departments* to come forward with suggestions for saving money and initial proposals have included streamlining the use of forms in the Inland Revenue and paying social security payments through banks as well as post offices. It should be recognized, however, that such an approach is not the same as attempting to allocate resources between departments on the basis of their competing social, economic and other purposes. Theoretically, at least, it is possible that such departmental 'efficiency exercises' might result in significant reductions in public costs which enable the government to achieve desired cuts in public expenditure commensurate with its macro-economic management plans. However, while they are contributing to increased 'value for money' from public expenditure, they only address such an issue in the narrowest of terms. The distinction between efficiency and wider notions of value for money will be discussed later in this paper.

Another weakness of PESC is its tendency to emphasize the continuation of future spending rather than to act as a brake on it when economic growth slows down. This has been a problem which has only arisen in recent years. Moreover, PESC, until 1976, involved no mechanism for financial control—that is comparing out-turn with the budget with reasoned explanations. Nor did it control the amount of cash spent as distinct from a given volume of services. Nor, in earlier years, did it include any assessment of future resources (i.e. what the country could afford). The last defect was remedied in the early 1970s by an annual medium-term economic assessment (MTA) prepared, but unpublished, by the Treasury. However, that has been abandoned since 1976, as the predictions became too inaccurate with the less stable economy.

Paradoxically, the main crisis for PESC came just after Wildavsky's book praising it was published. The economic uncertainties emphasized the inadequacies of PESC for cash control purposes and the cash-limit system was superimposed over PESC. This simply meant that blocks of expenditure were given fixed cash sums after production of likely price increases and then those responsible for the expenditure had to ensure (with a few exceptions) that the cash sum was not exceeded. Cash limits now cover the major part of central government vote expenditure. In addition, after 1976, more regular (i.e. monthly) information flows on cash spent were developed to enable cash control. At this point, the future of PESC stood in the balance, and perhaps still does. Wright (1979, p. 43) says that it is not clear whether there will eventually be a return to the 'solely cash system' similar to that used by Gladstone in the 19th century. Such a movement would interpret the Treasury role as one simply trying to keep expenditure down, with no commitment to promises of expenditure levels for future years. Alternatively, the cash controls might be combined with PESC to form a more integrated and sophisticated financial resource planning system including wider notions of effectiveness and measures of outputs. Further reference will also be made to these concepts later in the paper, but for the moment it suffices to note that this seems to suggest the desirability of a movement back towards PPBS (although perhaps still a long way from the full application of it) and as Wright concludes:

> 'It still seems to be the case that the distribution and level of public expenditure is very largely a rationalization of the bi-lateral negotiations with departments . . . nor is there much evidence that departments have developed techniques of programme and project appraisal which enable them to make more rational choices' (Wright, 1979, p. 50).

This outline review of U.K. central government budgeting serves to identify various additional aspects which would need to be taken into account in attempting to pursue the research questions on local authority budgeting raised earlier. Most local authorities now undertake some form of 'continuation budgeting'—a process of budgeting resource allocation to spending departments for existing activities for several years ahead. This development was probably the inevitable reaction to requests to comply with the national government's information requirements for PESC. Indeed, the evolution of 'continuation budgeting' might be investigated and compared with that of PESC. Research might also examine the strengths and weaknesses of PESC in relation to 'continuation budgeting'. However, it should be noted that local authorities are not compelled to use such a process to control their affairs and it is known that different authorities use different modes of continuation budgeting. For example, one authority uses a two-stage process which, first, calculates projected expenditure for current activities and then makes projections allowing for the maintenance of the same service standards for increases which have occurred in the beneficial population. Other authorities have only one level of projection. Does this indicate simply a different budget presentation or does it imply different underlying budget negotiation processes? Moreover, is there the same difficulty in defining 'existing policy' at local level as there obviously is with PESC or does the less extensive nature of local affairs, the closer proximity of service officers to the centre of operations and the closer involvement of elected members in executive action mean that this is less problematic? Do local authorities attempt to overcome weaknesses in 'continuation budgeting', if they exist, by PAR and MTA exercises? If so, is prediction for MTA purposes, with its greater dependence on rates and government grants, easier at local level? And does PAR work at local level—once again as a result of the smaller size of the administrative unit. All these questions are central to local authority financial planning and control, and yet very little published academic material is available on them. In addition, it could be argued that control through PESC and cash limits would itself be improved if answers were available to these questions since one weakness of the PESC system, not previously mentioned, is the limited ability of national government to control local authority spending. Certainly, further local authority expenditure controls are being introduced by the present government, but that merely seems to provide yet a further research possibility in terms of assessing the impact and likely reactions to such controls.

Is the 'Bounded Rationality' Theory too Limiting?

A few U.K. researchers have attempted to move beyond Wildavsky's general analysis at the local authority level. Greenwood, Hinings and Ranson (1976), for example, criticize Wildavsky's insistence that budgets are simply incremental, and raise the question of the different degree of incrementalism which may occur in different situations. They conducted a series of interviews with officers in eight local authorities in order to substantiate that environmental contingencies and organizational characteristics influence the degree of incrementalism. However, whilst their study is a pioneering one which incorporates a good theoretical discussion of likely organizational and environmental variables, it can be questioned whether the broad contingency framework which they used can provide any detailed insights into the political and officer negotiating processes which are an essential part of local authority budgeting.

The same criticism can be made of a paper by Greenwood (1979) who concludes that, while local authorities are generally 'incrementalist' in approach, the imposition of recent financial restraints 'has pushed them towards a greater measure of rational analysis'. Again, it is doubted whether survey methodologies can be depended upon to elucidate such facts. Local authorities may claim to be attempting greater 'corporate analysis' to provide a 'rational analysis of explicitly inter-departmental policy alternatives' but only a close observation of the processes involved can determine whether the end product was the result of a careful attempt to balance the arguments for and against competing interests rather than the result of political in-fighting and trade-offs which has existed previously only in a different guise. The Greenwood *et al.* studies widen the horizons of research in the area, but there is a need for further enquiries to corroborate or refute their conclusions. Indeed, early evidence from our own studies seem to indicate that the 'newly poor' situation serves to emphasize the strains involved in corporate integration rather than strengthen 'rational' planning of competing goals.

One other notable contribution to understanding the U.K. local authority budgeting process has been provided by Danziger (1978). In a study which involved a statistical analysis of budgets and interviews in four English county boroughs, he attempted to show which of five different models of budgeting best described practice. The five models were (a) a pure demographic approach, (b) a naive econometric model (extrapolating constancy of proportions, etc.), (c) and organization-process approach, (d) a cognitive-limits approach, and (e) an individual-level influence approach. Despite some success in explaining differences between boroughs by methods (a) and (b), none of the five approaches adequately explained longitudinal changes of budget allocations across services and, because of this, Danziger concluded that future research should be based on a series of studies using the different models that he had presented. He also noted that it is too early to fuse the strengths of the different approaches. Once again, we are faced with a pioneering study which leaves much scope for future researchers. The relevance of Danziger's ideas on future research methodology should be considered alongside the comments in the last section of this paper.

Seeking better Value for Money

The previous section described how PESC ran into trouble and needed modification as the U.K. ran into economic crisis in the mid-1970s and faced an urgent need to control the rate of inflation which is still running at about 20 per cent per annum. One prescription advocated for reducing such a rate of inflation is a considerable reduction in the public sector borrowing requirement. While it is a reduction *per se* which is seen as being capable of bringing short-run macro-economic benefits, quite naturally it is hoped that the development of better ways of achieving 'value for money' in the public sector will help to reduce expenditure levels. This is of concern to local authorities just as much as central governments.

The Use of Input Statistics

In addition to the introduction of the 'efficiency exercises' mentioned earlier, the pressure for better 'value for money' has led to senior politicians calling for an open debate of cost and operating statistics relating to local authorities. However, there is reason to question how effective such a process would be in achieving better value for money.

The Chartered Institute for Public Finance Accountants have for many years produced regular financial statistics showing unit costs and expenditure patterns analysed by service, and the practice of making comparisons between similar authorities is both long-standing and widespread. When the statistics are published each year, it has almost become a ritual with the relevant staff in local authority treasurers' departments to turn to last year's file, select the same authorities for comparison, and write for the relevant committee a brief report on cost comparisons with the same suggested reasons for cost differences (differences in regional characteristics, populations, age of assets, etc.). It is, therefore, suspected that service officers have stock arguments for explaining their 'league positions'. The high cost department claims success in running a high quality department, while the low cost department claims success in running an 'efficient ship'. However, it must be added that the picture just painted is one as perceived by the author without solid research evidence. It is a view based upon personal experience working in local authorities, and long-standing acquaintances with local authority treasurers and their staffs through both professional activities and research. The views stated are, therefore, more in the nature of hypotheses in need of formal corroboration.

Nevertheless, it is not difficult to see why such a situation might exist as a general phenomenon rather than in isolated pockets occupied by inefficient officers. To begin with, it is notoriously difficult to measure the outputs of most local authority services and, despite the efforts of academics and professional institutions over many years, very little progress has been made at producing reliable and useful output measures. Usually, the difficulties are inherent in the nature of the service supplied. For example, how does one measure the prevention of crime rather than its detection or the creation of a sense of security in the local community? Alternatively, how does one measure the value of the 'social visit element' of a meals-on-wheels service as distinct from the nutritional value of the food supplied? Consequently, very few useful *output* statistics exist and without the ability to match inputs to outputs in measured form there is always scope for 'rationalizing away' differences in inputs alone.

Superimposed upon the output measurement problem is the more practical problem of even achieving comparable *input* statistics. Despite the fact that most local authorities adhere to a fairly detailed standard accounting classification, treasury accountants have argued publicly that variations of accounting classification practices are so marked, even within the CIPFA standard code, that comparisons are of little use if one is trying to tie service departments down to a sensible debate on difference between authorities. The service departments are quite aware of the statistical imperfections, and are apparently quite capable of pointing out to the accountant the usual disclaimer printed in the front of each statistics booklet that the user should avoid making precise conclusions from the figures given!

There is, therefore, a need for more systematic work to establish to what extent it is relevant to compare input statistics, and how much effort would be needed to attain an acceptable degree of comparability. In addition, it would be useful to know *how* statistics are used at present in both private and public 'debates' over resource allocation and accountability. Without such evidence the call for a public debate on comparative local authority statistics may create wider public interest, but this will probably do little more than encourage a growth in the 'market for excuses' suggested by Watts and Zimmerman (1979).

Moreover, there is some evidence from the U.S.A. which suggests that even setting up such a public debate may be more problematic than some politicians believe. After studying U.S. local authority productivity exercises in some depth, one author commented that:

> 'There is no instance of which I am aware . . . of any significant pressure from citizens, citizen associations, or any other private organisation to set up productivity programs . . . not even the . . . vociferous opponents of higher taxes and spending have picked up the cudgels to fight for productivity improvement' (Hayes, 1977, p. 243).

On the other hand, the head of the U.K. District Audit Service recently told the author that while some might doubt that statistical comparisons can achieve much, it is clear that the recent stance by politicians has heightened awareness of the need for greater efficiency and was making the importance of the job performed by his staff more readily accepted.

All one can say at present, while awaiting more research based evidence, is that it seems unwise to place too much relevance on a statistical approach and that other means of achieving value for money should also be sought.

Alternative Ways to Improved Value for Money

Value for money is best thought of as an all-embracing term which encompasses both efficiency (more outputs per unit of input) and effectiveness (better selection of outputs to satisfy objectives). Obviously, there are various agencies and methods which have some impact upon local authority efficiency and effectiveness. Agencies internal to the local authority will include internal audit, O & M sections, treasury financial controllers, performance review committees and *ad hoc* productivity improvement exercises. External to the authority, some pressures come from government department inspectorates, the District Audit Service (responsible for auditing most U.K. local authorities) and, in a few instances, professional auditors from the private sector and management consultants.

Looking at internal organizations first, O & M sections have been far more concerned with conventional job evaluation and operative bonus schemes and work methods than with questions of effectiveness. Internal audits, on the other hand, are usually said to undertake both anti-fraud checks and 'management audits'. However, it is suspected that the majority of work on management audit relates mainly to work of a straightforward systems variety. Internal audit staffs of U.K. local authorities usually have neither the status nor the training to deal with broader 'value for money' questions. Also in terms of cut-backs in financial resources, it is probable that the need to keep basic anti-fraud investigations going, which arises from society's apparent desire to make public authority officers more accountable in terms of spending money for purposes authorized, will act as a constraint upon even the more straightforward aspects of management audit. In a restricted sense, therefore, the cuts in expenditure aimed at inducing better value for money may injure some activities which aim to achieve it. This, in itself, would be an interesting research hypothesis to pursue.

Regarding the more *ad hoc* internal processes which might be employed to improve 'value for money', Hayes' (1977) study of eight U.S. local authorities provides the most comprehensive evidence available so far and concludes that political leadership is the main requirement for successful initiations of productivity improvement programmes. However, he stresses that these programmes interact with the political process and they are, therefore, more easily achieved in some services than in others:

> 'Program efforts seem, for example, rarely to place much pressure on police departments, and the fire department will typically be handled with rather more circumspection than, say, the water department' (Hayes, 1977, p. 244).

and

> 'Relationships (of the city manager) with some department heads require protecting those departments from the direct scrutiny of the productivity staff' (Hayes, 1977, p. 345).

Hayes also highlights the resistance of spending department managers to ideas imposed from outside and their unwillingness to jeopardize internal relations by undertaking efforts which would cut back the department's budget or work force. On the basis of such ideas it is easy to assume that spending department managers are simply acting in an empire-protecting role and, no doubt, there always will be an element of such behaviour. However, even if positively motivated to improve productivity despite the managerial consequences, spending department managers look upon themselves as professionals who are experts in their own chosen work. As such, they are more expert than politicians, accountants or any other outsiders. Consequently, it is hypothesized that while they have to accept that politicians should decide broad allocations of funds, questions of productivity relating to the service are matters over which they should have discretion. If they can, like the police, call also upon wider political or social support, the local politician or treasurer tries to impose productivity exercises at his peril. Research is, therefore, also needed to examine the importance of conflicting values attached to different professions and politicians and the fluctuation of their popularity and how this is reflected in financial planning and control. At the national level, the problem is, it seems, essentially handled by mutual trust between the Treasury and the spending department. One way forward might be the re-location of financial controllers from the local authority treasurer's department to the spending department in line with the controllership function structure employed by many divisionalized companies. Space prevents a full analysis here but, there is some evidence that a trend towards building such a 'bridge' between departments may be developing in the U.K. The reasons, problems and processes of his development are analysed in Rosenberg, Tomkins and Day (1980). Studies such as those by Simon *et al.* (1954) and Sathe (1978) with respect to the private sector might, therefore, have considerable relevance for local authorities, and perhaps even at national level as well.

In addition, taking a broader exploratory perspective, Hayes has claimed that productivity programmes seem to arise in two instances: in authorities where a low-effort profile can be maintained and where potential opposition to such a programme is minimal and, secondly, where there exists a flamboyant political entrepreneur coming in on an 'evangelistic ticket'. This gives rise to another set of research hypotheses relating to the roles played by such contingent factors as political, organizational and environmental structures in enabling or hampering the ability to introduce 'value for money' exercises.

An examination of the external agencies which supposedly contribute to the achievement of value for money also highlights the difficulties involved rather than providing instant remedies for success. A recent example is the exercise conducted on Cheshire County Council by a firm of management consultants (see P.A. Management Consultants (1979)). Their report clearly recognizes the distinction between efficiency and effectiveness, but all the specific proposals relate to improving the former. With regard to improving effectiveness, there are simply exhortations about the selection of policy options on a rational basis and criticism of budget incrementalism; this is reminiscent of the early PPB and ZBB literature. As a result of such a report one wonders whether consultants primarily operating in the private sector would, given a free hand in the public sector, head off down that familiar road unaware of the crucial private and public sector differences described so clearly by van Gunsteren (1976).

If that latter hypothesis were proven it would seem that agencies with a much longer tradition of association with local government, and hence a deeper understanding of its professional and political functioning, stand a better chance of success in this area. However, there is also reason for unease with what can be achieved by such agencies. Once again, evidence being collected in our own west of England study suggests that government departmental inspectorates are mostly staffed by professionals appropriate to the service concerned and, therefore, have the same lack of finance expertise as the planning department officers themselves. For example, it seems clear that the inspectors for social services are more concerned with the well-being of old people in houses than in whether value for money is being achieved. On the other hand, external professional audit or District Audit lack the professional skills to question departmental policy. Consequently, no one agency attempts to take a co-ordinated view of value for money. Research might be conducted in more depth to discover whether these perceptions are valid and whether, despite the near absence of any contact between government inspectors and external audit, the two different types of agencies do, indirectly, achieve co-ordinated pressure for better effectiveness. In addition, researchers might consider whether a new combined audit/service department inspectorate with dual professional status would stand a better chance of overcoming the problems of professional jealousies and territories.

An alternative area for research, closely connected with this question, would be the comparison of the styles of operation of the local authority District Audit and the national Exchequer and Audit department. Colville and Tomkins (1980) have made a start at analysing these differences and, indeed, extended their investigation to include the national audits of the U.S.A., Sweden and Canada. It appears that each one operates under a different philosophy. Such variations may be accounted for by constitutional differences, but, on the other hand, it is suspected that, in part, the wide differences reflect the fact that no-one yet has the answer how best to conduct value for money audits; there is vast scope for further research in this area.

A Research Opportunity and a Warning

This paper has merely attempted to raise issues. A comprehensive analysis would have been quite impossible in such a short paper. Nevertheless, there appears to be a need for more research efforts into a variety of local authority accounting matters relating to budgetary practice, the use of statistics for control and the contribution which various internal and external agencies have made and can make to efficiency and effectiveness.

However, the overriding message of this paper is that research into these questions based only upon notions of 'rational decision analysis' and a systems analysis of planning and control procedures is unlikely to penetrate the veil of human interaction, professional defensiveness and political manoeuvre. The results of such research are, therefore, likely to have little impact upon practice. If accounting researchers are to offer anything in terms of improving local authority effectiveness, they must take these factors into account and this possibly means that they must collaborate with researchers from other disciplines. This will probably involve work in multi-disciplinary research teams and the introduction of new research methods into accounting which place greater reliance upon the analysis of qualitative rather than quantitative data. However, the recognition of what is needed does not mean that it is easy to do. Very little truly inter-disciplinary work has taken place anywhere in the social services and, in the same way as different professionals in local authorities have problems in 'merging' their different 'views of the world', so also will researchers from different disciplines (see Tomkins *et al.* (1980)). Additionally, even academics recently charged with the task of writing about research methodology in accounting (see Abdel-Khalik and Ajinkya, 1979, Ch. 2) only pay passing regard to qualitative research methods, their fundamental premises and the difficulties involved. (Readers interested are referred to the *Administrative Science Quarterly* (December 1979) and *The Sociological Review* (November 1979) which are virtually entirely devoted to this question.) The challenge offered, therefore, involves both new tools and new areas of study. But be warned, the path has risks for the accounting researcher trained in positivistic, quantitative research methods. When ice meets fire, one or other, or both, vanishes!

References

Abdel-Khalik, A. R. and Ajinkya, B. B., *Empirical Research in Accounting: A Methodological Viewpoint*. American Accounting Association, Accounting Education Series, vol. No. 4 (1979).

Colville, I. and Tomkins, C., *Value for Money Audits*. University of Bath, School of Management, Discussion Papers (1980).

Danziger, J. N., *Making Budgets: Public Resource Allocation*. Sage (1978).

Greenwood, R., 'The Local Authority Budgetary Process', in T. A. Booth (ed.), *Planning for Welfare: Social Policy and the Expenditure Process*. Blackwell (1979).

Greenwood, R., Hinings, C. R. and Ranson, S., *The Politics of the Budgetary Process in English Local Government*, presented to the Political Studies Association Conference, Nottingham University (1976).

Hayes, F. O'R., *Productivity in Local Government*. Lexington Books (1977).

Jablonsky, S. F. and Dirsmith, M. W., 'The Pattern of PPB Rejection: Something about Organisation, Something about PPB', *Accounting, Organisations and Society*, vol. 3, No. 3/4 (1978).

Novick, D., *Current Practice in Program Budgeting*. Crane Russack (1973).

P.A. Management Consultants, *Value for Money: Report on Cheshire County Council*. Confederation of British Industry (1979).

Rosenberg, D., Tomkins, C. and Day, P., *The Accountant in a Social Service Department: Values and Interpretations of Work Role*. University of Bath, Centre for the Study of Organizational Change and Development, working paper 80/04 (1980).

Sarant, P. C., *Zero-base Budgeting in the Public Sector—A Pragmatic Approach*. Addison-Wesley (1978).

Sathe, V., *Controllership in Divisionalised Firms: Structure, Evaluation and Development*. American Management Association (1978).

Simon, H., Gretzhow, H., Koznetsky, G. and Tyndall, G., *Centralisation vs. Decentralisation in Organising a Controller's Department*. Scholars Book Co. (1978); original copyright Controllership Foundation (1954).

Tomkins, C., Rosenberg, D. and Colville, I., 'The Social Process of Social Science Research with Specific Reference to a Multi-disciplinary Project in Accounting', *Accounting, Organisations and Society*, vol. 5, No. 2 (1980).

Van Gunsteren, H. R., *The Quest for Control: A Critique of the Rational-central-rule Approach in Public Affairs*. Wiley (1976).

Watts, R. L. and Zimmerman, J. L., 'The Demand for and Supply of Accounting Theories: The Market for Excuses', *The Accounting Review* (April 1979).

Wildavsky, A., *Budgeting: A Comparative Theory of Budgeting Processes*. Little Brown (1975).

Wright, M., 'Planning and Controlling Public Expenditure', in Booth, T. A. (ed.), *Planning for Welfare: Social Policy and the Expenditure Process*. Blackwell (1979).

14 Research issues in accounting for non-business organizations

Peter Bird
Professor of Accounting, University of Kent at Canterbury

It is convenient to follow the Financial Accounting Standards Board (Anthony, 1978) in using the term 'non-business organizations' to encompass the whole area of concern of this session, i.e. both the public sector and private, non-profit organizations. Together these comprise roughly half of the British economy; but the allocation to them of one of the ten sessions of this conference is a fair, if not even a generous, reflection of the proportion of accounting research effort that has been devoted to them.

In these circumstances, it is not surprising that the authors of the two papers agree that the question: 'What research needs to be done in this area?' should be answered along the lines 'Almost anything; our ignorance is too profound to allow us to propose a research strategy yet'. But surely positive reasons need to be given to justify putting research effort into this area and there are only two possible types of such justification:

(a) relevant characteristics differ between business organizations and some or all types of non-business organizations so that the non-business sector throws up accounting problems that are not encountered in businesses;

(b) problems which are common to business and non-business deserve study in a non-business context because they appear there in sharper focus, or more dramatically, and/or because comparative study is possible of the different practices currently adopted in business and in various types of non-business organizations.

It seems likely that most issues falling under the first heading, above, will be in financial accounting, arising from the legal or institutional framework; for instance, many types of non-business organizations receive financial resources which are restricted as to the use to which they may be applied, a feature rarely encountered in business. Management accounting problems are more likely under the second heading above; for instance, conflicting loyalties to an operating unit and to a functional specialism or profession occur in all sorts of organization, but show up particularly vividly in local government, as illustrated in Cyril Tomkins' paper.

John Perrin points out the wide diversity of institutional classes within the title of 'non-business organizations'. This point deserves to be stressed and its implications drawn out. The following list of classes is not exhaustive nor is the classification implicit within it definitive:

1. Central government departments;
2. Government trading organizations;
3. Nationalized industries;
4. Water authorities;
5. Health authorities;
6. Local government;
7. Universities;
8. Charities;
9. Friendly societies;
10. Building societies;
11. Housing associations;
12. Professional associations;
13. Trade unions;
14. Pension funds;
15. Non-charitable private non-profit organizations (e.g. Automobile Association, BUPA).

Even these classes may not be mutually exclusive; some charities are also housing associations or friendly societies or universities, and many charities are also companies or trusts. A class may not be even approximately homogeneous; charities include fund-raisers and endowed foundations, regional arts councils and independent schools, direct service providers and pure allocators of funds for others to use.

Each of these classes is a sub-culture with a legal, institutional and social context which must be studied and absorbed in some detail before you can say anything sensible about its accounting and financial management. The author has found this an eye-opening and humbling experience in relation to the world of charities. In the light of this, the Warwick report on the National Health Service is even more impressive than is apparent from the face of it (Royal Commission on the National Health Service, 1978). A researcher needs to make a substantial investment in working his way into a class of non-business organization; it follows that, in general, a researcher would be well-advised to specialize, for some time, in one such class rather than trying to study a particular problem across a range of classes.

But does this imply that nothing useful can be said about non-business organizations as a whole or any sub-division greater than one of the classes listed above? In his 'exploratory study' for the Financial Accounting Standards Board, Anthony (1978, pp. 8–10) starts by dividing non-business organizations into Type A 'whose financial resources are obtained entirely, or almost entirely, from revenues from the sale of goods and services' and Type B which obtain significant amounts of financial resources from other sources (e.g. taxes, grants, subscriptions, donations). He suggests that

Type A may be able to be treated for financial accounting purposes as if they were businesses. He also asks whether governmental organizations should be considered separately from private non-profit organizations. (The purpose of the study was to identify issues and arguments, not to propose prescriptions.)

Anthony's 'top-down' approach contrasts with the 'bottom-up' research practice recommended above. Answers will be forthcoming only from study of the specifics of individual classes of non-business organization. There will then be a need for a medium of communication among those conducting research in individual classes so that any potential for more generalizable results can be recognized and developed.

It seems quite likely that some generalizable results will be able to be found, since all non-business organizations share at least two characteristics that contrast with those of business and which give rise to many of their financial control problems:

(a) money surplus is not an indicator of success;
(b) money surplus is not distributable to individuals.

Also, where financial reporting is concerned, non-business organizations (other than a few nationalized industries) cannot plead commercial competition as a reason for keeping information confidential, especially forecasts and budgets.

Present practice in financial accounting in the private, non-profit sector is a mixture of over-regulation and under-regulation. Some classes of organization are subject to detailed and inconsistent legislation; a housing association which is also a friendly society will find that accounts prepared in accordance with the recommendations of the Housing Corporation will be rejected by the Registrar of Friendly Societies. On the other hand, accounting practices by charities, subject only to the Charities Act, are so variable that those who try to compile aggregates for the charity sector complain bitterly about the inadequacy of the data and produce wildly different estimates of the total annual income of the sector (Charities Aid Foundation, 1977–78 and 1978–79; Falush, 1978; Austin and Posnett, 1979a and 1979b). Even these researchers do not seem to appreciate all the deficiencies in the figures they are using.

All this may be summed up by asserting that, while research proposals in the non-business sectors should be processed through the filter of the two headings of justification for such research outlined above, there is enormous scope for fruitful research of almost every type in this largely uncharted area.

References

Anthony, R. N., *Financial Accounting in Non-business Organisations: An Exploratory Study of Conceptual Issues*. Financial Accounting Standards Board (1978).

Austin, M. and Posnett, J., 'The Charity Sector in England and Wales—Characteristics and Public Accountability', *National Westminster Bank Quarterly Review* (August 1979).

Austin, M. and Posnett, J., 'Charitable Activity in England and Wales', *Social Policy and Administration* (1979).

Charities Aid Foundation, *Charity Statistics* (1977–78 and 1978–79).

Falush, P., 'Trends in the Finance of British Charities', *National Westminster Bank Quarterly Review* (May 1977).

Royal Commission on the National Health Service, *Management of Financial Resources in the National Health Service*, Research Paper No. 2 (1978).

List of contributors

John Arnold has been Professor of Accounting at the University of Manchester since 1977. He was previously Senior Lecturer (1975–77) and Lecturer (1971–75) in Accounting at the same institution, before which he was Lecturer in Accounting at the University of Kent (1969–71) and Teaching Fellow in Management Studies at the London School of Economics and Political Science (1967–69). He holds the degree of M.Sc. in Accounting and Finance (with distinction) from the University of London and is a Fellow of the Institute of Chartered Accountants in England and Wales. He is the author of a number of journal articles, and of a book, *Pricing and Output Decisions* (Prentice-Hall, 1973), and co-author of *A Study of the Relative Usefulness of Six Accounting Measures of Income* (ICAEW Research Committee Occasional Paper, 1978). He is co-editor of *Topics in Management Accounting* (Philip Allan, 1980). He is a member of various working parties of the Institute of Chartered Accountants in England and Wales. His main current research interests are the identification of the factors influencing the setting of accounting standards and the evaluation of alternative methods of reporting enterprise performance to external users of accounting statements.

Krish Bhaskar is Professor of Accountancy and Finance at the University of East Anglia. He was appointed to this position in 1978 to establish a new programme with a special emphasis on the use of computers in accountancy and finance. Previously, he had worked at the University of Bristol and the London School of Economics, in both institutions being interested in the use of computers both for the routine processing of accounting information and to help in the decision-making, planning and control fields. His publications reflect both areas of interest. A peripheral research area has been the motor industry. Major book publications include *The Future of the World Motor Industry* (Kogan Page, 1980) and *Building Financial Models: A Simulation Approach* (Associated Business Press, 1978). Current research work includes the application of modern data base techniques, decision support systems theory and computing techniques to accounting.

Peter Bird is Professor of Accounting, University of Kent at Canterbury. He is a member of the Council of the Institute of Chartered Accountants in England and Wales and vice-chairman of its Research Sub-Committee. Previously he served with Arthur Andersen & Co., and taught at the London School of Economics. He is the author of *Accountability: Standards in Financial Reporting* (Haymarket, 1973) and *Understanding Company Accounts* (Pitman, 1979), and is the accounting editor of the *Journal of Business Law*. Currently, he is working on research into financial reporting by charities.

Richard J Briston is Reader in Accountancy and Finance at the University of East Anglia. He previously taught at the Universities of Hull and Bradford, and from 1972 to 1979 was Head of the Department of Accountancy and Finance at the University of Strathclyde. In 1977 he was Visiting Professor at the Centre for International Accounting Development in the University of Texas at Dallas. The author of *The Stock Exchange and Investment Analysis, A Practical Introduction to Business Investment Decisions, Growth and Impact of Institutional Investors* (with R. Dobbins) and *Business Finance* (with F. W. Paish), Richard Briston is also Joint Editor of the *Journal of Business Finance and Accounting*. His main current research interests are in the areas of international and comparative accounting.

Michael Bromwich is Professor of Finance and Accountancy at the University of Reading. During the period 1970–77 he was Sir Julian Hodge Professor of Accountancy and head of the Department of Business Administration and Accountancy at the University of Wales Institute of Science and Technology. Before entering teaching he worked as an accountant for Ford Motor Company, to which organization he has acted as consultant. His previous teaching post was as Lecturer in Accounting at the London School of Economics. His present research interests include management control and capital budgeting; his publications include a Penguin book, *The Economics of Capital Budgeting*, which was also issued by Pitman in a cased edition in 1979.

Jeffrey B Coates is Senior Lecturer in Finance and Accounting at the University of Aston in Birmingham. Educated at the Universities of Nottingham and Birmingham, he is a member of the Institute of Cost and Management Accountants. He previously served on the staff of the Department of Engineering Production at the University of Birmingham. His current research interests are in the economics of production process, with particular reference to advanced technology, and the current state of practice in management accounting.

David Cooper has recently been appointed Senior Lecturer at the University of East Anglia. Previously he has undertaken research and taught at the Universities of Manchester, Sheffield, Kent, British Columbia and California (Berkeley). He obtained a B.Sc. (Econ.) in 1970 from the London School of Economics and a Ph.D. in 1979 from the University of Manchester. He has conducted research and published in political economy and its relationship to accounting and auditing, organization theory, information disclosure to employees and the organizational aspects of accounting. Currently he is involved in two research projects; one on the cultural and symbolic uses of accounting systems and the other on the relationship between shareholder power and corporate performance.

David Flint was appointed Professor of Accountancy in the University of Glasgow in 1964. He graduated from the University of Glasgow and served for seven years in the army from 1939 to 1946, before qualifying as a member of The Institute of Chartered Accountants of Scotland. A partner in a firm in public practice for twenty years until 1971, he was President of The Institute of Chartered Accountants of Scotland in 1975/76 and as a Vice President of that Institute was one of the first members of the Consultative Committee of Accountancy Bodies when it was instituted. He is presently Convenor of the Institute's Research Advisory Committee. Among other appointments, David Flint is a Vice President of the Scottish Economic Society, a member of the Scottish Committee of the Institute for Fiscal Studies, and of the Company Law Committee of the Law Society of Scotland. He has been a member of the Commission for Local Authority Accounts in Scotland, the Management Training and Development Committee of the Central Training Council, the Executive Committee and Council of the Scottish Business School of the Management and Industrial Relations Committee of the SSRC. His major research interests are in audit theory and financial reporting; he is currently completing a text on audit theory and editing a book of audit readings.

J Chris Higgins is Director and Professor of Management Sciences at the Management Centre, University of Bradford. A graduate in physics from Gonville and Caius College at the University of Cambridge, Professor Higgins took up a short service commission in the RAF in 1953. After a number of years in physics and electronics, he joined the Department of the Chief Scientist (RAF) in the Ministry of Defence, working on operational research and information systems problems: during this time he gained an Honours Degree in Statistics and Psychology from London University. He joined IPC in 1967 as O.R. Manager and then became Director of Economic Planning and Research for IPC Newspapers Ltd., his work largely comprising corporate planning, information systems design and operational research in the fields of marketing, distribution and finance. He is a member of several government committees including the

Final Selection Board for the Civil Service Commission, the Defence Scientific Advisory Council's Assessments Board, and the University Grants Committee Sub-Committee on Management and Business Studies. He is chairman of the Social Sciences Research Council's Accountancy Steering Committee and is a member of its Management and Industrial Relations Committee. Professor Higgins is the author of six textbooks and some three dozen papers and articles on corporate planning, information systems and related topics.

Anthony G Hopwood is Institute of Chartered Accountants Professor of Accounting and Financial Reporting, and Director of the Doctoral Programme, at the London Graduate School of Business Studies. He is also Professor of Management at the European Institute for Advanced Studies in Management, Brussels. Educated at the London School of Economics and the University of Chicago, Anthony Hopwood previously held positions at the Manchester Business School and the Oxford Centre for Management Studies. He is the author of *An Accounting System and Management Behaviour* (1973), *Accounting and Human Behaviour* (1974) and numerous articles, and is Editor-in-Chief of *Accounting, Organizations and Society*. His current research focuses on the organizational and social aspects of accounting and information systems.

Gerald H Lawson is Professor of Business Finance and in 1978–80 was Director of the Doctoral Programme at the Manchester Business School, University of Manchester. He is a fellow of the Association of Certified Accountants in the U.K. During 1971–72 he was Visiting Professor at the University of Augsburg, Germany, and during the Fall of 1977 at the University of Texas. He was a visiting professor at the Ruhr Universität, Bochum in the Autumn of 1980 and is currently at the University of Texas. Professor Lawson was a British Council Scholar at Wirtschaftsuniversität, Vienna, Austria, in 1967 and at the University of Louvain, Belgium, In October 1978. He is a member of the editorial board of the *Journal of Business Finance and Accounting*. His main research interests are business valuation, cash flow accounting, inflation and relative price changes, taxation and company law reform. He has written numerous articles on these and other subjects. Professor Lawson is a member of the UEC Valuation Committee and he has acted as a consultant to British and foreign government ministries and to many industrial firms.

Tom Lee is a Scottish Chartered Accountant who worked for several years in practice before taking up a lectureship at the University of Strathclyde. He is presently Professor of Accountancy and Finance, and Head of the

Department of Accounting and Business Method at the University of Edinburgh. He has served on various committees and working parties of academic and professional bodies, including the editorial boards of the *Journal of Business Finance and Accounting* and *The Accounting Review*. He is the author of several books in his main teaching and research areas, including *Company Auditing* (Gee), *The Funds Statement* (ICAS), *Income and Value Measurement* (Nelson), and *Company Financial Reporting* (Nelson). He is also co-author with Professor Tweedie of *The Private Shareholder and the Corporate report* (ICAEW) and co-editor with Professor Parker of *The Evolution of Corporate Financial Reporting* (Nelson). He has contributed numerous papers and essays to other texts and to professional and academic journals throughout the world.

Tony Lowe spent a number of years in practice as a Chartered Accountant before taking a first class degree at the London School of Economics. During this early period of working life, he helped found a provincial practice for a London firm and subsequently became managing clerk of a City of London professional practice and Secretary of a London Stock Exchange quoted company. He has been Professor at Sheffield since 1971, before which he was at the University of Leeds, the Bradford University Management Centre and the Manchester Business School. He has also held visiting appointments at the Massachusetts Institute of Technology School of Management, Harvard Business School, the University of California (Berkeley) and the University of British Columbia. He has been Chairman of the Council of Departments of Accounting Studies and the Association of University Teachers in Accounting. His research interests are wide, and he has published extensively in the fields of management control, organization theory, systems theory, internal auditing, financial management and business forecasting.

David Otley is Lecturer in Accounting and Finance at the University of Lancaster. He was educated at Churchill College, Cambridge and worked for some years in the Operational Research Executive of the National Coal Board. He then joined the Doctoral Programme of the Manchester Business School where he developed his interest in the behavioural sciences and their application to management control systems. He is the author of *Behavioural Aspects of Budgeting* (ICAEW) and of papers in the *Journal of Accounting Research, Accounting, Organizations and Society*, and the *Journal of Management Studies.*

R H (Bob) Parker has been Professor of Accountancy at the University of Exeter since 1976. He has previously been associated with the London School of Economics, the University of Adelaide, the University of

Western Australia, the Manchester Business School, INSEAD and the University of Dundee. He graduated from University College, London, in 1954 and qualified as an English chartered accountant in 1958. He is editor of *Accounting and Business Research* and on the editorial board of the *Accounting Historians Journal.* He was a member of the Working Party which organized the Third International Congress of Accounting Historians, London, August 1980. Professor Parker's research interests are in accounting history and international accounting. His most recent publications are *The Evolution of Corporate Financial Reporting* (1979, with T. A. Lee) and *Accounting Thought and Education: Six English Pioneers* (1980, with J. Kitchen).

Ken V Peasnell is Wolfson Professor of Accounting and Finance and Head of the Department of Accounting and Finance, at the University of Lancaster. After qualifying as a Chartered Accountant in 1967, he studied at the universities of Sheffield, London and Lancaster. His academic positions, all at Lancaster, were successively P. D. Leake Research Fellow, ICRA Research Fellow, Lecturer and Professor. He is a past member of the editorial board of the *Accounting Review* and is a current member of the editorial board of the *Journal of Business Finance and Accounting*. His research interests are in the fields of accounting theory and finance. He is the (single or joint) author of three ICRA Occasional Papers, and articles in various academic and professional journals including the *Accounting Review*, *Journal of Accounting Research*, *Abacus*, *Accounting and Business Research*, *Journal of Business Finance and Accounting*, and *Journal of Accountancy*.

John R Perrin is Professor and Director, the Centre for Industrial Economic and Business Research, University of Warwick. He was educated at the University of California, Los Angeles (B.Sc. and MBA), and the London School of Economics (Ph.D. 1958) and previously held positions at Mount Allison University, Canada, the Department of Industrial Economics, University of Nottingham and the University of Lancaster. Founder editor of the *Journal of Business Finance and Accounting* in 1969, and now co-editor, he was also editor and co-author of *Management of Financial Resources in the National Health Service* (Royal Commission on the NHS, London, HMSO, 1978) and co-author (with G. Bevan *et al.*) of *Health Care: Priorities and Management* (London, Croom Helm, 1980). He is a member of the Council and the Accounting Panel of the Chartered Institute of Public Finance and Accountancy (since 1974). His principal research interests are in resource allocation and financial control in public-sector institutions, and problems of industrial productivity and performance.

John Samuels is Professor of Business Finance at the University of Birmingham, where he served as Dean of the Faculty of Commerce from 1975 to 1978. He is a member of the Accounting Standards Sub-Committee of the Association of Certified Accountants, the Research Sub-Committee of the Institute of Chartered Accountants in England and Wales, and was on the Working Party on Finance for Investment of the National Economic Development Office. Among his many publications are *The Management of Company Finance* (Nelson, 3rd edn., 1980), *Company Finance in Europe* (ICAEW, 1975) and *Savings and Investment in West Germany and the United Kingdom* (Wilton House, 1978).

Robert W Scapens is Senior Lecturer and Research Co-ordinator in the Department of Accounting and Business Finance at the University of Manchester where he has been since 1970. In 1975/76 he was visiting Lecturer in Accounting at the Ohio State University. He is author of *Accounting in an Inflationary Environment*, the second edition of which was published in 1981, and he has published articles in various professional and academic journals in both England and North America, including *The Accounting Review*. His current research work includes the development of a profit measure from the economic theory of the firm and a study of the control of financial performance in divisionalized organizations.

Jack Shaw graduated in Law from Edinburgh University in 1953 then qualified as a Scottish Chartered Accountant and as a Fellow of the Institute of Cost and Management Accountants. In 1960 he became a partner in a local firm which is now the Edinburgh office of Deloitte Haskins & Sells. He held a part-time teaching appointment in the Department of Accounting and Business Method at Edinburgh University from 1965 until he was appointed to the Johnstone Smith Chair of Accountancy at the University of Glasgow in January 1977. He continues to practise as a partner in Deloitte Haskins & Sells. His major publication is *Bogie on Group Accounts* and he contributes extensively to the professional press and to conferences and courses.

Edward Stamp is Research Professor in Accountancy and Director of the International Centre for Research in Accounting at the University of Lancaster. Educated at Cambridge University, he has previously held Chairs at the Victoria University of Wellington, New Zealand, and the University of Edinburgh. His publications include (with C. I. Marley) *Accounting Principles and the City Code: the Case for Reform* (1970), *Corporate Financial Reporting* (1972), (with M. Moonitz) *International*

Auditing Standards (1978) and *The Future of Accounting and Auditing Standards* (1979).

Cyril Tomkins is Professor of Accounting and Finance at the School of Management, University of Bath. Educated at Bristol University and the London School of Economics, he is a member of the Chartered Institute of Public Finance and Accounting. Previously holding positions at the Universities of Hull, North Wales and Strathclyde, Professor Tomkins is the author of many books and articles including *Financial Planning in Divisionalized Companies* (1973) and *An Economic Analysis of the Equipment Leasing Industry* (1979). He currently serves as a member of the Management and Industrial Relations Committee of the U.K. Social Science Research Council.

Geoffrey Whittington has been Professor of Accounting and Finance at the University of Bristol since 1975 and currently holds a Social Science Research Council Research Fellowship in Inflation Accounting. After graduating from the London School of Economics, he qualified as a chartered accountant and then spent ten years as a member of the research staff of the Department of Applied Economics, Cambridge, where he was also a Fellow and Director of Studies in Economics at Fitzwilliam College. From 1972 to 1975 he was Professor of Accountancy and Finance at the University of Edinburgh. His publications include two books, *Profitability, Growth and Valuation* (with A. Singh), 1968, and *The Prediction of Profitability*, 1972, and a number of papers in economics and accounting journals. He was also a signatory of the Meade Committee Report on *The Structure and Reform of Direct Taxation*, 1977. He is currently on the editorial boards of *Abacus*, *The Accounting Review*, and *Managerial and Decision Economics* and is an honorary associate editor of *The Journal of Industrial Economics*.